PRAISE FOR *ECONOMICA*

"Victoria Bateman's *Economica* is a must-read for anyone interested in women's history and economic justice. Bateman powerfully argues that women have always been central to economic life, from 18th-century shoemakers like Ann Askew to pioneers like Priscilla Wakefield, who founded the UK's first bank for women and children. For centuries, laws and social norms have constrained women's economic freedom, not only limiting individual potential but also undermining prosperity for all. Her research reminds us: economies thrive when women have the autonomy to work, earn, and control their wealth."

—Amanda Foreman, author of *The Duchess*

"Ambitious, wide-ranging, and absorbing—this book sets a new standard in economic history."

—Tim Harford, author of *The Undercover Economist*

"Taking readers on an enthralling journey from prehistory to the modern world, Victoria Bateman rightly emphasizes the importance of women's economic agency in human history. Filled with fascinating details, from the Mesopotamian traders whose wives ran the family business back home to the female factory workers of the industrial age and the twenty-first century care workers whose labor has been so frequently overlooked, *Economica* puts women's work back into the story of the global economy. Making the case for women's central importance, readers will be left wondering how economic history could ever be studied without reference to one half of the world's population."

—Elizabeth Norton, author of *The Hidden Lives of Tudor Women*

"The economic history of half of humankind has broken out of its ghetto. The time has come for Victoria Bateman's comprehensive stocktaking of how women figured in the economy, from the caves to the computers. And the time has come for you to read it."

—Deirdre McCloskey, author of *Economical Writing*

"Who are the wealth-creators? Victoria Bateman shows that the standard image of heroic male entrepreneurs or inventors could not be more misleading; in *Economica* she tells a gripping tale of all the unsung female industrialists and workers who are missing from conventional economic histories."

—Diane Coyle, author of *GDP: A Brief but Affectionate History*

"Victoria Bateman's revelatory and compelling new book puts women at the very heart of mankind's economic history. *Economica* should help ensure that's where they will remain."

—Ben Chu, BBC

"This wonderful book is not just a much-needed economic history of women but an economic history of everyone—for in Bateman's eyes giving freedom, equality, and dignity to women leads to high productivity and economic growth. The economic success of men is not down solely to their own abilities and efforts but is a joint product of the economic success of their mothers, sisters, and daughters. This thesis is defended with a wide-ranging familiarity with world history and an acute analysis of the economic incentives and forces at play. *Economica* is also a pleasure to read."

—Robert C. Allen, author of *Global Economic History: A Very Short Introduction*

"An entertainingly readable, well-evidenced global history that places women at its heart. Taking a grand sweep across the ages, it delivers a powerful message about freedoms and challenges us to shape our planet in the interests of all our citizens."

—Sara Horrell, professor of economic history, London School of Economics

ECONOMICA

ECONOMICA

A GLOBAL HISTORY OF WOMEN, WEALTH, AND POWER

VICTORIA BATEMAN

New York

Cover design by Chin-Yee Lai
Cover image © Fine Art Photographic / The Image Bank Unreleased via Getty Images

Seal Press
Hachette Book Group
1290 Avenue of the Americas, New York, NY 10104
www.sealpress.com
@sealpress

Printed in the United States of America

Originally published in 2025 by Headline in the United Kingdom

First US Edition: September 2025

Published by Seal Press, an imprint of Hachette Book Group, Inc. The Seal Press name and logo is a registered trademark of the Hachette Book Group.

The Hachette Speakers Bureau provides a wide range of authors for speaking events. To find out more, go to hachettespeakersbureau.com or email HachetteSpeakers@hbgusa.com.

Seal Press books may be purchased in bulk for business, educational, or promotional use. For more information, please contact your local bookseller or the Hachette Book Group Special Markets Department at special.markets@hbgusa.com.

Print book interior design by Bart Dawson.

Library of Congress Control Number: 2025009086

ISBNs: 9781541606067 (hardcover), 9781541606074 (ebook)

LSC-C

Printing 1, 2025

For all of the women—and men—in history
whose work remains invisible

CONTENTS

LIST OF MAPS

INTRODUCTION

WOMEN ARE, QUITE LITERALLY, THE ORIGIN OF THE WORLD. The survival of the human race depends intimately on women's reproductive efforts. While sixty percent of women's prime age years have historically been spent either in pregnancy or breastfeeding, men have, instead, been expected to 'bring home the bacon', sustaining their wives and children with the money earned by working in fields and factories or as butchers, bakers and candlestick makers.[1] Men have been the 'producers', paid in money, while women have been considered the 'reproducers', paid in an altogether different currency—the love that makes the world go around. Or so the story goes.

The journey of humanity from poverty to prosperity—a journey that is still ongoing today—is bursting with men who have become household names: from Giovanni de' Medici, John D. Rockefeller and Henry Ford through to Vladimir Lenin, Mahatma Gandhi and Bill Gates. But how many female entrepreneurs, merchants, industrialists and economic revolutionaries can you name? You would be forgiven for thinking that, until very recently, there were none at all. Even today, if we gathered in one room all those who have gone from rags to riches, it would be a room full to the brim with men: fewer than six percent of the world's self-made billionaires are women.[2]

Unsurprisingly, rather than being seen as the creators of wealth, women are commonly assumed to be the passive beneficiaries of the economic growth created by their fathers, husbands and brothers. We assume that economic history is made by men: that it is male entrepreneurial talent, their hard labour on farms and in factories, and their revolutionary ideas that have, generation-on-generation, lifted us from a time when life was 'poor, nasty, brutish and short'.[3]

But what about Phryne, the richest woman in ancient Athens, who offered to finance rebuilding the walls of Thebes after the city was razed to the ground by Alexander the Great? Or the canny businesswoman Khadija, better known as the first wife of Muhammad, who, after employing him to look after her troop of trading caravans, proposed to the prophet-to-be? And what about Johanna Ferrour, who helped orchestrate the Peasants' Revolt in fourteenth-century London? Or Priscilla Wakefield, the writer who set up the first English bank for women and children, or Madam Tinubu, in her time the wealthiest and most influential trader in Lagos, driven into exile by the British, or Ching Shih, a sex worker turned pirate who amassed a fleet of ships that controlled trade in the South China Sea? And have you ever heard of Helen Walton, who grew her 'five and dime' store into an American supermarket empire, Sarojini Naidu, who led an economic campaign of resistance against British rule in India, or Zhang Xin, 'the woman who built Beijing'?[4] And, just as importantly, what about the everyday women who laboured for the profit of others: the women who helped to build the Egyptian pyramids, the female slaves who worked on plantations or as domestics, the bare-breasted coal miners of the British Industrial Revolution, the 'convict maids' who laid the foundations of modern-day Australia, the female market-traders of Senegal, and the teenage girls who by day spun cotton in Boston's factories and by night penned their own literary journal? And, of course, the women who labour in many a sweatshop in places like Bangladesh and Vietnam today?

When I first set out to write this book, I thought that I would be racking my brains—and endlessly scouring historical sources—in an effort to find enough women to fill the pages that follow. Once I began to look, though, I quickly realised that I could fill not just one book but multiple volumes. Women have never been 'missing' from economic life; they have simply been hidden from view by those writing the history books. Given that, until relatively recently, most universities did not admit women, this is hardly surprising; most historians, and most economists, were men. Even today, there are twice as many men as there are women writing about the economy.[5] Fortunately, change is happening. It is thanks to the work of modern-day historians, archaeologists and archivists that the women workers and entrepreneurs of the past can be brought back to life and given the recognition that they deserve.

But, ultimately, this book isn't simply about placing the spotlight on women. Having spent twenty years teaching economic history at the universities of Oxford and Cambridge, it is also driven by a passion to weave together the threads of history into a single narrative that includes not only the lives of men but also the lives of women. We cannot understand the progress of our economies just by looking at the lives of men, nor can we simply supplement our current economic histories with a few additional lines—littered here and there—on what the other fifty percent of the population were doing with their time. The whole is, as ever, more than the sum of its parts. Once you 'add women and stir', our understanding of the past changes forever. What follows isn't simply a history of women; it is instead a more accurate economic history of us all.

As we delve into the past and span the globe, we will transport ourselves to the centres of prosperity in each period of human history, taking in ancient Egypt, Mesopotamia, Norte Chico Peru, the Indus Valley, ancient Greece, the Roman Empire, the Islamic 'Abbāsid Empire, Song China, Spanish America, the Dutch Golden Age, Industrial Revolution Britain, colonial West Africa, twentieth-century America, twenty-first-century China, and more. We will consider what types of work women were doing in different periods of history, what obstacles they faced and how women's pay—and treatment—compared with their male counterparts. We will immerse ourselves in all of the important economic moments of the past twelve millennia—the birth of farming, the invention of bronze and iron, the transition from feudalism to capitalism, the emergence of empires and global trade, the American War of Independence, the French Revolution, the Industrial Revolution, the rise and fall of European colonisation, the Russian Revolution, the Great Depression, the advent of computing, the Global Financial Crisis, the rise of modern-day China, and today's clean-tech revolution—all told through the perspectives of women as well as men.

Despite the many forces that have conspired against our female forebears, and their undeniable contributions within the home—without which, as we will see, the economy could not function—we will find that women have featured in almost every aspect of the economy. Amongst the numerous other roles and occupations, we will meet the female hunters of Stone Age Peru, the women plumbers of ancient Rome, the lady brewers of medieval London, the merchant queens of eighteenth-century West Africa, and the female computer engineers of the twentieth century. The sources that we will encounter in the process of documenting women's working lives are eye-opening: ancient seal impressions (the product labels and signatures of the ancient world); fingerprints on centuries-old pottery; petitions to kings and queens; court records; government tax registers; bank-account records; tombs, sculptures and paintings; marriage records; and even women's business cards from eighteenth-century London. Taken together, these sources help to provide a compelling and undeniable account of women's long-standing contribution to our global economy.

By spanning time and place, we will find ourselves asking: How involved have women been in the business world? What type of jobs were women doing in the past? Is women's hard work enough to guarantee that women themselves are recognised and rewarded for their efforts? Does *where* women work—whether inside or beyond the home—matter in terms of how much they are valued by society? What are the greatest obstacles to women's full participation in the economy? Is paid work exploitative or liberating? How does the gender pay gap today compare with that in the past? And have the most successful economies—those that have accomplished the most—been those where women have been able to participate most fully? The answers not only inform the present, but they will also help us to navigate our way to a more prosperous—and hopefully more equal—future.

At present, only one in two of the world's working-age women are in receipt of a pay cheque, compared with more than three in four men.[6] Globally, women who do work earn an average of only seventy-seven cents of every dollar earned by men.[7] Women occupy only a fifth of corporate board positions and run only ten percent of Fortune 500 companies.[8] While men are climbing the career ladder, women are still busy in the home providing three-quarters of all unpaid care.[9] Every day of the week, women spend an average of 2.4 hours more on care than men.[10] And not all of this care has been chosen. While many women might be making their own choices when it comes to the size of their families, many others are denied that choice. Only a half of women in developing countries are able to access contraception or have the right to say no to sexual intercourse with their husband.[11] Since fewer women go out to work than men, when combined with the gender wage gap it means that women take home only fifty-seven percent of what men earn each year, leaving them financially dependent and at greater risk of poverty.[12] Even more substantial than the gender gaps in employment and pay is the disparity in wealth between men and women. Women own far less of the planet than men: across the world, women constitute less than fifteen percent of agricultural landholders—in North Africa and the Middle East, it is fewer than five percent.[13] And, if there were as many female global billionaires as there are male billionaires, we would have six times as many Taylor Swifts, Sheryl Sandbergs and Oprah Winfreys.[14] Importantly, and as we will see, economic inequality isn't purely the result of women being busy in the home; it is also a product of legal and social practices that limit women's freedom to work, their ability to access bank accounts or credit, their right to own property and their right to inherit. The notion that a woman should be able to earn money, to keep and invest the money she earns, to do so proudly and to spend it as she pleases cannot—sadly—be taken for granted.

The issues that women face today are not new. As we will see, employment gaps, seniority gaps, pay gaps and wealth gaps have been a feature of many societies in the past. In the royal cloth workshops in ancient Sumeria, women dominated on the factory floor while men were more likely to be found working as overseers, and even women who did make it into senior roles were paid only a third as much as men.[15] In ancient Egypt, where men and women were relatively equal compared with many other civilisations, it was nevertheless the case that only twelve percent of landowners were women.[16] In ancient Athens, women faced a level of seclusion that rivals modern-day Afghanistan. In the Roman world, where women had far greater freedoms than in Greece, Emperor Augustus—employing a rhetoric that resembles modern-day social conservatism—launched an attack on working women and encouraged them instead to reproduce for the good of Rome.

As we will see, rather than being one long march towards economic liberation for women, history has been a roller-coaster ride for women. The pendulum has swung between periods in which women's involvement in the economy has been welcomed and rewarded to periods when it has been obstructed and rendered invisible. After all, patriarchs typically did not want to admit that women were the source of their riches. Success was instead attributed solely to men—the astute rulers, brave warriors, savvy merchants and creative geniuses that populate the history books. Legends developed that warned of uncontrollable women who distracted emperors, leaving their nation vulnerable to invasion, or of women who wreaked havoc—Pandora-style—by refusing to obey. The ancient Greeks, the Islamic Empire and numerous Chinese and Indian dynasties adopted the same mantra: that women's freedom was the cause of past ruin and that only by restricting women—their bodies, their movements and their choices—could future prosperity be guaranteed. The irony, as we will see, was that it created a vicious cycle of economic ruin that led to the collapse of many a civilisation. Indeed, in what were once some of the wealthiest economies of the world (including ancient Egypt, Iran and India), women live a far more restricted life today than they ever did—and their economy has paid the price. China has been one of the few historic civilisations to realise its mistake, resulting in what is the greatest economic success story of the modern day. And it was also, as we will see, by increasing women's freedoms that the West was able to make its way from being a global economic backwater to dominating the global economy.

From the most successful women of their day to those who struggled to make ends meet, this is the story of how, throughout history, millions of women have managed to financially support themselves, their families and their communities, providing food to fill stomachs and clothes and fuel to keep warm, along with the plays, books and songs that have kept everyone entertained. It is the story of how *women* have made the world rich.

CHAPTER 1

HUNTERS, FARMERS AND CLOTHIERS

THE WOMEN OF THE STONE AGE

LONG AGO, WHEN WE MORE CLOSELY RESEMBLED APES THAN we did human beings, the male of the species could not be relied upon to 'provide'. Mating males roamed the land and impregnated females who were quite literally left 'holding the baby'. Deadbeat dads generated economic needs in the form of extra mouths while single mums had to meet these needs by foraging for food and searching for a suitably dry cave in which to shelter their brood. Men provisioned for themselves, whereas women provisioned for the next generation. The economic survival of the human race thereby depended on the hard work of mothers—work that was more of a necessity than a choice. Then, between eight and five million years ago, something changed. As Africa—the homeland of the earliest humans—experienced drought, food became harder to source, and the most successful communities were those where men cooperated with women rather than abandoning them.[1] We began to work

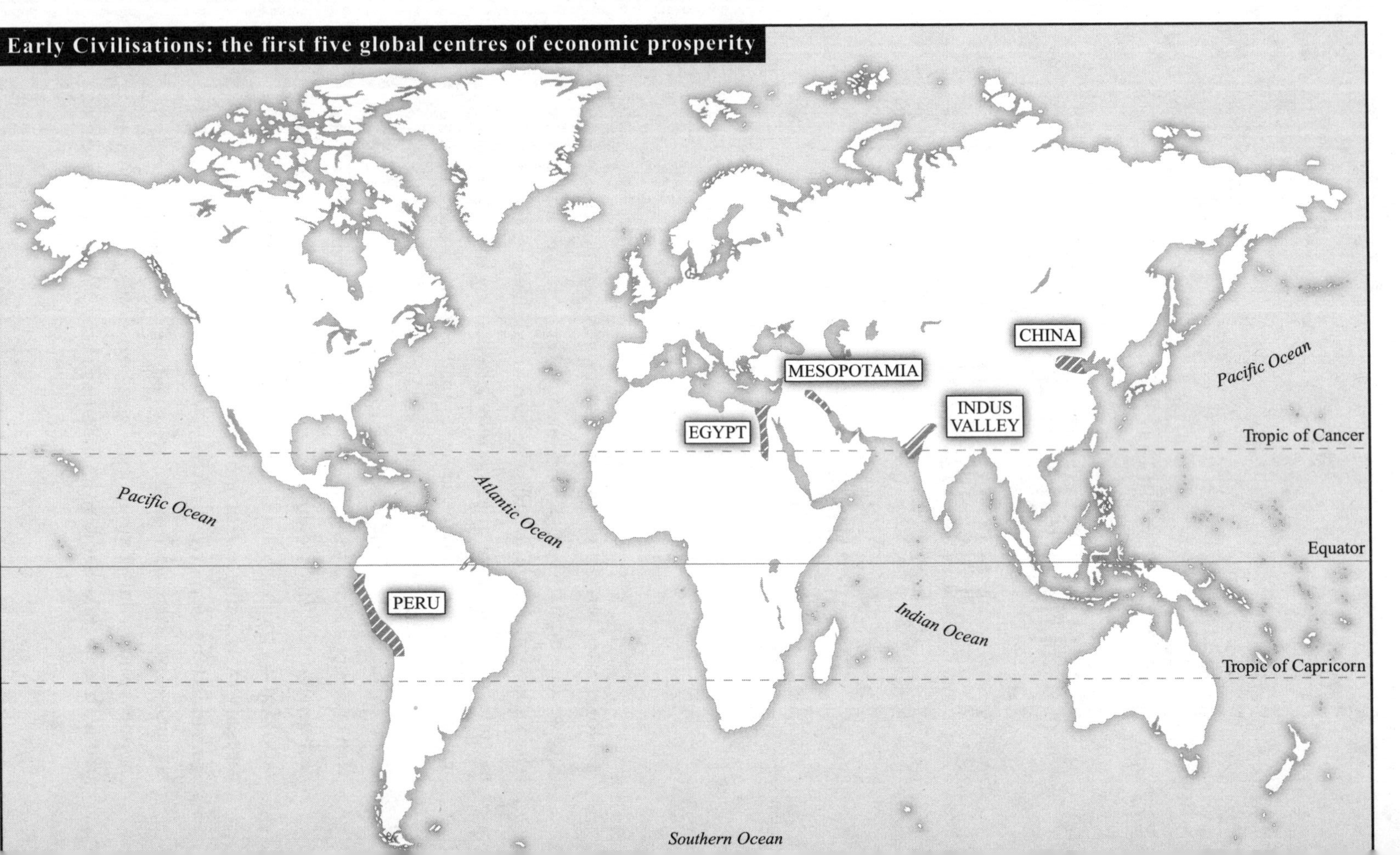
Early Civilisations: the first five global centres of economic prosperity
CHINA
MESOPOTAMIA
INDUS VALLEY
EGYPT
PERU
Pacific Ocean
Atlantic Ocean
Pacific Ocean
Indian Ocean
Southern Ocean
Tropic of Cancer
Equator
Tropic of Capricorn

together to source food and, in the process, evolved to walk on two legs. As fathers learned to share parental responsibility, doting dads replaced cads in what was an age of primitive stone tools, woolly mammoths and sabre-toothed tigers. With time, as global warming made other parts of the world more habitable, these early bands went in search of new land, crossing into the Middle East, with some venturing eastwards to China and others westwards to Spain.[2] Some time between 30,000–15,000 BCE, our ancestors reached the Americas.[3] The 'Flintstones' were populating the globe.

This chapter places women at the heart of the Stone Age. Contrary to the popular image of muscular and hairy men who journeyed far and wide to hunt for wild beasts in order to provide for meek women—dressed in animal skins—who pottered around their caves caring for infants, we will see that our understanding of the past has recently undergone a sexual revolution. Not only did women hunt alongside men; they also had their hands quite literally to the grindstone, grinding as well as planting the seeds that helped transform foragers into farmers, ushering in the first economic revolution in history. But, as we will also see, it was in this transition to a more settled life—one that we might recognise today, with chickens and pet dogs—that patriarchy began to take root. This is the story of how sexism first began.

REINDEER IN PARIS

The story of mankind passed down through the generations is one of distinct gender division; of strong men and docile women who took on completely different roles within their hunter-gatherer communities.[4] Still today, when it comes to understanding gender inequalities, appeal is often made to our historic past: that men behave one way because they were the hunters and women behave another because they took on an altogether different role, sealing the fate of generations to come. Gender equality, we are told, is at odds with human evolution; social conservatives instead would like us to aim for complementarity—a world in which men and women continue with the different roles they were ascribed in the Stone Age. It is a story of the past that is, however, now being overturned.

In 2018, high in the hills of Peru, some thirteen thousand feet above sea level, archaeologists uncovered the remains of a young woman. She was buried alongside a twenty-four-piece hunting kit, including long, pointed projectiles, a knife and meat-processing tools. Initially, the young woman was presumed to be male. It has long been standard practice in archaeology to assume that any skeleton found with hunting gear or weapons was, by default, male. While some thought otherwise, the woman's skeleton had deteriorated so badly that it was, in fact, difficult to prove. But, through new scientific analysis—which uses teeth instead of bones—archaeologists were, at last, able to establish the truth: that the remains of this particular hunter were in fact female.[5]

Known to archaeologists as 'Wilamaya Patjxa individual 6' (WMP6), we can say more about this spear-throwing young woman than might initially meet the eye. She lived nine thousand years ago, as part of a hunter-gatherer community in the Andean highlands, where the land was barren, speckled only with the occasional tuft of grass and—of course—the infrequent wild beast. In a constant battle to find food to stave off hunger, she would have been continually on the move, hunting deer and vicuña—a small member of the camel family—and sharing the resultant meat with her wider community. The mountains would have looked like they continued forever and would have offered little in terms of natural vegetation, though they did afford a diet of wild potatoes. Feeling cold would have been an everyday occurrence, and hypoxia (shortness of breath caused by a lack of oxygen) would have been a constant risk. Exactly why she passed away between the age of seventeen and nineteen we can only hypothesise, but the fact that she was ceremoniously laid to rest with her tools—which were still in full working order and so could easily have been put to use by another hunter—suggests that she was respected and held in high esteem. Her life and her contribution to her community were being honoured.

This Peruvian huntress, named Warawara ('star') by today's local population, was, it turns out, not alone. Of the twenty-seven big-game hunters uncovered in archaeological sites across the Americas dating to the period between 12,000 and 8000 BCE, eleven—some forty percent—have now been identified as female.[6] While some have questioned whether women buried with tools really were hunters, the hunting technology of the day is entirely consistent with the evidence that women did indeed hunt. The weapon of choice amongst early hunters was a spear-thrower known as the *atlatl*, a precursor to the bow and arrow. Proficiency could be achieved at a young age, meaning that females could become adept hunters well before the onset of childbearing. Furthermore, hunting was a communal task, one which involved not only throwing spears but finding and droving big game. Everyone could make a valuable contribution to the hunt.

On the left bank of the Seine, about forty kilometres outside present-day Paris, archaeologists have uncovered an almost perfectly preserved hunting ground and butchery camp occupied by a group of about thirty people some thirteen thousand years ago. Perhaps the most standout feature of the site is that it is filled to the brim with the bones of around seventy-six reindeer. This isn't a random location along the Seine; it is located at a ford in the river, providing a natural place where wild animals could cross from one bank to another, albeit slowly as they battled the currents in the water. Rather than requiring humans to set their own animal traps, the river acted as one big snare, allowing groups of hunters to capture multiple big game in one go.[7]

While the fruits of the hunters' labour could be quickly gained, the processing of the captured beasts required an immense team effort. In addition to a combination of spear-wielding and droving, numerous hands were needed to process, butcher and preserve the meat. Each unlucky reindeer needed to be cut up and cured, with their antlers harvested and hides removed. The resources yielded from the hunt went well beyond meat, and the archaeological remains suggest that this involved people of all ages, sexes and talents.[8]

While big game hunting has left its mark, the contribution of Stone Age gatherers has—until recently—gone under the radar. Unlike hunting, gathering was something archaeologists and anthropologists long assumed to be women's work. As a result, it is also the area of work that they considered the least important. Recent research, however, indicates that plants, shellfish and small creatures snared in nets and traps formed the mainstay of the hunter-gatherer diet, particularly in landscapes more hospitable than that inhabited by our Peruvian huntress. The historian Merry Wiesner-Hanks suggests that it might therefore be more accurate to refer to early humans as 'gatherer-hunters' rather than 'hunter-gatherers', while some have dropped the term hunting altogether and instead refer simply to 'forager societies'.[9] The assumption that hunting was key—and was carried out by men—is rapidly being overturned, and so too is our wider understanding of the Stone Age economy.

DECOMPOSING WOMEN'S WORK

In some ways, it wasn't the ancestors of engineers and inventors who instigated the first 'industrial' turn in human history, but instead the humble cook. Crunchy, naturally occurring plants and chewy, raw meat—freshly removed from the carcass of an animal—can wreak havoc with digestion. Most primates spend hours of their time simply chewing. Gorillas chew for six and a half hours every day, while grazing animals have little time for either work or play as they are constantly eating in order to fulfil their calorific needs.[10] It is little wonder that cattle produce up to 500 litres of methane a day, most of which is the product of burping. The invention of cooking—the ability to soften food and to render it less toxic—aided human digestion and freed up time for other types of productive activity.

Cooking involved harnessing the power of fire. Meat and fish could either be placed on an open fire—barbecue-style—or in a pit in the ground lined with heated stones and covered with plant matter, where the food could instead be roasted. By about 30,000 BCE, early cooks had also invented flatbread.[11] Not only did cooking free the human race from a life of indigestion; the ability to cook food down into a mush liberated women from a much lengthier period of breastfeeding.[12] As stomachs of all ages were filled with hot cooked food, life's little luxuries were born. Time previously spent chewing, digesting and breastfeeding could now be devoted to other tasks. This creation of 'spare time' meant that our growing brainpower—fuelled by protein—could be put to good use. In the course of the Stone Age, fibres, reeds, animal skin and leaves were turned into a plethora of new products: cloths, mats, animal traps, fishing nets and blankets. This was an age of creativity and—unlike today—everything was organic.

While the chipped stone tools more commonly associated with the Stone Age have survived the ravages of time, the much wider material culture of the era has disintegrated and decomposed. In today's forager societies, nine in ten objects are produced using perishable materials, and much of their production is carried out by women.[13] The artisanal skill involved is impressive, but any such items produced in the past have long since vanished, fuelling the impression that the economy was dominated by men who, when they weren't hunting, were instead chipping away at stone. Perhaps, as a result, the Stone Age has been misnamed. Once we recognise the plethora of work carried out by women, this period of human history might be better referred to as the Stone *Plus* Age.

A piece of string helps to unlock the secrets of this perishable past. Discovered only recently, it is the oldest surviving fibre-based artefact from human history, dating to around 40,000–50,000 BCE. Only 6.2 mm long and 0.5 mm wide, the string was found three metres underground on the surface of a stone tool fragment at the archaeological site of Abri du Maras, France, on a tributary of the Rhône River.[14] The string was constructed by twisting together three pieces of tree-bark fibre, displaying the same skills that would later lead to the development of spinning and weaving. While the earliest pieces of woven cloth have long since decomposed, evidence of their existence is visible in the neatly woven textile impressions found on 28,000-year-old fragments of clay in the region spanning from Moravia (in modern-day Czechia) down to Mesopotamia in the Middle East.[15] It is likely that the criss-cross checkerboard impressions were accidental rather than intentional—the result of handling clay while holding a piece of cloth. Some of the first fired-clay items in human history were small sculptures of animals and humans, and their fragments can in turn reveal quite a lot about who produced them. Those found in abundance in archaeological sites in Czechia, dating to between 25,000 and 15,500 BCE, bear fingerprints with fine ridges, suggesting that women were the ones working the clay.[16] Indicative of their creation by women, early pots had a distinctly female flavour of decoration, featuring numerous symbols of fertility.[17]

The processes used in the production of perishable items have also left another kind of mark: on the jaws of female skeletons.[18] Basketry—which was vital for everything from fishing to fetching—required the careful preparation of plant fibres, such as stripping rushes of their outer layers. When carried out orally, and at great speed, the stripping process creates grooves on human teeth. Evidence suggests that the female mouth was also all-important when working animal hides into leather goods: chewing was part of the process used to soften the skins. Similarly, when it came to weaving cloth while on the move, teeth could be helpful as a third hand—something which would not surprise any modern-day seamstress.[19] While the products of these women's labour have since decayed, looking carefully at the toll taken on their bodies, the evidence of their contribution to the 'gatherer-hunter' economy is abundantly clear. Not only were women hunting and gathering alongside men; they were pivotal to the invention of manufacturing.

FASHIONING THE FARM

When life was nomadic, belongings needed to be kept to a bare minimum. As today, there was a limit to how much people could carry while on the move—albeit in the age of baskets rather than suitcases that limit would have been somewhat less. Once humans began to settle down in one place, this constraint was lifted and 'manufacturing' could reach a whole new level. In Turkey, Syria and Israel, permanent homesteads started to appear by around 10,000 BCE, millennia ahead of the colder northern parts of the continent, where people continued to wander the grassy plains. The first villages comprised between ten and fifty families, who likely worked together—Amish-style—to clear the land, to construct shelter and to create pens for animals.[20] With this more sedentary existence, people could now possess much more than they literally 'stood up in', ushering in a material world like never before.

After forming settled communities, and as a step on from hunting and gathering, our ancestors began collecting the seeds of wild cereals and planting them on land suitable for human habitation, where—for the first time—we grew our own food. Alongside, animals were captured, placed in pens and bred for their meat. Land was increasingly enclosed, fenced off and farmed, no doubt making life more difficult for those who continued with the more nomadic way of life. Unsurprisingly, the assumption has been that the development of farming—like hunting—was a largely male endeavour. But, in the legends of the Inca, it was a woman—Mama Huaco—who first introduced corn to the Andes and, according to no less an authority than Charles Darwin, it would have been strange if women had not been involved in the invention and diffusion of farming more generally.[21] Women were perfectly capable of using a hoe and a digging stick, which was the height of farming sophistication in the Neolithic.[22] Since women were hunters, why indeed could they not also have been some of our earliest farmers? And, for those societies where men really were more likely to be away from the village hunting for animals or fishing in the seas, isn't it then even more likely that the women—left behind—would have been the ones collecting and planting the first seeds? Indeed, if women were, like today, the people most likely to be cleaning the toilet, then they would have been the first to notice the way in which seeds naturally sprouted from the human excrement deposited in latrines, which likely provided the first natural example of the potential on offer by planting (rather than simply eating) seeds.[23] As the archaeologist Dani Nadel writes, when it comes to planting the first crops 'it's impossible to say who had the idea first, man or woman . . . It's difficult to know for certain what happened 20,000, 12,000 or 10,000 years ago . . . But perhaps we have denied women a very important role'.[24]

While we will never know for sure who fenced off and sowed the first fields, archaeological evidence suggests that women were the ones on the front line, milling the grain and transforming it into something edible. Female skeletons from the 9,500-year-old Abu Hureyra settlement in Syria show visible joint damage and lesions on the ankles, toes, knees and the lower backs.[25] More or less every home had its own grindstone, and grinding cereals was no mean feat: it involved kneeling at a grinding stone fixed to the floor, moving back and forth while exerting physical force for a prolonged period of time. To produce enough flour to feed a family of six, you would need to grind grain in this way for two to three hours a day every day.[26] No wonder that it took a toll on the female body.

Recent research has also revealed something rather radical: that farms existed to supply us with clothing as much as they did to supply us with food. Around the time that humans settled down to farm the land, the climate underwent a mighty shift. The end of the Ice Age had brought warmer weather, leading to the release of glacial meltwater that created a sudden and unexpected drop in global temperatures, which presented quite a challenge for a scantily clad species that had long since lost its own fur.[27] Not only were our ancestors left feeling cold, but as sea levels rose, evaporation increased and rains became more frequent, meaning that we needed a form of clothing that could breathe in the humid weather and protect us from the rain. At the same time, woolly mammoths and other sizeable beasts did not much like the change in the climate, and those that did manage to survive were quickly hunted to extinction for their skins.[28] Societies in the Middle East, the Indus Valley and China therefore hatched a plan: to domesticate sheep and goats, which could in turn be bred for their fleeces.[29] In the Andean highlands of Peru, llamas and alpacas provided an equivalent source of wool.[30] Farm animals were, in other words, 'walking wardrobes' as much as they were walking larders.[31] That may well explain why, for the Incas, killing an alpaca has traditionally been considered criminal.[32] Alongside using animals, people ingeniously began to turn plants into cloth: Egypt cultivated flax, China grew hemp and the Indus Valley domesticated cotton.[33] So too did northern Peru, where cotton cultivation—which began 8,000 years ago—predates both corn and the chilli pepper.[34] Nearby in Mexico, the earliest textiles were woven from the cactus-like maguey plant, while in Papua New Guinea, where the signs of an early civilisation are only just being discovered, the first domesticated banana—which was somewhat less edible than modern-day varieties—was likely grown for its fibres more than for its flavour.[35] Across the world, our ancestors were cultivating plants and breeding animals in order to clothe our wet and cold bodies, not just to fill our stomachs.[36] For the first time, clothing was becoming big business. Farming and cloth-making were inextricably linked.

Weaving cloth required serious equipment, providing further reason to pursue a more sedentary lifestyle. Looms loom large: whether it is conducted horizontally or vertically, weaving takes up space. In parts of the world where the weather suited courtyard and rooftop living, weaving tended to take place on the floor, with the fibres stretched out horizontally on a large frame. With these 'warp' threads in place, the weaver could then weave the 'weft' in and out between the parallel strands. Funerary art from ancient Egyptian tombs suggests that horizontal looms were being used by women from as early as 4500 BCE.[37] Where the weather was less well suited to the outdoors, looms instead stood tall—as if flipped ninety degrees—with the fibres stretched across a vertical as opposed to horizontal frame. In the case of these vertical looms, the weaver typically used a set of weights attached to the bottom of each set of warp threads, to hold them in place during the weaving process. While the wooden frames have disintegrated with time, the weights—typically made from clay—have been found by archaeologists in the residential living quarters of both Chinese and Middle Eastern homes, and in many a woman's grave.[38] Cloth was a woman's business—and it was a business that could not have gone unnoticed given the scale of the equipment involved.[39]

For women with small children, the production of cloth had a rather important feature: it could easily be conducted from the home, where it could be combined with childcare. Spinning and weaving can be very repetitive, and—at least in the hands of a skilled person—can therefore be easily interrupted and resumed; something of a necessity while taking care of infants. Unlike working with stone or metals, there was no need for sharp or dangerous tools of a kind that could injure a child. While there was, of course, no reason why men were not equally as capable as women when it came to producing cloth, there was a doubly good reason for childbearing women to specialise in cloth production: fertility was soaring. Since a settled existence meant that baby-making became a more regular occurrence, women had to juggle work and childcare.

The home was the bedrock of the Neolithic economy. While in more recent history, working from home has been seen as secondary and trivial, in Neolithic times the home was the main arena of production. The economy started and ended with the family unit: to ensure that the basic needs of their families were met, women had to provision their households, ensuring sufficient food, clothing and other necessities. Women were, in other words, the 'chief operating officers' of their families.[40] They wove their own cloth, produced their own food, brewed their own beer and made their own pots, ensuring every step of the way that the muscle and brain power of each family member was put to good use. That included young children, who could help by brushing and preparing raw wool before it was spun by their mothers. The home was the workplace and the workplace was the home.

INHERITANCE RULES

Once humans began to lead a settled existence, saving for the future became a distinct possibility. Not only was it possible; it was necessary. The natural world was unpredictable—as was our own health. Rather than consuming everything at once, it made sense to save surpluses for a later date. Grain could be stored, milk could be churned into cheese, and cloth could be rolled up to trade for future needs. Unlike forager societies, farming societies could more easily accumulate and preserve wealth, and no more so than in the form of land and livestock. While saving solved one problem, it also begged a question: how to pass on the contents of your barn to future generations. While the custom of legacies—along with family names—passing through the male line has become reasonably standard practice in recent history, this 'patrilineal' (or more generally patriarchal) way of life is neither natural nor inevitable. In fact, Victorian anthropologists proposed that all societies were, in their early days, matrilineal, with names and property passing from woman to woman.[41]

Societies had good reason for passing lineage and property through the female line. While the father of a child could never be known for sure, the mother was the one who physically gave birth, meaning that a mother always knew that a child was her own. The greater responsibility that a mother might therefore feel towards her children in turn meant that many societies felt that mothers should be the ones in charge of the land, so that they could secure sufficient food for their family. The wife was the custodian of her children, and so it was she—not her male partner—who had effective usage or ownership rights over the land the family inhabited. As a result, before the American founding fathers, there were the clan mothers: the women of the Haudenosaunee people (the Native American confederacy of the Mohawk, Oneida, Onondaga, Cayuga, Seneca and Tuscarora nations), who were customarily in charge of both land and government.

Farming in North America traditionally involved hoes and digging sticks made from animal bones, and women—not men—held the right to farm the land, a right that they could pass on to their daughters. Women controlled both the production and the distribution of food and clans were named after animals or birds and followed the female line. Women remained within their family's community, rather than moving into the community of their husband. Communities were 'matrilocal': husbands—rather than wives—were, therefore, the ones who were expected to relocate upon marriage. Families lived communally in bark-shingled longhouses, with shared hearths and partitions that offered privacy when sleeping.[42] Even after marriage, men were expected to continue helping their mothers and their sisters when needed; men, in other words, worked for women, rather than (as is more usual in today's economy) women for men.[43] This continued outside the home too. While men were the ones who held seats on political councils, they were selected by women who could depose them if they acted against their interests, and war could not occur without female consent.[44] Evidence of society being similarly female-centred in Britain has also recently come to light as a result of an in-depth study of human skeletons found in an Iron Age burial site in Dorset. Using DNA evidence and carbon dating to reconstruct family trees, researchers have found that—compared with men—deceased females were more closely related to other people in their community, suggesting that women (not men) continued to live in the same community throughout their adult life.[45] In the Pacific, genetic evidence suggests that society has been similarly women-focused for millennia.[46] Societies in which descent passes through the female line are also deeply rooted in parts of West Africa, southeast Asia and in the grassy hills of northeast India, home to the Khasis.

But not all societies in the distant past were akin to female communes. There is plenty of evidence of 'Big Man' societies headed by male chiefs, including in the form of lavish male burials.[47] There is also evidence from some parts of the world, including large parts of continental Europe, that women were being 'exchanged' between communities. Scientists have recently studied the remains of more than a hundred people buried in a makeshift graveyard in central France around 5000 BCE, finding that family members were related through the male as opposed to female bloodline. Unlike fathers, mothers had been brought into the community during their youth, and while sons remained within the community, daughters did not.[48] This means that either at or before puberty, girls were being moved between communities. The fact that the female skeletons did not display evidence of violent abduction suggests that a 'peaceful' exchange of girls was taking place, albeit we can never know the degree to which the girls (as opposed to their parents) had a choice in the matter. The analysis of DNA from an even older—50,000 year old—Neanderthal site in Spain similarly reveals that men were much more closely related than women, again indicating that it was women—not men—who were the ones being 'exchanged' between communities, consensually or not.[49]

Since early humans lived in small bands of between twenty and thirty people, they needed to mix with those beyond their own circle.[50] Inbreeding could be highly destructive, and so surviving generation-on-generation meant meeting new people. The question is: Why did some societies exchange women more than men? Perhaps it was because women were understood to be valuable property before other forms of property—land, cattle and farms—even existed.[51] At a time when the world's total population numbered in the thousands rather than the billions (only reaching a million about twenty thousand years ago), food and resources were abundant and extra hands could be put to good use. This meant that women were considered in possession of a special gift: the gift of fertility. Parallels were drawn between women's fertility and the fertility of the natural world, and the 'mother goddess' was praised and revered across the world. Given that more than a third of children died in infancy and that childbirth itself was a risky business, a mother with a babe in arms was a sight to be celebrated.[52] Since that which is most prized is also most vulnerable, fertility was a double-edged sword: it could lead women to a situation of power but also to a situation of being captured and controlled. Women's lives were on a knife-edge, which explains why Stone Age societies were so varied and why historians present us with two diametrically opposed visions of the past: at one extreme, the matriarchal societies in which women commanded power and, at the other extreme, a society in which men dressed in animal skins, club in hand, abducted unsuspecting women as they foraged for food.[53]

Not every Stone Age society was the same—there was certainly plenty of room on the continuum between matriarchy and patriarchy. But, with time, it appears that more societies moved in the patriarchal direction, with descent, rank and property passed down the male rather than the female line, and women being absorbed into their husbands' families.[54] The result is that seventy percent of societies today exhibit such patriarchal features.[55] The question we therefore need to ask next is: Why did some societies abandon more women-friendly practices in favour of more patriarchal ones? As we will see, the plough, pastoralism and property rights—the three P's—all had a role to play.

PLOUGHS, PASTORALISM AND PROPERTY RIGHTS

Farming was not an easy life. Working the land often required being in the fields from dawn until dusk. The skeletal remains of foragers tell us that they were better nourished than our first farming ancestors—and had more time to spare. Foraging was part-time work: in around three hours a day, you could find enough food from the natural environment to fill your stomach.[56] It's not surprising therefore that, for a long period of time, foraging and farming continued to exist side by side. Some foraging societies lived their lives regardless of their more sedentary peers—a diverse range of such societies continue to exist today. Those who did settle down to farm the land supplemented their food needs with food acquired from naturally foraging the surrounding environment. But, starting in the seventh millennium BCE, a new invention transformed the farming world, resulting in the virtual extinction of the forager way of life in large parts of North Africa and Eurasia. That invention was the plough.

By attaching a wooden frame with sticks that dragged on the floor to the back of a strong muscular animal, such as a water buffalo or a cow, a farmer could cut furrows into the land. This meant that seeds could be planted more easily. Angular strips could also be attached to the frame and dragged across the land, allowing the soil to be turned more easily. The result was that each farmer could cultivate a larger area of land, producing food that went beyond the needs of their own family.[57] While the plough raised productivity, it also had a serious downside. The earliest artistic depictions of ploughs—which include models and paintings from Egyptian tombs—show that men were almost consistently the ones in charge of ploughing the land. Handling a plough required more muscular strength than the older farming technology of using digging sticks and hoes. The result was that—in areas where the plough was adopted—farming became seen as men's work.[58] Women were instead pushed into the domestic sphere, grinding grain and making cloth. In Sipar, not far from present-day Baghdad, millstones were treated as women's property, gifted either from the husband to the wife or from the father to the daughter.[59] It was the equivalent of being gifted an oven or a vacuum cleaner for Christmas. History casts a long shadow: in regions which have historically made greater use of the plough, the gender gap is highest today.[60]

The plough wasn't suited to all terrains. Where more traditional methods of farming continued, women continued to work and maintain rights over the land. On more inhospitable terrain—in the mountains, deserts and expansive arid grasslands that stretch from eastern Europe to Mongolia—herding grew in popularity, whether of sheep, goats, yaks, reindeer or cattle.[61] In some places, such a life remained, by necessity, nomadic. Where the land was arid and water was in short supply, it was easier to take animals to water (and fodder) than it was to bring water (and fodder) to animals. In other places, the pastoral life required the seasonal movement of livestock: spending summers on higher land and then moving down the mountainsides as the winter set in. For men who lived in matrilineal societies, herding offered a potential way out: a chance to escape matrilineal control and to build their own property in the form of a herd. Like ploughing, nomadic pastoralism became dominated by men. And, so as to guarantee their own patrilineal family line, some of these pastoralists went to great efforts to acquire women and to shield them from impregnation by other men. Even today, women living in the parts of the world with a long history of nomadic pastoralism experience some of the greatest restrictions on their participation in wider society. They have less freedom of movement, experience higher rates of male violence and adhere to stricter and more restrictive sexual norms, such as veiling and female genital cutting.[62]

According to Friedrich Engels—the famous compatriot of Karl Marx—private property was at the root of the sexist turn. Foraging communities, in Engels's view, offered a primitive form of communism, in which land was communally owned and people worked cooperatively to achieve common goals. This more egalitarian society began to disappear in parts of the world where farming was invented. What was key for Engels was that farming brought ownership. Previously communal land was fenced off and made inaccessible to everyone except the owner. The herds of animals that were being shepherded across mountains and plains also became privately owned. With fields and herds therefore came the invention of private property. In the way that Marx saw private property as being at the root of wealth inequality, Engels saw private property as being key to understanding gender inequality. Where men were the ones in charge of ploughing and herding, it was men—not women—who were granted property rights. Land on which they had previously been able to freely wander—foraging and hunting—was now 'enclosed' in private hands. Activities that had previously been part of everyday life were now branded as poaching and trespassing. Rather than being able to fend for themselves, women were left dependent on their menfolk—who in turn wanted to ensure that 'their' women were producing heirs to whom the land could pass. In Engels's own words, the result was that women 'became the slave of his [man's] lust and a mere instrument for the production of children'.[63]

FROM SEXISM TO STATES

Whether it was the plough, pastoralism or property rights, the uptick in patriarchy is visible in one shocking fact: between 7,000 and 5,000 years ago, the genetic diversity of human males collapsed across the Middle East, Africa, Asia and Europe, to the point that the male population had only one seventeenth of the genetic diversity of the female population.[64] The reason for the extinction of such a large number of Y chromosomes is that men were increasingly living with their own relatives—in patrilineal groups—and competition between these groups (which included killing each other) therefore had the power to wipe out entire male lineages. Since women were scattered—expected to move to their husband's communities upon marriage—their DNA could not be extinguished if the community they married into faced destruction. In other words, since brothers lived together but sisters were dispersed across numerous communities, it was the survival of male lineage that was dealt a fatal blow as societies began to compete with one another.

The creation of wealth—in the form of land, livestock and other property—incentivised theft and so destruction on a grand scale.

Not only was land increasingly attractive; so too were people. Not everyone wanted to do the hard work of ploughing fields, looking after livestock or weaving cloth, particularly if they were men in the game of acquiring more land and herds. In a world which was far less populated than it is today and which lacked labour-saving machines, people were scarce and valuable. As the people who could in turn produce even more people, women were particularly prized. Men raiding villages and capturing their female inhabitants was an all-too-common occurrence. As a result, women could be removed from the safety of their own clan and transported to a new society in which they may have been unable to speak the language, with no claim on either land or property. In order to guarantee paternity, their firstborn child was typically killed, with all successive children being treated as the property of the father. Daughters could be gifted to neighbouring societies as a means to maintain peaceful diplomatic relations.[65] Whenever diplomacy failed, full-blown warfare ensued—the ultimate means to gain ownership of more land and people. In this process, as we will see in the next chapter, not only were a large number of male chromosomes wiped out, but the first states and empires began to emerge.

CHAPTER 2

DOCTORS, SCRIBES AND INNKEEPERS

THE WOMEN OF THE BRONZE AGE

WHAT WAS THE FIRST CITY IN HUMAN HISTORY? IT WASN'T Beijing, Rome, London, Athens or New York, however great those cities might be today. Instead, Jericho—of biblical fame—dating to at least 8000 BCE, is one of a number of cities that could lay claim to the top spot.[1] So too is the much lesser known Çatalhöyük, a city that grew up at the foot of a volcano in modern-day Turkey. Nine thousand years ago, it housed family homes, constructed from brick and clay and entered via a ladder up to the roof. Rooftops functioned not only as meeting places but as streets. Each home had its own hearth and some also had their own shrines, decorated with paintings of livestock, hunting scenes and goddesses. Inhabitants of the city herded livestock, farmed with hoes, drank alcohol, wore jewellery and could see their reflections staring back at them in mirrors.[2] It was a relatively equal society, both in terms of wealth and gender. Women worked outdoors as well as indoors, were as well nourished

Mesopotamia
Black Sea
Caspian Sea
GREECE
Troy
Thebes
Athens
ANATOLIA
Kanesh
Çatalhüyük
Knidos
Urkesh
Karana
MESOPOTAMIA
Ashur
SYRIA
Euphrates
Tigris
Mari
AKKAD
PERSIA
Mediterranean Sea
Babylon
Jericho
Jordon
SUMER
Lagash
Ur
N
Giza
Nile
ARABIA
EGYPT
Persian Gulf
0 50 100 150 200 250 miles
Red Sea

as men and were sent into the afterlife with the same degree of ceremony as their menfolk.[3] The city's shared wealth was built on selling obsidian, the glass deposited by volcanic lava, which was highly prized by tool-makers.[4] Obsidian—along with amber, jade and lapis lazuli—was one of the first traded items in history.[5]

While impressive, Çatalhöyük lacked the kind of governmental structures and geographic scale of the societies that developed later in history.[6] It was in the Bronze Age—starting around five thousand years ago—that the world's first such 'civilisations' began to emerge. These civilisations were much more substantial in size than the societies that had come before, and developed sophisticated systems of administration that could plan public works, from grain stores and large-scale irrigation systems to defensive structures and networks of temples. Borders were defined and tightly guarded, writing systems and legal codes developed, and the economy became more complex—and with that, more capable of producing surpluses.[7] In some societies, these surpluses were used to enrich those in power, resulting in lavish palaces and glorified monumental structures that came at the cost of poorly paid workforces and enslavement. Inequality—both in terms of wealth and gender—had the potential to reach higher levels than ever before, although, as we will see, the extent to which it did varied greatly from one civilisation to another.

This chapter depicts life in five of the earliest civilisations: the ancient Egypt of the pyramids; the historic heart of the Middle East known as Mesopotamia; the Indus River Valley spanning modern-day Pakistan and India; China, the home of magnificent tombs filled with pottery, jade and tiger heads; and Peru, the home not only of corn and chilli but also of wool and cotton. Five millennia ago, these were the five great centres of prosperity, and they spanned the entire spectrum from warmongering Mesopotamia to the more peaceful and idyllic Indus. Notable for its absence from our list is any part of Europe or North America. While today the West features at the top of the international economic league tables, for most of history it was a backwater of little consequence. And the world has changed in more ways than one. While women in Egypt, India, Pakistan and the Middle East today are often considered marginal to the economy, the lives of their distant ancestors—as we will see—could not have been more different. This is the story of women's working lives in some of the most formative years of human history.

ANCIENT EGYPT

Ancient Egypt—a land blessed by the River Nile—existed in splendid isolation for thousands of years, protected by the surrounding deserts. It was a place of peace and tranquillity, and created its own unique civilisation. Egyptian wealth was ploughed into pyramids, commissioned by Egyptian rulers in order to provide a safe route into the next world. Central to the Egyptian belief system was the notion that creating a visual record of life on earth would aid the transition to the afterlife. Whether or not this helped the ancient Egyptians, it has certainly helped historians by providing a wealth of images of daily scenes. Tomb paintings from burial sites in ancient Egypt depict men, women and children in vivid colour. The women have long black hair and are dressed in long, white linen dresses. During festivities—such as in banqueting or musical scenes—they wear makeup around their eyes, bangles on their arms and necklaces that form collars around their necks. Sometimes their linen clothing is so fine that it is virtually translucent—something that would be considered unacceptable in modern-day Egypt. Carved stone reliefs and statues from the tombs add further to the mix. Despite being thousands of years old, the scenes look remarkably modern. We see women not only occupying domestic roles, but also working in fields, weaving in workshops and entertaining the royal court with musical performances.[8] One statue of a woman—with her left hand lifted and placed on her right breast—is inscribed with the name Sitsnefru. Archaeologists believe that she was a wet-nurse for an elite family. The fact that she was memorialised suggests that she was a respected and valued member of the household.

Not far from the opulence of the pyramids, one can find more evidence of women's working lives. The construction of a pyramid took a workforce of between ten and thirty thousand people a period of around twenty years.[9] Some of these workers lived permanently on site, for which an entire camp—much like a modern-day town—was created. Others worked on temporary contracts for three or four months at a time, for which suitable lodgings needed to be found.[10] These worker camps were, until recently, off the archaeological radar, but are now being explored. The results have shocked archaeologists. While traditionally the pyramids were assumed to have been built by 'whip-driven' slaves, evidence from the camps suggests that the majority were in fact paid labourers.[11] While slavery no doubt existed in Egypt, it was less of a slave-based economy than some of the other societies that we will encounter. For labourers, the standard daily pay was around ten loaves of bread plus beer, some of which could be traded for meat, fish and clothing.[12] Much of what was consumed was produced on site, creating opportunities for all kinds of craft producers and market stall holders. Given the scale of the workforce—and the twenty-year period involved in building a pyramid—death also needed to be dealt with. Every workers' camp therefore had its own cemetery, which included miniature pyramids and tombs. What is notable, however, is that half of all skeletal remains found in the workers' cemetery at the Great Pyramid of Giza are female.[13] While some presume that women lived on site to look after their husbands, the fact that female—and not just male—skeletons show signs of heavy labour suggests that women were very much involved in construction, whether directly or indirectly, such as by mixing mortar, making food or producing uniforms for the workforce.[14] The pyramids were not just a spectacular achievement of architectural ingenuity; they also owe a debt of gratitude to the labours of both men and women.

In the settlement at Deir el-Medina, home to some of the people who built the Valley of the Kings and Queens, we get a taste of Egyptian family life higher up the social ladder. This was a 'middle-class' settlement for some of the better-paid workers, including many of the leading artists and stonemasons of the day. Its residents occupied four-room family homes, each with its own oven and grindstone. In the hot summers, people would sometimes sleep on their roof, which would also be home to the family's pet geese and pigeons. A love poem found at the village reads: 'He does not know my desire to embrace him / And that he would write to my mother'. It suggests that, at that time, young men were expected to ask a young woman's mother for permission to marry.[15] Egypt was neither patrilineal nor matrilineal; it practised bilateral descent, meaning that people could trace their lineage through both their mother's and their father's kin.[16]

While women in middle-class homes were considered the 'mistress of the house'—not just at Deir el-Medina but also elsewhere in Egypt—they were also free to pursue a life beyond the home.[17] Though the daily lives of many Egyptian women involved sweeping the mud floors of their homes with reed brushes, shaking out mats to remove sand and dust, baking bread and brewing beer, they could alongside these domestic tasks also earn an income.[18] Egyptian women could own property, start their own businesses, were free to divorce and were equal to men before the law.[19] One of the economic activities most associated with women was the production of linen, whether within the home or on a more industrial scale. Linen was the cloth of choice in Egypt as it suited the hot and humid climate. While linen did not hold dye as well as wool, meaning that clothing was plain, the Egyptians introduced colour into their wardrobe via jewellery, such as collar-style necklaces.[20] Linen also had another advantage: it was easier to wash and keep clean. Tomb paintings and miniature wooden models—often found in the burial sites of the less well-off—depict women spinning and weaving in workshops while men not only collect the raw material—flax—but also tend to the laundry in the waters of the Nile, braving the crocodiles.[21] What is notable—based on the items that appear in their graves—is that women from poorer families were buried on more equal terms to their husbands than was the case with women from wealthier families.[22] Women's weaving clearly made a crucial contribution to their household, but that could easily be overlooked when the husband's salary started to grow.[23]

Not all higher earners, however, were men. Around a fifth of Egypt's elite were women.[24] Women held responsible and senior positions in the workforce, as government administrators, managers of royal family households and doctors.[25] A woman by the name of Peseshet—who lived almost five thousand years ago—can lay claim to being the world's first known female physician. Not only was she a doctor; she also taught at Egypt's medical school in Sais.[26] Egypt was at the forefront of medical knowledge in the ancient world.[27] Medical papyri detail symptoms, diagnoses and treatments for all kinds of illnesses and diseases, and include the first known treatise on gynaecology.[28] The skeletal remains of the pyramids' workers' villages show that complex surgery was carried out in response to accidents and illness. One cemetery includes the remains of two people whose bones properly healed following amputation—one the left leg and the other the right arm.[29]

Women could be found throughout the Egyptian economy but, as we will see next, they were more likely to be free in the land of the pyramids than they were in the land of empire-building Mesopotamia.

MESOPOTAMIA

Rising from the mountains bordering Turkey, and then winding through the Syrian and Arabian desert and out into the Persian Gulf, are the two great rivers—the Tigris and the Euphrates—between which lies the fertile crescent of Mesopotamia. Encompassing modern-day Iraq and parts of Turkey, Syria and Iran, Mesopotamia became the trading centre of Eurasia in the fourth millennium BCE. It is known to archaeologists and historians as the 'cradle of civilisation'.

At first sight, Mesopotamia might appear to have been an unlikely place to play host to one of the world's first civilisations. The soil was marshy and there was little in the way of trees or stone from which to construct buildings. But, despite the odds, it was the place where the civilisation of Sumer emerged, at the mouth of the Persian Gulf.[30] Six thousand years ago, farmland in the region was communally owned by extended family groups.[31] Women farmed, fished and caught small game.[32] With time, land became concentrated in the hands of fewer people, in a process that was not always even-handed.[33] By offering generous-seeming loans to fellow landholders but on extortionate terms, the most successful families were able to magnify their wealth not only through interest payments but by forcing anyone who could not repay to give up their land—and themselves—in lieu of their debt.[34] The process snowballed until every part of Sumeria had its own wealthy elite, who in turn declared themselves kings and queens. Their rule was legitimised not only by wealth but by an insistence that they could offer a special relationship with the heavens, one that would guarantee their people a prosperity similar to that with which they had themselves been blessed.

Rather than managing the land themselves, the elite often left this task to temples. Temples were the business-places of the day: they organised irrigation and drainage to improve the productivity of agriculture, they managed the system of sowing and harvesting, and they doled out basic rations to the servile workforce.[35] Much of the hard labour on temple or palace estates was provided by servile labourers in the form of enslaved prisoners of war or local people who had fallen on hard times and become dependent on temple authorities. In addition, the ruling elite insisted on collecting not just tribute but compulsory labour service from peasant families who leased or owned their own land—the equivalent of a rent or tax collected in kind rather than in money.[36] Anyone who attempted to escape their obligatory labour service could be punished with enslavement. Where peasant families faced financial difficulty, wives and daughters could find themselves in debt bondage. The death of a patriarch provided no escape from servitude: widows who had not produced a male heir could become locked out of the chain of patrilineal inheritance, leaving them landless. It was through such impoverishment that women found themselves institutionalised as servile labourers on temple estates.[37] Taken together, enslavement, impoverishment and debt bondage meant that close to a half of people lived their lives in some form of servitude.[38] It was the immense administrative effort involved in this system of labour coercion that helped give rise to the written word. Starting life in the fourth millennium BCE as simple pictorial representations, and written on soft clay that then hardened, the cuneiform language employed the 'rebus principle' in which, for example, the sketch of a bee followed by a leaf can be read as 'belief'. The fact that clay was used as opposed to parchment has fortuitously provided historians with a wealth of written documents, a large proportion of which relate to the economy of the day. It was also around this same time that Egyptian hieroglyphs developed, making the written words of Mesopotamia and Egypt the oldest known languages in the world.[39]

Flourishing agriculture wasn't, however, the most distinguishing characteristic of Sumeria. Instead, it was its cities and its trade: more than thirty cities emerged across southern Mesopotamia, each with its own landed elite, craft producers and merchants. Since Sumeria lacked wood and stone, trade was important from the start. The elite tasked merchants with going in search of raw materials for the building of palaces, temples and water systems. In their trading missions, merchants also discovered copper, which was imported from Anatolia in the north (in present-day Turkey) and also, via the Persian Gulf, from Oman.[40] It was by building on these trading connections—by sea and by land—that the region was able to prosper in the course of the Bronze Age.

From around 3500 BCE, Anatolians began smelting copper and tin to produce a new, stronger substance: bronze. Pure copper had long been worked by coppersmiths—as is clear from the presence of copper crowns and axes in archaeological digs—but was extremely difficult to cast. Metal production was, as a result, limited to either the barest necessities or the most prized luxuries. One option was to combine copper with arsenic, which achieved a more workable and at the same time harder metal, but with somewhat poisonous consequences. Tin provided an alternative, but was much harder to source, requiring long-distance travel to Central Asia—to Afghanistan and the surrounding region—either via Persia by land or from the Persian Gulf by sea via India.[41] Sparking the first long-distance trade boom in history, this search for tin not only saved the lives of Anatolian blacksmiths who would have otherwise continued to die from arsenic poisoning, but also created the first globally connected economy, and it was Mesopotamia that provided the vital trading link with Central Asia.[42] The presence of clay 'tablets' written in Sumerian throughout the region is testament to the trade which took place.[43] The trade in metals stimulated all other forms of trade, and with it manufacturing. Caravans of draught animals—loaded with all kinds of cargo—journeyed to and from Anatolia. The written records from Sumerian palaces—lavishly decorated, with multiple courtyards and shrines—reveal that the wives of male rulers were active in this growing economy, not only owning their own land and livestock, but commanding their own industrial workshops, and arranging purchases of leather, wool and cloth.[44]

Booming trade brought a flourishing interconnected economy across Mesopotamia, with the only downside the creation of intense rivalry and competition. As alliances developed and waned, Mesopotamian city-states veered between cooperation and conflict. The land to the north of Sumeria—Akkad—was increasingly jealous of Sumeria's more favourable coastal position and the prosperity that came with it. By the third millennium BCE, their ruler—Sargon—was on the rampage. Not only did he conquer Sumeria; he also conquered land further north—in modern-day Syria and Iran—uniting the whole region between bronze-producing Anatolia and the Persian Gulf. It was the world's first empire. Sargon parachuted his daughters into temples as priestesses, thereby placing them in positions of immense power. One of these daughters—Enheduanna—can lay claim to being not only a priestess but also the first known literary author in history. Enheduanna wrote extensively about her life, her admiration for the goddess Inanna, and her experiences of sexual abuse. Having been captured by a warlord in the course of her father's rise to power, she described how his 'slobbered hand' covered her 'honey mouth' and turned her body to 'dirt'. Despite their intimate nature, her words were used for centuries to teach others how to write—including Mesopotamian women. Based on the clay tablets, we know that women were amongst the earliest scribes in the region. Writing wasn't just for men.[45]

While cuneiform gave birth to the world's first stories—the Epic of Gilgamesh and the Enuma Elish, in which the Garden of Eden and the Fall of Man feature long before the Old Testament—the vast majority of tablets relate to economic dealings. Women's names are present throughout these legal documents, many of which involve property disputes, suggesting that women were able to seek justice if family members misappropriated their land or other assets.[46] Early Mesopotamian women could own their own land, start their own businesses and file for divorce. A large number of the cuneiform tablets also document everyday business, taking the form of letters between merchants and suppliers, financial demands, loan contracts and rental agreements, with women visible in a number of the documented transactions. The private letters between a businesswoman named Lamassi and her husband, Pusu-ken, reveal that textiles were central to the boom in long-distance trade.

From the letters, we know that Pusu-ken moved to a merchant colony in the Anatolian city of Kanesh around 1900 BCE, while Lamassi, his wife, remained behind in Ashur to look after the family's business interests in the city: they were 1,200 km apart, and kept in touch by letter. In addition to sending family news, Lamassi's letters also contain her business dealings, including lists of the cloth she had gathered together ready to send to her husband and estimates of when he could expect it to arrive by caravan. At this time, tin sourced from Afghanistan was commonly packaged up with textiles and then taken—along the caravan route—all the way to Anatolia. Softer, bulkier and lighter than tin, cloth was wrapped around the precious metal, cushioning the tin and the donkeys that carried it. Not only did tin and textiles provide the right balance in transportation terms—perfect for the side packs of a donkey—but without the textiles, there would have been no bronze. Cloth was traded for the raw material—tin—as well as for finished bronze and for other desirable items. It formed a currency of its own.

The letters between our husband-and-wife duo reveal the scale of family businesses at the time and the involvement of daughters as well as wives. A letter from Pusu-ken to his daughter tells her that her cloth is selling well and includes feedback on which styles and patterns are most fashionable in Anatolia, helping the family to adjust their cloth-production patterns in a way that maximised their sales. Pusu-ken says that he would be sending a mina (approximately a pound) of silver as payment for his daughter's cloth, and that it could be expected to arrive by donkey on the next caravan returning to Ashur. A third letter—this time between the daughter and one of her brothers—chastises the brother for failing to pay for the batch of cloth entrusted to him. She writes: 'All this is my production, my goods entrusted for [sale with] profit . . . My gold you have taken! I beg you . . . send it to me with the first caravan and give me courage'.[47] This young woman would, indeed, have been anxious to receive her payment, as without it she would not have been able to buy the wool needed to make her next batch of cloth, and the success of the family business depended on it.

At this time, the Sumerian city of Ur, located at the mouth of the Euphrates on the Persian Gulf (which then reached further inland), was the largest city in the world, with a population of one-hundred thousand people. It was the central hub of twelve thousand female weavers, many of whom lived and worked in the surrounding villages. Even Girsu, a somewhat smaller city, was home to six-thousand female weavers.[48] The demands placed on cloth production by the boom in long-distance trade meant that the industry underwent a profound shift: production increasingly moved out of the home and into the workshop. A couple of generations on from Lamassi, Queen Iltani of Karana (a small city-state on the caravan trail between Assyria and Anatolia) was running her own textile workshop, with twenty-five spinners and weavers. The majority—fifteen of the twenty-five—were women, two of whom brought their children into work each day.[49] Her husband wrote to her on one notable occasion to announce: 'The king of Shirwun has arrived; he asked the caravan that was going out of Karana, but it had no garments fit for presents available. Now send me quickly any garments that you have available, whether of first-rate or second-rate quality, for presents'.[50] Cloth was vital for political relations, but recognition was not always paid where it was due. In the Sumerian city of Lagash, the royal workshop was manned entirely by women, though men often took on the role of overseer, for which they were paid handsomely: male overseers received three times the earnings of female overseers.[51] Women worked, but the gender pay gap was many times greater than we are used to in the modern world and, since many of Mesopotamia's workers were in servitude, they had no choice at all over their labour, leaving them 'overworked, underfed, and poorly housed'.[52]

Beer was another sector dominated by women. Beer was considered the drink of the gods—and was believed to promote health and wellbeing—which made brewing a vital part of the economy. Taverns were situated along the caravan route to quench the thirst of merchants, and the law prosecuted innkeepers who sold short measures to unsuspecting guests with punishment by drowning. Women were the archetypal innkeepers of Mesopotamia and, through their taverns, became intricately involved in the wider business world.[53] In addition to serving beer, these 'tapstresses' sourced dates and barley for brewing, engaged in lending—including lending their own grain in the event of food shortages—and dried and sold their waste sediment as fodder for cattle and pig farmers. Queen Kubaba of

Sumeria—the first female ruler ever recorded in history—had herself been a brewer of beer, and, according to cuneiform tablets, ruled for a hundred years, having been blessed by the gods for diverting some of her grain to feed hungry fishermen.[54]

In addition to their appearance on clay tablets, women's presence throughout the Mesopotamian economy has also been revealed by another type of item found in abundance in archaeological digs: seal impressions. In a world before the lock and key, seal impressions—stamped onto clay by a cylinder seal—were used to secure all kinds of wares. These impressions operated like a signature or guarantee, sealing shut containers filled with everything from beer to flour, and acting as a stamp of ownership or maker's mark. Every person of importance had their own cylinder seal—onto which their name and image were carved—that could be carried with them and rolled over clay to create seal impressions whenever needed. The visual markings on the seal impressions allowed someone to verify the contents, to identify the owner or supplier, and to be safe in the knowledge that the produce had not been interfered with. Excavations from the living quarters of a royal palace in Urkesh have revealed numerous cylinder seals as well as associated seal impressions—the equivalent of today's packaging labels—littered across the working areas of the palace. From the kitchen and utility area to the adjoining courtyard, seal impressions were dropped and discarded as bottles were opened and sacks were emptied. The seals depict everyday scenes, and they show some of the key members of the queen's staff at work, including Zamena the wet-nurse and Tuli the cook. Each senior staff member in the palace had their own seal, allowing them to take charge of the produce they needed for their everyday work. Unlike the seals of female staff members, which depicted their work, the seals of male staff members depicted their heraldry.[55] While this is a sign that patriliny was on the rise—that the line of descent was by now passing through the male line—it also tells us that women remained a significant part of the economy. The guarantees issued by women—in the form of the impressions formed by their seals—were accepted and trusted.[56]

In its quest for tin, Mesopotamia became linked with another of the world's first civilisations: that of the Indus Valley. But, as we will see, this was a civilisation that managed to combine economic prosperity with a much greater degree of equality, both in terms of wealth and gender.

THE INDUS VALLEY

Between the Middle East and Central Asia, in the valley of the Indus River, covering an extensive area of modern-day Pakistan and India, was a civilisation that might have appeared to be something of a utopia. Here, there were no elaborate tombs, no huge monuments, no splendid temples, and no spectacular palaces of a kind found in either Mesopotamia or Egypt. Unusually, no artistic depictions of royalty or of slavery have been found, and quality objects—and precious rocks and minerals—are spread across all types of housing; housing which was much less varied in size and grandeur than was the case in these two other civilisations.[57]

Five millennia ahead of New York, the Indus Valley's two main cities—Harappa and Mohenjo-Daro—housed tens of thousands of people in multistorey homes that were built in an impressive grid-like fashion. The typical home had baths and flushing toilets, connected by systems of communal sewers, and internal walls were not bare brick but were instead covered in plaster.[58] There was a mix of residential areas, connected by narrow streets, and a much longer and wider main shopping street, which would once have been alive with haggling shoppers, stallholders, merchants and the occasional elephant. Different sectors of the city were associated with different types of activity, from cloth-making to ceramics. Sizeable granaries suggest that the cities were well provided for in terms of food supplies.

Aside from the main cities, the Indus was home to numerous well-connected towns and a thousand or more villages, in total covering a geographic area that was larger than either Egypt or Mesopotamia. The Indus River provided the underlying sustenance, but needed to be managed, as its natural strength risked flooding homes and fields. An extensive water management system succeeded in taking control, turning dry, baked and cracked land into fertile plains while alleviating the risk that they would become unexpectedly drenched in water. Barges, carts and water buffalo were a common sight on the land, and as crops from the fields and salt fish from the coast made its way into the cities, pottery and cloth moved in the opposite direction.[59]

While political structures were clearly capable of town planning and water management, and took care of a geographical area that was both large and populous, it seems that those in power did not exploit the many in order to enrich the few.[60] There were, for example, no self-glorifying monuments of a kind found in other civilisations.[61] While the Indus and Mesopotamia were linked by trade, on the Indus side this trade tended to be much more in the hands of private merchants rather than palaces and temples, which acted to limit the accumulation of wealth by the political elite.[62] Both economies were prosperous, but in the Indus that prosperity was far more evenly distributed.[63]

Like Mesopotamia and Egypt, the Indus civilisation—which archaeologists only began to explore in the 1920s—was unearthed at a time when the territory was under European rule. When British archaeologists—dressed in their linen suits—supervised the removal of layers of soil and the careful brushing of the bronzes, bones and relics that lay underneath, they soon were forced to admit that India had a history and heritage that was much older than their own. But while Indus society was clearly complex, it still remains relatively mysterious. Like Egyptian hieroglyphs and Mesopotamian cuneiform tablets, it has left archaeologists with a wealth of written sources. The only problem is that archaeologists have yet to find an equivalent of the Rosetta Stone, which means that the Indus script remains—for now—undeciphered. Lacking the written evidence, there is therefore a limit to what we know about the lives of the men and women who lived in ancient India and Pakistan. But, based on other types of archaeological evidence, the relative equality of wealth appears to have been matched by a similar degree of equality when it came to gender. Indus society remained matrilocal, which meant that men—not women—moved into their spouses' communities upon marriage.[64] We can see this from scientific analysis of skeletons which reveals that women were more highly related in their communities than were men. This meant that women were surrounded by a tight female network throughout their lives. In addition, terracotta figurines of Indus women are both plentiful and realistic in form, unlike those found in some other time periods, where reproductive body parts were exaggerated for artistic effect. The 'mother goddess' continued to be praised in the Indus civilisation at a time when, in other civilisations, godlike figures were being promoted.[65] Just as significantly, male and female Harappan graves were equal in terms of their opulence.[66] Compared with Mesopotamia and Egypt, the Indus appears to have been the most equal civilisation of all. Sadly, as we will later see, it was a civilisation that did not last.

CHINA

Cut off from the rest of Eurasia by the Himalayan mountains and the Tibetan highlands lay China's own unique civilisation, located in the valley of the Yellow River.[67] Meandering downhill from the Tibetan plateau, then through the desert and into the north of China, before turning southwards into the lower-lying plains and then eastwards towards the sea, the Yellow River was aptly named: the plains that surrounded it were almost as yellow as sand.[68] This yellow-tinged soil—or loess—was soft and full of mineral nutrients, making it highly fertile. According to Chinese mythology, it was Huang Di—the Yellow Emperor—who secured the Yellow River valley from nomadic tribes, giving birth to the Chinese civilisation in the third millennium BCE.[69] It was a period which archaeologists describe as one of gated and walled villages, geometric pottery and human sacrifice.[70]

It was on a fine summer's day during this reportedly ordered and tranquil time that Lady Hsi-ling, the wife of the Yellow Emperor, sat quietly sipping her tea in the gardens of the palace, when her quiet contemplation was, all of a sudden, disturbed by a cocoon from an overhanging mulberry tree falling into her cup. As she removed the unexpected intruder, the cocoon began to unravel, moistened and warmed by her favourite drink. By chance, Hsi-ling had—according to the legend that followed—invented sericulture, the cultivation of mulberry trees and the care of silkworms. Though fate had offered a helping hand, it was curiosity and commitment that made Hsi-ling the mother of silk production—not just in China but across the world.[71] While it was her husband, the emperor, who was instead popularly credited with clothing the Chinese people in something other than animal skins, it was his wife he had to thank for this history-changing invention.[72]

For centuries to come, Chinese empresses sacrificed a pig and a sheep to give thanks for the mulberry trees that burst forth each spring.[73] The mythological association of silk production with a woman—and one with regal associations—suggests a long-standing connection between women and silk in Chinese history. So too does the association of silk-production with goddesses. As sericulture spread to the rural regions of Nanking and Chengdu, silkworm breeders built shrines containing life-size goddesses, where they made their own sacrifices of wine and fowl.[74] Cheaper forms of fabric—of a kind more likely to be worn by peasant families—were produced from wool and hemp: sheep imported from Mongolia and Kazakhstan were domesticated and fed on grain, providing a ready supply of wool, and the Yangtze River basin became the first part of the world to grow hemp.[75] By the first millennium BCE, tax was being collected from peasant households in the form of cloth and grain.[76] Every peasant woman could expect to spend up to six weeks a year producing cloth for the state. This cloth was in turn used to clothe the army, to pay for state officials, and for diplomatic gifts—bribes to discourage enemy states and northern tribes from launching an attack. Textile manufacture—fibres that needed to be disentangled, ordered, smoothed, spun and woven together in a pattern—became a metaphor for good governance. In Chinese script, 'to govern' and 'to reel silk' are pictographically connected.

Unlike the Indus Valley, China was a place of stark divisions between rich and poor. Much as in Egypt and Mesopotamia, queens in China were buried in an opulent style, surrounded by vast quantities of pottery, precious metals and precious stones. Large numbers of female sacrificial victims, likely drawn from their own servants, also accompanied the female elite to the grave.[77] The lives of wealthy women were clearly much longer and much more comfortable than those of poorer women, and involved a greater range of economic opportunities. Cloth was the one thing that united all women. While elite women owned and supervised cloth workshops, poorer women spun and wove the cloth, whether as servile labour in palace workshops—as in Mesopotamia—or as peasants within their own home.[78] The resultant cloth provided a currency with which to trade with the outside world. In that sense, Chinese women were laying the foundations on which the 'Silk Road' would be built, enabling the integration of China's vast civilisation with the wider world.[79]

PERU

Textiles were also at the heart of the final one of our first five centres of global prosperity, nestled between the Pacific Ocean and the Andes in the parched valleys and plains of modern-day Peru. In fact, it was only towards the end of the twentieth century that Peru was identified as having had its own complex and independent civilisation in ancient times, making it the civilisation about which we know the least but with the most exciting potential for new discoveries.

In addition to sharing China's focus on cloth, ancient Peru was, like Egypt, the home of mummies and pyramid-builders and, like the Indus Valley, it appears to have been a reasonably peaceful society. One of its most important centres was the city of Caral. Now said to be the oldest city in the Americas, Caral's discovery has succeeded in extending back in time the origins of complex society in the Americas. Five thousand years ago, Caral was home to three thousand people across a 626-hectare site. Today, it is an archaeological site that stands in the middle of the arid desert plains of Peru, in an environment that could not seem more inhospitable. The ancient architecture was on a monumental scale, featuring sunken plazas—with concert-style acoustics—and seventy-foot-tall, terraced mounds that resembled Egyptian pyramids.[80] Constructed from stone and tightly packed bags of boulders, the pyramids were colourfully covered in fine clay, some with a red-pink tinge and others yellow-beige in colour.[81] Caral was not alone in its magnificence. The Norte Chico region—which consisted of four river valleys—was dotted with thirty such monumental sites, with pyramids that loomed large across the landscape.[82]

Whereas civilisations elsewhere in the world developed in river valleys that were disconnected from their surrounding highlands—which were the preserve of nomadic enemy tribes—ancient Peruvian civilisation consisted of a much more integrated whole. The coast, the lowlands and the highlands supported one another. Anchovies, sardines and shellfish were brought inland and exchanged not only for plant-based produce such as squashes, beans, corn, avocado and chilli—produced with the help of irrigation channels that brought water to the parched land[83]—but also for something of equal importance: cotton. It was cotton—worked into fishing nets—that enabled greater catches out at sea, in turn providing the foundation for population growth and, with it, an increasingly dense and sophisticated society.[84] Cotton was key to making the most of what the sea had to offer, creating a symbiosis between mountain and sea: a whole that was more than the sum of its parts.

The inhabitants of Peru had been honing their cotton-making skills for some time. Six thousand years ago, the people of Huaca Prieta ('Black Pyramid')—a settlement situated along the northern coastline—were eating popcorn and corn-on-the-cob while weaving a striped fabric consisting of three different colours of thread: tan, blue and white.[85] Tan was the natural colour of cotton, the white thread came from the fibres of a bright-white vine and the blue thread consisted of dyed cotton. It was the world's earliest known use of blue indigo dye.[86] Dental remains from the Huaca Prieta site reveal that—over the generations—the diet of those producing the cloth became increasingly varied, to include the produce of the sea as well as the land.[87] Cotton underpinned the economic integration of the diverse landscapes of ancient Peru.

The politics of the Norte Chico civilisation remain something of a mystery. Arranging and managing the construction of pyramids and irrigation networks likely required some form of state structure. Evidence of communal feasting during the construction process is apparent in the huge cooking pits and sizeable piles of buried refuse—consisting of fish bones and shellfish—found close to excavated monuments.[88] But this wasn't entirely a pescatarian commune. Some residences were large and consisted of plastered stone walls, while others were smaller and constructed from simple wattle and daub. Whether the relationships between such city dwellers—and similarly between the coast and cities like Caral—were based on trade or on compulsion remains an open debate.[89] The fact that there were no defensive structures—no city walls—suggests that warfare and conquest were not, however, the chief occupation of whatever form of state existed. Like early Egypt and the Indus, this was primarily a peaceful civilisation.

Whether men and women were equal in the Norte Chico civilisation is still relatively unknown. The recent discovery of a mummified forty-year-old woman—buried with eight flutes—suggests that women could achieve positions of wealth and power.[90] We also know that in the much later and less peaceful period of the Inca Empire, women were supervising state weaving workshops manned by the daughters of defeated communities.[91] In the societies conquered by the Incas, the presence of textile tools doubled following invasion, indicating that conquered peoples were expected to spin and weave as payment to the state.[92] In the Aztec and Mayan societies which developed further to the north, female gods were depicted spinning and weaving, fibres in hand.[93] Wherever states sprung to life in the Americas, cloth remained integral, and it was clear who was producing it: women.

While there is still a lot to be discovered about the economy of ancient Peru—making it one of the most active archaeological centres of the world today—we know that thousands of years before the Incas, cotton was already king. Whether the system of producing cotton textiles was based on servile labour—as in Mesopotamia—or on the home production of peasants—as in China—remains, for now, a mystery.

PATRIARCHY PROLIFERATES

Five thousand years ago, women were busy building the world's first five civilisations in Egypt, Mesopotamia, the Indus Valley, China and Peru. In some of these societies, they were more likely to be enslaved, while in others they were more likely to be free peasant women or even members of a burgeoning middle-class whose wealth depended on trade. This meant that not all women were fully rewarded for their efforts: their hard labour sometimes showed in the splendour of palaces and pyramids—or in the flourishing businesses of their husbands—rather than in their own pay packets. One thing, however, is clear: with time, gender—and class—divides began to widen.

Warfare was a harbinger of change. Towards the end of the third millennium BCE, the bearded herdsmen of the Syrian mountains—a people known as the Amorites—descended from their highlands in search of greener pastures for their flocks. Travelling along the Euphrates River, they were described in cuneiform tablets as giants who knew neither home nor grain, though they were soon happily making themselves comfortable in the towns and cities that dotted Mesopotamia's fertile crescent.[94] In an attempt to prevent their onward march to Sumeria, the king of Ur built a wall between the Euphrates and the Tigris. Despite it being 155 km in length, the Amorites simply walked—or, rather, rode—around it. Transforming themselves from conquerors to rulers, these Syrian interlopers gave rise to some of the most notorious kings in Mesopotamian history. By 1755 BCE, King Hammurabi was in command of the vast swathe of land between Syria and the Persian Gulf, creating the Babylonian Empire that features in the Bible.

Best known for the 'Code of Hammurabi'—a set of laws which the King claimed to have received from the gods—Hammurabi transformed the legal landscape by shifting the focus of law from the victim to the perpetrator. Harsh punishment replaced compensation as payment for crime, and, as a precursor to the Law of Moses, was applied in an 'eye for an eye' fashion. Under the auspice of protecting the weak, the code also created what was arguably the first legalised system of patriarchy, one that made women the property of men—supposedly for their own protection. By the Late Babylonian era, women beer sellers had disappeared,[95] women no longer appeared as witnesses in legal documents,[96] and cloisters previously run by women were under male administration.[97]

Women were instructed to veil and to seclude themselves from the rest of society, and the amount of bodily coverage became a means of distinguishing between women on the basis of wealth, rank and occupation.[98] The later Assyrian Law Code described in detail which women should and should not veil, and assigned punishments for those transgressing the rules. In sum, all women were legally obliged to veil, with the exception of 'harlots' and 'slave girls' and 'daughters who lacked status' (i.e. were poor). In order to maintain the distinction between these groups of women, any 'harlot' who was caught veiled was to be stripped of her clothing, caned fifty times, and have 'pitch poured on her head'. Any slave girl caught doing the same was to have her ears chopped off. If a man failed to report a veiled harlot or slave, he was also to be stripped and caned, and would have his ears 'pierced [and] threaded with a cord tied behind him' while doing a month of 'hard labour for the king'.[99]

In a move paralleling the invasion of the Amorites in Mesopotamia, the people of the 'steppes'—the pastoral nomads from the extensive mountainous terrain that lay between India, China and the Middle East—descended across Eurasia in the course of the second millennium BCE. Their mighty weapon was the horse-drawn chariot—the tank of its day. It was at this time that the peaceful and relatively equal Indus civilisation disappeared. How and why such a sophisticated and prosperous society suddenly vanished are questions that continue to evade historians and archaeologists, but the descent of the steppe people ranks highly amongst all explanations.[100] Wherever they invaded, the chariot riders sent shock waves through the societies they conquered. Some historians have argued that they brought an uncivilised, brutish and patriarchal culture that was responsible for a sexist transformation across Eurasia.[101] Whether or not they did, the very act of invasion certainly gave added impetus to patriarchy, as it meant that homes and farms were raided and wives and daughters were raped, kidnapped and sold as sex slaves. In response, some communities introduced greater restrictions on women, limiting their ability to leave the home and enforcing stricter dress codes when they did. There were also implications for sons. In times of unrest, families wanted to keep their sons at home to act as protectors, tipping the balance away from matrilocality and further towards patrilocality. This meant that wives were expected to move to their husband's home or community—rather than vice versa—which deprived them of their own family network and left them under the watchful eye of their parents-in-law.

Patriarchy was, however, also on the rise in civilisations that managed to keep the chariot-riding nomads at bay. While Egypt was still relatively 'woman friendly', by the Middle Kingdom (2030–1786

BCE), lists of government administrators featured fewer women supervisors and overseers.[102] Weaving was still considered women's work, but workshops were increasingly being run and controlled by men rather than women.[103] Being a good wife and mother—wearing the title 'Lady of the House' with pride—became a woman's principal role.[104] In the subsequent New Kingdom (1567–1085 BCE), when Egypt became less politically isolated, women featured less prominently in artistic depictions of everyday scenes and, while they could still in theory own property, relatively few did in practice.[105] The ten-metre-long Wilbour Papyrus, a survey of fields in Middle Egypt undertaken by Egyptian administrators in the reign of Ramesses V, includes the names of 131 female landowners, which equates to only twelve percent of the total number of landowners listed in the papyrus.[106] And as Egypt expanded eastwards into Palestine and Syria, enslaved women became a part of the booty and were allocated work as servants, weavers, brewers, agricultural labourers or cloth makers.[107] As surrounding communities sought to appease the Egyptians, they sent women as a form of tribute, some of whom found themselves housed in a royal 'harem'.[108] Egypt was becoming more like Mesopotamia in both its use of slave labour and in its lack of women's rights.

Around the same time in China—when the Yellow River valley was ruled by the Shang Dynasty—sexism was also on the rise. It was a period of China's history about which we knew very little until, a century ago, a Chinese official was feeling unwell and requested ancient 'dragon' bones, which could be ground into a herbal medicine. He noticed that one of the bones was marked with an inscription, which read that 'Lady Hao would give birth to a girl, which would not be good'.[109] The bones were subsequently dated to the second millennium BCE, making them China's earliest known example of 'son preference'. At that time, Chinese emperors communicated with the heavens through the cracks that were generated when heat was applied to the bones of the dead. The cracks were interpreted as containing secret messages from the afterlife.[110] Curious about the strange messages contained on the ancient bones, archaeologists began to dig, and, in the process, unearthed the tomb of Lady Hao. Containing objects made from bronze and jade, along with weapons, sixteen human skeletons and the remains of four tigers—likely human and animal sacrifices—the tomb's scale and opulence is indicative of a society with stark divisions between rich and poor. While the contents suggest that Lady Hao—one of the emperor's sixty-four wives—owned her own land and led military campaigns, she lived in a society in which women like herself were losing ground.[111] Royal women—people who had previously helped to administer their territories—were being replaced by a new class of administrator: the male eunuch—castrated males whose sterility meant that they could not pose a paternity threat to male leaders.[112]

Ironically, wherever the marginalisation of women occurred, women's remaining freedoms were held responsible for the resultant economic misfortune, creating a vicious cycle of further restrictions. In China, it was a woman—named Daji—who was held responsible for the entire collapse of the Shang Dynasty. According to legend, Daji—a kidnapped slave girl—distracted the last Shang emperor from his battle planning. Rather than keeping a close eye on his military campaign, he drank and partied with Daji, leaving the Shang vulnerable to attack. The Zhou—who succeeded the Shang—in turn blamed a woman for their own downfall, this time Bao Si, the wife of King You. Legend has it that as a form of entertainment, in order to alleviate her boredom, she repeatedly encouraged the king to light the nation's warning beacons, misleading people into believing that there was an imminent attack. When the Zhou did finally face attack, people presumed that the fires had once again been lit by way of a prank and so refused to respond. The fate of the Zhou was, we are told, sealed in a precursor to 'The Boy Who Cried Wolf' tale, but where the protagonist was female: a silly woman who misled an honourable man.[113]

Thereafter, a well-ordered society in China was felt to depend on well-ordered families. A strict hierarchy—based on gender as well as age—was considered key to maintaining this order. Confucian scholars preached that women should obey and that those who did not were a disruptive force in society. According to Confucius (551–478 BCE): 'Women are as different from men as earth is from heaven . . . Women are, indeed, human beings, but they are of a lower state than men'.[114] The dominance of men over women was codified in Confucianism's Three Obediences: unmarried women were obliged to obey their father; married women their husband; and widowed women their sons. The patriarch was at the top of the family hierarchy, followed by sons, then the mothers of sons and finally—at the bottom of the tree—daughters-in-law, most of all those yet to bear a son. Women's behaviour was judged according to the Four Virtues, which involved being chaste, being agreeable (but not talkative), having a modest and tidy appearance and possessing embroidering skills.[115] In her second-century CE *Lessons for Women*, Ban Zhao re-popularised these teachings by preaching that women need not possess 'brilliant talents' and should instead be hardworking, humble, yielding and modest.[116] Anything that upset the patriarchal order did not just have consequences for the present; it also had consequences in the heavens as well as for the nation as a whole. According to the Confucian philosopher Mencius, 'The root of the empire is in the state [and] the root of the state is in the family'.[117]

The sexist turn across numerous Bronze Age civilisations is in part explained by the fact that women's reproductive powers were considered more—not less—important as political and religious structures developed.[118] A woman was not only key to producing descendants who could take care of her and her husband in old age; she was also key to supplying the manpower needs of the state.[119] States needed armies—even more so as life became less peaceful—meaning that one of a woman's principal duties was to provide sons who could fight. These male warriors were increasingly glorified, seen as essential to a successful economy, enriched by the booty of war.[120] Larger numbers of people also meant more tax revenue and more people who could perform compulsory labour for the state's building schemes.[121] Where states lacked people—or just wanted more of them—it was therefore in their interest to encourage women to focus their efforts on baby-making. They did so through the legal system—for example by depriving women of access to the professions and of rights to land, effectively forcing them into the role of housewife—or by favouring religious ideas that emphasised women's role as reproducers. In Egypt and Mesopotamia, women's bodies were described as fertile fields and male sexual activity was depicted as sowing these fields.[122] In China, ancestor worship was popularised by the state. Descendants were, in other words, believed necessary to keep the souls of their deceased ancestors alive by making appropriate offerings.[123] And since the primary goal of sexual activity was considered to be the generation of new life, heterosexual relationships were favoured.[124]

As wealth disparities grew, more so in Eurasia than in the Americas, the sexist turn was magnified. Over time—and whether through good luck, hard work, wise investments or, instead, as a consequence of force, extortion and corruption—some families were able to amass a fortune while others were left in poverty. Not only did this have clear consequences for the daughters of the poorest families—those most liable to be left hungry and vulnerable to exploitation—it also had consequences for the daughters of better-off families. Wealthy families felt that they had two good reasons to crack down on their daughters. The first was to 'save' them from seduction by a sweet-talking handsome stranger who might have an ulterior motive.[125] Unlike a son, a daughter could potentially find herself with a child in arms, making her less desirable to a future husband. Seducers were aware that if their seduction succeeded, a family had little choice but to allow their daughter to marry her seducer. Perhaps in response, land across the Middle

East was increasingly held by—and divided between—men rather than women, reducing their 'financial' attractiveness. The second somewhat related reason for the sexist turn was that families wanted to 'protect' their daughters from outside 'pollution' in an effort to control growing inheritances. As wealth grew, inheritance became more important, which in turn meant that potential—more reputable—husbands were keen to guarantee that their future children were truly their own. This created a demand for 'pure' wives: women who had been secluded from other men. As the rich became richer, restrictions on women's participation in the wider economy—working, shopping and selling alongside men—therefore grew. While on one level, ordinary women were able to escape such restrictions—as their families had less wealth to protect—they of course experienced poverty more sharply than their female social superiors. Moreover, once seclusion and veiling became a common practice amongst the ruling elites, it acquired a prestige that social climbers—those slightly further down the hierarchical ladder—also wished to copy. Families who could bear the potential loss of earnings of female members began to adopt the same practices in an effort to ensure the best matches for their daughters—matches that could bring better job and business prospects for their male relatives. Once restrictions on women began to emerge at the top of the ladder, they diffused throughout society.[126] Patriarchy finally had all the excuses it needed for treating women as second-class citizens—something that even women born into privilege could not, as they had done in the past, escape.

Growing warfare, the state's desire for more people, and increasing inequality were the three factors that combined to push societies in a more patriarchal direction, depriving a growing proportion of women of the freedom to choose how and where they worked. By restricting women's economic options—in large part by limiting their freedom to mix with men—fathers and husbands were able to exert control over their wives and daughters, leaving women economically dependent despite the immense value they created for their families and economies.

~

AS THE ANCIENT GREEKS EMERGED AND—UNDER ALEXANDER the Great—conquered Egypt, Mesopotamia and the Indus Valley, one could be forgiven for thinking that things would take a turn for the better. After all, the Greeks are credited as the founders of modern civilisation and democracy. But, as we will see in the next chapter, the ancient Greeks actually moved the dial further in the direction of patriarchy.[127]

CHAPTER 3

COURTESANS, POETS AND POTTERS

THE WOMEN OF ANCIENT GREECE

IN 1350 BCE, THE MEDITERRANEAN SEA WAS AT THE CENTRE of a web of trade that connected the Egyptians, Babylonians and Assyrians with the kingdoms and empires developing along its eastern shores—the Hittite Empire in Anatolia, the Kingdom of Mitanni further south, and the Minoans, Mycenaeans and Trojans who feature in Greek mythology. So that they could profit from the flourishing trade, rulers established diplomatic relations with one another that helped to underpin a period of peace and prosperity. But by 1177 BCE, drought, famine and earthquakes had wrecked prosperity and peace had given way to rebellion and war.[1] With food in short supply, hungry hordes rose up against their rulers and took to the seas on small boats in a never-ending search for a better life. In the associated revolts and invasions, pyramid builders went on strike, palaces were set alight, tombs were robbed and statues were decapitated. Like a pack of cards, one kingdom after another fell. As

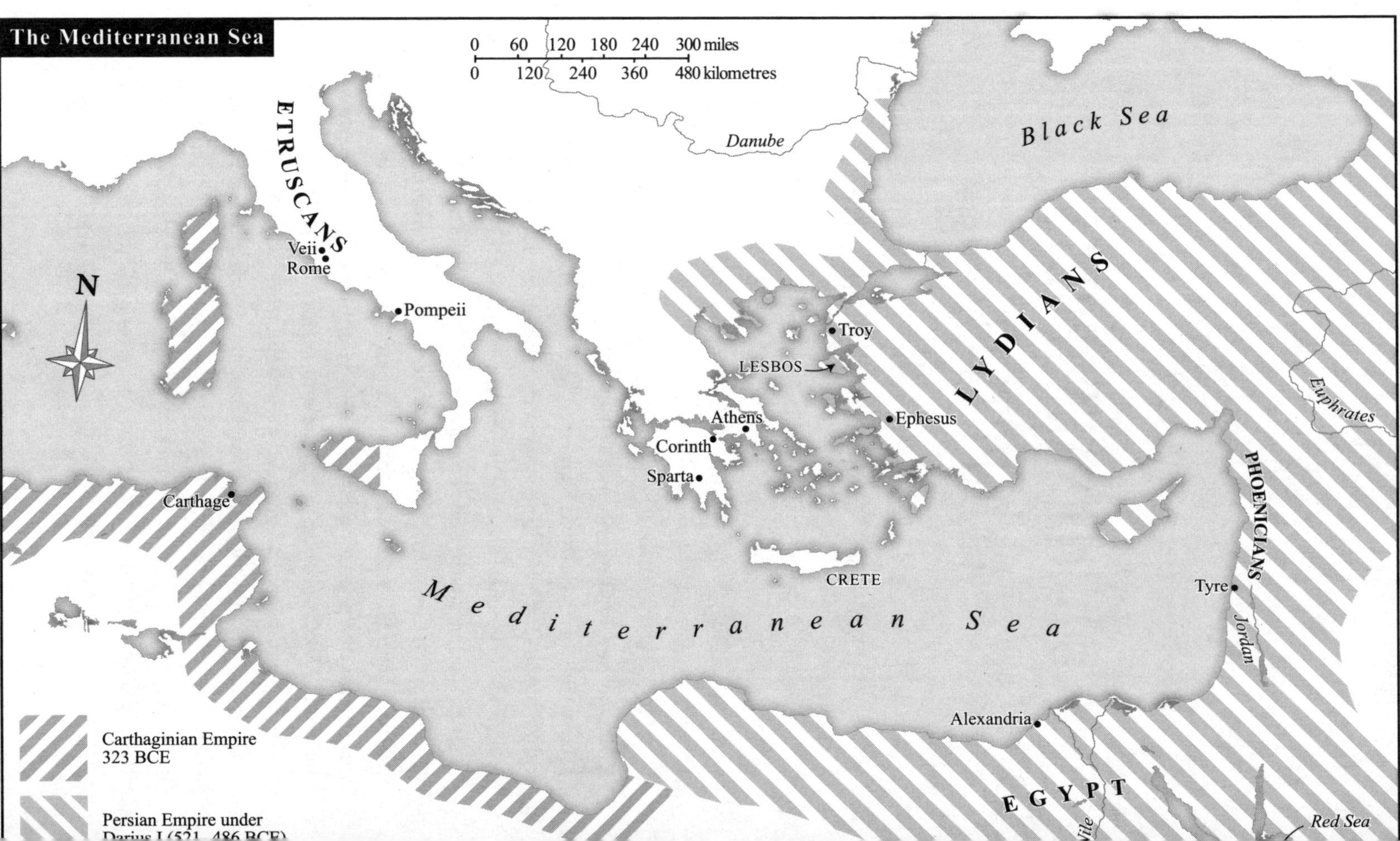

The Mediterranean Sea
0 60 120 180 240 300 miles
0 120 240 360 480 kilometres
N
ETRUSCANS
Veii
Rome
Pompeii
Carthage
Danube
Black Sea
LYDIANS
Troy
LESBOS
Ephesus
Athens
Corinth
Sparta
CRETE
Euphrates
PHOENICIANS
Tyre
Jordan
Mediterranean Sea
Alexandria
EGYPT
Red Sea
Carthaginian Empire
323 BCE
Persian Empire under

diplomatic connections were torn asunder, so too were trade agreements. Whole writing systems—the means by which the great powers communicated about politics and trade—disappeared. Of the 'club of great powers', only Egypt survived, albeit in a much-weakened state, having spent the last of its wealth fending off the invading 'Sea Peoples'.[2] A 'Dark Age' descended, lasting for some 300 years, out of which emerged a new age: the age of iron.

While difficult to melt, iron—one of the most commonly found elements in the earth's crust—had the advantage that it was much more widely available than tin. As the trade networks of the Bronze Age collapsed, making the sourcing of tin to produce bronze more difficult, societies channelled their efforts into developing iron. As iron replaced bronze as the metal of choice, weapons became deadlier and tools became more useful. Longer and stronger nails enabled the building of bigger and better boats. Iron-tipped ploughs allowed thicker soils to be farmed and sharper sickles made clearing land, as well as harvesting, easier than ever before. And the development of the work toolkit—still familiar to carpenters, builders and plumbers today—supported all kinds of crafts. Free from the dependence on tin, economies could develop in regions well beyond the cradle of civilisation, including in the outer reaches of Europe. Unlike tin, iron was an equalising force. Previously barely inhabited, the British Isles became dotted with more than three-thousand hill forts, along with numerous farmsteads and villages, comprising timber and wattle-and-daub-walled 'roundhouses' topped with conical thatched roofs. Celtic designs—the intricate and repeated geometric motifs used to decorate brooches, mirrors, swords and shields—spread across Europe, emblematic of newly developing connections and trade.

As Europe began to awaken from its slumber, economic life in the Eastern Mediterranean was starting to be rebuilt. As we will see, this was the era in which the Lydians invented coins, the Phoenicians pushed Mediterranean seafaring out into the Atlantic and the toga-wearing ancient Greeks went from strength-to-strength. As the Greek city-states jostled with one another for supremacy, Athens emerged triumphant. It was the birthplace of democracy, the location of the Parthenon, and the place of learning that gave rise to the philosophers, poets and playwrights whose works continue to be studied today.

In this chapter, we explore what life was like for iron-age women in the flourishing Eastern Mediterranean. As we will see, although Ancient Athens has been credited with laying the foundations of the Western world, it was a place where women and business were treated with equal disdain. Women faced seclusion and veiling, and merchants and bankers—of whatever sex—faced stigma and exclusion. It was in the lesser-known kingdoms of the Eastern Mediterranean—in Lydia, the Phoenician city-states, Crete, Lesbos and Sparta—that women were able to exercise far greater freedoms. It's time for the ancient Greeks to face a historical reckoning.

THE MIDAS TOUCH

From the Great Pyramid of Giza to the Hanging Gardens of Babylon, some of the Seven Wonders of the Ancient World are still famous today. At least one of the Seven Wonders was, however, far better known in the ancient world than it is now. This was the Temple at Ephesus, which was dedicated to the 'mother goddess', known in Greece as Artemis. According to Antipater of Sidon—who composed one of the earliest lists of the Seven Wonders—the Temple of Artemis put all other wonders to shame. The original temple was rumoured to have been built by the Amazons—a tribe of women who lived their lives on horseback and abandoned their sons, raising only their daughters. After being destroyed by a flood, it was rebuilt by the Lydian King Croesus in the sixth century BCE. The rebuilt structure was 377 feet long and 151 feet wide, and consisted of columns—in double rows—that reached forty feet into the sky. Visitors to the temple included not only the devout but also merchants, who offered gifts to the goddess in the form of coins, jewellery or other precious wares. It is on this site that some of the world's oldest coins can be found.

Lydia—the region where the temple was built—was a princely kingdom in Anatolia, not far from Greece. In the second millennium BCE, it was part of an Indo-European empire known as the Hittite Empire—an empire built by nomadic tribes who migrated from the Black Sea steppes. But after the disintegration of the empire during the Bronze Age collapse, Lydia was left to make its own way in the world, which it wisely chose to do by developing its economy. It became the original nation of shopkeepers: the home of the first retail shops, and—according to the Greeks—the inventor of the first gold and silver coins.[3] Coins minted in Ephesus bore the stamp of Artemis, her face on one side and her sacred animals (the stag and the bee) on the other, making Artemis arguably the first—albeit mythical—woman to be represented on money in history.[4] Other Lydian coins bore the head of a lion or a lion's paw.[5] This tiny but valuable invention revolutionised trade.

Before the development of money, buying and selling took the form of barter. Traders would line up their wares and agree upon a swap, such as cloth for tin. This meant that trades could only occur where both parties had something that the other person wanted in return. Since cloth was produced everywhere, was non-perishable (unlike food) and could easily be judged by sight and by touch for its quality, it was the de facto currency of the barter economy. But cloth had its limits as a medium of exchange, as not all buyers had cloth to hand and not all sellers wanted it in return for their wares. Finding a 'mutual coincidence of wants' wasn't always easy, which left goods unsold and meant that most people had to be reasonably self-sufficient in their effort to meet their basic needs. In a world of barter, the economy is therefore less productive, as fewer 'trades' take place and we are less able to 'specialise'. With money, this problem is overcome: we can all be paid in money and can then take that money to buy whatever we want or need, which a grocer—or whoever else—can use in turn to make their own purchases. With it, people can focus their time and efforts on what they are best at, rather than spreading themselves thin in a way that is unproductive and inefficient. It was, therefore, thanks to the Lydian invention of coins that the global economy was able to further expand.[6]

Before the invention of coins, lumps of precious metals were sometimes used as payment, but there was always a question mark about purity. While a piece of cloth could be quickly examined to establish its fineness and translucency, establishing the quality of a lump of precious metal was much more difficult, and required an expert analysis. Nuggets of gold and silver were rarely pure in form, as they naturally occur in the earth's crust mixed with other less precious metals. Before being used as payment, each lump therefore needed to be tested in an effort to identify its true content, something which slowed down transactions and made trade costly and cumbersome. When Lydian traders first began to strike coins from precious metals, they faced a similar problem. The innovation of the Lydian state was, therefore, to mint coins in standard weights out of what it could guarantee was pure silver or gold. While Lydia was blessed with its own naturally occurring supplies of gold, transforming this into coinage required impressive technical know-how in terms of removing impurities from precious metals and heating the metal to 800 degrees Celsius or more to create the coins. In addition to the competence of its metalworkers and artisans, the success of the Lydian mint was also dependent on the trust that people placed in the Lydian state. Rather than undertaking the process of weighing and checking the purity of payment for themselves, people allowed the state to take on this role. Trust meant that buyers and sellers could be certain about the value of the coins, and certain that other people would accept the coins they used, and so coins became a popular means of payment, one that made trade easier and less risky.[7] This made Lydian cities such as Sardis attractive places in which to trade in the first millennium BCE.[8]

So synonymous was Lydia with money that the Greeks invented the myth of a Lydian king called Midas who, in return for doing a good deed, was granted a wish by the Gods—famously asking for everything he touched to be turned into gold. Lydian wealth was much talked about in ancient Greece.[9] So too were Lydian women. While relatively little is known about the position of women in Lydia, the observations of Greek travellers suggest that women were relatively free in comparison with women in Athens. Herodotus, the Greek geographer and historian, was shocked that Lydian women—unlike those in Athens—were free to decide for themselves who to marry or even whether to marry at all. So alarmed was he by the independence of Lydian women—including their presence on the streets—that he assumed they must all be sex workers and concocted stories of how Lydian women built up dowries by prostituting themselves. Needless to say, this is something of an exaggeration: it is more a sign of women's invisibility on the streets and marketplaces of Athens than a sign of how Lydian women actually spent their youth.[10] Only in the most conservative societies are women going about their ordinary business presumed to be sex workers, and ancient Greece, as we will see, was mostly on a par with modern-day Afghanistan in its treatment of women.

Through trade, the Lydians were connected with the Phoenicians, who lived along the Lebanese coastline. Like the Lydians, the Phoenicians were much talked about in ancient Greece. It was from the Phoenicians that the Greeks learned their alphabet, albeit switching the direction of writing from right-to-left to left-to-right. It was this alphabet that in turn provided the foundation for the Western writing system. We also have the Phoenicians to thank for the white work shirt, which was donned as a uniform by its sailors.[11] But, more than anything else, the Phoenicians were known for the colour purple. The word 'Phoenician' translates as Purple People, and they were so named because of the valuable dye originating in the sea snails that inhabited the seas around Lebanon. The value of this dye served to make purple cloth the most prized of all colours. Its great expense meant that it was donned only by the elite, whether by royalty or by religious authority figures. In fact, societies commonly banned anyone beyond the elite from wearing purple, so as to maintain class distinctions between the rich and the poor.

Like the mysterious Lydians, we still know relatively little about women in the Phoenician economy. But, as with Lydia, there are clear signs that this was an economy in which women were relatively free compared with ancient Athens. Historically, while women have always been involved in spinning and weaving, dyeing was a sector of the economy almost entirely left to men. But, archaeological evidence from Phoenician settlements has revealed that women—and not just men—were buried with the shells of the valuable sea snails, alongside equipment for spinning and weaving, suggesting that women were active at all levels when it came to the production of the lucrative Phoenician cloth.[12]

Aside from purple dye, the Phoenicians had another string to their bow: timber. This was a material that had always been sorely lacking in the Middle East, where the terrain consisted largely of deserts or, in Mesopotamia, of swamps. It was with their cedar forests that the Phoenicians were able to build cutting-edge ships.[13] Armed with their fleets and their valuable purple dye, the Phoenicians became the expert handlers of trade between Egypt and Mesopotamia, and it was a goddess—Tanit—whom Phoenician sailors worshipped on their travels.[14] Around the time that the Lydians were inventing coins, the Phoenicians began to spread their sails even further across the Mediterranean, setting up trading colonies that reached as far as the Atlantic. Most prized of all was the city of Carthage, in North Africa, which went on to develop its own flourishing empire across the western part of the Mediterranean.

According to the founding myth of Carthage, it was an enterprising woman named Dido that the Carthaginians had to thank for their prosperity. The mythical Dido had crossed the Mediterranean Sea from her Phoenician homeland on the Lebanese coast and landed in the middle of the North African coastline, where she purchased the land on which Carthage was built from an African chieftain named Iarbas. Her freedom to travel and to invest in new land paid off. For centuries, Carthage was a roaring success.

BEWARE THE ANCIENT GREEKS

As the Lydians and Phoenicians were rebuilding the Mediterranean economy, the city-states of ancient Greece were still in their infancy, backward and poor and jostling with one another for primacy.[15] The ancient Greeks were more interested in warfare than they were in trade. Greek migration and expansion into the wider Mediterranean, including to the Anatolian coast in and around Lydia, was driven more by necessity—the need to flee war and unrest at home—than it was by an interest in trade.[16] Greek mythology glamorised the warrior—a figure who featured highly on the pottery of the period. Greek potters smothered their clay pots in a black glaze, on which—in silhouette—they carved images of men with shields and spears fighting to the death. But as this eye-catching black and red figure pottery became much admired, Greece became ever more drawn into trading networks. Greek traders learned seafaring practices from the Phoenicians, eventually pushing the Phoenicians out of Greek waters to take charge of their own trade. The Greeks also borrowed ideas from the Lydians, including adopting coinage. Some of Greece's first coins came from the Greek island of Aegina, close to the Greek mainland, which traded extensively with the Lydian coast. They were stamped with a turtle. In Athens, silver coins were stamped with the face of Athena or her sacred bird, the owl. Though later to be developed than the coins of Aegina, Athenian coins were considered some of the purest of all Greek coins, which made them the premier currency of ancient Greece.[17] Athens was on the rise but, before it could extend its reach, it had to first face off against an almighty enemy.

By the middle of the first millennium BCE, there was a new player on the Mediterranean stage, one that popularised the tradition of celebrating birthdays and introduced desserts after dinner (for which I am personally very thankful).[18] It was woman-friendly Persia (modern-day Iran), and it succeeded in building an empire larger than any the world had previously known, bringing three of the world's oldest civilisations—Egypt, Mesopotamia and the Indus Valley—under one umbrella. And Persia did not stop there. As Persian armies marched towards the Mediterranean, they also swallowed up Lydia and Phoenicia. Phoenician harbours were turned into shipyards for the Persian military and in around 546 BCE King Croesus of Lydia was captured and put to work as the economic advisor to King Cyrus of Persia, rolling out coinage across the Persian Empire.[19] Key to Persia's success was that it was humble enough to recognise and adopt superior tools, knowledge and ideas. It assimilated the best bits of every society it conquered, not just coinage and seafaring techniques but also Egyptian dress, which was considered more practical for military uniforms.[20] Persia's 'iron fist' was contained in a 'velvet glove'.[21] Rather than expunging local rulers, the Persian king saw himself as the 'king of kings', something which enabled a degree of local autonomy.[22] According to the historian Tom Holland, Persian occupation 'could be compared to a light morning mist . . . you were aware of it, but it was never obtrusive'.[23] Altogether this greater flexibility, compared with previous empires, made the Persian Empire a seemingly unstoppable force. So too did the fact that Persia was not a place in which the talents of half the population were sidelined. Women in Persia lived lives that were much freer than those of Iranian women today. They could own land, start businesses and travel alone. Since its economy was thereby firing on two cylinders, Persia had the financial wherewithal to support its imperial dreams. And, by the fifth century BCE, it was at the heart of this empire that King Darius and his son—Xerxes—made plans to conquer Greece.

The Athenians knew that they faced a formidable enemy, leaving them with little choice but to evacuate their beloved city. Women and children—travelling by foot, by ox-cart and by boat—were sent to safety fifty miles away. All able-bodied Athenian men were ordered to make their way to a fleet of new naval vessels, fresh out of the shipyards and paid for—in one of the greatest flukes of history—by a newly discovered silver mine. As the Persians entered an abandoned Athens, where they sacked the Acropolis and burned the city to the ground, the Greeks waited patiently on their boats as smoke and flames billowed into the night sky. Their hopes were pinned on a desperate but ingenious plan: lulling the Persian fleet into the narrow straits between mainland Greece and the island of Salamis, where the smaller but also more agile Greek boats would have at least some chance of taking on the larger—and more numerous—Persian vessels.[24]

Having succeeded in taking Athens, Xerxes—who had by then inherited his father's throne—consulted his confidantes, who urged him to take on the Greek fleet, with the aim of eliminating Greece's last line of defence. Only one person—a woman named Artemisia, who commanded her own naval squadron on the Persian side—advised the king not to engage. 'Why need you run the risk of naval actions at all?', she asked. Persia had already achieved so much on land that gambling it all on a naval battle—even if the odds were in its favour—seemed foolhardy. Artemisia's advice was prescient but ignored, and the result was the first great naval battle of history: the Battle of Salamis. As the eight-hundred-strong Persian fleet entered the narrow straits between the island of Salamis and mainland Greece, they became a tangled mess. In order to manoeuvre, Persian vessels found themselves ramming one another, inflicting damage and injuries to their own side. Artemisia's ship was one of the few to escape unscathed. As Xerxes looked on, aghast from atop a nearby rock—head in his hands—the Greeks were in equal shock. Not only had they snatched victory from the jaws of defeat, but, in the words of the writer Herodotus, they found it 'remarkable that a woman should have taken part in the expedition against Greece'.[25]

Artemisia—named after the goddess Artemis—brought back to life the mythical woman to whom Lydia's Temple at Ephesus paid homage.

In celebration of their victory against the Persians, the Greeks built a magnificent columned structure that continues to dominate the skyline of Athens today: the Parthenon. Its stone reliefs and sculptures depicted mythical battles in which the Greeks were styled not only as mere mortals but as gods who had taken on giants and minotaurs. But men were not the only ones to feature in the battle scenes. Carved into the frieze on the western side of the temple—facing the afternoon sun—were images of Greek warriors fighting the women known as the Amazons.

Having met Artemisia in battle, the Greeks drew parallels with the fierce warrior women of the Eurasian steppes—those rumoured to have first built Lydia's Temple of Artemis. Their ability to travel long distances on horseback while wielding weapons that magnified their physical strength made them a force to be feared. And we now know that rather than being mythical, these warrior women were in fact real. Archaeologists have uncovered the remains of numerous female warriors dating from the sixth century BCE, buried alongside riding gear and weaponry. One burial site is home to a girl aged thirteen or fourteen, with an arrowhead embedded in her body, and bowed legs that are typical of a life spent on horseback.[26] The Greeks were, it seems, haunted by the prospect of women who fought back, and, as we will see, it was for good reason. The Athenians were, whether by intention or not, doing everything within their power to make enemies of women.

WIVES AND MOTHERS

Ancient Athens might have invented democracy, but it was a democracy only for men. Women were barred from politics, law and the military. Greece's founding myth tells of a divine world in which women initially dominated but were eventually usurped by Zeus, who on Mount Olympus established a new patriarchal order, denying women not only political power but also the power of creation.[27] Unlike the sexually promiscuous gods, most Greek goddesses were virgins.[28] In order to overcome the obvious practical difficulty, the gods were granted life-giving powers. Athena was born from the head of Zeus and Aphrodite rose from the ocean on a shell after the severed genitals of Uranus were thrown into the sea. And it was after unsuccessfully pursuing Athena, who was determined to remain a virgin, that Hephaestus's semen fell to the ground to create Erichthonius—according to Greek mythology, one of the first rulers of Athens. According to ancient Greek writers, it was men—not women—who were the creators of new life.[29]

While in real life women were needed to create the next generation, Athenian men made sure that they were in charge. Greek patriarchy took the form of a guardianship system, in which women were under the legal control of men, with the control passing from a girl's father to her husband upon marriage. Rather than being a free choice, marriage was arranged, and typically occurred by the time a girl reached fifteen, to a husband twice that age. Women could not inherit unless no immediate male descendants existed and, on the rare occasions when they did inherit, they were forced to marry their closest male relative in order to ensure that their family property remained in male hands. To guarantee that wealth was passed onto 'true' heirs, women's virginity was considered paramount. This meant that freeborn 'citizen' women—unlike those in the Persian Empire—were not allowed to mix with men. Female slaves carried out tasks that involved venturing beyond the four walls of the home, as well as the usual domestic drudgery. In the warrior world of ancient Greece, women captives were the prizes of war. While men captured in battle were typically ransomed or killed, women were the ones brought back home to carry out the work that was considered taboo for freeborn women.[30] But when it came to higher-status work, women—whether freeborn or enslaved—were nowhere to be seen. It was men—not women—who signed their names on the famous black and red pottery that Athens exported to the rest of the Mediterranean, and of the numerous Athenian writers and poets, not a single one was female.[31]

Since chastity was considered an Athenian woman's primary virtue, it had to be guarded at all costs. Ancient Athens was an unruly place and so, in order to achieve some kind of order, lawmakers turned to bribing men with sex.[32] By building a system of brothels, staffed by female slaves and poor—typically migrant—women, the Athenian state believed that it would 'strengthen democracy'.[33] In the words of the ancient Greek poet Philemon, the lawmaker Solon wanted to offer sex cheaply and in abundance, in response to 'seeing that the state was full of randy young men whose natural appetites were leading them where they had no right to be'.[34] The price of sex was set at one obol—a sixth of a day's wage for a male labourer. While sex work therefore became legitimate—to the point that it was taxed—there were clear boundaries between sex workers and 'respectable' women, and the existence of the former became a means to control the latter.[35] Any woman who lost her virginity before marriage was condemned to a life of sexual slavery, thereby preventing her from polluting the pool of 'respectable' women and ensuring that the male citizens of Athens did not have to fear whether or not their children would truly be their own.

CLOTHING GREECE

In the middle of the fourth century BCE, a woman by the name of Phryne cast off her clothes and walked naked into the sea at the Festival of Poseidon. Born into a family of caper farmers, Phryne had moved to Athens in her youth, where she supported herself by entertaining elite men with a combination of wit and beauty. While she was free to use her body to sexually gratify the Athenian ruling class, it turns out that she was not free to skinny-dip. Her naked seaside antics brought her before a court, where she was charged with impiety, for which the punishment was death. Just as she was about to be convicted, her lawyer reached over and ripped the gown from Phryne's body, leaving her nude in front of the all-male jury. The bold and brazen strategy worked, as Phryne was found not guilty on the basis that her body was so goddess-like that the gods would be offended if she were sentenced to death.[36]

Phryne had more than one string to her bow. Not only was she a successful courtesan; she also modelled for the first full-size nude statue of Aphrodite. Sculpted by Praxiteles, the Aphrodite of Knidos became an instant tourist attraction.[37] The shock to moral authorities was palpable—and no doubt contributed to her charge of impiety. The goddess Aphrodite had previously been depicted not only clothed but veiled.[38] Mortal women in Athens were expected to cloak every part of their body. Terracotta figurines of everyday women and girls draped in endless folds of cloth graced many a Greek residence.[39] Fragments of the ten-inch-tall, mould-made statuettes—painted in red, orange, purple and pink tones—are frequently found in the archaeological remains of ancient Greek homes, typically alongside loom weights and cookware. Naturalistic in style, these 'tanagra' figurines offered a feminine ideal for the women of ancient Greece.

The female citizens of ancient Athens were not only expected to veil their bodies and even their hair; they manufactured the cloth to do so themselves. Despite their exclusion from the public sphere, the historic association between women and cloth continued unabated in ancient Greece and the designs that women wove into their cloth—from zig-zag shapes to repeated curls—inspired the geometric emblems that graced much of the earliest prefigurative Greek pottery.[40] While cloth-making was conducted behind closed doors, its influence penetrated the workshops of the most celebrated sector of the Greek economy, which suggests that women themselves may have been some of ancient Greece's first potters, until men came to dominate production, at which point designs shifted from geometric decoration to warrior scenes.[41]

According to legend, Helen of Troy—who we will meet later—wove her own cloth, and archaeological excavations in the city have revealed beads made of gold alongside a loom containing half-finished cloth: the weaver was clearly hard at work when the city was sacked and burned.[42] The goddess Athena was also portrayed as a weaver, and ancient Greek loom weights are often found stamped with her sacred bird, the owl.[43] In ancient mythology, Athena's cloth-making acumen was famously put to the test by the mortal Arachne, who was turned into a spider—left to weave webs for the rest of time.

At the yearly Festival of Athena—the Panathenaia—Athens's female elite presented the goddess with a dress that they had specially woven for the occasion. Preparations began nine months beforehand, when girls nearing puberty were specially chosen and set to work, in seclusion, in the Acropolis.[44] The resultant dress consisted of a large rectangle of patterned fabric designed to be wrapped around the body, with the corner pinned at the shoulder by a brooch, thereby preventing the cloth from coming unwrapped. It was known as a *peplos* and while it had once been a traditional form of dress for Greek women, by the fifth century its use was reserved for Athena. Why that was the case is open to speculation: Was it changing fashion on the part of women, or was it the result of male paranoia? Some Greek accounts suggest that the brooch was seen as a danger by men; a weapon that women could remove and use as a form of defence. Indeed, stories abounded of a group of women who, upon receiving bad news, stabbed the messenger to death with the pins of the brooches removed from their *peploses*.[45] Male fear of women could, it seems, have gone as far as banning dresses that needed to be pinned with a brooch. If so, it is fortunate that the celebratory *peplos* woven for the Festival of Athena was not designed to be worn by a mere mortal.

Athena's *peplos* was paraded through the streets of Athens, possibly on a life-size boat, in place of a sail.[46] To take part in the procession, women gathered at the large arched entrance to the city and then proceeded to the Acropolis—the home of Athena's altar—before continuing on to the civic and shopping district of central

Athens.[47] For the festival, Athens came alive with music competitions, poetry readings and Olympic-style sporting contests in what was one of the few times each year that 'respectable' women were able to venture out of the home and enjoy themselves in public.[48] Temporary stands were constructed for onlookers, many of whom travelled to Athens to soak up the atmosphere. Since the festival took place at the height of the summer, the air would have been thick with heat, music and the sound and smells of bleating animals—animal sacrifice was a common part of ancient festivals, and so representatives from Athens' dependencies brought live animals into the city to be sacrificed in Athena's honour.[49]

After being presented to the goddess, the specially woven robe was placed on public display in Athens—like a painting or sculpture—so that the stories it captured could be admired.[50] Woven into the cloth were scenes of the heavens, showing Zeus and Athena battling for victory against the giants. The primary colours were yellow and purple. Saffron was used to colour the yarn yellow and the colour purple was courtesy of the valuable Lebanese sea snail. Spending the best part of a year weaving for the goddess was considered a privilege for young women. For Athens's most 'respectable' women, weaving was not to be undertaken for money but instead for clothing themselves and their families or for gifting to the goddess.[51] Paid work was considered unbecoming—as sullying the soul.

When it was conducted for money, cloth production was typically carried out by slave women—including in home-based workshops—and by sex workers, with some overlap between the two.[52] A half of the women freed from slavery in the fourth century BCE were described in their manumission inscriptions as 'wool workers'.[53] Female slaves were often expected to spend their evenings selling sex and their days spinning wool as a means to financially support their owners.[54] Between two-thirds and nine-tenths of the time taken to produce a finished piece of cloth was accounted for by spinning, which made it extremely labour-intensive.[55] Unlike weaving, spinning was thankless, repetitive and mind-numbing. On the side of Greek vases can be found not only looms with female weavers at work, but also baskets of wool—ready to be spun—in the background of scenes depicting the sale of sex.[56] A Greek vase unearthed in Italy from the fifth century BCE depicts a woman making cloth as a man offers her a jewellery box filled with jewels. A cup from the same era shows a woman preparing wool for spinning while male clients or suitors attempt to distract her. Once again, a Greek man bears gifts, including a string of jewels.[57] Muscular analysis of the statue Venus de Milo (the Roman equivalent of Aphrodite) has indicated that her missing arms were posed in a position to spin, her lower right hand working the spindle as her left hand, lifted high, held the distaff wrapped in wool.[58] While cloth-making was an essential part of women's daily lives, it was smeared by associations with female sexuality, placing power back in the hands of the patriarchy.

By devaluing women's work, Athenian men not only turned women into financial dependents but were able to cultivate the belief that men were superior beings—it is a strategy that has sadly been repeated throughout history.

EQUAL CONTEMPT

In ancient Greece, the distaste for women was matched by a distaste for business. Writing in the fourth century BCE, Aristotle noted that money-making had taken over the Athenian world and was converting 'every aspect of life into monetary considerations'.[59] Commerce jarred with Athenian conceptions of the good life, which revered the leisurely pursuit of cultural interests. Men aspired to be warriors, politicians or philosophers, not traders, financiers or entrepreneurs.[60] The pursuit of wealth for wealth's sake was frowned upon and the philosopher Plato—who set out a plan for an 'ideal society'—argued that leaders and soldiers should be completely forbidden from owning property and amassing their own wealth, so as to insulate them from corruption and ensure that they had the best interests of their city-state at heart.[61] While Aristotle was less opposed to private property than Plato, he argued that there were 'natural' and 'unnatural' ways of making money. Exchanging something physical—like wheat or pottery—for money was, he believed, perfectly natural, but using money to make more money was, he felt, unnatural, and no more so than lending money at interest.[62] While farmers and potters were considered virtuous, merchants and bankers were not.[63]

Those who sought to defend Greek civilisation against the rising tide of commercialism drew a connection between women and money in an effort to discredit both. The poet Hesiod warned men that women were gold-diggers: 'Do not let a woman with a sexy rump deceive you with wheedling and coaxing words; she is after your barn', he wrote.[64] According to Hesiod, women spent their days 'munching', taking too many baths, smothering themselves in perfume and 'filching' items reserved by their husbands for sacrificial offerings.[65] The result of all this luxury is, we are told, that women risk driving men into poverty. Simonides of Amorgos, the Greek poet of the seventh century BCE, warned:

> *For Zeus designed this as the greatest of all evils: / Women. Even if in some way they seem be a help; / To their husbands especially they are a source of evil. / For there is no one who manages to spend a whole day / In contentment if he has a wife, / Nor will he find himself able to speedily thrust famine out of the house*[66]

With no small irony, this fear of women may reflect the fact that women were in reality heavily involved in household finances, making decisions about household expenditure and overseeing home-based production.[67] This was more of a reflection of Greek attitudes to business than it was of their faith in women. Since business was looked down on by the Athenian elite, women were left playing a central role in the home-based economy of ancient

Greece, one in which workshops and agricultural estates centred on the home. The definition of a good wife was one who—from behind closed doors—could capably manage household expenditure and revenue streams, balancing incomings and outgoings in a responsible way. Unlike today, there was no difference between home economics and economics. Indeed, the word 'economics' derives from the Greek word *oikonomikos*, which translates as 'household management'.[68] Wives and daughters provided the free and invisible management that in turn kept agricultural estates and workshops running, enabling their husbands and brothers to spend their days engaging in what were considered 'higher' pursuits. After all, the male politicians, philosophers and warriors needed some way of financially supporting themselves, and they were happy to leave that to someone else. But making money beyond what was required to live a 'good life' was nevertheless seen as corrupting to the soul, and so business activities were expected to have their limits.[69] 'The type of character which results from wealth is that of a prosperous fool', Aristotle wrote.[70] Women's business successes were, in other words, not to be celebrated.

The dislike of women and business placed women in an impossible situation. On the one hand, since men didn't want to waste their time on business, it automatically left women with more of a role in family enterprises. On the other hand, women's involvement in business could not risk their or their family's reputation. After all, claims of citizenship depended on the 'respectable' behaviour of women, as is clear from one particular legal case.

In the middle of the fourth century BCE, a man by the name of Euxitheos appeared in court to defend his claim to citizenship. At this time, the official 'citizen' lists were being purged of anyone who was considered of impure descent. Athens was at war, resulting in anti-foreigner sentiment of a kind that typifies periods of nationalism. This provided a perfect opportunity for anyone who wanted to settle a personal vendetta to do so by accusing their personal enemies of being of 'impure descent'. Since only citizens were entitled to rights and freedoms, a lot was at stake—including the right to remain a free man rather than to be enslaved. Euxitheos was amongst those whose citizenship was being contested, leaving him at risk. He turned to the orator Demosthenes to make his case before the court.[71] The case that was made against him hung on the fact that his father had a foreign accent and that his mother had worked as a seller of ribbons and as a wet-nurse.[72] While Euxitheos was able to defend his father's accent by pointing out that he had been taken prisoner in a foreign land, the fact that his mother had engaged in paid work was considered demeaning, degrading and embarrassing.[73] A woman who engaged in paid and 'menial' work was, according to Greek authorities, not worthy of being a Greek citizen, and so neither was her son. Rather than contesting the court's attitude towards women's work, Demosthenes apologised on behalf of his client and explained that it was a result of the family having fallen on hard times at a moment when 'the city was suffering misfortune, and everyone was in a bad way'.[74]

While women from the 'citizen' families of ancient Athens lived their lives in seclusion, poorer women—as well as those from citizen families who had fallen on hard times—had little choice but to cross the boundaries between the home and the outside world, which naturally meant mixing with men. Greek literature is filled with women selling garlands as well as food such as bread, vegetables and porridge, and working as washerwomen, seasonal agricultural labourers or nurses. Such employment was, however, poorly paid and small-scale. Better-paid occupations—such as medicine, politics and the law—were closed to women. So too was trading on a larger scale than street peddling, as any transaction beyond the value of 'one *medimnos* of barley' (the equivalent of a family's weekly food shop) required authorisation by a male guardian.[75] If a woman wanted to build her own independent fortune, her only real option was, therefore, to monetise her body and climb to the top of the sex-work hierarchy, becoming a *hetaera*.[76] Whether better described as female companions or escorts, *hetaerae* had a handful of male clients with whom they engaged in long-term relationships, exchanging sparkling conversation and intimacy for living expenses and gifts. It was by becoming a *hetaera* that Phryne—the woman who posed for the naked statue of Aphrodite and revealed all to the courtroom—was able to amass a personal fortune, making her arguably the richest woman in Athens.[77] While the work of women such as Phryne has been expunged from the more sanitised versions of history, legal testimonies allow us to peer into the business dealings of one of her peers, a woman by the name of Antigone.

Antigone came to the attention of the courts after becoming embroiled in a business deal. When one of her male clients—Athenogenes—decided to sell his perfumery business, which was riddled with debt, Antigone agreed to act as a broker, encouraging a man called Epicrates to purchase the perfumery. It was a substantial business deal, worth several hundred thousand dollars in today's money, and thanks to the subsequent legal wrangling it became the most documented business deal in ancient Athens.[78] After experiencing 'buyer's regret', Epicrates charged Antigone and Athenogenes with fraud. He claimed that he had been caught 'in a trap', 'persuaded by Athenogenes's courtesan' to enter into the deal while being entertained in her home.[79] We can imagine the scene: copious amounts of wine, pleasant conversation and who knows what else. In his defence, Epicrates noted that—according to Greek law—'if someone, while persuaded by a woman, writes a will for the disposition of his own property, the will shall be invalid' and that, equivalently, since he had entered into the business deal in similar circumstances of 'persuasion', the deal should be rendered null and void.[80] Sadly, while the speeches made in this particular court case were documented, the verdict of the jury has been lost in history.[81] What it nevertheless tells us is that in Athens, the law was not on the side of women: as with cloth production, the ancient Greeks struggled to separate women's paid work from sex work, which thereby tainted any form of paid endeavour with which women were involved. Women who worked for money were, quite simply, assumed to be sexually unvirtuous.

One practice more than any other serves to convey the disdain that Athenian men felt towards both women and commerce: when the male owner of a bank passed away, their business was commonly passed not to their son but, instead, to their surviving wife and a male slave—and the two were expected to formally seal their partnership with marriage.[82] Banks were, in other words, not fit to be inherited by male citizens. This contempt towards banks—like the contempt towards women—was not exactly beneficial for the economy. While the Greeks treated bankers with suspicion—as people who made money from nothing—banks are an essential part of any thriving economy. They provide a place where people can save their hard-earned money and, more importantly, a means through which those savings can be channelled into the hands of people who wish to borrow. Without banks, only those born into money can afford to make their way in business, which acts as a sharp brake on the economy. It also, however, serves to shelter the incumbent elite, protecting them from facing competition from those who would otherwise be able to rise up the social ladder—the nouveaux riches. While the Athenian world has gone down in history as a place of arts and culture, it was also a place in which women and business were pushed to the margins.

A DIFFERENT WORLD

In his epic mythical poem *The Odyssey,* written in the eighth century BCE, Homer tells of a wise and brave warrior called Odysseus—the King of Ithaca—returning to his beloved Greek island after a hard-won victory in the Trojan War. For ten years the Greeks had besieged the city of Troy—in present-day Turkey—and their victory was only ensured by tricking the Trojans, by appearing to withdraw whilst leaving behind a large wooden horse as a gift. Once the Trojans had heaved the horse through the gate in the city walls, Greek soldiers burst from it, massacred the men of Troy and enslaved Troy's women. It was a war with a woman—by the name of Helen—at its heart.

In the story, Helen was the daughter of Zeus. She was also the heir to the throne of Sparta—a city-state in ancient Greece—and renowned throughout Greece for her beauty, which brought many suitors to her door. Princes from across Greece sought Helen's hand in marriage, showering Sparta with gifts in an effort to win her favour. After much jostling, Menelaus—the youngest son of the King of Mycenae—was chosen to be Helen's husband, which earned him the title of King of Sparta. The details of Homer's poem suggest that Sparta was something other than a patriarchy. The royal bloodline passed through Helen, rather than through either of her brothers; her husband's kingship was the result of their marriage; and her throne was to be inherited by her daughter.

While mythology should not be confused with reality, in Sparta women had far greater freedoms than in Athens, so much so that they were considered outspoken and promiscuous by other Greeks.[83] Physical fitness was considered as important for Spartan women as it was for men, which meant that girls were encouraged to exercise and were well nourished. Spartan women did not have to hide their bodies and commonly wore a skirt with slits to the side that revealed the thigh and enabled the legs to move unconstrained.[84] Girls did not marry until they were eighteen and did not reside with their husbands until they were thirty, with the years in between treated as something of a 'trial marriage'.[85] Women owned forty percent of Spartan land and property and were able to spend their inheritances as they wished, including on racehorses and the latest fashions.[86]

In *The Iliad*, Homer writes of how, while her husband was away, Helen had left Sparta for Troy with the son of the Trojan king, a man called Paris, who had fallen madly in love with her.[87] When Menelaus realised that his wife had gone, he challenged Paris to a duel. Despite Menelaus winning the duel, the goddess Aphrodite conspired against him, saving Paris, and as a result Sparta and Troy ended up at war, drawing the warrior Odysseus into battle. After Sparta's victory, Odysseus embarked on his return journey home, during which time he was sent a set of challenges as tests from the

Gods, resulting in a gruelling ten-year-long return trip. For seven of those ten years, Odysseus found himself captive on the island of Ogygia, from which he escaped by building a raft and navigating by starlight. After his raft was destroyed at sea, Odysseus was washed up on a new Greek island—Phaiakians—where he was awoken the next morning by the voices of women laughing and giggling as they washed their clothes and played games on the seashore.[88] While on the island, Odysseus met women working on the river bank, women who owned property and women who ran their own homes. The island was a veritable paradise in which women were happy and free. Like Sparta, this was a very different world to that of patriarchal Athens, and it appears that it was the real-world island of Crete that provided Homer with the inspiration.

While Crete is perhaps best known for its minotaur, it also deserves to be known as the birthplace of dance. In Greek mythology, Minos—the King of Crete—commissioned not only a labyrinth to contain the minotaur, but also a dance floor for his daughter.[89] Unlike in Athens, women in Crete were free to dance in public and scenes of women dancing can be found in abundance on the frescoes that decorated Cretan palaces.[90] Unlike Athenian women, these Cretan women are not veiled, and instead have their long hair—which hangs over their puff-sleeved dresses—on show. In addition, Cretan fresco scenes depict women hunting, farming, commanding a ship and engaging in buying and selling.[91] In some, we see women with exposed breasts; perhaps breastfeeding in public was already an accepted practice on the island of Crete, enabling women to balance childcare and work.[92]

Dating to the seventh or sixth century BCE, the law code of Crete's city of Gortyn allowed women to own, control and inherit property. Women also had a say in who they married, could live in their own family home—rather than moving in with their parents-in-law—upon marriage and were able to divorce, in the event of which they were entitled to take half of the value of the couple's jointly held property. And, unlike the kinds of horrific punishments we find elsewhere in the ancient world, the punishment for adultery was a simple fine.[93] Rather than being a patriarchy, Crete was closer to a matriarchy, and the mother goddess had long held a prominent place in Cretan culture.[94] Women's fertility was recognised and revered, and connections were made between the fertility of women and the fertility of the natural world.[95] Battle scenes appear to be absent in Cretan art, suggesting that Crete was something of a peaceful island paradise.

This more peaceful history seems to have worked to the advantage of women. In fact, Crete is the only part of ancient Greece known to have been home to a female potter.[96] While sadly we do not know her name, she has been identified as a potter based on her skeleton, which was buried some time between 900–650 BCE in a cemetery on the slopes of Mount Ida. She died in her late forties, and her remains suggest that she was unusually muscular on the right side of her body and had worn out the cartilage in her hip and knee joints, an injury of a kind that could occur from repeatedly and purposefully kicking the mechanism that drove her potter's wheel. Using the motions of a modern-day female potter on the island and comparing these with the motions created by washing, baking, weaving and harvesting, archaeologists have been able to show that the muscle and the wear and tear on the skeleton were an exact match for the profession of potter.[97] The archaeologist Julie Hruby, based at Dartmouth College, is currently pioneering the analysis of fingerprints left on some of the most valuable and detailed pottery of the Greek world in an effort to see if other such female potters can be identified.[98]

Moving from female potters to poets, we need look no further than Lesbos, home to the poet Sappho.[99] While in Sappho's time the word 'Lesbian' simply meant 'a woman from the island of Lesbos', it is thanks to her poetry that the word came to acquire an altogether different meaning. Sappho was born in 612 BCE to an aristocratic family. Her poetry expresses love for other women, which has made her the lesbian icon of the ancient world, though since homosexuality was normalised in Greek society, whether she was writing from her own perspective or to appeal to her readers cannot be known for sure.[100] Sappho's poems were floral, natural and romantic and speak of trembling hearts, of tongues so frozen by love that they are unable to speak, and of flames trickling under the skin.[101] Designed to be sung, the poems became popular at dinner parties and social gatherings, where hosts and guests alike could sing along while accompanied by an instrument known as the lyre (a stringed, lute-like instrument from which the word 'lyric' derives).[102] While much of Sappho's more erotic poetry appears to have been lost in time—some of it destroyed by the medieval Church by order of Pope Gregory VII—one surviving fragment includes mention of a leather phallus.[103] Whether Sappho was paid for her writing we cannot know for sure, but her reputation and renown meant that wealthy families invited her to teach their daughters, suggesting that she may have established her own school, through which she would have been able to make a living.[104] While Athens—commonly seen as the seat of art and culture in the classical world—cannot lay claim to a single female poet, Lesbos was home not only to female poets but to female choirs who performed works written by women like Sappho.[105]

The peace and prosperity of the islanders who haunted Greek myths and the greater rights and freedoms that they offered to women were likely not coincidental.

BUILDING ALEXANDRIA

While Aristotle had baulked at the way making money was taking over the Greek world, one of his students had a more open attitude to business and trade. His name was Alexander—the son of the King of Macedonia—and upon his father's death, he became leader of an alliance of Greek city-states known as the League of Corinth.[106] Not all of Greece accepted his rule, and that included Phryne. When Alexander's armies destroyed the Greek city of Thebes, which mounted a resistance, Phryne offered to fund the rebuilding programme, albeit under one condition: that the walls be inscribed with the words 'destroyed by Alexander, restored by Phryne the hetaera'.[107] For Phryne, 'hetaera' was not a badge of shame; it was a badge of honour. And so too was standing up to Alexander.

After successfully conquering wider Greece, Alexander went on to tackle the almighty Persian Empire, earning himself the title 'Alexander the Great'. His success on the battlefield meant that Greek influence spread as far east as India and as far south as Egypt, where he made himself pharaoh.[108] It was in this land of pyramids, crocodiles and linen that Alexander established a new port city—in 332 BCE—which he, somewhat egotistically, named after himself. Alexandria became Egypt's principal port and the largest city in the Greek world. It was the commercial centre of Alexander's 'Macedonian Empire', and became famous not only for its trade but also for its library and its scientists.[109]

By establishing his own city, Alexander the Great was able to bypass the antibusiness elite in Athens. There were in fact two good reasons for choosing Egypt as the new heart of the Greek world. Not only was Egypt more friendly to commerce; it was also more friendly to women. Unlike in Athens, women in Egypt had managed to hold on to many of their historic freedoms. Rather than being patrilineal, Egyptian families traced descent through the female as well as the male line.[110] And, at least to begin with, Egyptian law was allowed to coexist alongside the imported Greek legal framework, which meant that Egyptian women were able to avoid Greece's guardianship system.[111] But, while Alexander was in Babylon, where he was making plans to improve irrigation throughout the 'fertile crescent' and to build a Mesopotamian version of Alexandria at the mouth of the Tigris, he fell ill and died, aged only thirty-three.[112]

Alexander's empire was divided up between his Greek generals. Under this continued Greek influence, Greek culture began to penetrate Lower and Middle Egypt, both as a result of intermarriage and as a consequence of Egyptian families adopting Greek practices as a means to align themselves with, and seek favour from, their overlords. By the first century CE, the legal and economic affairs of most Egyptian women were under the supervision of a male relative in the form of a guardianship system.[113] Nevertheless, unlike in Athens, gender segregation did not take root. Alexandria was home to women doctors, teachers, scholars, poets and philosophers.[114] Women also worked as nurses, beer sellers, dancers, musicians and camel keepers.[115] When it came to the home, women and men were still able to occupy the same rooms, and women were not expected to veil when in public.[116] Indeed, on the mummies housed in Egyptian tombs dating to the Greco-Roman period, we find lifelike portraits of women of all ages, with curly hair, large earrings and necklaces of pearls. Painted on wood in vivid colour and with wreaths and jewellery adorned with gold, these portraits were placed on the face of the linen-wrapped and embalmed bodies of the deceased.

~

FEW SOCIETIES IN HISTORY HAVE DONE MORE TO RENDER women invisible than ancient Greece. Not only did women's hard work in family businesses go unrecognised and unrewarded; men even attempted to take credit for reproduction. This distaste for women proved inseparable from the antibusiness culture that pervaded ancient Athens. It's therefore not the Athenians but lesser-known civilisations such as the Lydians and Phoenicians who are truly deserving of a place in economic history, while Persia, the empire that has traditionally been painted as the great enemy of Greece, was in fact far more successful—in part because it embraced rather than constrained women's freedoms. While the subsequent spread of Greek culture across the empire amassed by Alexander the Great has been one of the great talking points of history, it was—thankfully for women and for the economy—a short-lived success. As Greece jettisoned its one big opportunity by failing to appreciate the recipe for economic success, somewhere else was waiting in the wings: Etruria in Italy, where women were so free that they were dismissed by Athenian colonisers as 'promiscuous drunkards'.[117] It was here, as we will see in the next chapter, that the Romans were to emerge and to usurp the Greeks as inheritors of the ancient world.

CHAPTER 4

MERCHANTS, PROPERTY DEVELOPERS AND MONEYLENDERS

THE WOMEN OF ANCIENT ROME

WHILE IN THE FIRST MILLENNIUM BCE, NORTHERN AND Western Europe—distant from the trading arena of the Eastern Mediterranean—were relatively backward, they were starting to look attractive to budding conquerors.[1] The Iron Age had roused the outer expanses of the continent from its sleep, turning uninhabited wildernesses into farmed and settled land, giving rise to expanding populations. Lacking its own cities, empires, writing and coinage, the region was ripe for takeover by those who were already a step ahead. In search of new opportunities, the ancient Greeks had set up colonies along the Western Mediterranean coastline, founding what is today the city of Marseille (in the south of France) along with the Italian cities of Taranto and Syracuse in southern Italy.[2]

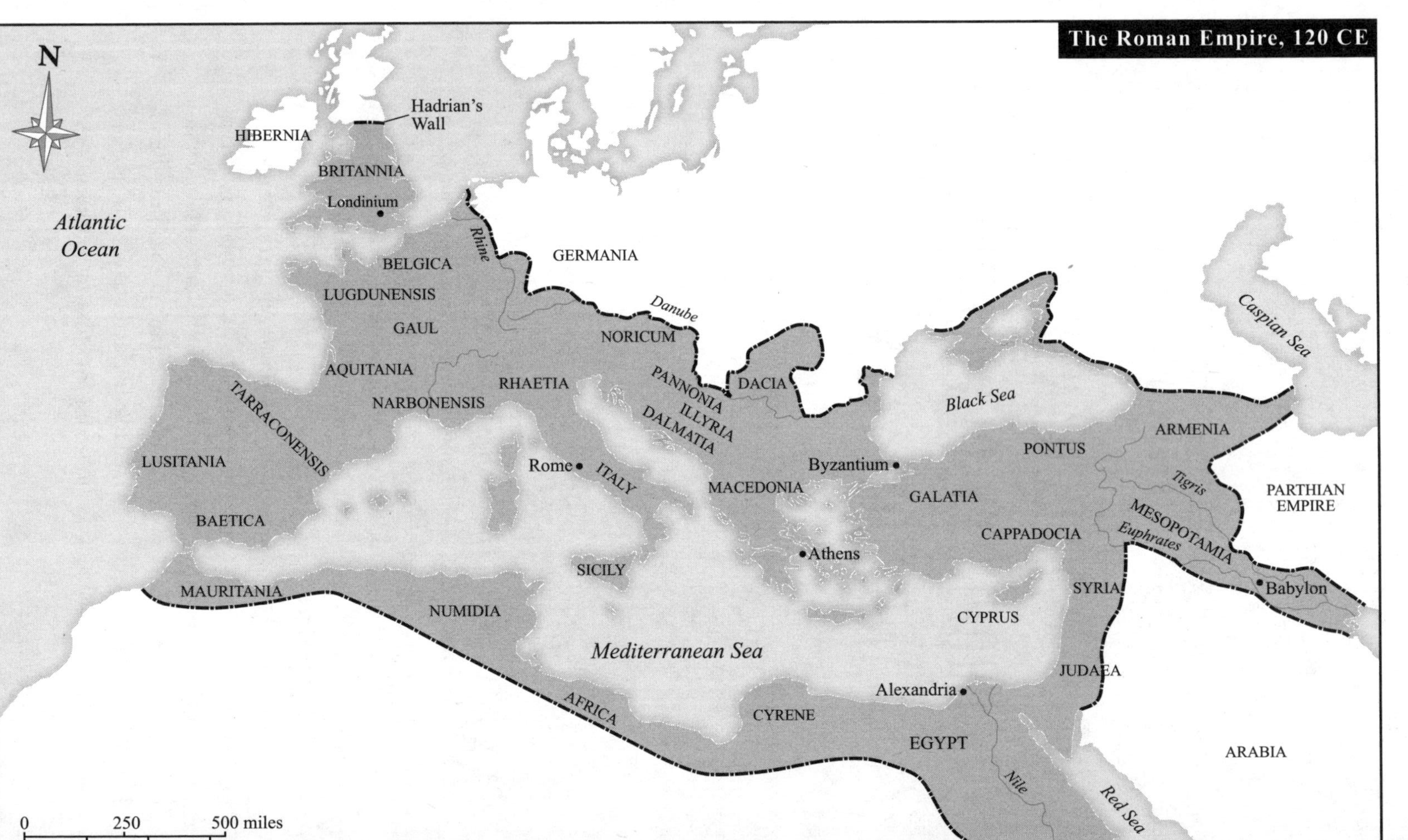
The Roman Empire, 120 CE
N
Hadrian's Wall
HIBERNIA
BRITANNIA
Londinium
Atlantic Ocean
Rhine
GERMANIA
BELGICA
LUGDUNENSIS
GAUL
Danube
NORICUM
AQUITANIA
TARRACONENSIS
RHAETIA
NARBONENSIS
PANNONIA
ILLYRIA
DALMATIA
DACIA
Black Sea
Caspian Sea
ARMENIA
PONTUS
LUSITANIA
Rome
ITALY
Byzantium
MACEDONIA
GALATIA
Tigris
PARTHIAN EMPIRE
MESOPOTAMIA
Euphrates
BAETICA
CAPPADOCIA
Athens
SICILY
Babylon
SYRIA
MAURITANIA
NUMIDIA
CYPRUS
Mediterranean Sea
JUDAEA
Alexandria
AFRICA
CYRENE
EGYPT
ARABIA
Nile
Red Sea
0
250
500 miles

Greek migrants, pottery and coinage had therefore begun to flow into wider Europe. But, it was the Romans—the inhabitants of a small town on the Tiber River in central Italy—who soon usurped the Greeks to become the supreme colonialists of the era. By 43 CE, the Roman army had reached the British Isles and, despite Queen Boudica's valiant attempt at resistance, the Romans eventually came to rule an area that encircled the whole of the Mediterranean and stretched from the North Sea to the Red Sea. Roman territory was vast. It included modern-day England and Wales, France, Spain, Greece, Turkey, the Near East and North Africa—a total area so large that it would have taken seven weeks to travel from east to west (an equivalent distance to that between the states of Washington and Florida).[3]

Compared with ancient Greece, women had a far better deal in Rome. They were not restricted to the home, and could be found on both sides of the counter: shopping and serving customers. Women could bathe alongside men and could sit at the dinner table with their guests, feasting on wine, dates, bread and fish. And they certainly did not need to veil, making women's elaborate hairstyles a feast for the eyes. Roman women owned shops and ships, they imported wine and olive oil, and their seal impressions can be found on the storage jars—or amphorae—that have since been dredged from the Tiber River. Women even helped to build the city of Rome itself: a third of the clay beds that supplied the capital's bricks were owned by women and twenty-seven of the water pipes that spanned the city were etched with women's names.[4] In fact, women constituted ten percent of all 'plumbers' in Rome—four times the proportion of plumbers that are female in Britain today.[5] The lives of women in Rome were a world apart from those in ancient Athens.

As we will see in this chapter, not only did women help to sow the seeds of Roman success, but the eventual erosion of their freedoms—along with the plight of the enslaved—served to undermine the economic stability of the Roman Empire. The rise—and fall—of Rome depended on the fortunes and freedoms of women.

ETRUSCAN REALISM

Deep inside the British Museum, within a lavish sarcophagus, is the skeleton of a noblewoman dating to the second century BCE. On top of the sarcophagus is a large, reclining terracotta figure, wearing earrings and pulling back her veil. As the figure reveals her hair, we catch sight of her bare arm, adorned with bracelets decorated with snake motifs. The woman's name was Seianti Hanunia Tlesnasa and she died, in her mid-fifties, in a land that was home to the first great 'superpower' of the Western Mediterranean: the Etruscans.[6]

Forerunners to the Romans, the Etruscans inhabited the Italian region between the Arno River and the Tiber of Rome, an area which today comprises Tuscany and parts of Umbria and Lazio. Rich in mineral resources, Etruria had long attracted traders from across the Near East, making it renowned not only for its iron, bronze, silver and gold but also for its commerce. Etruscan burial sites were stocked with weapons and jewellery crafted from the region's rich resources, and Seianti's skeleton provides the most complete set of bodily remains from this era. It is, in fact, so complete that, until recently, it was considered a fake. Some suspected that the original skeleton had been replaced in the nineteenth century to enhance the value of the sarcophagus at a time when ancient artefacts were being sold to private buyers. Radiocarbon dating has, however, confirmed that the bones do indeed date to the time of the tomb. Unlike the skeleton, the silverware that accompanied the burial—which also made its way to the British Museum—survives only in photographic form, having disappeared when the museum was evacuated during World War Two.

Seianti was clearly important and respected, and her presence in an opulent burial site is testament to the position of women in Etruscan society. Thanks to the careful research of archaeologists, we know quite a lot about her life. Her bodily remains suggest that Seianti was 154 cm (60 inches) tall—taller than me—and that she had been well nourished but suffered from arthritis and dental abscesses. It seems that she had also suffered a severe physical trauma in her teens, leaving a fracture around her right eye, tooth loss on the right-hand side of her jaw, and damage to her joints and pelvis along one side of her body. The damage is consistent with a horse-riding accident in which the rider's horse had fallen to the ground, trapping one half of her body underneath. The strong muscle attachment points on Seianti's upper leg bones certainly suggest that she was a keen horsewoman. Rather than being driven around in a carriage, protected by a parasol, Seianti was—we can hypothesise—free to make her own excursions on horseback, albeit with the associated hazards.[7]

Facial reconstruction based on Seianti's skull reveals that the terracotta figure that graces her sarcophagus closely resembles her real-life appearance, making it the first realistic portrait in Western art.[8] Whereas the Greeks at this time were focused on the ideals of youth, Etruscan portraits were not afraid to show sagging skin and wrinkles, valuing authenticity over superficiality. Much as in Palaeolithic depictions of women, Etruscan images of women were natural, not stylised. In contrast, the Greeks shied away from depicting women nursing or bearing children and instead, as we have seen, attributed birth to men, as a metaphor for masculine creativity. The representation of a woman breastfeeding or in labour would have been shocking in the Greek world, adding to women's invisibility. The Etruscans, in contrast, not only placed motherhood on display; they did so with gusto.

A seal impression from Poggio Colla in northern Tuscany shows an Etruscan woman crouching, with her legs spread apart and her knees raised, as a newborn baby emerges from her body. Another graphic representation of childbirth can be found on the relief of a decorative bronze Etruscan wine bucket, presumably used at banquets, which tells the story of a young couple meeting, kissing and engaging in sexual intercourse (in all manner of positions) before the woman gives birth, flanked by two midwives.[9] Small statuettes of nursing mothers can be found throughout Etruscan archaeological sites and across Italy more generally, and while women's tombs in the ancient world tended to contain tweezers, which archaeologists presume were for depilation rather than the removal of splinters, when an Etruscan woman's skeleton was excavated replete with pubic hair, they were left startled.[10]

Artistic depictions of married couples and of family scenes place emphasis on the wife as well as the husband, and daughters as well as sons, and a mother could pass her own family name on to her children, something which no truly patrilineal society could possibly allow.[11] Indeed, Theopompus—the Greek writer—noted that Etruscan women brought up all of their newborns 'even if they did not know the father', which would have been unthinkable in his own world, where fathers made decisions about whether a newborn should live or die, and the 'exposure' of babies was an accepted practice. A woman's involvement in decisions concering her children was, at this time, remarkable. And, importantly, Etruscan women maintained legal autonomy once married.[12]

According to Theopompus, even appearing naked was not considered a 'disgrace' for a woman in Etruria.[13] While Theopompus might have been prone to exaggeration, it does suggest that women's bodies in the region did not carry the same shame as women's bodies in ancient Greece, and—with this—women were much more free to engage in the wider economy as they did not have to fear being seen in public by men. Women's respectability was not tarnished by being visible, which in turn meant that they were on more equal terms with men when it came to accessing opportunities beyond the home. Moreover, in Etruscan society, spinning was neither belittled nor diminished; even tombs of elite women were filled with tools such as spindle whorls and distaffs, albeit encrusted with gold and amber.[14] The fact that women were relatively free and equal in Etruria helps to explain why its economy prospered as, unlike in Athens, women and business were welcome. The more inclusive environment acted as an attracting force for anyone seeking an escape from more repressive societies, in turn adding to the dynamism of the economy.

Around 650 BCE, Demaratus—a merchant from Greek Corinth—settled in the region, accompanied by a band of Greek potters, and married an Etruscan princess.[15] Their descendants went on to rule nearby Rome for generations to come. That was until, in 509 BCE, Tarquin—the king's son—raped a young noblewoman by the name of Lucretia, causing a rebellion that resulted in the overthrow of the royal family and the establishment of the Roman Republic. The Romans were about to begin their march across the pages of the history books.

THANK YOU, DIDO

In 396 BCE, the Romans successfully besieged the Etruscan city of Veii, where they loaded its precious bronzes onto carts destined for Rome. The tables had turned and Rome was now on top. This left just one other enemy in sight—that of Dido's Carthage—a civilisation that was every bit as keen on trade and on women's rights as Etruria.

By 300 BCE, Carthage had built a maritime empire that encircled the southern and western reaches of the Mediterranean, incorporating large parts of the North African coastline as well as Spain, Corsica, Sardinia and Sicily. This was an empire of equals, not one of dominance and submission: an 'all for one, one for all' free-trade association of allied but autonomous states who stood in defence of one another with the aim of maintaining peaceful trading relations. These relations extended to the Etruscans, with whom they had a trade treaty.[16] Commerce—not power—was the goal of the Carthaginians.

As Rome expanded into Etruria and beyond, fireworks began to fly, resulting in a series of wars between Carthage and the Romans, known today as the Punic Wars. Carthage was Rome's nemesis. According to Roman legend, Dido had cursed Rome following a tragic love affair with Aeneas, the son of Aphrodite, who chose to abandon her so that he and his descendants could found Rome.[17]

Rather than engaging in peaceful trading relations, the mythical animosity was the excuse the Romans needed to obliterate their greatest rival. The Roman statesman Cato the Elder did not hold back when he pronounced, '*Carthage delenda est*': Carthage must be destroyed.[18]

To defend its trading partners across the Western Mediterranean, including the Etruscans in Italy itself, the Carthaginians had no choice but to go to war with Rome. Given the seafaring might of the Carthaginians, the Romans expected to be attacked by fleets of vessels travelling across the ocean waves. But instead, to take them by surprise, a Carthaginian general named Hannibal attacked by land. He marched from northern Africa through Spain and France before crossing the Alps atop an elephant and inflicting serious losses on Rome's military in northern Italy. 'I have come not to make war on the Italians, but to aid the Italians against Rome', he explained.[19]

To help ensure that all resources were available for the war effort, Rome instituted a crackdown on 'frivolous' spending and public displays of luxury—a crackdown that applied only to women. Women were no longer free to ride in carriages in the city centre; they were prevented from wearing the colour purple (the colour associated with the Phoenicians); and they were limited to carrying no more than half an ounce of gold.[20] As women adjusted to the new restrictions, Roman soldiers were busy moving the battle lines closer to Carthage, where they slaughtered their enemies and took their elephants captive.[21] Rome—despite Hannibal's valiant march—had, in the end, triumphed. But, seven years on from Rome's victory over Carthage, the curtailment of women's freedom to travel and to spend continued.

Some argued that restraining women's spending at a time of war when men were making their own sacrifices was simply a means to level the playing field between the sexes: that for women not to experience some form of pain would have created tensions between the sexes, potentially leaving women open to physical attack on the streets from men who judged them to be overly ostentatious and carefree. Since large parts of the male population were away at war, women already stood out on the streets of the city. But the fact that the restrictions continued into peacetime suggests that there were other motives. Once again, the statesman Cato the Elder had a great deal to say, with his speeches offering much more than a whiff of misogyny. He argued that limiting women's spending power prevented them from being in a 'clothing contest' of a kind that risked 'corrupting' those with means and shaming those who lacked the funds to spend. In other words, Cato believed that the restrictions instituted on women during wartime should continue indefinitely. That women, in other words, could not be trusted with money and so needed to face greater constraints than men. Roman women disagreed. They were tired of the double standards and so, in 195 BCE, they protested at the Roman Forum, the centre of all political life in the city.

The Forum was just a stone's throw from the imposing Temple of Vesta, where Rome's 'Vestal Virgins' kept the holy fire burning in honour of the Goddess of the Hearth, Vesta. The flame housed in the temple was considered so important to the prosperity of Rome that it required full-time supervision by the hand-picked virgins. But, rather than keeping their own home fires burning, Roman women—dressed in sleeveless long white dresses and with neatly coiffured hair—were flooding into Rome's political heartland from the surrounding towns and rural areas.[22] It was there at the Forum that Roman statesman were gathering to debate whether or not to repeal the wartime restrictions on women. Fuelled by a breakfast of bread, dates and honey, the women congregated in the warm Italian air, begging the statesmen who passed by to restore their freedoms and besieging the homes of statesmen like Cato who lobbied in favour of maintaining the restrictions. Rome's male elite continued to debate the matter in the Forum for some days, but the women did not give up, with their numbers increasing with each passing day. So many women gathered that the main approaches to the Forum became blocked by the female crowds, whose gowns picked up dust as they brushed against the floor and whose hair began to work its way loose after days of relentless protest. With the women having such strength in numbers, the statesmen had no choice but to listen. Roman women had done themselves proud, successfully regaining their freedom to spend.[23]

HORTENSIA SPEAKS

By the first century BCE—by which point Roman rule was well established—Rome was coming under attack from within. According to one Roman writer, Rome's defeat of its enemies removed the common foe that had bound together the Roman elite and, with it, prepared the ground for civil war; military success, in other words, had bred self-indulgence and corruption.[24] Women were to pay the price. In 42 BCE, following the assassination of Julius Caesar, a three-man dictatorship consisting of Mark Antony, Octavian and Lepidus was busily devising a plan to pile the cost of civil war on women.[25] They proposed appointing a tax assessor to estimate how much the state could reasonably—or unreasonably—extract from Roman women. This was a monumental change. It was men—not women—who had historically paid taxes to Rome on behalf of their families. There had been only one exception: that of wealthy widows of equestrians, who had historically paid a tax—known as the *aes hordearium*—that kept the state's military horses fed in lieu of their deceased husband's military contribution.[26]

For men, political rights—the right to vote—came with the duty of defending the realm. Men either had to fight in the army or pay a tax to fund those who did. Since they were the ones both serving on the front line and funding the military, it was considered only fair that men should have a say in political matters—most importantly, in matters of war. Rome had begun life as a 'warrior community', and so, historically speaking, citizenship for the Romans meant being a warrior and having a vote on wars in which you would yourself participate. War made the Roman state, and the Roman state made war. Since women were not considered warriors, they were denied citizenship and, with it, both the right to vote and the responsibility of paying tax.[27] Not paying tax was, in a sense, the quid pro quo of not having a vote. It therefore made sense that if the state were to insist that women now pay tax, then they should also be granted a say in political matters: either women deserved equal political rights, or they deserved not to be taxed. 'No taxation without representation' as Americans would say, centuries later, when fighting for their freedom from Great Britain. To make their case, Rome's wealthiest women began lobbying Flavia, the wife of Mark Antony. Such behind-the-scenes politics—women appealing to the wives of statesmen who in turn had the ear of their husbands—was one of the key ways in which women could make their voices heard at a time when they were locked out of politics.[28] In this case, Mark Anthony would not listen.

A woman by the name of Hortensia—the daughter of a Roman lawyer—was incensed. Perhaps inspired by the women who had demonstrated in the previous century, she took to the Forum—where she was surrounded by men—and delivered a public speech that sent ripples across Rome. As her voice echoed across the open space, the statesmen stopped and listened. She noted that women had 'no share in magistracies, or honours, or military commands or in public affairs at all' and so should not be expected to fund the wars caused by men.[29] Mark Antony and Octavian were furious with her audacity, but her speech was so compelling that they had little choice but to change their plan.[30] The women of Rome had—once again—been heard. While they didn't achieve the right to vote, they did manage to fend off taxation.

Despite women's victory, taxes remained a hot topic in Rome. Rather than relying on thieving the wealth of their defeated opponents, the Romans were increasingly turning to taxation. Tax could provide a steadier and more predictable income stream for the Roman treasury than booty—so long, that is, as the economy was not smothered by the tax burden. Rome seems to have achieved about the right balance. In order to acquire the money they needed to pay their taxes, conquered territories had no choice but to produce and export surplus food, wine and manufactures, boosting the economy.[31] Meat, wine, oil, metalware, pottery, glassware and cloth were traded not just short but long distances. Between the third and the first century BCE, shipwrecks in the Mediterranean trebled—not because the ocean waves were more tumultuous but because far more trading voyages were taking place.[32] At around twenty percent, Roman taxes were high enough to support the infrastructure that underpinned such trade but not so high as to discourage economic activity.[33] Trade and tax were two sides of the same coin and, as we will see, the Roman world's booming economy of trade was as much instigated by women as it was by men.

ROME GOES GLOBAL

By the time Hortensia was delivering her protest speech at the Forum, the former territories of Etruria, ancient Greece, Carthage and Lydia were under Roman rule. Even Mesopotamia was in sight. France, Spain, Greece, Turkey, the Near East and North Africa were combined within a single empire, and it was the Roman acquisition of Egypt that brought Cleopatra to the lusty attention of Mark Antony.

Egypt was the jewel in the crown of the Mediterranean. During the fourth century BCE, it had been a part of the Persian Empire, after which it was conquered by Alexander the Great. After Alexander's death, one of his top generals—Ptolemy—took charge.[34] Despite the Greek influence, elements of the more gender-equal Egyptian culture lived on. This meant that rather than being overlooked, Cleopatra ruled alongside her brother, Ptolemy XIII. As the two siblings battled for supremacy, Mark Antony—who styled himself on Alexander—fatefully took the side of Cleopatra. With trading links that ran down the East African coastline and out as far as India, the commercial reputation of Alexandria continued through

Roman times. Mark Antony even considered making it the capital of the Roman empire.

Egypt opened the door to another world. Its Red Sea coastline offered connections not only with Africa's Aksum Empire and the Arabian coastline but also with India. And so, it was to India that Roman ships began to set their course. Guided by the weather patterns of the annual monsoon, more than a hundred ships a year journeyed all the way from Roman Egypt to India, amounting to one a day in the peak sailing season.[35] The *Periplus Maris Erythraei*—a Roman shipping manual—offered advice for those newly traversing the Red Sea route and the results are clear: an abundance of Roman coins have been found along the Indian coastline.[36] And through their trade with merchants in Afghanistan, Uzbekistan and Tajikistan, India was able to extend Rome's reach all of the way to China.

Despite its great prosperity, China had lived in relatively blissful isolation from the rest of Eurasia. Trade was severely hampered by the surrounding deserts and mountains. Merchants took their lives into their own hands when they attempted to beat a path from China across unwelcoming territories that were home not just to extreme weather conditions but also to nomadic tribes for whom raiding was a way of life.[37] These nomads had something of a reputation, including for drinking the blood of their victims and incorporating the scalps of their enemies—animal-skin style—into their clothing. Their notoriety wasn't helped by the fact that the leader of the Persian Empire—Cyrus the Great—had been killed by Scythian nomads who lived to the north and east of Persia.[38] China had in fact built a Great Wall in order to keep the nomads out.[39] Where the wall proved insufficient, the Chinese state would bribe nomads not to attack, offering young royal women as brides, along with silk—manufactured by women—and anything else it could scramble together.[40] But, by the second century BCE, the Chinese state—under the new Han Dynasty (206 BCE–220 CE)—was making its own incursions into nomadic territory, where it built a system of forts and secured travel routes through which traders could pass to the oasis city of Dunhuang.[41] The Silk Road (or what historians today prefer to call the Silk Routes) was brought to life.

Silk—produced by Chinese women—was the currency of the Silk Routes. This precious cargo would pass through the hands of numerous middlemen in the process of making its way along the caravan route. All traded items—which included incense, gold, silver, livestock and slaves—were priced in terms of bolts of silk, which comprised forty-foot-long pieces of strong and lustrous silken fabric that could be folded into a lightweight package.[42] The Romans had an immense appetite for silk, so much so that they referred to the northern Chinese as Seres—the silk people. As payment for silk, the Romans had to offer their own wares. In the Afghan trading post of Begram, at the crossroads of the caravan trade between India and China, an astonishing array of Roman treasures have been unearthed in what was once presumed to have been the treasury of a great palace. Newly interpreted as a customs depot, the treasures include Roman glassware, bronzes and plaster casts that date to between the first century BCE and the second century CE.[43] While any silk that was present has sadly degraded with time, within the stockpile can also be found fragments of Chinese lacquerware.

Similarly buzzing with the caravan trade was the region of Sogdia, in present day Uzbekistan and Tajikistan. An abandoned mailbag of Sogdian letters dating from the early fourth century CE—found in the rubbish dump of a watchtower—is evidence of a postal and trading network that connected the Far East with Central Asia. Filled with letters that contain the names of the senders as well as the recipients, it tells of the exploits of the Sogdian merchant families in China. The mailbag included two letters from a woman who had been abandoned by her merchant husband in Dunhuang, the Silk Route city in northwest China on the outskirts of the Gobi desert.[44] The woman's name—Miwnay—translates as tiger cub.[45]

In the first letter, which is addressed to her mother, the Sogdian woman writes: 'I, unfortunate[ly], live without clothes, without money. I ask [for] a loan, but no one agreed to give me, so I had to beg

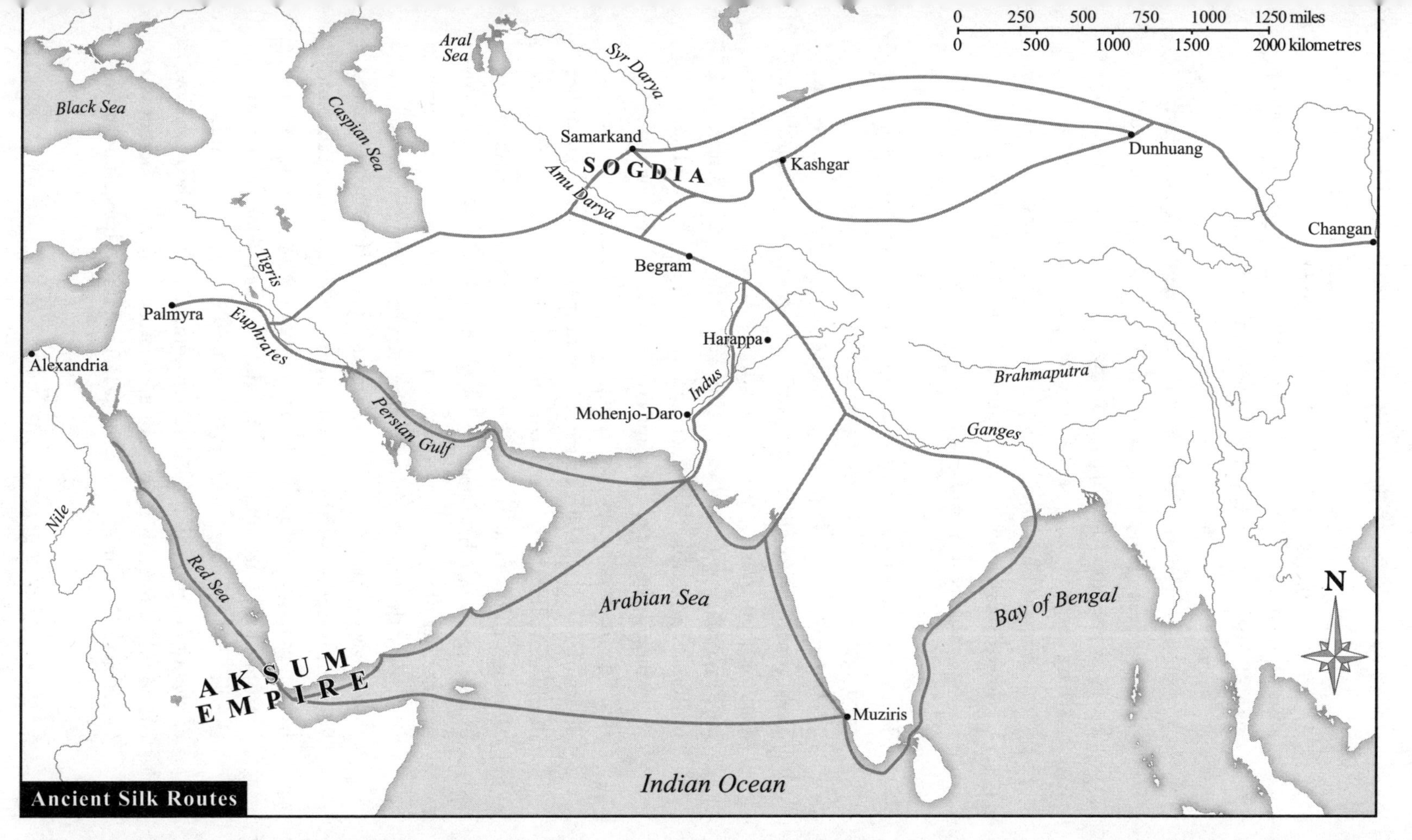

Ancient Silk Routes

alms of the priest'. The second letter—with a date that corresponds with 21 April—is addressed to the woman's husband:

> I am doing badly, badly, and I consider myself dead. I send you letters again and again, but do not receive a single letter from you, and I lost hope of seeing you . . . all these years, I have obeyed your orders, I came to Tun-huang [Dunhuang] despite the objection of my mother and brothers . . . I followed your words in everything. But then I should have better become the wife of a dog or a pig.[46]

This particular letter, as with the one to her mother, remained in the mailbag, unread. What happened to the woman is unknown.

Other letters in the Sogdian mailbag are less personal in nature. They contain information on shipments ready for dispatch and deal with purchase requests, including for silk that would likely have eventually made its way to India and then on to Rome. Back in Rome, and despite both men and women being avid spenders, it was women who faced constant criticism for buying foreign luxuries. Purchases of everything from perfume to pearls were said to be diverting Roman wealth to 'strange or hostile nations'.[47] Upon her death, Priscilla, the wife of a courtier, was praised for resisting the 'alluring wealth of Indians, Chinese or Arabs'; the poet Statius wrote of how 'she would have preferred to die in poverty and chastity, to sacrifice her life so as to save her honour'.[48] What was conveniently ignored by the literary elite was that women contributed to Rome's coffers every time they went on a spending spree. The discovery of the 'Muziris' papyrus—which contains financial accounts of incense and ivory imported from India—suggests that the tax paid by Roman consumers on wares imported via the Red Sea alone equated to a third of the Roman state's entire military expenditure.[49] Standing at twenty-five percent, the Roman customs tax was fairly reasonable compared with tariffs in more recent history and, by not acting as a brake on trade, managed to earn the Roman state a handsome sum.[50]

Funerary inscriptions reveal that women were, in fact, not only buyers of foreign wares but also sellers. While we still know very little about the role of women in Sogdian merchant families, the epitaph of a merchant's wife from Roman Africa reads: 'my companion and partner in business'.[51] Touchingly, the husband notes that he has 'no hope of living without such a wife'. An inscription in the Temple of Medamud, in modern-day Egypt, honours two female merchants of the Red Sea, Aelia Isidora and Aelia Olympias.[52] An epitaph from Rome—dedicated by an adult daughter to her parents—reads: 'Coelia Mascellina made [this tomb] for her parents, for [her mother], a woman of unequalled purity, a negotiatrix of oil and wine from the province of Baetica [and] for her most dutiful father'.[53] Not only was Coelia's mother an importer of oil and wine from Baetica (Spain); Coelia followed in her footsteps. Pottery baring Coelia's seal have been found in the Tiber River while those of at least twelve other women have been unearthed in the Monte Testaccio—the rubbish heap for amphorae in the city of Rome, now a grassy mound, estimated to contain fragments from more than fifty-three million amphorae.[54] The presence of women in the shipping trade is also attested by an imperial order of Emperor Claudius, who asked women with ships to come forward to help transport food to Rome at a time when the city was struggling with food shortages.[55] While women lacked political rights, Roman laws relating to buying and selling stated explicitly that they applied to women as well as men, something which is apparent in the relics of Pompeii—perhaps the most important archaeological site of the Roman world.[56]

MATRIARCHAL MALLS

In 79 CE, on the morning of 24 August, the city of Pompeii was humming with everyday hustle and bustle. Ten thousand of its residents were going about their daily business—shopping, visiting bathhouses and exchanging pleasantries as they passed on the streets, perhaps commenting on the fact that the sky was unusually grey. As bakers placed their loaves in the oven in time for the lunchtime rush, volcanic debris began to shower the city, crushing and asphyxiating its population, who had no time to make haste. Mount Vesuvius had erupted and Pompeii had become buried under a mountain of ash. Preserved in time, it offers historians a glimpse of everyday life in the Roman world, allowing us to shine a light on women, rich and poor.

Amongst the ashes can be found an advertisement on the facade of a building, which reads: 'to rent for the period of five years'.[57] Consisting of baths, a bar, shops and apartments—all accessed via a grand entrance replete with columns—this was the property empire of Julia Felix, a first-century-CE businesswoman. Felix was the self-made woman par excellence of the Roman world. According to her rental advert, she was the 'daughter of Spurius', which suggests that either Julia or her father were illegitimate—a fact which she did not choose to hide in her advertisement.[58] Some historians think that she had descended from freed slaves.[59]

Once a noble house, Felix's building, which occupies a double lot, was divided into apartments, with the lower floors consisting of an extensive entertainment and recreational complex. Whereas exclusive property was, historically, decorated with images of famous battles or mythological scenes, at the heart of Julia's building were murals representing business life. These murals included a still life—in the private dining quarters—depicting a money bag, piles of carefully sorted coins, a papyrus scroll and writing implements.[60] Positioned in the atrium, and visible to bathers, diners and drinkers alike, was a twenty-metre-long frieze illustrating an extensive array of market scenes. We see the transportation of goods by mule and cart, the sale of cloth and bread, and a good deal of browsing on the part of potential customers. By making the market the artistic highlight, the choice of ornamentation elevated the everyday world of business. Moreover, by showing buyers and sellers dressed in similar attire, it placed the two parties on an equal footing, suggesting that this was a society where the boundaries between those who had money to spend and those who needed to sell something for a living were somewhat blurred compared with more hierarchical societies.

The decoration tells us that those who frequented Felix's mall would not have been offended by business and had likely made their way in the world not through military or political means—as was typical of the elite class—but instead through commerce. This was a building owned by a woman whose ancestors had likely risen from the class of slaves and one that served the Roman bourgeoisie: people who had, like Julia herself, amassed a degree of wealth but were nevertheless lacking in elite 'status'. And its clients were not only men; they were also women and, unlike in earlier history, the bathhouse was not gender segregated: men and women bathed alongside one another.[61]

Women were active in the economy of Pompeii. Women dressed in tunics with uncovered hair, shopping for everything from shoes to fast food, featured prominently in the city's murals.[62] On the colourful frescoes that decorated the numerous shop fronts, we also find images of women selling a whole array of everyday items. The shop of Verecundus featured a fresco in which a woman stood behind a large L-shaped counter, with a table to her front displaying cloth and shoes, and cabinets to her rear filled with countless jars; a male client is sitting on a bench and gestures to the female assistant as she holds up items for his consideration.[63] Inscriptions on everyday objects found in Pompeii reveal the names of female vendors: the name Gavia Severa appears on containers of honey and jars of cosmetic lotions, and one Umbricia Fortunata—a woman who had been freed from slavery—appears on containers of fish sauce.[64] Where they contain mentions of an occupation or business, funerary reliefs and epigraphs provide another source of evidence as to the types of jobs occupied by women. While they suggest that the majority of dealers of luxury items were men, they also tell us that women were not entirely excluded from such work. Even the most valuable luxury items—such as purple dye, silk and perfume—were sold by women as well as men.[65]

BANKING ON WOMEN

In a butcher's shop at the heart of the city of Rome stood a man dressed in a tunic chopping meat on a butcher's block. He was surrounded by joints which hung from a tall wooden rack and a plethora of sharp butchery knives. To his far side—on a throne-like chair—was an elegantly draped woman wearing a long dress with unveiled hair arranged in a neat 'up-do'. In her hand was a wax tablet, on which she was finishing the company accounts. This daily scene was—like so many others—memorialised on the side of a Roman tombstone, and it shines a light on the female bookkeepers of the Roman world.[66]

With all of the buying and selling that was taking place in the Roman economy, an army of people were needed to keep track of the numerous daily transactions. Accountants and bookkeepers were as important in the Roman world as they are today. While the names of those who looked after the accounts of the numerous shops and enterprises of cities like Rome and Pompeii have been lost in time, we do know the names of those who looked after the accounts of the Roman imperial family. Huge marble slabs—known as *fasti*—from the estates of the emperors Claudius and Nero reveal that it was women who looked after the books. The names Julia Secunda and Claudia Hellas are inscribed on the slabs alongside the job title NUMM, short for *nummularius*—person who handled money.[67] Appearing on a marble-inscribed slab such as this was a mark of status. Not everyone who worked for the imperial family was included, only those who had been specially chosen for inscription. Those chosen were in a position of authority—the equivalent of trade union representatives, guild masters or society networkers. The fact that two female bookkeepers made their way onto the *fasti* suggests that they commanded power and respect within the imperial household. Some have nevertheless doubted whether the two women really were working for the emperor, with one historian having proposed that the title NUMM could be short for the much simpler word *nummus* (coin) instead of *nummularius*, implying a giver of money instead of a handler of money. The suggestion is that the two women had bought rather than earned their position of authority—their seat at the table—by making a benefaction. But the fact that these women's inscriptions take on the exact same form as all the other entries on the list speaks for itself. Women can frequently be found in the numerous archaeological relics that survive from the past; the question is whether or not we choose to take them seriously.

Roman women didn't only work as accountants; they also borrowed and loaned money, including through banks. Unlike the Greeks, the Romans were welcoming both of women and of bankers. The emperor Augustus, who ruled the Roman Empire from 27 BCE to 14 CE, was in fact born into a family of bankers.[68] Banks were big business in the Roman world. Not only did Roman elites deposit large sums with banks, Roman soldiers were encouraged to place a portion of their own earnings into savings accounts, with some of the first banks emerging close to Roman legions.[69] Bank loans were used to buy land, vineyards and buildings, to purchase the items that filled retailers' shelves, and to repair or equip ships. And Roman banks did not merely serve the economic interests of men. The surviving accounts of one financial institution—the Sulpicii of Puteoli, dating to the first century CE—reveal the names of numerous female clients, from the aunt of Nero to women freed from slavery. A woman by the name of Caesia Priscilla borrowed money on two separate occasions. In fact, women appear in a quarter of the Sulpicii's financial dealings, including on money transfers for purchases made at the famous auction houses of Puteoli.[70] The Sulpicii also acted as intermediaries in financial deals between women: a surviving tablet documents a loan made by one Titiana Antracis to a borrower called Euplia.

Female moneylenders also operated in the world beyond banking. A wax tablet from Pompeii provides details of a loan made by Didicia Magaris to Poppaea Note, with slaves—valued at 1,400 sesterces—having been used as collateral. The deal was carried out in front of four witnesses and a male representative. The fact that the tablet was found under the stairs of a private home—alongside silverware and gold jewellery—suggests that Didicia's money-lending business operated from her own home.[71] Graffiti found inside another residential property in the city lists loans made by a woman called Faustilla alongside various numerical workings that indicate a keen eye for mathematics. Clothing and earrings were recorded as collateral for two of her loans.[72] Elsewhere in Pompeii, public graffiti advertises that a woman named Somene had fifty denarii available to lend. While women like these were not operating from the plush offices of an imposing bank, and might today be dismissed as pawnbrokers, they were nevertheless providing banking services, filling a gap in the market that the banks had left wide open.

ENSLAVING THE ECONOMY

In 38 BCE, a woman named Livia divorced her husband—a Roman senator with whom she had two sons—and married the future emperor, Augustus. Augustus's ruthlessness and ambition may well have attracted a woman with dreams of becoming Rome's first empress. While Augustus was not the first man to rule the Roman world, he was the first official emperor, one who—much in the style of a *Star Wars* script—plotted to bring down Rome's republican regime and replace it with something far less democratic, all while justifying his actions as being in its defence. It was in Augustus's hands that the Roman Republic had morphed into the Roman Empire, and Livia didn't just stand by and watch: she was Augustus's ally and political confidante, and became the first woman to feature prominently on Roman coinage.

In a display of wealth and status for visiting guests, Livia's imperial household was awash with servants. An army of doorkeepers, cleaners, cooks, gardeners and maintenance staff helped to ensure that her Roman town house ran like clockwork. Livia even had her own personal dresser, doctor, masseuse and hairdresser.[73] Her army of domestic staff was so large that her estate even had its own sick-bay for staff, with separate wards for male and female staff, and a teacher for the slave children on the estate.

When a member of Livia's domestic staff passed away, they were cremated and their ashes were placed—in urns—in a giant mausoleum on Rome's Via Appia, the oldest Roman road, which is lined with many of Rome's tombs. In this *Monumentum Liviae* can be found the ashes of more than a thousand of the servants who worked for Livia and her wider family. Many were placed in pairs in their own little niche, honouring relationships that had formed between staff members. Small plaques placed alongside each niche reveal the names of Livia's domestic staff, along with their status and—in some cases—occupation. Around thirty-six percent of the staff working in households such as Livia's were women.[74] The majority were either slaves or freed slaves. Of the freed slaves memorialised in Livia's staff mausoleum, a third were women. Many of these women would have been granted their freedom as a form of promotion after distinguishing themselves in the imperial household or, instead, upon marriage or retirement.

As Livia's mausoleum helps us to appreciate, not all women in the Roman Empire were free to choose how they engaged with the economy. As Rome conquered territory across the Mediterranean, slave dealers accompanied the military, enslaving defeated peoples in their thousands and sending them for sale in specialised slave markets. By the start of the first century CE, the slave population had grown to between one and two million people, or up to thirty percent of Italy's total population.[75] Instead of building its economy on a platform of expanding liberties, an economy of exploitation took root in the Roman world.

Prisoners of war from Rome's conquests overseas included the skilled as well as the unskilled, while those who were born into slavery or who were enslaved at a young age were sometimes trained for skilled work. Apprenticeship contracts help to make visible the lives of a handful of female slaves. A surviving contract between a female slave owner and a master weaver from the time of Antoninus Pius tells us that a slave girl named Taorsenouphis was apprenticed for a period of fourteen months in the workshop of Pausiris. We see that she was to be fed and clothed by the weaver and that in the event of illness she was to remain in the weaver's care in order to make up time.[76] A similar contract for a slave girl called Helene—from the first century CE—apprenticed her for a longer period of two and a half years and came with the condition that if, after that time, she had not gained sufficient skill in weaving, the slave owner could recoup the cost of the apprenticeship from the weaver.[77]

In the fanciest residential quarters of Pompeii, an army of women weavers could be found hard at work in light-filled atriums and porch-like colonnades. Archaeological remains from the house of Marcus Terentius Eudoxus include loom weights and graffiti etched with the names of eleven textile workers: Amaryllis, Baptis, Damalis, Doris, Florentina, Heraclea, Iuanuaria, Lalage, Maria, Servola and Vitalis. Dyeing and cloth-cleaning workshops—identifiable from their tanks and vats—were located close to family homes, an indication that spinning and weaving took place in private residences. While this slave-based economy of domestic manufacture has been disparaged as 'unorganised' and 'informal', its position at the heart of the most exclusive homes is evidence of its importance to Roman households.[78]

Where slave owners did not want to busy themselves with the day-to-day running of their business, the most trusted and skilled slaves found themselves in managerial positions, making business decisions which included sourcing and purchasing raw materials. While slaves lacked any form of legal right, and so could not by law undertake business transactions, a legal vehicle known as the peculium made the impossible possible. The peculium was a personal fund that could be set up by a household head in the name of someone under their care, allowing the beneficiary to engage in a range of financial transactions without requiring approval. What made this legal vehicle popular was that the household head could never be liable for more money than was within the fund itself, meaning that the beneficiary of a peculium could never make deals or run up business debts to an extent that risked the financial security of the household. Where a peculium was granted in the name of a slave, and if the business with which they were involved proved particularly successful, the money and assets within the fund could grow to the point that the slave could purchase their own freedom from their master.[79] A funerary monument for a female weaver from Aquileia, named Trosia Hilaria, describes her as a freed slave who ran her own weaving business. It also notes that she had herself become the owner of slaves.[80]

As the slave economy reproduced itself, inequality increased. On average, a senator's income was two hundred times that of a peasant's subsistence wage.[81] In the first century CE, half of Roman Tunisia—once the home of Dido's Carthage—was owned by six men alone.[82] Conquest, enslavement and political networking concentrated wealth in the hands of a few while depriving the majority of basic freedoms. It was no way to build an economy that could withstand the tides of history.

FOR THE LOVE OF ROME

Rather than building on Rome's equality-loving and republican foundations, the emperor Augustus—the husband of Livia—set about undermining the economic contributions of half of the population. Despite women's significant economic presence, Augustus felt that they should be 'producing' in an altogether different sense, giving birth to the next generation. When it comes to women's work, there has always been a trade-off: since there are only so many hours in the day, spending more time performing paid work means less time available to care for infants. But, rather than letting women make their own choices about how they lived their lives, Augustus wanted to make the choice for them. Much as in the present day, social conservatives were in a moral panic about falling fertility rates, divorce and a reluctance amongst young people to marry. Rome, they thought, risked failing not because it was increasingly exploitative—with an economy that depended on slaves—but because women were too free. As part of his programme of social reform, Augustus's marriage laws punished all those who did not marry and procreate. The penalties for not doing so were financial, designed to hurt the bottom line: those who were unmarried were no longer allowed to inherit; those who were married but childless were only entitled to a half of any inheritance they received; a childless spouse could only inherit a tenth of their partner's property; widows and the divorced were expected to remarry if they had not produced at least three children (four if formerly enslaved) and, where they did not, lost their inheritance rights.[83] The financial incentive was not only to marry, but to marry young and to procreate quickly—whatever the risk to a woman's own health and wellbeing. Not only did childbearing affect inheritance rights; it also affected day-to-day family income. While women were barred from politics, their husbands' careers increasingly depended on their wives' childbearing efforts; when it came to political or bureaucratic offices, those with at least three legitimate children were given preference and offered a wider choice in terms of the provinces to which they were posted. For doing their 'duty', the political wives of Rome were kept onside through the introduction of punishment for adulterous senators. Naturally, the emperor did not turn to the Senate to introduce his adultery laws, but instead to the Tribal Assembly—the body that represented ordinary Roman citizens as opposed to members of the elite.[84] To avoid hypocrisy, Augustus was even forced to send his own daughter—along with her lovers—into exile following accusations of extra-marital sexual activity. Much like modern-day conservatism, valuing women's efforts within the family was just one side of the coin; the other side stoked not only moralism but nationalism. The baby boom that Augustus was engineering was welcomed by all those who felt that Rome was becoming too cosmopolitan. According to Augustus, it was 'neither right nor creditable that our race should cease, and the name of Romans be blotted out with us, and the city given over to foreigners—Greeks or even Barbarians'.[85] This growing anti-immigration rhetoric points, perhaps, to the real reason why Augustus valued what women could produce with their wombs more highly than what they could produce with their hands.

In addition to lumbering women with extra baby-making, the Roman emperors of the first century CE also made life difficult for female entrepreneurs in other ways.[86] Under Roman law, women had long been the subjects of a 'guardianship' system, and so, in theory at least, were unable to enter into any deal or contract without the authorisation of a father or husband. This was, the law explained, because of 'the frivolity of their minds'.[87] Upon the death of their guardian, a woman did become legally autonomous and so was able to inherit, but she still needed a replacement guardian to oversee her financial dealings. While in theory women as a result faced 'perpetual wardship', in practice they had greater freedom. Marriages where the husband was *not* granted guardianship over his wife had become increasingly common, and, where women did have guardians, they were progressively taking a laissez-faire approach, letting women make their own decisions and automatically approving them.[88] But, perhaps in response to women's increased presence in the business world, the traditional view that women's business activity was too risky, both for themselves and for their families, began to gain traction. Women were increasingly portrayed as lacking judgement, potentially leaving male relatives lumbered with debt and other obligations. A backlash against the independent working woman was underway, and the emperors Augustus and Claudius happily threw their weight behind it. Rather than phasing out the guardianship system, they agreed to make only one exception: only women who had given birth to at least three children (or, as with the marriage laws, four if formerly enslaved) were freed from guardianship, as a reward for having done their duty.[89]

With the renewed emphasis on guardianship, women became locked out of the Roman banking establishment, as a woman's signature on a financial deal could no longer be considered to provide sufficient authorisation. According to the jurist Callistratus, whose writings date to the turn of the third century CE, women were 'removed from the office of the banker, since this is man's work'.[90] Women were left on the sidelines, filling in the gaps left by the big banks by providing lending services on the black market, including pawnbroking from their own homes. Women like Julia Felix—who had run her own commercial mall, making her own business deals without a male guardian—were becoming more of a rarity. A papyrus from third-century-CE Egypt gives details of two female owners of a pottery—Aurelia Leontarous and Aurelia Plousia. Their workshop contained a potter's wheel, a kiln, storage space and raw materials, and was leased to a fellow potter for a period of two years. In return for occupying the workshop, the contract stated that the female owners were to be supplied with around 15,000 pots a year. Their contract was, however, agreed to and signed by a male guardian.[91]

As women's paid work increasingly came second to childbearing, women's contribution to the economy became hidden from view—something that occurred behind closed doors. The result was that of all the Roman gravestones studied by historians which mention an occupation, only fourteen percent belonged to women.[92] While men were remembered for their businesses, their wives—who often worked alongside them—were instead memorialised only as wives and mothers, unable to proudly announce their occupations to the world.[93]

ROME PAYS THE PRICE

Enslaving large portions of the empire and attempting to lock women out of the economy were never going to be a recipe for weathering the storms that history inevitably brings. For a century or two, the Roman economy managed to escape the consequences by pure luck. From the vineyards of Italy to drizzle-soaked Britain, the sun shone on the Roman Empire. Warm and wet weather filled Roman fields with wheat and pushed olive production to whole new altitudes.

Land that is today desert was brimming with crops and livestock. As fields burst forth, so too did population, and with abundant supplies of food, wool and wine, trade boomed. By the end of the first century CE, Romans were—for the first time—getting drunk on French as opposed to Italian wine. The first French vineyards—those of the Rhône Valley—were harvesting their grapes and the consumption of French wine quadrupled in Rome.[94] A quarter of Italy's own home-produced wine made its way to North Africa, with grain filling the bowels of the ships for the return journey.[95] But, by the third century CE, the climate took a turn for the worse. Cooler and drier weather hurt harvests year-on-year, leaving the population hungry and less healthy and, with that, more prone to disease. War disrupted trade routes that would have otherwise helped alleviate famine, while marauding soldiers, in search of food to fill their stomachs, spread disease. Lower tax revenues—a result of there being fewer crops to tax—meant that defence and infrastructure were wasting away.

Fewer ships took to the waves and—in response to the associated shortages of all kinds of everyday items—inflation began to escalate. People complained about the cost of living, in response to which the state increasingly intervened, to the point that, to quote one historian, 'exceptions from market economy principles became the rule'.[96] This was 'Caesar madness', with a series of desperate interventions that aimed to solve problems but instead made them worse. In 301 CE, Emperor Diocletian resorted to an emergency economic plan, issuing a price edict that set maximum prices for more than a thousand everyday products. Simply ordering inflation to stop was—as many a government has found since—not enough to solve the underlying economic problems. Instead, businesses were ruined as they were unable to sell their wares for a price that covered costs, which in turn further reduced supply, worsening shortages and creating more inflationary pressure. As people continued to struggle with rising prices, the state put pressure on banks to lower their interest rates in an effort to help businesses and households. But by limiting the interest rates that banks could charge, it turned lending into a loss-making activity, so banks simply closed their doors. By the end of the third century CE, banks had completely disappeared.[97] Accessing credit became almost impossible, adding to the woes faced by businesses. As the economy faltered, the situation began to spiral out of control. The Roman economy descended into ruin.

No longer blessed with sunshine, the damage that Rome had inflicted on its own economy began to reveal itself. Slavery and the increasing marginalisation of women deprived the economy of much needed dynamism. When times were good, that was less of a problem. When times were bad, the lack of economic nimbleness was a recipe for disaster. Had women not been living under the constraints imposed on them by emperors and slave owners, they could have risen to the challenge that the changing climate created, from shipping grain to help alleviate shortages to experimenting with new types of drought-resistant crops. The erosion of their freedoms instead tied their hands, leaving all too many women looking on helplessly while unable to act. And having already adopted a mindset of coercion and control when it came to women and slaves, the only way that the state knew how to react in response to economic disaster was to exert further coercion and control. As banks and businesses were ruined by the state's heavy-handed rulings, invaders took the opportunity to prey on the economy's weakness and its increasingly underfunded system of defence.

Why an empire that had lasted for centuries collapsed so spectacularly is a question that has long entertained historians. Numerous explanations have been put forward, from marauding barbarians to corruption at the heart of the Roman state and, most recently, climate change. But all the numerous explanations share one thing in common: they ignore the half of the population that is women. From the beginning, women had been at the heart of the Roman economy but, rather than appreciating the contributions they made, Roman emperors sought to sideline them, robbing the economy of the talents that women could offer at the time when they were most needed.

~

IN THE FOURTH CENTURY CE, WITH THE ECONOMY IN TATTERS, the Romans gave up on Rome and moved to a new city that the emperor—Constantine—chose to name after himself: Constantinople, in the historic region of Anatolia. Situated in the more prosperous, eastern part of the empire, this new Roman Empire, known as the Byzantine Empire, left Western Europe in a state of abandonment.

In addition to shifting Rome's axis towards the east, Constantine also converted to Christianity. Venus, Jupiter, Apollo and Juno—along with the numerous other gods and goddesses—fell out of favour, replaced by a single deity known simply as God. In this new version of the heavens, one male god was in sole charge and goddesses were gone for good. By the end of the sixth century, Christianity had a new competitor in the form of Islam, a religion which similarly said good riddance to goddesses. As the Islamic world expanded northwards from the Arabian desert, a clash ensued, one in which the Muslims—not the Christians—came out on top. It is to women's role in this expanding world of Islam that we turn next.

CHAPTER 5

BROKERS, CONCUBINES AND WET-NURSES

THE WOMEN OF THE PAX ISLAMICA

As the Byzantine Empire attempted to carry forward the mantle of Rome from its capital in Constantinople, Western Europe descended into an era once ominously termed 'the Dark Ages'. With the Romans no longer in charge, control was increasingly localised and peace was continually interrupted, both by local conflict and by invaders, including the infamous Vikings. Trade was increasingly risky, not helped by the unmaintained and so crumbling Roman transport infrastructure, which meant that markets gave way to barter and self-sufficiency. As economic life in Western Europe unravelled, the Middle East entered a new dawn. Within a century of Muhammad receiving his first revelation, Islam spread from the sacred city of Mecca, through Mesopotamia and the southern reaches of Byzantium, out to the outer reaches of India, and across the North African coastline into Spain. By 800 CE, the majority of Western Eurasia's largest cities—ten out of thirteen—were under

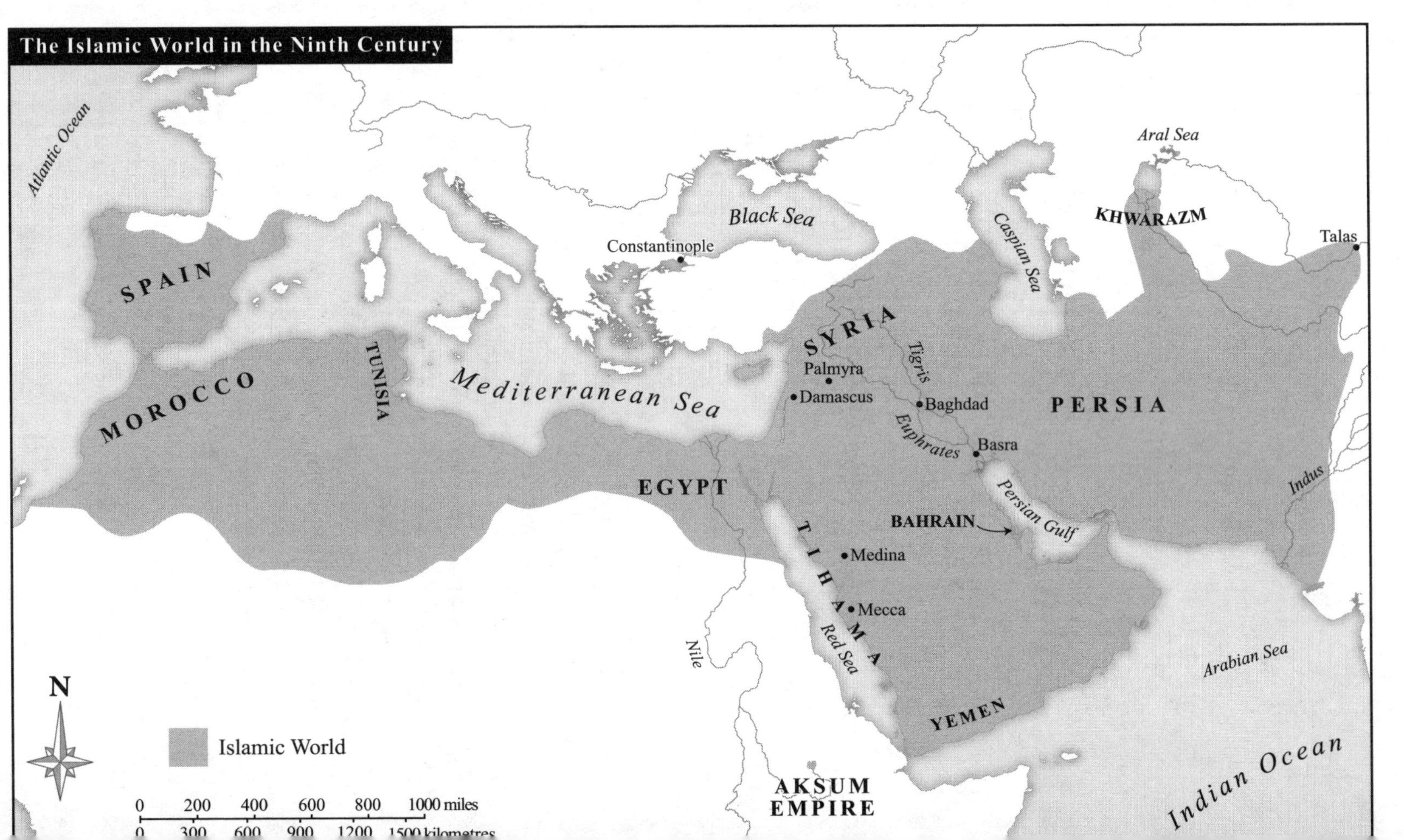
The Islamic World in the Ninth Century
Atlantic Ocean
SPAIN
MOROCCO
TUNISIA
Mediterranean Sea
Constantinople
Black Sea
EGYPT
Nile
SYRIA
Palmyra
Damascus
Tigris
Baghdad
Euphrates
Basra
Caspian Sea
Aral Sea
KHWARAZM
Talas
PERSIA
Indus
Persian Gulf
BAHRAIN
Medina
Mecca
TIHAMA
Red Sea
YEMEN
Arabian Sea
Indian Ocean
AKSUM EMPIRE
N
Islamic World
0 200 400 600 800 1000 miles
0 300 600 900 1200 1500 kilometres

Muslim rule, and the largest of all, Baghdad, had a population more than thirty times the size of London.[1]

From the start, women and business were at the heart of Islam. Muhammad's first wife, Khadija, was a wealthy merchant who employed the prophet-to-be to take care of her caravans. Not only was she 'the boss'; she initiated her marriage, proposing to Muhammad.[2] Born in the middle of the sixth century CE, Khadija was the first Muslim convert and her business acumen funded the spread of Islam across the Arabian desert. Embracing her respect for business, the Islamic world entered an economic golden age that lasted from the eighth to the eleventh century. This chapter shines a light on the numerous ways in which women drove the Islamic economy forward, highlighting the rights offered to women by the Quran, their subsequent battle with those who sought to deprive them of their freedoms, and how they allied themselves with slave armies in order to fight back.

ISLAM'S FIRST BUSINESSWOMAN

In 595 CE, Mecca was a bustling centre of trade, and one of its richest and most respected merchants was the forty-year-old Khadija. From Syria in the north to Yemen in the south, travellers flooded into the city from far and wide, creating opportunities for buying and selling everything from gold, frankincense and myrrh to pearls, cloth and spices. Situated between the warring Byzantine and Persian empires, Mecca not only skilfully juggled trade with both sides, it also reaped the financial rewards as ships from the Indian Ocean were diverted away from the Persian Gulf to the Red Sea.[3]

Making the most of Mecca's geographic location, Khadija operated a sizeable fleet of camels that moved animal skins, leather and cloth northwest along the coast of Arabia up to the Byzantine trading hub of Damascus. Each camel carried up to 160 kilograms in weight and a system of nose rings, ropes and saddles linked together up to forty camels at a time.[4] Running a caravan business was risky as well as potentially lucrative. Transport overland was physically demanding, for people and pack animals alike. Walking at the speed of a camel (around three miles per hour), a caravan travelled for up to fourteen hours a day—sometimes overnight when the weather was particularly hot.[5] It took up to fifty days to travel the roughly thousand miles between Mecca and Damascus.[6] Livestock could easily tire on the journey, which risked the abandonment of cargo en route, and banditry was a constant threat. To lessen the risks, traders transported their wares in convoy, offering safety in numbers. While Khadija did not accompany her caravans, she funded and arranged the trips, connecting the Arab world with Byzantium.

Like Khadija, Muhammad was born into a family of merchants within the Quraysh tribe, albeit less commercially successful ones. His childhood was grief-stricken: his father passed away while he was still in the womb and his mother died when he was only six years old. Still a child, Muhammad passed into the care of his paternal grandfather and his uncle, who were—successively—chiefs of the Hashim clan. The Hashim led a league of small-scale traders, attempting to compete with the wealthier and more powerful clans who monopolised trade.[7] Muhammad's first business trip was a journey to Damascus with his uncle, who was not only a chieftain and a trader but also a poet. Thereafter, Muhammad ventured to Bahrain, Yemen, and across the Red Sea to Ethiopia.[8] By his early twenties, he was well-travelled but, lacking his own funds to invest in trade, supervised the transportation of other people's wares, gaining a reputation for honesty.

Trust was all-important in long-distance trade: since a caravan of camels could be away for months, merchants needed people they could rely on to make journeys on their behalf. Khadija tasked the young Muhammad with travelling to the Hubasha fair in Tihama—on the Red Sea coast—to purchase cloth. He subsequently undertook trips to Yemen and, eventually—the most prized of all journeys—to Damascus, accompanied by Khadija's servant and a trusted relative. Impressed by the success of his trip to Damascus—not only its financial fruitfulness but also Muhammad's integrity—Khadija invited Muhammad to become her business partner. The partnership they entered into was known as *mudarabah*: a business contract in which one person offered capital and the other offered their labour, with the distribution of profit between the two parties agreed in advance.[9] It was a common means through which people with talent but not wealth were able to access the cash that they needed to fund their business ideas.

Once married, and while contemplating in a cave on Mount Hira near Mecca, Muhammad reportedly came face to face with the Angel Gabriel and began to receive the revelations of Allah. Trusting in his claim to be the messenger of God, Khadija became Muhammad's first convert. Her financial, as well as emotional, support was crucial to the spread of Islam.[10]

ISLAMIC CONSOLIDATION

From the Mesopotamians to the Romans, early civilisations were known for their plethora of gods and goddesses. By claiming that there was only one God, Muhammad—like Jesus before him—challenged the polytheism of the ancient world, including the teachings of his own tribe, the Quraysh. His emphasis on integrity in business and on using wealth to help others riled the 'great merchants' of wealthier clans, who threatened to cut ties with the smaller-scale traders who supported the Prophet, forcing them into financial hardship.[11] In 622 CE, after his much-loved uncle had passed away and the chieftainship passed to another uncle—one who was more closely connected with the most powerful merchants—Muhammad lost the protection of his family and was forced into exile.[12] He fled Mecca by night for the oasis town of Medina, more than two hundred and fifty miles northwards; his growing army of supporters in the town made for a warm welcome, but only after a multiday journey in which Muhammad and his companion—Abu Bakr—had to evade capture at every turn.[13]

Taking the opportunity to gather the faithful and to forge military alliances, by 630 CE Muhammad was ready to make his return to Mecca. His military strategy was simple: hit his enemies where it hurt most, by persistently raiding their trading caravans. His successful raid on a caravan escorted by the leader of the Quraysh tribe became known as the Battle of Badr.[14] While targeting trade in and out of Mecca was not good for Khadija's old caravan business,[15] depleting the fortunes of Mecca's other merchants allowed Muhammad to capture the city and, from there, to unite a large chunk of the Arabian peninsula.

In this new world of Islam, women did not take a back seat.[16] One modern-day historian has uncovered the work of eight and a half thousand female scholars from the early days of Islam—enough to fill a fifty-three-volume biography.[17] Muhammad's hideout town of Medina was home to numerous independent women who, having converted to Islam, deserted their tribes and sought refuge there; infringing his tribal peace treaty obligations, Muhammad refused demands for the women to be returned.[18] From the beginning, women were free to accept or reject Islam independently of their fathers or husbands. They went on pilgrimages, attended mosques and listened to the Prophet's speeches.[19] Even on the battlefield, women were active in both supporting and opposing Muhammad. When her male relatives were killed by one of Muhammad's men at the Battle of Badr, a woman named Hind bint Utba found the perpetrator and proceeded to cut off his ears and rip out his liver.[20]

After more than twenty years of marriage, Khadija passed away in her late fifties or early sixties. The Prophet was devastated.[21] When one of his subsequent wives scorned her as 'that toothless old woman', he replied, 'Allah has not replaced her with a better'.[22] With a new army of wives—married in part for reasons of tribal alliance—Muhammad seems to have acquiesced to those of a more patriarchal persuasion.[23] It was in this post-Khadija phase that he received the revelations that instructed his wives to stay in their homes and to greet visitors only if concealed by a hijab.[24]

Once Muhammad passed away, his successor, Abu Bakr—the first of the 'Pious Caliphs'—faced numerous revolts from grand and notable women who took the opportunity to contest Islamic rule.[25] They included a tribal revolt in the north led by Sajah bint Al-Harith, an Arab Christian woman who claimed to be the true prophet, and a resistance movement led by Yemeni women in the south. After defeating these, as well as numerous other rebellions, Abu Bakr took advantage of the war between the Persians and the Byzantine Empire to make territorial gains. Islamic power was growing. The second caliph, Umar (634–44 CE), continued the geographic expansion, conquering Egypt from the Byzantines, which brought lucrative tax revenues and grain for Mecca and Medina. Despite having been Muhammad's father-in-law, Umar had encouraged the Prophet to take a harsher line towards his wives.[26] Once caliph, he instituted a new legal code which included 'more stringent laws involving punishments for women and restrictions on their movements': he forbade Muhammad's widows from joining pilgrimages, prevented women from attending mosques and introduced death by stoning in the case of female adultery.[27] After his policies were met with opposition, including from his own wife, Umar compromised on segregation and seclusion in place of full-scale bans. The third caliph—Uthman (644–56 CE)—attempted to undo some of the damage, allowing women fuller participation in society.[28] Despite successes on the battlefield, his rule was, however, troubled, both by those who resented women and also by those who were envious of the merchants who profited from Islam's territorial expansion.[29] Much as in ancient Athens, antibusiness types also tended to be antiwomen, perhaps because they believed that money wasn't only tainted but risked challenging patriarchal control by giving women options outside the home. Women and business were increasingly under the spotlight and, when Uthman was murdered, civil war followed: Ali, the son-in-law and cousin of the Prophet, took the reins of power, while Aisha, the surviving wife of Muhammad, mounted her camel to lead a revolt against him in the fiercely fought

'Battle of the Camel'. While she lost the battle, she may have won the wider war.[30]

Aisha's supporters—the Sunnis—went on to found the first united Islamic Empire: the Umayyad Empire (661–750 CE). The Umayyads transferred political power from the Arabian desert to Syria, establishing their capital at Damascus, where the Christian cathedral of St. John the Baptist was demolished and replaced with the Great Mosque. Despite the initial destruction, the Umayyads gained a reputation for religious tolerance. Jews and Christians were free to practise their own religions—so long as they paid a poll tax from which Muslims were exempt. Conversion to Islam was therefore not actively encouraged, as it risked reducing the state's tax revenue.[31] The Umayyads also became known for their competent administration. They expanded the capacities of the state, centralising defence as well as taxation, and welcomed non-Muslims within the civil service. One of the finance secretaries for the first Umayyad caliph was, in fact, a Christian.[32] Religious tolerance not only helped to create a political meritocracy, it also made good business sense. In turn, the practice of buying and selling across religious divides encouraged a common humanity and so tolerance for one another.

The global spread of Islam—faster and further than Christianity—was a consequence not only of military conquest, but also of trade.[33] The territorial reach of the Umayyads was impressive, extending as far as Armenia in the north, India in the east, Yemen in the south and Spain in the west. Trade proved to be a successful religious diffuser because—rather than relying on intermediaries—Muslims went out into the world and traded directly with non-Muslims, thereby bringing a wide array of people into contact with the religion.[34] From merchants to middlemen, and from animal riders to sellers of pack animals for the caravan trade, there were more than 233 different occupations within the commercial sector alone.[35] The spread of Islam as a religion was, in other words, inherently tied to its pro-business culture.

The production and circulation of money helped to grease the wheels of Islamic trade and the Middle East became known for its financial innovations, many of which were later adopted by Europeans. In newly conquered territories the Umayyads made sure that local mints remained open and, where none existed, established new mints.[36] Churches and monasteries were taxed for the first time, resulting in the release of precious hordes of gold and silver, which were in turn minted into coins.[37] Unlike in Roman times, Islamic mints were operated with private—not just state—initiative, and the state welcomed independent prospectors who scoured the land for suitable mining opportunities.[38] After initially continuing with the use of pre-Islamic coins, the Umayyad caliph 'Abd al-Malik (685–705 CE) introduced a common currency, consisting of the gold dinar, the silver dirham and the copper fals, for use across the Islamic territories. The availability of coins—and so the avoidance of problems intrinsic to barter—helped to sustain market exchange. In Western Europe, Islamic coins were minted on the black market, testament not only to the greater sophistication of the Islamic economy but also to the western desire for Middle Eastern produce—and the lack of their own money to pay for it.[39]

While women lacked recognition as political leaders, behind the scenes they played an important diplomatic role, appearing in front of the first Umayyad caliph to make representations on behalf of their communities. Sawda bint 'Amara, well-known for her anti-Umayyad poetry, complained about her newly appointed regional governor, saying to the caliph Mu'āwiya: 'Were we not obedient, we would be forceful and insurgent. Dismiss him and we shall thank you. If not, we will know you for what you are'. Also appealing to the new caliph's sense of justice, Umm Sinan bint Haytama, similarly known for her poetic attacks, complained about unfair treatment, including the imprisonment of her grandson. After granting her an audience, the caliph asked: 'What brings you to my region, after I was used to you cursing me and encouraging my enemies against me?' She replied that his tribe 'are not insolent after they have shown clemency, and they do not seek revenge after they have been forgiven'. Seemingly dazzled by her courage, the caliph ordered the release of her grandson and—upon her request—gifted her a camel for the return journey home.[40]

Since the Islamic Empire united a vast region, it brought together territories with rather varied histories of women's rights, from Egypt, where women were relatively free, to the much more patriarchal Mesopotamia and parts of the Eastern Mediterranean where the ancient Greek influence lived on. On the one hand, the political regime of the Umayyads appears highly patriarchal: men, not women, ruled; men could have multiple wives; and the number of concubines was rapidly growing—in large part because Islamic expansion created fresh opportunities for the enslavement of foreign women. On the other hand, excavations of an Umayyad mansion in Syria have brought to light luxury household manufactured goods inscribed with the names of female makers and historical records reveal that women were free to meet with male political figures.[41] In the late seventh and early eighth century, for example, the caliph's wife castigated the provincial governor of Iraq and Iran for his attitudes towards women, after hearing via one of the court's slave women that he believed that women existed just for pleasure and were not worth consulting on political matters. Having brought this to the attention of the caliph, she demanded that the governor come to see her for a lesson in gender politics. After leaving him waiting for a lengthy period outside her office—perhaps in an attempt to show who was boss—she invited him in and told him in no uncertain terms that 'the caliph will not take your opinion about his women seriously'.[42] In the more patriarchal parts of the Umayyad Empire, it is therefore very possible that Islamic rule improved rather than hurt women's rights.

THE DINNER PARTY

In 750 CE, Abu al-Abbas invited the family of the Umayyad caliph to a spectacular dinner. While the guests reached for the platters, the hosts drew their weapons and slaughtered them.[43] Descended from the uncle of Muhammad, and claiming to have a closer connection to the Prophet than the Umayyad caliph, Abu al-Abbas declared himself the rightful ruler.[44] His dynasty—that of the ʿAbbāsids—reigned from what would become their new capital of Baghdad for the next five hundred years. It was during this time that the Islamic economy truly witnessed its golden age.

Following the territorial expansions of the Umayyads, the Mediterranean was rapidly becoming a 'Muslim lake', alive with trade.[45] Islamic scientists, cartographers and shipbuilders provided the maps and instruments that merchants needed to cross the oceans and travel even further afield. This included the astrolabe—the precursor to the compass and the computer of its age—which was perfected by, amongst others, the female astronomer Mariam al-Astrulabi. Away from the ocean waves, agriculture prospered. Legal records in the form of fatwas reveal that women bought date plantations, orchards and grain stores.[46] By investing in agriculture, they were amongst those who provided funds for new crops and irrigation schemes in Egypt and Iraq, revolutionising farming. With the greater availability of food, increasing numbers of people were freed from growing their own produce and so migrated to towns to work in manufacturing. Food processing (from baking to making sweetmeats) and cloth production were the two largest manufacturing sectors, in total accounting for forty percent of all manufacturing output. These were also the sectors with the largest concentration of women workers.[47] Though women occupied a much smaller range of occupations than men, the sectors in which they worked accounted for a sizeable share of economic activity.[48] Literary works feature female pedlars selling foodstuffs in ninth century Basra, suggesting that women were a visible part of the urban economy.[49] Where gender segregation was practiced, it resulted in women performing skilled and sophisticated work—including as doctors and brokers—of a kind that only men, with very few exceptions, undertook in Europe.[50] Wealthy women, who were less likely to work for a living, invested in retail outlets and workshops, which they rented out to male shopkeepers and male artisans, making a less visible but equally important contribution to the urban economy.[51] By 800 CE, the Middle East and North Africa as a whole was more than twice as urbanised as Europe, and by 1300 there was a tenfold difference.[52] Up to a quarter of the population of Iraq alone lived in towns and cities.[53] The growth of the economy is equally visible on the pages of cookery books from the time, which featured increasing amounts of meat and dairy in place of cheaper grains.[54]

Part of the secret to its success was that Islam managed to avoid many of the antibusiness tendencies of Christianity. Christian clerics preached the renunciation of worldly pleasures, not just by monks and nuns but by society more generally. Material goods were seen as a distraction from spiritual life, placing a barrier between God and the soul. Those who retreated from wider society to live as hermits in the desert were celebrated and even beatified. The Christian response to famine and disease was not wise economic policy but to pray for a miracle. Since poverty and self-denial were idealised, there was little pressure to grow the economy, and moneylenders and merchants were treated with suspicion. By contrast, the business partnership entered into by Khadija and Muhammad provided a model for business within the Islamic world, allowing those with talent and experience to access the funds they needed for entrepreneurial endeavours. Commerce carried high regard, and a new merchant class emerged in place of landowners and the clergy. Rather than being 'antibusiness', Islam embraced business ethics, believing that if business was conducted with integrity, it would be for the good of all.

Consistent with Islam's respect for business, and in stark contrast to Rome's 'Caesar madness', the ʿAbbāsid state took a laissez-faire approach that allowed private enterprise to flourish.[55] As their territories expanded, new marketplaces were established, with inscriptions on mosaic-covered entranceways that carried the blessing of religious rulers. Large numbers of buyers and sellers served to compete down prices, including at the famous bazaars.[56] Supervisors known as *muhtasibs* were appointed to ensure that business ethics were upheld and that fraud was punished.[57] Having grown up in a tribe of small-scale traders, Muhammad understood the importance of competition as a means to avoid power being concentrated in the hands of the few. Not only were all kinds of goods more widely available than ever before, prices were lower, making them more accessible for a wider segment of society. Business was for everyone. And that, as we will shortly see, included concubines.

THE STORYTELLER AND THE SLAVE

One day, a king beheaded his adulterous wife and married for a second time, ensuring that his new wife was young and virginal. After spending their wedding night together, the next morning the king killed his new bride for fear of once more being cuckolded. The next night, he took a third wife, whom he also quickly executed. This barbarous practice became a daily routine—the revenge the king inflicted on womankind. Eventually, there were so few women left that the king turned to his advisor and asked to marry his daughter, Scheherazade. Despite being urged to flee, Scheherazade agreed to the match. On her wedding night, the king overheard his new bride telling her sister a story and, eager to hear the finale, spared her life the next morning. The next night, Scheherazade finished her tale and began a new story, and was again spared another day. Telling one story after another—of Aladdin, of Ali Baba and of Sinbad—Scheherazade managed to captivate the king for one thousand and one nights, by which point he was so besotted that he made her his forever queen.[58]

The resultant book is, after the Quran, the most widely known book of the Islamic world.[59] It tells of a woman succeeding not through her beauty but through her brain. Only by entertaining the king with her mind was Scheherazade spared the fate of death. While the story is, of course, fictional, the character was modelled on a real-life eighth-century woman, al-Khayzurān.[60] Captured in Yemen and sold in Mecca, al-Khayzurān was a *jarya*—a sex slave—in Baghdad's court. Since the court harem was already full of women, the caliph gave al-Khayzurān to his son—al-Mahdī—on the basis that she was 'good for childbearing'.[61] Rather than keeping her as his concubine, not only did al-Mahdī marry al-Khayzurān; he made her his co-ruler.

When their son—al-Hadi—inherited the throne from his father, it resulted in a battle of wills. Despite her experience as a ruler, al-Hadi told his mother that: 'Whoever from among my entourage—my generals, my servants—comes to you with a petition will have his head cut off and his property confiscated. What is the meaning of those retinues that throng around your door every day? Don't you have a spindle to keep you busy?'[62] After reigning for just two years, al-Hadi passed away in suspicious circumstances. Leadership passed to another of al-Khayzurān's sons—Hārūn al-Rashīd—for whom she became a trusted advisor.[63] Under al-Khayzurān's influence, Baghdad blossomed into a centre of learning, home to a paper mill and a monumental library known as the 'House of Wisdom'.[64] Like Khadija, Khayzurān had a head for business, developing her own cloth-manufacturing business and amassing wealth to the point that she even helped to pay some of the treasury's bills.[65]

In the early days of Islamic rule, the sons of slaves were locked out of the line of succession, but times were changing—and not just for al-Khayzurān.[66] In the first centuries of Islam, outbreaks of plague had fuelled a heavy reliance on slave labour, provided by Islamic conquest. Active slave markets could be found in Basra, Baghdad and Khwarazm, and, in total, it is estimated that six million Africans were enslaved, along with several million Turks and millions of Europeans, Egyptians, Syrians and Persians.[67] But by 869 CE, East African slaves—at work draining the abandoned salt marshes of southern Iraq—were in open revolt, protesting that their harsh treatment violated the covenant between the caliph and God.[68] This rebellion was known as the Zanj Rebellion, and it lasted for fourteen years. In one notable incident, one of the leaders of the revolt corralled slaves into giving their masters five hundred blows as a demonstration of purpose.[69] As the rebellion spread, the slaves and their supporters successfully occupied the city of Basra and reached within twenty-seven kilometres of Baghdad, before the rebellion was eventually crushed in 883 CE. The bloodshed nevertheless made some people think twice about slavery. Increasingly—in both agriculture and manufacturing—the economy comprised a waged workforce.[70] And since the population of the Middle East had not yet fully recovered from past plagues, workers remained in short supply, meaning that they could bargain for a handsome pay packet: the average wage of unskilled labourers in Baghdad during the Islamic golden age was typically double what was needed to house and feed a family of four.[71]

Higher wages made a significant contribution to the economy, by encouraging the development of machines which raised productivity. In a low-wage economy, businesses have little incentive to develop or use machines as they can simply rely on employing more cheap labour. In a higher-wage economy, by contrast, it can be profitable to innovate as doing so allows you to produce more without needing to employ additional—expensive—people. The higher productivity that results from innovation in turn makes the higher wages of current workers more affordable, as they can produce more each day, thereby covering their cost. In agriculture, more crops were trialled, including rice, lemon, lime, sugar and cotton; in mining, new extraction techniques were developed; in manufacturing, 'manufactories'—super-sized workshops—emerged with tasks split, mass-production-style, between different parts of the workforce.[72] In Egypt, which had historically supplied the Roman world with wheat, Islamic tax collectors invested tax revenues in the production of flax, aiding the growth of the linen industry.[73] In Spain, as well as in North Africa, agricultural land that had previously consisted of large Roman *latifundias* worked by slaves was divided up into smaller plots, each of which was leased to peasants who hired waged labour.[74] Since wages exceeded subsistence, the average worker had enough money to buy the extra products that the economy was capable of producing. Rather than stagnating, the economy could keep on growing. Transitioning away from an economy of exploitation to a high-productivity, high-wage economy was key to the continuation of the golden age.[75]

It was the associated growing knowledge and skill base in the Islamic world that gave rise to the library. In Islamic Spain, no price was too high when it came to books. The tenth-century ruler—al-Hakam—sent people across the world in search of books with an almost limitless budget.[76] Not only were Greek scholarly works translated into Arabic, but Arabic scholars penned their own scientific works on astronomy, medicine and mathematics. Books were written for practical purposes as well as for a scholarly audience. The eleventh-century Islamic ruler of Tunisia came from a family of bookbinders and authored his own manual on how to bind books.[77] In manufacturing, where apprenticeships were the norm, technical manuals circulated on everything from soap-making to construction, indicative of high levels of literacy amongst the general population.[78]

While education and learning were dominated by men, the Islamic instruction from God 'to seek knowledge' applied equally to women. Not only did women found numerous schools, but it was a woman—Fatima al-Fihri—who, in the ninth century, founded the first educational institute to confer degrees: the University of Al Qarawiyyin in Fez, Morocco.[79] But, despite their intellect, manuals for women included little or no mention of paid work, focusing instead on their work as wives and mothers. There was, however, one notable exception.[80] In his love treatise *The Ring of the Dove*, published in 1022, Ibn Hazm spoke of how 'women plying a trade or profession, which gives them ready access to people, are popular with lovers—the lady broker, the coiffeuse, the professional mourner, the singer, the soothsayer, the school mistress, the errand-girl, the spinner, the weaver and the like'.[81]

Labour shortages no doubt encouraged the recruitment of women into numerous parts of the economy, but it also raised anxieties in terms of the risk to their sexual purity and marital fidelity. It was by emphasising this risk—thereby fuelling the anxieties of fathers and husbands—that those of a more patriarchal persuasion were, eventually, able to conspire to put women back in their box. Much as had happened in the Roman Empire, the women of the Islamic Empire witnessed a backlash—something that hurt not only them but, with time, the economy.

BEHIND THE VEIL

'Never will a nation prosper that makes a woman its ruler'.[82] After Muhammad's death, witnesses reported on his words and deeds, with each account known as a Hadith. By the ninth century, 600,000 Hadiths circulated, of which 590,000 were declared fake.[83] It is likely that some suspect statements slipped through the net. With so many accounts circulating, scholars could be selective when determining what Muhammad really did—or did not—say about women. The Quran was, however, clear on one thing: that men are granted a material advantage by God and, as such, are obliged to be the 'maintainers of women'.[84]

Women who earn a living do not feature in the Islamic holy book, with one exception: wet-nurses. Unlike Jewish women, Islamic mothers were not obliged to breastfeed, which created a possible job opening for other women.[85] Tenth-century obstetric manuals from Cordoba and Cairo offered nutritional advice for wet-nurses, to ensure optimal health for the infants under their care, and the Quran was clear that wet-nurses must be paid for their efforts. Islamic jurists provided model contracts, with a typical employment of two years for pay that varied according to labour-market conditions. Since there was no assumption that a wife should breastfeed, she was herself entitled to the equivalent pay of a wet-nurse if she did so herself. When it came to divorce, wages for breastfeeding also fed into alimony payments. There was, however, a caveat when employing a wet-nurse: a wet-nurse's husband had to formally give permission by signing the contract of employment himself. Wet-nursing could—naturally—only be carried out by a woman who had herself given birth and, since births were expected to occur within marriage and wet-nursing came with limitations on sexual activity, employment required the joint consent of husband and wife.[86]

Ultimately, a woman's milk was considered her own. Under Islam, women's ownership over their bodies also received emphasis in other ways. With only one exception, the legal schools of Islam were in agreement that a newly married woman had the right to refuse intercourse.[87] Birth control, unlike in Christian societies, was also acceptable under Islamic law, which meant that fertility was relatively low, in turn helping to prevent the population from expanding to the point that it undermined the high-wage economy.[88] In Shi'i law, husbands were expected to pay their wives for practising coitus interruptus at the rate of ten dinars a time—unless a wife consented to the practice. The payment was considered valid in view of the fact that the Quran granted women rights to children and to sexual pleasure.[89] By limiting the size of their families, women were making an invisible contribution to the high-wage economy—and they were being paid for it.

Wet-nursing aside, husbands were expected to provide for their wives, and fathers and brothers were obliged to provide for unmarried women. Historically, women were married young; whether or not they had the right to withhold their consent for marriage was debated by the different Islamic schools of thought.[90] While economically dependent on their husbands, women could, in theory at least, expect equal treatment when it came to the material comforts of life. In the words of the Prophet, giving advice to a husband: '[Her right upon you] is to feed her when you eat, buy her clothes when you buy for yourself, not to smack her on the face, not to curse her and not to ignore her'.[91] Women's financial reliance on men, along with their lesser legal rights when it came to divorce, nevertheless placed the balance of power firmly in male hands, and women were expected to obey their husbands.[92] Whether in religion, in politics or within the family, men had authority over women.

While women were not expected to provide for their families, they did, however, have a right to their own assets. A wife had control over her dowry, and inheritance did not pass purely through the male line: a daughter was entitled to inherit half of the share that went to her brother.[93] This meant that even though they did not in general earn a wage, women from better-off families had access to their own wealth. In comparison with Jewish law, Islamic law granted women far greater ownership rights, and, importantly, legal records reveal that these rights were upheld and respected.[94] One fatwa relates to a married woman whose fields had been cultivated by her husband. The woman had recently passed away, leaving her husband unsure as to whether he should proceed with sowing the next season's crops. The fatwa ruling was as follows:

> If his cultivation of the land in question was done with his wife's knowledge and consent, and this has been confirmed, he has to pay rent. If, on the other hand, he has no proof of that . . . then the heirs have the right . . . to take the land away from him. His cultivation of her land without her knowledge amounts to usurpation, and the value of his work is annulled.[95]

In other words, the husband had no automatic right to continue to cultivate the land and risked losing his time and energy if he did so; this was his wife's land and only her heirs were entitled to reap its rewards.

WHAT'S YOURS IS YOURS

Women's paid labour was not actively encouraged by Islam, but when women did earn, their money was considered exclusively their own.[96] One piece of evidence of women's paid work comes in the form of a fatwa ruling from Islamic Tunisia, which reveals that women were commonly employed to spin flax. Islamic jurists were asked to rule on whether spinning during the month of Ramadan was permissible. The issue was that, while spinning, the mouth was commonly used as a third hand, with saliva helping to moisten the flax, which necessarily meant that threads touched the tongue. Taking a pragmatic approach, the jurists declared that this was not equivalent to consuming food—so long as the flax had no flavour. The fatwa recognised that many women spun out of economic necessity and that forbidding such work would threaten their livelihood. Only women who were not considered needy were asked to refrain from the practice during the holy month.[97]

Spinning flax, cotton, wool and silk was a popular occupation for poorer women, who also worked as dyers, lacemakers and embroiderers. Virtually all of this activity did, however, take place within the home; women were less likely than men to work in workshops.[98] Women's domestic labour in the cloth industry was typically arranged by male tax collectors, who offered to supply women with raw materials such as flax and pay them for their work, while at the same time collecting the tax on their activities.[99] Rather than collecting taxes itself, the state 'farmed out' tax collection, granting to private individuals the right to collect taxes in return for paying a lump sum to the Treasury. This system offered two advantages: it gave state finances a degree of stability and left the difficult administrative process of actually collecting taxes to others. In return for guaranteeing a fixed amount of tax revenue from their own pockets, the tax collectors were free to keep for themselves anything they managed to collect above and beyond that amount; it was, effectively, their reward for administering tax collection and compensated for the risk they were taking that tax revenues might fall below their personal payment to the Treasury. Encouraging economic activities which generated tax revenue was therefore a top priority for tax collectors, and that included the hidden economy of domestic manufacture.[100]

In addition to conducting paid work from their own homes, women also worked in female-segregated areas of public life, which created many skilled as well as unskilled forms of employment. This included everything from working as secretaries for other women and as assistants on the women-only days at the public baths to providing medical and brokerage services for the female half of the population. A medical textbook from the fifteenth century depicts a female doctor treating a patient[101] and in 1332, the king of Aragon was treated by an Islamic female doctor.[102] According to Ibn Khaldun, author of the magisterial economic treatise the *Muqaddimah*, published in 1377—four centuries ahead of *The Wealth of Nations* by the man more commonly considered to be the father of economics, Adam Smith—midwifery was the highest form of employment.[103] Midwives were treated as expert witnesses when it came to the court of law.[104]

Though sex-based segregation necessarily constrained women's economic participation, Islamic jurists at times made arrangements to cushion the blow. In some cases, markets were established to serve women to the exclusion of men and, at city gates, female inspectors checked that female pedlars were not concealing items to escape the sales tax.[105] For contracts which required both parties to an agreement to identify themselves before a notary, women with covered faces were granted permission to appear so long as they had two witnesses.[106] Where women were felt to have been at a disadvantage by not being able to appear in person for market-based transactions, courts tended to rule in their favour. In one case a women rented a silo in which to store her wheat and, not being able to check its suitability in person, was unable to see that it was infested with mice. After she discovered the nibbled wheat, she refused to pay her rent, for which she was taken to court. The judge found her not guilty.[107] While women were expected to minimise mixing with men, those who had reached menopause—and so were no longer of childbearing age—had greater freedoms, which opened up a wider set of business and job opportunities for older women. According to the Quran: 'The women who are past their youth (and can no longer bear children) and do not look forward to marriage will incur no sin if they cast off their outer garments'.[108] *Hisba* manuals—which provided practical guidance on how to align working life with Islamic law—recognised 'maturity and old age' as qualifications for textile brokers, as well as for female prison wardens.[109] Wherever and whenever seclusion became increasingly popular, it fuelled an army of mature female brokers who could buy and sell goods on behalf of other women, acting as go-betweens when it came to deals between younger women and the male half of the population.[110]

While married women had full rights to their wages within Islamic law, ensuring that the home was a place of peace and comfort—in order to support their husbands—took priority.[111] If a woman's paid work overly interfered with her domestic duties, husbands had the right to forbid it. Legal records from the eleventh to the fifteenth centuries indicate that an increasing number of women were, in response, including a 'right to work' within their marriage contracts. Mashita—a woman hairdresser who lived in Tunisia in the fourteenth century—included in her marriage contract the clause that she be permitted to continue to practise her trade.[112] Women hairdressers were, as now, popular amongst bridal parties, meaning that Mashita's work was in high demand. The frequency with which the 'right to work' appeared in marriage contracts suggests that while paid work was common for women, it was also in need of protection.

As the economy grew and wealthy families became even wealthier, paternity uncertainty became a growing concern. Husbands did not want to risk their wealth being passed on to children who were not their own, leading to increased levels of seclusion, veiling and sex-based segregation for wives. To provide the excuse they needed, the Quran was reinterpreted to provide a stricter dress code for women and to discourage them from leaving their homes, and the 'superior' status which it offered to men was justified by portraying women as less mentally fit and sexually untrustworthy.[113] Not only were women losing out, it was, they were told, their own fault.

SINGING SLAVE GIRLS

A thirteenth-century Muslim traveller to the Arabian port of Aden described in distressing terms the sale of enslaved women and girls in the local souk:

> *The slave girl is fumigated with an aromatic smoke, perfumed, adorned and a waist-wrapper fastened round her middle. The seller takes her by the hand and walks around the souk [market] with her; he calls out that she is for sale. The wicked merchants appear, examining her hands, feet, calves, thighs, navel, chest and breasts. He examines her back and measures her buttocks in spans. He examines her tongue, teeth, hair and spares no effort. If she is wearing clothes, he takes them off; he examines and looks. Finally, he casts a direct eye over her vagina and anus, without her having on any covering or veil.*[114]

Though slavery had become less popular in agriculture and manufacturing compared with the early days of Islam, it was not extinguished in other parts of the economy.[115] The enslavement of women and girls for domestic purposes is an area that has long been neglected by historians despite its effects on large numbers of women.[116] Indeed, in a world in which wives were increasingly secluded, female slaves helped to bridge the gap between the outside world and the inner realm, enabling the mistress to remain pure. While the slave trade between the Islamic world and Africa is much less well documented than that between Africa and the Americas, it appears to have focused more on women than it did on men, with the purpose being domestic servitude as opposed to agricultural labour.[117] In addition to numerous hands that could help with labour-intensive, everyday drudgery, skilled female cooks and bakers were in high demand, and could command double the price of an unskilled slave.[118] Sex and reproduction were also on the minds of those who purchased slaves. An eleventh-century Islamic doctor, Ibn Butlan, penned an advice book on the purchase of foreign slaves for this purpose, writing that:

> He who wants a jarya [slave] for pleasure should choose a Berber [North African]; he who wants a reliable woman to look after his possessions should take a Roman. For the man who wants a jarya to bear him children, the best choice is a Persian. If he wants a jarya to suckle a child, he should choose a Frankish [Western European] woman.[119]

The Muslim world clearly drew its slaves from a wide area, and European merchants—as well as others—willingly supplied European women to Islamic merchants in return for the fancy and sophisticated wares that the Middle East could source from the rest of the world.[120]

Slave girls could also provide entertainment in other ways. In the Middle East, music was, historically speaking, women's work: until the late seventh century, men were prohibited from performing professionally as singers and musicians unless they were enslaved.[121] A culture of singing slave girls developed that continued with the Umayyads and ʿAbbāsids.[122] Acquired through conquest and trade, enslaved girls were trained in music, poetry and Arabic. When a father and son duo set up a school to formally educate slave girls, they found that they could make a handsome sum from their onward sale: up to twenty-six times their original price.[123] The repertoire of their best students included up to four thousand poems and songs as well as passages from the Quran. Their students were bought by wealthy men, either to perform for their own amusement or to be hired out to others. Muslim caliphs paid large sums to procure the most beautiful and most educated pupils, or received them as diplomatic gifts and as part of the booty of conquest.[124] The musical and instrumental performances slave girls provided were central to court-based entertainment, making their patronage and ownership even more of a status symbol at a time of growing economic wealth.

Some slave girls developed social connections that led to wealth and marriage.[125] According to the eleventh-century writer Ibn Hazm, the mothers of more than ninety percent of 'Abbāsid caliphs were, in fact, slave women: 'among the 'Abbāsid only three caliphs were sons of a *hurra* [a free woman], and among the Umayyads of Andalusia not a single son of a free woman succeeded in becoming caliph'.[126] The mothers of Islam's ruling elite came not only from the Middle East but also from Africa, Europe and Central Asia, indicative of the vast geographical extent of the slave trade. Becoming a favourite of a caliph was, however, a risky business. Caliph Adud al-Dawla became so besotted with a particular slave girl that his governmental in-tray reached a bursting point, upon which he ordered that the girl be killed in order to prevent future distractions.[127] The lives of other slave girls ended in beatings and banishment for poor musical performances, and some suffered death by poisoning at the hand of fellow slave girls, with whom competition for favours could be fierce.[128]

Despite being the mothers of many a caliph, and having had no choice in the matter of their enslavement, slave girls were depicted by many writers as wicked seducers who led Muslim men astray and drained them of financial resources.[129] According to the ninth-century writer al-Jahiz, author of the satirical *Epistle on the Singing Girls*, owners of singing slave girls were guilty of debauchery and greed. While Islamic jurists did not prohibit the practice, they did eventually rule that the slave girls' owners could not benefit from their earnings; that, in other words, slave girls could not be 'rented out' and, upon their death, any income or gifts they accumulated could not be inherited by their master.[130] As the rules tightened, singing slave girls went out of fashion, and, by the eleventh century, male musicians were—for the first time—taking over musical entertainment in court.

FATIMA'S LEGACY

While Sunni Muslims dominated Umayyad and ʿAbbāsid rule, the descendants of Ali (the Shias) claimed a connection with the Prophet that rivalled the ruling caliph, since Ali had married Muhammad's daughter, Fatima. Their claim was fiercely contested: as far as the ruling ʿAbbāsids were concerned, succession could not take place through the female line.[131] But in North Africa, far from Baghdad, the Shias established a sizeable following and, by tapping into the lucrative Saharan caravan trade, were able to build the wealth they needed to expand their rule. By 969 CE, these 'Fatimids' had conquered Egypt, and, much to the chagrin of Baghdad, appointed their own rival caliph. The period of two caliphs had begun, and, with it, the deep divide between the Sunnis and the Shias.[132]

Egypt was, in fact, already ripe for takeover. The golden age was fast fading. Egypt had not only become increasingly independent of Baghdad; it was poorly run.[133] The economy had been neglected, the population felt exploited and corruption was rife. In the absence of competent administration, tax collectors had personally pocketed large sums, depleting the treasury of the revenues it needed and causing taxes to rise to unbearable levels. Under Fatimid rule, the tax system was reformed and the economy prospered once more.[134] Rather than interfering at whim, the Fatimids took a hands-off approach to the economy, pursuing a liberal course, both economically and socially.[135] Religious tolerance became a hallmark of their rule. Trade was encouraged—including through the development of new harbours—and the new capital, Cairo, came to rival Baghdad as the commercial hub of the Islamic world.[136]

By the third generation, Fatimid rule was steering off course, until a young woman by the name of Sitt al-Mulk placed it back on an even keel. Her ruling brother—al-Hakim—was a wild child. As a night owl, al-Hakim declared that night was day and day was night, insisting that everyone live according to his daily routine.[137] Since he disliked barking, he also ordered the mass killing of all dogs.[138] He did not much like women either, and so banned them from public spaces, even forbidding shoemakers from making shoes for women so that they were compelled to stay at home. For seven years and seven months, it is said that no woman was seen on the streets of Cairo.[139] Women pleaded with the ruler, noting that some amongst them had no choice but to leave their homes for reasons of economic necessity. In response, the caliph devised a cumbersome system of home shopping, ordering merchants to go door-to-door with a long-handled soup ladle on which they would place their wares, allowing women to remain hidden behind their front doors.[140] The onerous nature of the practice riled women and merchants alike. Bans on singing, wine, shellfish, pleasure boats and even having a nice view from windows followed.[141] Outlawed food items were burned or dumped into the Nile, creating food shortages and inflation as the price of what food remained soared. Illiberal policies created economic ruin, and the caliph made women, Jews and Christians the scapegoats.[142]

On 13 February 1021, al-Hakim disappeared while out walking in Cairo's hills. The reign of terror had—at last—come to an end. Stories circulated that his older sister, al-Mulk, was responsible.[143] Whether or not that was the case, we can never know for sure, but the women of Egypt had not taken kindly to being secluded, and neither had the economy. Despite the rumours, al–Mulk—born to her father's sex slave—assumed leadership of the Fatimid kingdom. Having been a confidante and advisor to her father, she was already well primed.[144] She reinstituted women's freedoms—including the right to leave their home—and restored religious tolerance, sending an envoy with gifts to the Byzantine Emperor as an apology for al-Hakim's treatment of Christians in Egypt. By making a clean break from the tyranny of al-Hakim, al-Mulk managed to re-establish order in the cities and villages, returning the economy to normal service.[145]

Female monarchs also helped to underpin economic prosperity in another part of the Shia world closely allied with Egypt: Yemen. As the Crusades disrupted trade routes through the Near East, Yemen became increasingly important to Egypt as an alternative route to India. Not only did Egypt and Yemen develop strong trading connections; they also had a common enemy in the form of Baghdad. Just as in the days of Muhammad, Yemeni women were infamous for their revolts against Arabian rulers.[146] After escaping 'Abbāsid rule, Queen Asma governed on equal terms with her husband. Not only did she attend political councils, she did so unveiled. Upon her death, her daughter-in-law—Arwa—became queen, and ruled Yemen for half a century. The royal title of the two women—*al-sayyida al-hurra*—translates as the noble lady who is free and independent; it was appended with the words *balqis al-sughra*: little queen of Sheba.[147] The reign of the two Yemeni queens is remembered as a period of peace and prosperity, and one in which education was championed.[148] While the education system in Baghdad was male dominated, the Fatimids were much more welcoming of women's education, and Queen Arwa in particular was known for her intellect and knowledge.[149] With her people behind her, Queen Arwa ruled until her death at the age of ninety-two.[150]

A century later, with the Crusades still in full swing, Egypt was the subject of a Christian invasion. According to the history books, Saladin was Egypt's saviour. Regaining territory lost to marauding European knights, he famously reunified the Muslim world and, by prohibiting Christian merchants from the Red Sea, employed economic warfare to sap the crusaders of funds.[151] For his ultimate victory, Saladin recovered the holy land from the crusaders, leaving them with little more than Tyre—the city that Dido had abandoned in favour of Carthage.[152] There was, however, a woman who resisted the attacks of crusaders with equal strength: a woman whose name translates as tree of pearls and deserves the same recognition as Saladin. She was called Shajar al-Durr.

Born in tribal Central Asia—a region which faced the ravages of Mongol invasion—al-Durr had been taken captive as a girl and sold to the harem of the Baghdad caliph. From there, aged only eleven, she was gifted to al-Salih Ayyub, the ruler of Egypt, whom she went on to marry.[153] After his death in 1249, al-Durr kept the news of his passing top secret in an effort to avoid damaging morale during wartime, ruling incognito in his place. Using her slave heritage to bring Islam's slave army—the Mamluks—to her aid, she then successfully routed the crusaders and captured their leader, King Louis IX.[154] By negotiating his release, al-Durr was, in turn, able to replenish Egypt's coffers.[155] After her victory, al-Durr was appointed official ruler of Egypt, and became the first woman in an Islamic country to have her name minted onto coinage.[156] Baghdad, however, was not ready to legitimise a female ruler. Instead, the ʿAbbāsid caliph sent a letter addressed to all Egyptians, which read: 'If you have no man to rule over Egypt mayhap we can send you one'.[157] Lacking the caliph's approval, al-Durr was eventually deposed. The Mamluks, however, made sure that a Mamluk remained in charge. Between them, women and the slave armies of Islam were fighting back.

Across the Islamic world, the tables were turning on the Islamic aristocracy. The muscle of the elite had long depended on the capture and enslavement of boys in regions bordering the Islamic world, who were in turn trained as soldiers in order to provide the empire with sizeable and highly skilled slave armies.[158] With time, these Mamluk armies began supplanting their masters and manoeuvring themselves into power, not only in Egypt but also in the Islamic territories within India.[159] The contemporary of al-Durr in Delhi was Sultana Radiyya. Radiyya's father was a Turkic slave who served as a general in the Islamic military during the establishment of the Islamic state in India.[160] His success on the battlefield led to an arranged marriage with an Islamic princess, after which he declared independence from his father-in-law and established his own—Mamluk—dynasty in India.[161] Rather than naming one of his sons as successor, he named his daughter, Radiyya, as his heir, selecting her on the basis of merit over gender. She ruled from 1236, and her first act as ruler was to unveil.[162]

Women and slaves were at the heart of the political revolutions that shook Islam from the late tenth century onwards, challenging the status quo and revealing what a truly liberal economy could involve. In the Islamic capital, scholars—departing from the spirit of Muhammad—struggled to comprehend rule either by women or by slaves. Indeed, the freedoms of women in Egypt 'shocked' visitors from Baghdad.[163] This creeping misogyny and illiberalism achieved only one thing: putting the brakes on the 'Abbāsid golden age. With a dying economy, Islam's historic centre was incapable of resisting invasion. The very caliph who had so brazenly refused to recognise the rule of al-Durr reaped his just desserts: in 1258, Baghdad was brutally sacked by the armies of Genghis Khan's grandson, Hulagu Khan.[164] Starting life in the tribal lands to the northeast of China, the Mongol Empire became the largest contiguous empire in world history.[165]

~

AS THE AXIS OF GLOBAL ECONOMIC ACTIVITY SHIFTED EASTwards, it is to China—to life before, during and after the Mongol dynasty—that we venture next.

CHAPTER 6

INVENTORS, WEAVERS AND SPINNERS

THE WOMEN OF CHINA'S GOLDEN AGE

WHILE THE MIDDLE EAST WAS EXPERIENCING ITS GOLDEN age, Tang Dynasty China was in the process of building its connections with the wider world. China and Baghdad were in fact virtual neighbours. The Islamic Empire extended as far as present-day Kyrgyzstan, which meant the 'Silk Road' traversed Muslim territory. Passing through the Gobi and Taklamakan deserts, this lively caravan trade left its mark with the pottery camels and bearded ceramic merchant figurines that can be found in Chinese tombs.[1] Not just by land but also by sea, it was Muslim merchants who were in charge of long-distance trade in the Far East.[2] The wreckage of a ninth-century Arab trading vessel discovered near the Indonesian island of Belitung in 1998 reveals the extent of the seaborne trade. This one ship alone was carrying sixty thousand items of Chinese pottery, including bowls, ink pots, and spice jars, all decorated with birds and flowers. It was just one of many ships that regularly

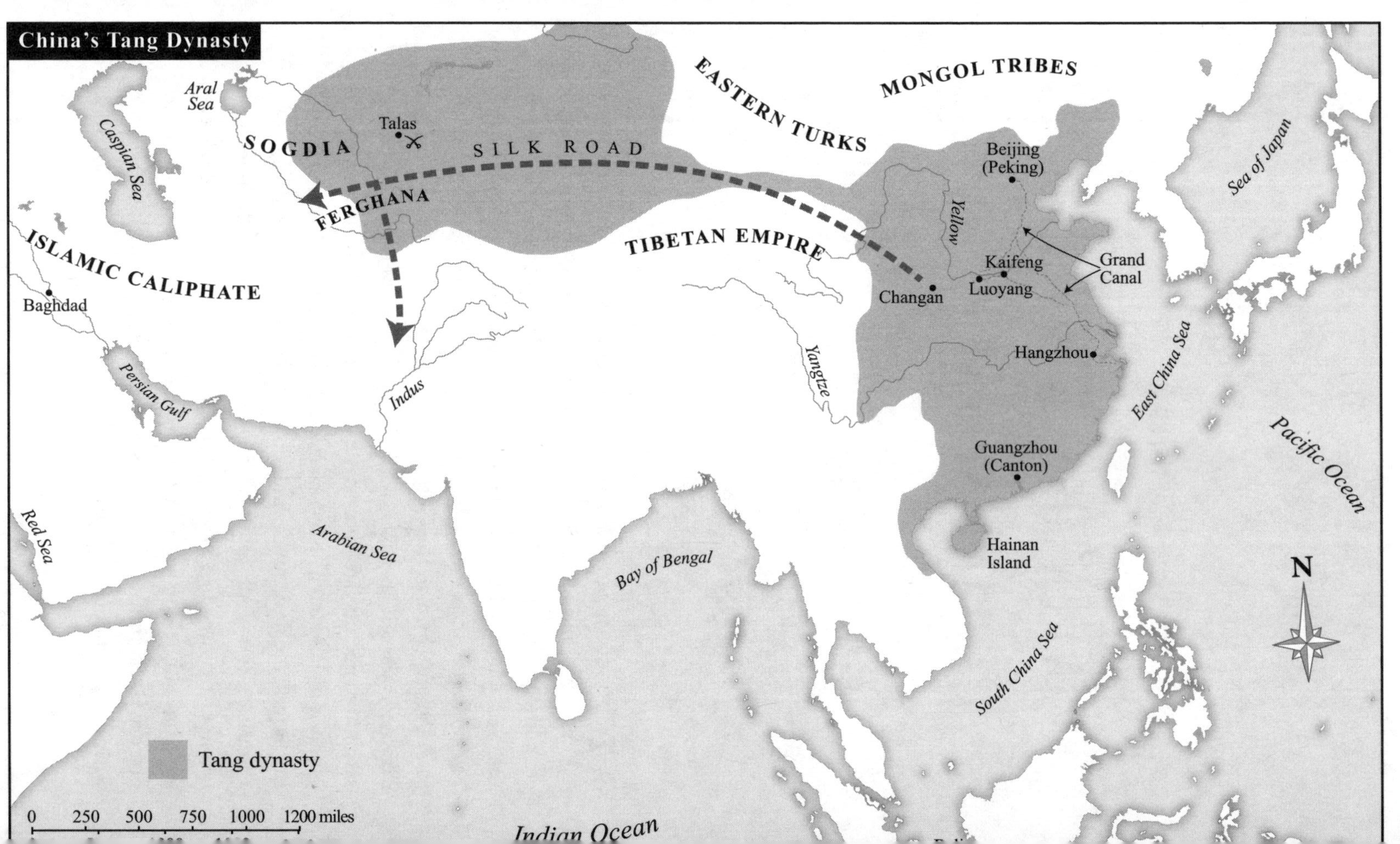
China's Tang Dynasty
Aral Sea
Caspian Sea
SOGDIA
Talas
SILK ROAD
FERGHANA
EASTERN TURKS
MONGOL TRIBES
Sea of Japan
Beijing (Peking)
Yellow
TIBETAN EMPIRE
ISLAMIC CALIPHATE
Baghdad
Kaifeng
Luoyang
Changan
Grand Canal
Hangzhou
Persian Gulf
Indus
Yangtze
East China Sea
Pacific Ocean
Guangzhou (Canton)
Hainan Island
Red Sea
Arabian Sea
Bay of Bengal
South China Sea
N
Tang dynasty
0 250 500 750 1000 1200 miles
Indian Ocean

navigated the maritime trade route between China, India and the Muslim world.[3]

Between the tenth and the eleventh centuries, as the state loosened its grip on the Chinese economy under the new Song Dynasty, an indigenous merchant class emerged and took to the seas in search of their own trade. With its economy booming, China overtook the Middle East to become the wealthiest part of the world between the eleventh and the thirteenth centuries.[4] By the late thirteenth century, the Mongols had deposed the Song and built an empire that stretched from China to Baghdad.

In this chapter, we uncover the lives of women during China's golden age. Not only did women breed silkworms and weave cloth, but they also pioneered new machines that lifted productivity and, with it, the economic fortunes of the nation. Women's work was at the heart of China's economic miracle and much more visibly so than in the golden age that had preceded it in the Middle East. But, as we will see, the more lucrative women's work became, the more patriarchal forces conspired to capture the rewards, leaving women not only increasingly closeted and veiled, but with their feet bound.

LADIES OF HORSEBACK

Housed in New York's Metropolitan Museum is a thirty-six-centimetre-tall statue of a woman on horseback. Her black hair is not covered and neither are her arms. She wears a wide-brimmed hat and a short-sleeved V-neck top and trousers, and she is certainly not riding side-saddle. As the rider sits proud and tall, the horse—properly saddled—has its head bowed. Modelled in clay, the figure dates to the seventh century, the period of the Tang Dynasty (618–906 CE).

Horses were greatly prized in China and were some of the first items that China imported along the Silk Routes—from Central Asia—in return for the silk produced by Chinese women.[5] The horses of the Pamir Mountains of Ferghana—spanning Tajikistan and Afghanistan—were considered some of the most valuable, as they were believed to be 'sired by dragons', and quite literally sweated blood.[6] In Chinese tradition, the silkworm and the horse were felt to possess the same vital energy, and one of the four goddesses of sericulture was commonly depicted with the head of a horse atop her shoulders.[7] Documents excavated from third-century-CE Loulan—an oasis along the Silk Route and the site of a Chinese military garrison—record one merchant's purchase of 4,326 bolts of Chinese silk, paid for with 319 horses, at a price equivalent to thirteen and a half bolts per horse.[8] Horses were not only valuable as a form of general transportation, they were essential for the defence of the realm: northern nomads were astute equestrians, and while nearly impossible to conquer, having their own horseback military did at least allow the Chinese to forge alliances and extend their territorial reach into the north and west. By the Tang Dynasty, the Chinese court was breeding its own stallions and mares. Starting with only three thousand horses in the early seventh century, the imperial inventory in the northwestern pasturelands reached 325,792 horses by the year 754 CE.[9]

The Tang Dynasty was not only famous for its horses; it was also the only period in Chinese history when China was run by a woman. Empress Wu, born into a family of timber merchants, began life as Wu Zhao. Well-connected politically, her family had benefitted from gifts of land and other valuable assets, meaning that she had a comfortable—if not regal—childhood. She had been encouraged to read and to take an interest in current affairs and, by the age of fourteen, became a junior concubine of Emperor Taizong. After the emperor's death, as was traditional, she was moved to a temple to live the life of a Buddhist nun, but, having already begun a relationship with the emperor's son and successor—Gaozong—she was soon back, walking the corridors of court. And, rather than being just one of many concubines, Wu was now the highest-ranking concubine of the new emperor and, much to the annoyance of the senior officials, assumed the duties of a top advisor. Her influence grew until, after the emperor's death, she was able to take the reins of power for her son. Her rise to become the de facto leader of the empire was not without challenge; some objected to her merchant—as opposed to aristocratic—roots, while others protested about the incestuousness of her relationship with father and son. However, by sidelining her enemies, Wu was eventually able to take full command, deposing not only one but two of her sons. By 690, she was empress in her own right.[10]

Empress Wu made the city of Luoyang her imperial base. Being close to China's Grand Canal—an engineering feat which rivalled the better-known Great Wall—it was well provisioned with food from China's agricultural heartlands.[11] The Tang's more westward capital was Changan. With close to a million people, it was the largest city in the world at the time.[12] Unlike Luoyang, Changan was situated on the Silk Route, meaning that its international connections reached as far as Damascus, Baghdad and Constantinople, the next most sizeable cities in Eurasia. Just like the Romans, the Tang were keen on roads: their road network was a total of 13,500 miles long.[13] In addition to maintaining the historic 'Silk Road', which they populated with numerous forts to defend it from attack by northern tribes, the Tang also built roads that ran northwards from the cities of Luoyang and Changan, enabling defence of the northern frontiers, as well as roads that reached outwards to the provinces. So as to keep itself informed, the state established a pony express, with stations positioned every ten miles along its road network. Deliveries were expected to be on time. If a message arrived a day late, the courier received eighty blows of a rod, and if life was lost as a result of tardiness, the courier was sentenced to death by strangulation.[14] Along with maintaining a postal system, the Tang state also set up customs points across its road system, to police the flow of people and goods using a system of trade permits and taxes. Records suggest that government—as opposed to privately owned—boats dominated the Yangtze River and the Yellow River, transporting rice and cloth that had been collected as tax and was destined for the capital.[15] The Tang economy was under tight control.

Unlike the Muslim world, the Tang were far less enamoured with private enterprise. The state was in charge of the economy's most valuable resource—land—which was allocated through land grants on an 'equal fields' basis. Every man aged between seventeen and fifty-nine was entitled to thirteen acres, with the exception of merchants. More than eighty percent of China's population lived off the land and every three years a census was undertaken, enabling the redistribution of land from those who had reached the age of sixty to those who had recently come of age.[16] Since it was men who owned the land, women were under male control. Upon marriage—which typically took place when a girl was in her teens—a young woman moved into her parents-in-law's household. Women were not, however, entirely without rights. A woman's key form of financial independence was her dowry, gifted to her upon marriage. The Tang Code—often seen as China's first code of law, written in 653 CE—specified that a woman's dowry was her own property and, as such, was not to be rolled into her husband's family property. In order to prevent her husband's family from claiming her assets, a daughter-in-law not only came into marriage with a detailed inventory, but the contents of her dowry—which could include jewellery and clothing—were placed on display at the marriage ceremony itself, making them common knowledge and so incontrovertibly hers.[17] Not only were women in charge of their own dowries, but when widowed they were free to return to their natal family. They could also remarry, and if a widow's parents had already passed away, she could arrange her own second marriage. The rights that women possessed under the Tang Dynasty softened the blow of an otherwise patriarchal system and may well have been a reward for their own particular contribution to the economy: not only producing sons but also producing the cloth destined for the Silk Routes.[18]

China's trade—like its land—was carefully controlled by the state. Merchants were seen as leeches—as people who produced nothing and who wandered from place to place, making them difficult to control.[19] They were, as a result, closely regulated by the state, only able to conduct business activities that the state considered essential. Unable to travel and trade without the required permits, their ability to buy and sell was severely constrained. To make matters worse, the state set prices for the goods traded in the economy, rather than leaving these to market forces, which gave merchants no control.[20] Since they were considered unworthy, they were not entitled to grants of land, were banned from having relationships with elites, and were not allowed to ride horses (which no doubt made their journeys much more onerous).[21] Since no one involved in business was permitted to enter the civil service or hold political office, few inside government could understand the benefits of allowing everyday people to 'truck, barter and trade'.[22] Even for the state, selling was considered undignified. When in 681 CE the Tang emperor became aware that his horse manure was being sold as a fertiliser to help pay for court expenses, he quickly put an end to the practice, worried that he might be remembered as the seller of manure—which, ironically, of course he now is.[23]

The suppression of an indigenous business culture created a vacuum into which foreign merchants could expand. Sogdian merchants from Central Asia dominated trade along the Silk Routes, and were provided with travel documents by the Chinese state.[24] On the eastern coast, and along China's Yellow River and Grand Canal, the Koreans set up their own trading hubs. Along the southern coast, trade was left to merchants from the Middle East, whose ships followed the winds of the monsoon to journey from the Persian Gulf. By choice, trade was entirely out of China's hands.[25]

Adopting Confucian ideas of order and control, the Chinese state commanded the economy from above, leaving people on the ground with little choice about where to live and what to produce. Entrepreneurship was discouraged, as was buying and selling. A simple life in which men farmed the land and women wove cloth was considered the ideal. Letting people make their own decisions about how they lived their lives—a policy of 'laissez-faire'—would, the state felt, create chaos and disorder. But, despite—and perhaps because of—its commanding control of economic resources, internal rebellion ensued and the Tang Dynasty was brought to a close.

GOING FOR A SONG

In 903 CE, the warlord Zhu Wen surrounded the imperial court of the Tang with his gang of bandits. Unhappy with the way the Tang state was managing the economy, and thinking that he could do a better job himself, he was determined to take charge. After beheading hundreds of senior officials, he invited the juniors to a feast in a tent, where they were all strangled. China's aristocracy had been eliminated. Changan, the Tang's most prized city, was dismantled building by building and its wooden building timbers floated off down the river to Luoyang. In reality, the rule of Zhu Wen was little better than that of the Tang, which meant that he soon faced a taste of his own medicine. In 960 CE, a coup d'état led to the start of a new dynasty, the Song (960–1279 CE).[26]

In the bustling city of Kaifeng, located on the Grand Canal, the Song emperors built an entirely new system of government. With the hereditary elite gone, they introduced a civil service exam to recruit a whole new generation of officials. Meritocracy now replaced family connections.[27] When warfare with the nomads to the north led to the capture of Emperor Huizong in 1127 CE, the Song declared Hangzhou—a southern centre of commerce—their new capital city. The Song had now become the 'Southern Song'.[28] Having lost direct access to the Silk Routes in the north, merchants instead took to the waves. As Chinese shipbuilding boomed, Muslim traders in the South China Sea faced new competition. The Chinese 'junk'—an innovative boat with fully battened sails—along with the invention of the compass put Arab shipping to shame.[29]

Despite territorial losses in the north, Song China witnessed a golden age.[30]

Compared with the stratified, aristocratic society of the Tang, meritocracy and an appreciation of commerce created a new dynamism during the era of the Song.[31] The expansion in coinage demonstrates the economic growth that was taking place. In 997 CE, 800 million new coins entered circulation; by 1085 CE, it was six billion.[32] For bigger transactions—of a kind that are more likely to occur in an expanding economy—carrying coins or cloth was becoming cumbersome. Merchants therefore began to offer receipts from deposit shops, where they safely stored the means of payment.[33] As these 'certificates of deposit' began to change hands from one trader to another, they became a trusted form of currency. Understanding the need for something lightweight, but wanting to avoid the circulation of fake deposit receipts that could harm trade, the Song authorities decided to regulate the system. In 1005 CE, they granted a small handful of carefully selected deposit shops the right to issue receipts, thereby inventing the first state-regulated paper money.[34]

The popularity of paper money was indicative of an economy in which trade was booming. In fact, not only was trade booming, so too was the population. By c. 1100 CE, little more than a century on from the start of the Song Dynasty, China's population had doubled to more than a hundred million and was becoming increasingly urban.[35] At least one in eight people lived in towns and cities, compared with no more than one in twenty during the Tang Dynasty.[36] By the thirteenth century, the capital city was home to two million people. Cities were so densely populated that watchmen patrolled the streets at night to keep them safe from fires.[37] Property was increasingly in private hands, allowing land and buildings to be bought and sold.[38] In the countryside, personal bondage gave way to contractual tenancy. Newly able to reap the rewards of bigger and more frequent harvests, farmers began to trial the introduction of winter crops, such as wheat, as well as planting cash crops—those grown to sell rather than to consume—such as tea, sugar, hemp and tobacco.[39] Sericulture also spread south across China, responding to growing demand for silk in the booming economy.[40] As the industry expanded, silk production became increasingly specialised. Some households focused entirely on raising silkworms, selling the resultant yarn to newly emerging silk workshops, where more sizeable looms could cater for the latest—lightweight—fashions.[41] Xu Wenmei—the wife of an official—was particularly instrumental in encouraging the diffusion of silkworm breeding. In her husband's *Book of Sericulture*, published in 1090, she is acknowledged as the source of all the latest techniques.[42] And this was not the only book available in China: China's printing industry boomed.[43] With developments in both the town and the countryside, underpinned by an expanding knowledge base, Song China became the richest nation in the world: on a per person basis, it was twenty-five percent richer than Italy and a whole sixty percent richer than England.[44]

Perhaps unsurprisingly, status increasingly revolved around money and this meant that as the economy grew, so too did the value of dowries.[45] With the aristocracy gone, the most eligible bachelors were those who passed the civil service exams, and families with daughters of marriageable age competed for them by offering ever larger dowries.[46] Marriage was central to the lives of Chinese women, and giving birth to a son was the key way in which women gained power and prestige.[47] While marriage was arranged—seen as a means to unite two families—companionship and affection were, however, also increasingly considered important. Families even arranged marriages for their deceased children so that they would have a soul mate in the afterlife.[48] Though many daughters-in-law were absorbed into the households of their in-laws, it was common for a married daughter to maintain contact with her own parents and sons increasingly left home to establish their own—nuclear—households.[49]

Whereas a man's property was treated as communal to the family, the dowry continued to be a woman's own property, providing her—and her future husband—with potential financial independence. It was, as a result, women's assets that were typically available to be invested in the growing economy. While business activities were considered unfeminine, giving birth to a son enabled a young woman to be economically ambitious, under the auspice that it was for the son's—rather than the woman's—benefit. And sons, even once grown up, did not often have much say in the matter, as they were expected to be obedient to their mothers. Song legal practice allowed mothers to take wayward sons to court to force them to behave as they wished.[50]

Alongside dowries, inheritance was also becoming more important as the economy grew. The Song state allowed daughters to inherit alongside sons. A rule of thumb developed in which women received a share that was half that of a brother and, for the first time, daughters were permitted to inherit in the event that there were no sons.[51] If parents passed away leaving only a young daughter, she was entitled to take all of her family's property into her future marriage as her dowry.[52] Song law also allowed young widows without in-laws to manage their husband's property upon his death, rather than it being passed into the hands of his brothers, so long as they remained chaste.[53] Widows collected rents, took charge of farmland and hired labourers until their eldest son came of age.

The fiscal needs of the state—particularly when it came to securing the country's borders—meant that it also took an active interest in inheritance. Instead of introducing a general inheritance tax, the state opted to target the property of families without sons, confiscating two-thirds of the property inherited by married daughters, leaving them with only one-third between them.[54] While married women might have had larger dowries than ever before, they now carried the burden of inheritance tax. Despite some positive developments for women, patriarchy still loomed large. A battle was brewing that would determine not only the fate of Chinese women but the future health of the economy.

THE BATTLE OF THE SEXES

Sometimes referred to as China's equivalent of the *Mona Lisa*, a delicate scroll from the twelfth century CE depicts a secure, well-ordered and well-governed society in which people potter about the streets with purpose, attend to market stalls and transport their wares to distant markets along the river. Known as the Qingming Scroll, it is more than five metres long and was painted by the artist Zhang Zeduan. With an impressive level of detail that features boats, livestock, fields, shops and a tax office, the artwork has been copied hundreds of times over the centuries. Out of the more than five-hundred people visible in the scroll—amongst them monks, carpenters, metal workers, innkeepers, jugglers, teachers, masons, traders and shoppers—only twenty are women.[55] Of the women who appear outside, whether on the city streets or in the fields, all are considered to be of a low social rank. According to some art historians, the scroll depicted real life in the Song capital. For others, it depicted the kind of society that conservative forces were committed to creating.[56]

Economic growth challenged the Chinese brand of conservatism, Confucianism. On one level, Confucian thinkers welcomed greater prosperity, seeing the satisfaction of human needs and greater material comfort as a force for stability. The Confucian philosopher Mencius had preached that only 'those with a secure means of livelihood will be steadfast in their hearts'.[57] For centuries, his work had guided rulers to provide the right conditions for the economy to prosper.[58] While in many ways, the Song era delivered on his economic advice, economic growth also changed the lives of women in a way that contradicted Confucian ideas of order and harmony. Whereas women were previously under the control of their families, producing cloth from within the home, in this newly booming economy, women carried out a wider range of economic activities. They worked in fields, traded everyday wares, fermented alcohol, worked in teahouses, sold medicine and found work as matchmakers, shamans, midwives and wet-nurses.[59] And it wasn't only the women who benefitted from the growing economy that gave 'traditionalists' the ammunition they needed to stoke society's fears of their rapidly changing world, but also the women who lost out. One practice more than any other provoked particular anxiety amongst fathers: the wives and daughters of 'respectable' families being sold into concubinage.

In the booming Song economy, concubines were becoming increasingly popular. While visiting brothels was shunned by the state official class, keeping a concubine was not.[60] Indeed, a third of officials seem to have had at least one concubine.[61] The Song state formalised such relationships: it recognised the sons born to concubines as equal to those of the primary wife, granted concubines a right to their own property and offered a degree of legal redress in the case of extreme mistreatment.[62] Since the commercial classes now had more money to spend on luxuries, they also adopted the practice of purchasing women, not only to please their own erotic desires but also to entertain business associates. Concubines were in greater demand and this greater demand was met by a growing supply of women. Money was fickle—it could be lost as well as acquired—and daughters bore the brunt when their families fell on hard times. Rather than preaching greater freedoms for women as a solution for their precarious situation, scholars instead preached that they should be more tightly controlled. The story of one particular eleventh-century young woman became the topic of poetry and literature.

Wang Qiongnu, the daughter of an eleventh-century judicial official posted to Huainan, had been raised in luxury. In the 1050s, her father lost his job 'for being too harsh' and subsequently passed away, together with her mother, while the family were returning to their home. Her brother then took control of the family's assets and abandoned Wang Qiongnu who, in view of her change in fortunes, lost the interest of her betrothed. By the age of eighteen she was starving, and so the elderly wife of one of the family's former servants arranged for her to become a concubine to a wealthy official. She was dressed in fine clothes and taken to his home, leaving the official's other concubines—along with his wife—jealous of her charm and beauty. Beaten regularly by these other women, she lived a life of humiliation. While accompanying her official to an inn, she wrote her suicidal thoughts—graffiti-style—on a wall.[63] We can imagine that she asked to use the bathroom, finding herself alone perhaps for the first time in a very long time, taking out her frustration as she inscribed her letters on a wall while thinking of her parents and her lost childhood. Whatever she was thinking as she wrestled with her suicidal thoughts, Wang Qiongnu's words touched a nerve. Her story gripped readers who had been happy to turn a blind eye to the practice of concubinage where it concerned women beyond their own social circle, but who had now been awakened to the prospect that their own daughters—born into luxury—could similarly be sold into such a life. Wang Qiongnu's journey from respectability to concubinage represented an upturned hierarchy, something which was at odds with the Confucianist obsession with a hierarchical and well-ordered society.

The increasing size of dowries further added to social anxieties. Neo-Confucian scholars such as Sima Guang saw dowries as a dual threat: as undermining the harmony of the family and compromising the dominance of men over women. Dowries allowed women to have access to property of their own—an 'enclave of freedom' from the family into which they married.[64] Since they were growing in size, the dowry increasingly gave women—and their husbands—a power and independence that subverted the rule of the father-in-law, undermining age-based as well as gender-based hierarchies.[65] By investing in real estate, funding bridges and irrigation schemes and donating to charitable causes, women were seen as 'flashing their cash'.[66] Wanting to crack down on women's financial power, Neo-Confucianists preached that large dowries were 'vulgar' and reduced marriage to a financial transaction.

The formation of smaller, more nuclear households in which women had greater influence also jarred with traditionalists, who instead favoured bigger and more extended households.[67] So too did the growing practice of 'matrilocal husbands': husbands who moved in with the bride's family. The other side of the coin to the dowry was the betrothal gift—or 'bride price'—paid by the husband's family to the family of the bride, expectations of which were growing alongside dowries. Where a potential son-in-law could not afford to offer gifts to the bride's family, they could instead consent to taking up residence in the bride's family home. It was an arrangement that was particularly popular where a family was wealthy but without sons, and it subverted traditional family practices by switching the roles of bride and groom.[68]

Neo-Confucian scholars also rebuked women's inheritance claims, praising those who rejected their inheritance and passed their claim to their closest male relative, thereby ensuring that property remained within the male line.[69] This attack on inheritance was not merely directed at women; it was directed at personal property more generally. Confucian thinkers believed that property should be in the communal ownership of a family so as to ensure harmony and to minimise conflict between sons. Daughters-in-law were encouraged to donate their dowry to the communal property pot of their husband's family, and funerary inscriptions praised those who did so for their generosity.[70]

The more women's economic position advanced, the more backlash they faced. The result was that while in some respects women's rights advanced during the Song, in other respects they began to retreat. For women, the golden age was an age of contradictions. As some in society worried that women were being 'sullied'—and increasingly demanded untouched brides to remove any doubt about paternity—veiling and seclusion started to spread. By the twelfth century, even doctors were complaining that elite households refused to let them see their womenfolk—the most they were able to do was to feel the pulse of a hand emerging through the curtains of a four-poster bed.[71]

In 1211, Ghengis Khan went on the rampage. By 1279, his grandson, Kublai Khan, had installed himself as emperor across the whole of China, having deposed the Song. The Mongol Empire became the largest continuously connected land-based empire in the world.[72] It reached across Central Asia into Eastern Europe and besieged Baghdad. The unity and security it offered enabled the Silk Routes to flourish like never before, and Chinese innovations—printing, gunpowder and the compass—spread westwards.[73] But the structural break from the Song created an opportunity for the conservatism that had been brewing. The patriarchal ideas of Neo-Confucianism would now become legal reality.[74]

MONGOL MANIA

Around the turn of the thirteenth century, a son took his widowed mother to court to strip her of her legal title to her fields. It wasn't because she was mentally infirm—as he might have claimed—but because he wanted the fields for himself. After the death of his father, his mother had returned to her natal family, leaving the son and his three sisters under the charge of their paternal grandparents, the Xu's. While the widowed mother had not been allowed to keep her children, she had taken her dowry, which consisted of fields long farmed by her own family, the Chen's. The son claimed that he had more of a right to his mother's fields than she did. Judges initially ruled in favour of his mother. On appeal, a judge by the name of Huang Gan reversed the ruling.[75] Women's rights to their own property were being challenged and, as the new Mongol 'Yuan' Dynasty absorbed Neo-Confucian ideals, the situation went from bad to worse. The Yuan—the ruling dynasty that emerged from the Mongol Empire—were intent on building a new and united China, and gained credibility and loyalty by appealing to the moral anxieties that had been building throughout the Song, focussing their rhetoric on reviving traditional Confucian values. It was a useful distraction from the fact that they exempted from taxation anyone of Mongol origin together with the merchants from the wider empire who operated in and out of China—which meant higher taxes for everyone else.[76]

Defence of the realm was the first priority. In order to ensure a sizeable army, land was set aside for military households, each of which was tasked with providing and financially supporting a soldier in return for the land their family occupied. Since soldiers—and the payers of land tax—were expected to be men, the state treated male-headed households as sacrosanct, which played to Confucian ideals.[77] If property passed into the hands of women, as opposed to a male relative who was eligible for conscription, the land was no longer doing its job of supporting the military. Yuan property laws therefore cracked down on the inheritance of land by daughters; where there were no surviving sons, the brothers of the deceased now inherited. The Yuan also attacked the financial independence which the dowry had customarily offered to women. The new property law, introduced in 1303 through the Ministry of Rites, stated:

> *Regarding dowry lands and other goods that a woman brings into her marriage: from now on if a woman who has once been married wishes to marry again to someone else, whether she is divorced while her [first] husband is alive, or is lying as a widow after her husband has died, her dowry property and other assets that she originally brought into her marriage should all be taken over by the family of her former husband. She is absolutely not permitted to take them away with herself, as was formerly done.*[78]

Women effectively became trapped forever in their husband's family. In place of the former practice of widows returning to their natal families and potentially going on to remarry, the state created a system of honours and financial support for widows who committed to chastity on the death of their spouse. To qualify for an award—which included door insignia—a woman had to have been widowed before the age of thirty and then to have remained chaste to the age of fifty. In the process of bestowing honours, neighbours and relatives were interviewed and asked to attest to a widow's 'virtuous' behaviour. What the Yuan state promoted became known as widow chastity.[79]

The rhetoric of widow chastity preached that women should sacrifice their own freedom and independence in order to serve their husband's household. It committed them long-term to their spousal household, and they were encouraged to help manage his family's resources, instead of their independent dowry.[80] Door insignia became a badge of honour for the household of a deceased spouse, but for some in-laws the financial value of a widow loomed larger. By 1309, a widow's in-laws were legally permitted to marry her off and to keep the betrothal gifts for themselves.[81] Not only had women lost rights to their own property, but they were themselves increasingly considered property. By 1313, Chinese courts were filled with lawsuits brought by women attempting to protect their property and contest arranged marriages; the state responded with a new act—to simply prohibit women from filing lawsuits.[82]

Through its changes to property law, the Yuan Dynasty institutionalised patriarchy. Unsurprisingly, from the point of view of the natal family, the birth of a daughter—as opposed to a son—was not the cause of celebration; it was the cause of disappointment. Daughters were now irrelevant both to the continuation of the male line and to the observance of filial piety through 'ancestor worship', both of which were the responsibilities of a son.[83] Through marriage, daughters were absorbed into their in-laws' household, to be vessels for the production of male grandchildren. Counter to tradition, they were now never to return to their natal household, even when widowed. This meant that girls were never more than temporary guests in their own home—who cost their parents money. Ensuring a profitable marriage match was the only economic benefit offered by a daughter, whether through the 'bride price' paid to her family or through the jobs, business deals and loans that the groom's family could offer the bride's family. Marrying into a family that was well connected also helped to protect the bride's relatives from political exploitation.[84] Families therefore did all they could to ensure that their daughters were attractive to potential in-laws. Rather than placing them on public display, this meant, firstly, signalling their chastity—to prove that a girl wasn't 'damaged goods'—and, secondly, emulating the practices of those at the top of the social ladder as proof of 'class'. Foot-binding ticked both boxes: small feet were a symbol of social standing—big-footed girls were, by contrast, laughed at and looked down on—and it served to ensure that women could not easily wander away from the home, limiting their ability to mix with men. Not only were women's economic rights under attack in the reign of the Yuan, so too were their bodies.

SPINNING THEIR CAGE

For centuries, the scourge of Chinese society was—apparently—the big-footed woman. The solution was for every five- or six-year-old girl to have her feet broken, her toes bent under her sole and her feet then tightly bandaged to the point that they were little more than short stumps on which she could, at best, hobble around the home, sometimes needing the help of a walking stick. The aim was to achieve a foot size of no more than three inches. Defeating nature could take two years and required regular rebinding, each time removing blood and pus and dousing the foot with perfume to hide the smell of putrescent flesh. According to legend, the first woman to have bound her feet was Yao-niang, the favourite court dancer of the tenth-century Emperor Li Yu, who was ordered to make her feet small and arched like the crescent of a moon. By the early twelfth century, foot-binding was spreading throughout society, starting with the upper classes—who could afford to render their daughters economically immobile—and then diffusing downwards to regions in which women's work could be performed within the home. It has been estimated that between sixty and eighty percent of Chinese women faced the pain and limitations associated with having had their feet bound. Some girls died as a result of the mutilation. In the process of achieving the desired look, a family could work its way through twenty sets of ever smaller shoes over the course of the two-year rebinding period. But aside from boosting the shoe industry, what foot-binding achieved was an increasingly sharp division of society along gendered lines.[85]

Only girls living in families where women's work took place outdoors—in the paddy fields—managed to escape the practice. In the parts of China suited to rice farming, rendering female members of the family incapable of movement was economically impractical. Potential in-laws would see a girl who was unable to move around the fields as economically burdensome.[86] Where foot-binding most took off was, therefore, in regions where more sedentary forms of labour dominated. More than anywhere else, that included the parts of China that specialised in cloth production, where, from the Yuan Dynasty onwards, a new technological revolution was taking hold, making women's work increasingly lucrative.

The revolution was led by Huang Dao Po, who introduced cotton cloth production to thirteenth-century China, centuries ahead of England's equivalent revolution. Aged only ten, Huang Dao Po had run away from her poverty-stricken family to escape an arranged marriage. She travelled along the Huangpu River in search of new opportunities and eventually boarded a boat for Hainan Island, where she met the women spinners and weavers of the Li people, who took her under their wing and taught her the secrets of their trade. Years later, she returned to her hometown of Songjiang (near Shanghai), where she set up a cotton cloth-making business and passed on her knowledge of the most advanced spinning and weaving techniques to local women.[87] The technologies she introduced included the treadle-operated spinning wheel, which raised productivity and transformed the financial prospects of Chinese women. Whereas the traditional spinning wheel painstakingly spun a single thread, the treadle-operated wheel introduced by Huang Dao Po enabled up to five threads to be spun by a single operator, making the production of cotton cloth more profitable for the producer and at the same time cheaper for the consumer. It was a win-win. Today, Huang Dao Po is celebrated across China as the mother of cotton; she has appeared on coins and stamps and even has a crater on the planet Venus named after her. Not only did she revolutionise Songjiang, transforming it from a poor region to a centre of cotton manufacturing, she revolutionised the Chinese economy.[88]

Silk had dominated the Chinese cloth industry, but cotton soon became the material of choice for all except the elite. Cotton could be woven at a rate of a bolt a day—much faster than silk—producing a strong, cheap and durable cloth that appealed to a mass market.[89] As the industry boomed, foot-binding provided the patriarchal family with a means to capture the economic value of their daughters and daughters-in-law, by preventing them from carving out an independent existence beyond the home.[90] The stakes were high: as the new spinning technology spread, the earnings of spinners tripled, to the point that women's income from spinning rivalled and even exceeded that of their husbands, who instead laboured in the fields.[91]

China's cloth production was not simply aimed at the domestic market; it was also clothing people across the world. This was an economy in which women were making a sizeable contribution to their household but were not themselves receiving the rewards: the profits went directly into the pockets of their parents and then their in-laws. Women were not only funding the families they married into, but were carrying the weight of the wider economy—all while being kept behind closed doors and with pained feet.

~

CHINA'S GOLDEN AGE HAD CULMINATED IN A SYSTEM BY WHICH the state and the family conspired to extract the value that women created. Just as with the ʿAbbāsid and Roman economies, growing restrictions on women's lives would act as a slow puncture that sucked the lifeblood out of China's future growth prospects. After all, the more that women were deprived of their freedom, the less they would be able to use their talents to pioneer new waves of innovation and new sectors of the economy.[92] As Chinese women were increasingly shackled, over in northwestern Europe, women's lives were about to take a turn for the better. It was, as we will see, this divergence in the lives of women that would sow the seeds of a spectacular reversal of fortunes, eventually leading to the rise of the Western world.

CHAPTER 7

DAIRY MAIDS, BREWERS AND SHOPKEEPERS

THE WOMEN OF THE EUROPEAN RENAISSANCE

COMPARED TO CHINA AND THE MIDDLE EAST, MEDIEVAL Europe had little to offer the world. Its economy was far less sophisticated, its scholars were far less knowledgeable and its technologies were far more basic.[1] In the late thirteenth century, Marco Polo—a Venetian explorer who travelled to China—marvelled at 'the noble and magnificent' city of Hangzhou, which, he wrote, 'might lead an inhabitant to consider himself in paradise'.[2] He described the city as being one hundred miles in circumference, with 12,000 bridges that criss-crossed canals, ten half-mile-long markets, paved streets, paper money (in place of the heavy and impractical coinage still in use in Europe) and a population of 1.6 million, making it many times larger than his home city of Venice—at the time the wealthiest city in Europe. Of trade along China's Yangtze River,

Polo wrote: 'I tell you that this river goes so far and through so many regions and there are so many cities on its banks that, truth to tell, in the total volume of traffic on it, it exceeds all the rivers of the Christians put together'.[3] Polo was in little doubt of the source of China's success: 'business . . . is on such a stupendous scale that no one who hears tell of it without seeing it for himself can possibly credit it'.[4] European visitors to the Middle East were similarly amazed. In the twelfth century, crusaders returned home not just with tales of *One Thousand and One Nights* but with books bursting with the latest scientific developments in everything from astronomy to medicine.[5] Given the opulence and knowledge on display, Europeans believed that it was by accessing the extensive markets of China and the Islamic world that they could plan their escape from the 'Dark Ages'.

Trade with the world's leading economies seemed to offer endless opportunities—so long as Europeans could find something of their own to trade in return for the tempting foreign produce. With little in the way of sophisticated manufactures to export, Europeans therefore turned to trading their own people. Eastern Europe and the Slavic communities became the source of so many slaves that the word slave derives from the word *Slav*.[6] Young women often fetched the highest prices.[7] The Caliphate, where Muhammad had forbidden the enslavement of anyone who converted to Islam, had quite an appetite for foreign women. While the Islamic slave trade is less well documented than the Atlantic slave trade, it seems likely that around two-thirds of African slaves in the Islamic world were women.[8] Similarly, in the late fourteenth and fifteenth centuries, around eighty percent of slaves sold in the Christian Mediterranean were women.[9] Europe's trade in women helped to pay for its entry onto the expanding world markets.[10]

The downside of Europe's growing trade with China and the Middle East was that disease could travel on the same ships that brought cloth, spices and porcelain to European shores. The result was the Black Death of 1347–51, with a death toll that ran into the tens of millions. People—particularly young, fertile women—had never been so valuable. From China to Europe, the state and society doubled down on the systems of exploitation that could extract maximum value from what women produced, not just in terms of the cloth that they could manufacture but also their reproductive potential. Enslavement and its lesser cousins—the system of serfdom and patriarchal control within the family—were pursued with renewed vigour. But, in a region that was distant from the global hustle and bustle, away from the Mediterranean ports that traded with the wider world, women began to wrest back control. This chapter tells the story of how northwestern Europe began to escape from an economic system based on exploitation, one in which ordinary women played a starring role. It is a story that set in motion the region's divergence not only from the rest of Europe but from the rest of the world.

BLACK DEATH

Just as in Roman times, Italy was the leading force in the European economy in the Middle Ages. However, rather than being a unified state, the Italian Peninsula had splintered to become a collection of numerous small competing city-states. Venice—the home of the gondolas that plied the palazzo-lined Grand Canal—was the most spectacular city of all. Lacking agricultural land to feed its population, but with an advantageous coastal position, Venice had a natural inclination to search for trading opportunities. After sending its fleet to help the Byzantine Empire resist Islamic invasion, Venice was granted trading privileges through Constantinople, giving its traders priority access to the lucrative Silk Routes. With its resultant monopoly on Europe's long-distance trade, Venetian merchants were able to sell Chinese silk—along with other foreign wares—at extortionate prices to the nobility of the Western world. Not only was the Chinese patriarchy extracting the value that Chinese women produced, so too were Venetian merchants, who pocketed the hefty markup that they placed on Chinese silk. And these same merchants, of course, paid for their foreign wares in part with the money they made from exporting female slaves. Venice was at the heart of Europe's slave trade.[11] Slavery had not died with the Romans but continued through to medieval times.

Venice's rival on the western side of Italy was the city of Genoa and, since Venice was known for its luxury trades, Genoese merchants instead focused their efforts on buying and selling bulky mass-market products, including grain, oil, soap, alum and woad. Sea connections through Gibraltar to London were first established by the Genoese, and by the late thirteenth century its trading vessels were regularly using the route, thereby connecting the north and south of Europe by sea.[12] Envious of Venice's more lucrative international trade, Genoa was, however, keen to expand its trade eastwards. In an effort to develop its own trade with the Silk Routes, Genoa established a trading colony in the Crimean Black Sea city of Caffa, from where it traded slaves as well as silk, spices and precious metals. It was a region under the control of the Golden Horde (the Central Asian branch of the Mongol Empire) which made the city a key terminus of East-West trade. While the Golden Horde initially welcomed the Genoese merchants, who paid them a large lump sum for their access, they took an increasingly grim view of their traffic in women, which included many young girls of Mongol origin.[13] Caffa, like Venice, had become one of Europe's biggest slave markets. As tensions mounted, the Golden Horde wanted its city back. In the middle of the fourteenth century, they besieged Caffa, isolating its Genoese inhabitants, in the hope that they would eventually run out of food and be starved into submission. To keep up the pressure, more troops were drafted in from across Central Asia, but they arrived ill with fever rather than ready for war. Soon, plague was spreading from troop to troop and, in an attempt to speed up victory, the military turned to biological warfare: catapulting the corpses of dead soldiers over the city walls, infecting the Genoese inhabitants inside. After escaping the siege, Genoese sailors subsequently returned to Italy via Constantinople, from where the illness spread onboard Italian ships to all corners of Europe.[14] This 'Black Death' was one of the most serious demographic shocks in history: between a third and a half of all Europeans perished, and it would take until the sixteenth century for the population to fully recover.[15] The loss of life created a bloody battle between serfs and lords, one in which the exploited majority came together, pitchforks in hand, to fight for greater rights. It was the outcome of this battle—a battle between the exploited and the exploiters—that would set northwestern Europe on an entirely new course.

Beyond the splendour of the Venetian and Genoese city-states, the majority of Europeans at this time lived a rural life, including in the British Isles. Europe was the land of knights and their castles, in which the mass of the population worked the land—often as slaves or as serfs—under the watchful eye of the local lord. Lords and ladies feasted and grew rich on the agricultural surpluses that they sold to any passing Italian merchants who lowered their anchors at nearby ports. Everyone else lived a hand-to-mouth existence, with relatively little control over their own lives. In Britain at the time of the Norman Conquest of 1066, around twenty percent of the population were enslaved.[16] An even greater proportion of the population lived a half-life, somewhere between slavery and 'freemen'. These were the serfs who, in return for a right to farm the land on which they lived, were obliged to provide 'labour dues' for the lord, from which there was no escape. Serfs were legally tied to the land; if they tried to flee, they could—like slaves—be captured, sent home and punished. By limiting the freedom of individuals to take charge of their own lives, the system of feudalism enriched elites but restricted the ability of the economy to grow. Peasants were unable to properly benefit from their own effort, and lacking freedom of movement they were restricted in their ability to hunt out new opportunities, whether in the countryside or in the towns. Only by ending this feudal system could Western Europe set its economy on a more prosperous course, and it was the shock of the Black Death that provided the ultimate test.

As more people succumbed to headaches, nausea, black lumps and fever, farming estates across Europe found themselves bereft of both nobles and peasants. Lords were left without heirs to take on and manage their estates, and peasants were either too ill or too dead to work the land.[17] Wheat was left rotting in the fields and any food that was harvested was not exactly in high demand. As the population of nearby towns collapsed, leaving fewer people in need of being fed, the prices of agricultural produce plummeted. At the same time, peasants who did survive the plague were in short supply and so were able to insist on greater rights and proper rewards for their hard work on the land. Taken together, this left the landed aristocracy in a financial crisis—along with Europe's treasuries, who now had a much smaller economy to tax. In England, the monarch compelled all free and able-bodied men and women aged fifteen or over to make themselves available to work, and capped their wages. Alongside these measures, and to help rebuild the state's coffers, a poll tax was imposed on every adult, which had to be paid without exception.[18] Peasants were angered when they heard of the new impositions through their local town criers and sheriffs. Gathering together from farms and villages, they took their fight for greater freedoms directly to the King—the fourteen-year-old Richard II.

Women led the initial charge, making them the first people to be arrested and imprisoned for 'helping people to rise up'. Joan Hampcok and Agnes Jekyn were placed in hand- and leg-cuffs in the dungeons at Canterbury Castle.[19] In June 1381, after Wat Tyler—a blacksmith—broke into the castle to free the two women, the gang of three together led one hundred thousand peasants on a march to London. Marauding through the city, they burned and plundered buildings as they hunted for the political elite.[20] A woman from Kent named Johanna Ferrour led a breakaway group of the protestors to the Savoy Palace, the home of the Duke of Lancaster—one of the king's top advisors. With a series of other female comrades, she tore tapestries, broke furniture and crushed porcelain before setting the palace on fire.[21] Continuing the rampage, Ferrour found and 'arrested' the Lord Chancellor and made plans for him to be beheaded at the Tower of London, which was by then under the control of the rebels. According to court accounts, Ferrour also stole a treasure chest of gold, which—after sailing it down the river on a stolen boat—she divided between herself and her rebel gang.[22] Other women similarly did not refrain from picking up 'staffs, sticks, and staves' and wielding them 'against perceived oppressors'.[23] From Yorkshire to Essex, they looted mansions, robbed shops and markets, incited mobs, and attacked prisons. In Cambridge, an elderly woman named Margery Starre broke into Corpus Christi College, seized its charter and set it on fire in the market square while shouting, 'Away with the learning of the clerks! Away with it!'[24] As soldiers and officials fled the capital, King Richard II was left alone to face the army of angry peasants. Despite reportedly telling the peasants that 'you will remain in bondage, not as before but incomparably harsher', the tides of history were not on the monarch's side.[25] The poorest members of society had taken on the King and won: serfdom had received its final blow and women had led the charge.

As English peasants were freed from feudal restrictions, workers were able to demand fairer rewards. After all, they had market forces—demand and supply—on their side. In response to the labour shortages, together with the associated demand for workers, wages doubled.[26] And since land—the source of aristocratic status—was now abundant compared with the shrinking population, its value moved in the opposite direction. While the decreasing value of land hurt the landed aristocracy, it helped everyone else. Rents fell by between twenty and thirty percent.[27] Since rents were more affordable, a growing number of people could work their own land, making the economy far more equal. With those who actually farmed the land now able to pocket the rewards, there was a clear incentive to produce crops and meat more effectively. The result was rising agricultural productivity, declining food costs and the ability of the economy to feed growing numbers of city dwellers. The fact that farms were becoming more efficient in turn meant that towns—where rents were also becoming more affordable—were better provisioned. In other words, as farms became more productive, towns began to flourish.

By the end of the fourteenth century, more than four in ten English people worked outside of agriculture.[28] In this new economy of buying and selling—one in which more people were free to earn and to spend—towns became hubs for all kinds of workshop activity and provided a focal point for markets that drew in produce from near and far. As cloth manufacture boomed, Italian merchants who were accustomed to supplying silks, linen and velvets to the rest of the continent began to worry. The Italian city-states faced new competition, not just from Britain but also from France and the Low Countries. Peasant women had opened the door to a new way of ordering the economy, one that replaced exploitation with liberation.

While ordinary people in northwestern Europe were freer than they had been for centuries, the triumph of the peasantry was not a story repeated elsewhere. In the vast grain-growing regions of Bohemia, Poland, Russia, and Egypt, nobles turned the screws on the peasantry, imposing an even harsher system of coercion and control in an effort to make up for their reduced numbers.[29] In order to prevent the peasantry from harnessing market forces to demand better rewards for their labour, ruling elites placed limits on their freedom of movement, preventing them from being able to move and find jobs. They were left with no option but to accept the harsh treatment and miserly rewards doled out to them by their masters. This was Serfdom 2.0.

In response to the growing shortages of people, the demand for slaves also grew, which meant that the price of slaves rocketed.[30] The slave market in Venice and Caffa, where slaves were stripped bare and, as recounted by one visitor, made to 'walk up and down to show whether they have any bodily defect', boomed.[31] The percentage of people who were slaves in the urban centres of the Western Mediterranean is estimated to have been between three and five percent, and as high as ten percent on the Mediterranean islands of Mallorca, Malta and Crete, where agricultural plantations would later provide a model for the Americas and the Caribbean.[32] The Black Sea remained the source of many a European slave, transported in chains onboard Italian ships, destined for slave markets in the Mediterranean cities.[33] Every year, between two and five thousand people were sold through the city of Genoa.[34]

As before, women featured highly amongst those who were bought and sold: four in five of the slaves sold in the Mediterranean between 1360–1499 were women.[35] Women were valued not only for the work they could perform in fields, in cloth workshops or as domestic servants but also—at a time when people were in short supply—for their sexual and reproductive services.[36] This practice wasn't only confined to the harems of distant lands. Closer to home, people who had lost their wives and children to the plague began to turn to female slaves to produce them an heir, a fact which is visible in the growing number of Italian wills that made provisions for the children born of slaves, including some in the form of dowries for slave-born daughters.[37] Rather than disowning the children they fathered by slave women, men of means were acknowledging and providing for them in order that they could continue their fathers' legacy. Cosimo de' Medici—the banker and ruler of Florence—bought a slave girl called Maddalena, with whom he had a son, Carlo de' Medici, who became a senior clergyman. Like China and the Middle East, the most historically prosperous parts of Europe were doubling down on a model of economic growth that relied on exploiting women. And it is for that reason that the future of European growth would not be found in Italy but instead in Europe's northwestern periphery, where women were breaking free from feudal shackles and, with it, shaking the foundations of patriarchy.

GIRL POWER

At the start of the fifteenth century, a woman dressed in blue—with a white head-covering concealing her hair, her neck and her breasts—was hard at work spreading mortar onto bricks handed to her by her builder's mate, a queen. Together, they were constructing the *City of Ladies*. From Sappho to the Amazons, each of the building blocks represented a different female presence from history. As the buildings took shape, they served to prove that women were the equals of men: able to build civilisations that reached high into the sky. Next to the construction site was a private study, where the lady dressed in blue and white could also be found, surrounded by books. On the desk in front of her was an open manuscript, visible to three visitors—the lady of reason, the lady of rectitude and the lady of justice—who had given the instruction to build.[38]

This colourfully illuminated scene is contained within Christine de Pizan's 'sumptuously bound' *The Book of the City of Ladies*—a book that predates the invention of the printing press, meaning that every copy was duplicated by hand onto vellum. Born in Venice, as a child Pizan had moved to Paris, where her father worked as physician to the French King, Charles V. She was raised in the royal court and by the age of fifteen was married to a royal notary. In her twenties, Pizan's life took a difficult turn. Her husband succumbed to the plague, and her father and the King also passed away in quick succession. Without any male relatives to support her, Pizan had to find work at a time of great instability, not only in her home life but also in the country as a whole. France was on the brink of civil war as different political factions jostled for power after the death of the monarch, whilst the country was also at war with the English. Using her privileged educational start in life, Pizan turned to writing books that appealed to those with money to spare, milking her contacts with courtiers across the network of European courts and palaces. It made her the first woman in European history to earn a living through writing.

While Pizan's start in life was a world apart from most other women in northwestern Europe, her feelings of sorrow and her need to take charge of her life would have been shared by a lot of women. Like Pizan, many women were able to turn misery into opportunity precisely because the Black Death disrupted traditional hierarchies, not just in terms of wealth but also in terms of gender. With shortages of men, women were in high demand across the economy. And, with feudal restrictions falling by the wayside, young people were increasingly free to move around and to find work that could offer them the best possible terms. Farms and workshops had to compete with each other for new recruits, which pushed wages and working conditions upwards. Whether you were a landowner or an artisan, if you needed someone to work for you, you had to make them an offer they couldn't refuse. In rural areas, farmers tempted teenage girls with renewable annual contracts that offered full bed and board together with a wage.[39] This meant that a girl could leave her family home and find a stable, long-term position that offered enough financial independence to escape being married off by her family. While men in agricultural service typically ploughed the fields, women were tasked with milking cows and running the dairy. Milkmaids were becoming the stereotypical sight of the age for a reason. People could now afford to fill their stomachs with something other than bread: with meat, meat and more meat.[40] Fields that had previously grown wheat were instead turned to pasture. In England, beef—roasted or otherwise—became the national dish. Pavement cafes emerged in Westminster and take-away beef pasties priced at a halfpenny were available day and night in the City of London.[41]

While milking and looking after cattle paid less than ploughing—women typically received between fifty and sixty percent of the male wage—it came with bed and board and offered long-term prospects.[42] Ten years working as a milkmaid offered a much-needed nest egg for any teenage girl with dreams of making her own way in the world. Rather than being married off by their father at a young age—as had been the fate of Pizan—young women were able to move out of their family home, find a stable job on a farm and decide for themselves whether, when and who to marry. By the time a young woman and her sweetheart reached their mid to late twenties, they could—if they both saved hard—amass enough money to purchase a small farm and get married.[43] Alternatively, they could invest their savings in education and training, such as by paying for an apprenticeship that offered access to skilled work in a local town or city, with the prospect of one day having their own workshop.[44]

Drinking habits also changed in ways that created growing opportunities for women. Not only were people eating more roast meat in the decades that followed the Black Death, but they were also consuming twice as much ale as before.[45] The increased consumption of beer combined with lower rents to create a rapid expansion in the number of inns and taverns, with beef and mustard being the most popular 'pub grub'.[46] Curious pub names such as the Bag O'Nails, the Pig and Whistle, the King's Head and the Scissors and Pin came to grace the city streets.[47] Brewing became big business. By the early fifteenth century, the brewers of London were so numerous that they founded their own guild, and women accounted for around forty percent of its membership.[48] Having started out on a small scale—the equivalent of today's home-brewing—the production of ale was increasing in scale, with married couples working together to meet the growing demand. Most of London's medieval breweries were run jointly by husband and wife teams, but while the husbands often dabbled with other business opportunities, wives specialised entirely in the production of the nation's favourite beverage.[49]

Of course, where there is alcohol, there is also fun and frolicking. Sex work was, alongside brewing, a growing enterprise in Europe's medieval cities. The Bishop of Winchester's brothel in London's district of Southwark was one of the most notorious in the Middle Ages.[50] Christianity had a somewhat complicated relationship with sex work. Sex was, in general, considered sinful, so much so that the bulk of the cases heard before England's Church courts revolved around sex.[51] But rather than seeking to abolish sex work, the Church sought to control it, believing it to be a 'necessary evil'—a safety valve against male lust that helped to maintain 'social order'.[52] As a result, not only did local Lord Mayors invest in brothels, so too did the Church. And it wasn't just sailors and foreign merchants who frequented the brothels, but clergymen themselves, as legal records help to reveal.

In 1516, Elizabeth Chekyn was convicted of being 'a common harlot and strumpet' who had 'lately taken [to] strolling and walking by the streets of the city in a priest's array and clothing, in rebuke and reproach of the order of priesthood'.[53] When she was arrested, she was found in bed with two priests.[54] The hypocrisy of the Church must have seemed so blatant to Chekyn that she had boldly and proudly 'borrowed' her clients' garments while taking her walks around the city. On another occasion, a London sex worker stole two rings from the purse of a priest; when he took her to court, he was himself charged with fornication.[55] In comparison with the typical daily wage of a female agricultural labourer—which was between one and a half and two pence per day, with board worth an extra penny—sex work paid at a rate of between half a penny and a penny per client.[56] While life as a sex worker was risky, the sums on offer attracted many women.

FEMMES SOLES

Brewing and brothels weren't the only businesses open to women in medieval towns. As towns struggled with shrinking populations, women traders came to the fore and were increasingly recognised and valued for their work.[57] There was, however, one problem that had to be overcome: while single women were considered their own free people, married women were by law considered appendages of their husbands, which meant that husbands bore financial responsibility for any business dealings conducted by their wives.[58] As feudalism gave way to buying and selling, the consequences of this system of 'coverture'—of women's liabilities being covered by their husbands—became abundantly clear. In 1377, a man by the name of John de Pekham was placed in a debtor's prison for a debt incurred by his wife; he was not the only husband to suffer this fate.[59] Coverture existed throughout Europe, and while it had obvious upsides for women, it also had a serious downside: the fact that it was legally difficult to force a woman to pay her debts acted as an impediment to women's participation in the business world. After all, who would want to risk trading with a woman who couldn't be compelled to uphold her word? Needless to say, a lot of husbands also worried about the personal ramifications if their wives were to set up their own businesses, no doubt causing many an argument. So, in an effort to get around coverture laws, London invented a practice by which married women could be officially registered as a 'femme sole', giving them an independent legal status, separate to that of their husbands and equivalent to that of a single—i.e. unmarried—woman. More and more towns followed suit in an effort to end the legal obstacle to commerce that women faced.

In 1457, Agnes Gower appeared before the mayor and aldermen of London to declare that she was a producer of silk and to request that she be free to 'merchandise' independently of her husband.[60] Her request was accepted and she was formally entered in the council records as a 'femme sole'. Like Gower, the majority of 'femmes soles' traded cloth, not just domestically but internationally, indicative of women's active presence as both cloth producers and cloth merchants.[61] Female silk producers—many of whom produced ribbons, tassels and fringes—were so numerous that they formed their own lobby group. In the fourteenth century, they had petitioned the King for the arrest of Nicholas Sarduche, an Italian merchant who had been buying up silk in an effort to control its supply, at a profit that was not being passed on to the women themselves. The authorities found in favour of the 'silkwymen'.[62] In 1455, female silk producers petitioned the King once more: noting that more than a thousand women worked in their industry and that their livelihoods were at risk from foreign competition, they demanded a ban on imports of foreign silk products that competed with their own trade. The King obliged.[63]

Not only were women launching themselves onto the business scene as 'femmes soles'; they were also actively involved in their parish guilds. These were the lifeblood of towns and cities by the late medieval period. Established in the name of saints, they played an active role in religious matters, organising the funerals of members and performing masses on behalf of the deceased, providing charity to those in need and holding meetings and annual feasts in their guildhalls. In addition to their religious functions, the influence of parish guilds extended into the local economy, and they provided a social network from which the more business-oriented guilds—such as that of the 'silkwymen'—developed.[64] The fact that membership was open to women as well as men is a sign of women's active role in the medieval economy.[65] In the town of Boston in Lincolnshire, one in five of the members of the town's Corpus Christi Guild were women, and they spanned the entire social spectrum from duchesses to former servants.[66]

Not far from Boston, in the English port of King's Lynn, a woman by the name of Margery Kempe was a member of her local guild, and traded not only with other English merchants but with those from overseas. Born in 1373, Kempe was the daughter of a local mayor and merchant,[67] and in her fifties, she penned the first English autobiography. A businesswoman and the mother of fourteen children, she tells of her struggles with her own health, the way she nursed her husband back to health after a fall down the stairs, her feelings of intense sexual passion and, with them, her struggles with the morality of sex. She tells not only of her business successes and failures but also of her arrest for heresy. As a woman with international contacts, Margery would no doubt have bought and sold wares from people who were critics of the Catholic Church. At a time when the Church held a dominant position within society, a life in business came with certain risks. Margery found herself being dragged before numerous bishops, expected to prove her devotion to the Catholic Church in order to avoid being burned at the stake.[68] Medieval Europe had one foot in the future and one foot in the past, but was also about to take a step into another world.

ATLANTIC DREAMS

On 2 January 1492, the Islamic Sultan of Spain handed the keys of the Alhambra palace to King Ferdinand and Queen Isabella. After seven hundred years of Islamic rule, Spain was back in Christian hands. Andalusian Muslims retreated to North Africa, where they formed an exile community in the town of Tétouan, Morocco. After taking on the governorship of Tétouan, a Muslim woman by the name of Sayyida al-Hurra allied with Barbarossa—the pirate of Algiers—to build a pirate fleet that targeted European ships crossing the Mediterranean.[69] As the 'pirate queen' of the Western Mediterranean, al-Hurra wreaked havoc, seizing goods and taking sailors captive.[70] She understood that there was only one form of warfare that mattered, and that was economic. There was, however, a limit to the damage that al-Hurra could inflict. The axis of European trade was about to undergo a radical shift: from the Mediterranean Sea to the Atlantic.

For millennia, the Mediterranean had been the beating heart of European trade. It was the home of the ancient Greeks, the Phoenicians and the Romans and was the place that connected Europe and Asia through its eastern ports. Since the fall of Rome, the world of Byzantium—centred on the city of Constantinople—had provided a safe Christian home for Venetian traders who wanted to bridge the gap between Europe and the expanding empire of Islam. This Byzantine Empire was the home of glittering golden mosaics, opulent churches and Italian merchants. But, in 1453, this all changed when the Ottoman Turks invaded Constantinople. When the Ottoman leader—Sultan Mehmed II—entered the city in triumph, he instructed that Friday prayers should take place in the city's cathedral, the Hagia Sophia. In a single stroke, the centuries-old cathedral was converted into the mosque that still stands to this day. Soon, the Ottomans had also taken Caffa, the historic centre of Genoese trade through the Black Sea. With Byzantium and the Black Sea now lost to the Christian world, Italy's door to the Far East was about to slam shut. Merchants from across Europe entered a race to develop alternative trade routes to China, India and the Middle East that bypassed the Mediterranean, hoping that they could reproduce the Venetian and Genoese success stories for themselves. Setting sail from Lisbon, Portugal's Vasco da Gama navigated all the way around Africa—rounding the Cape of Good Hope—and headed up into the Indian Ocean, where Portuguese merchants took command of trade with Europe. By 1557, Portugal had been granted permission by China to trade through Macao: for the first time, Western Europe had its own physical presence in the Far East. Spain followed Portugal into the Indian Ocean, seizing the fortified town of Manila in the Philippines from its ruler—Prince Sulayman—in order to establish its own trading base. The competition between the Portuguese and the Spanish was intense; neither party wanted to share the gains on offer.

Thinking outside of the box, Christopher Columbus devised an altogether different plan for reaching Asia. As a man of science, Columbus questioned the then-popular notion that the world was flat and reasoned that if instead the world was spherical, sailing westwards across the Atlantic would open a backdoor to China and India. Queen Isabella of Spain—the only monarch willing to listen to his radical scheme—turned Columbus's plan into reality.[71] After seventy days sailing across the Atlantic, Columbus landed in the Caribbean, where he took some convincing that his feet were not in fact on Indian soil.[72] Though the local inhabitants were, as a result, referred to as Indians—and the territory became thereafter known as the West Indies—the focus of Spain's international trade was now South America.

The Spanish 'conquistadors' who followed hot on the heels of Columbus were invaders as much as they were traders. Justifying their actions as spreading the word of God, what the conquistadors wanted even more than souls was something shiny and very valuable. Hernán Cortés—perhaps the best-known of the conquistadors—was tasked with finding the gold which was rumoured to have paved the streets of Aztec towns and cities. Without the help of a slave girl called La Malinche, however, the Spanish dream of El Dorado would likely have remained just a dream. While lesser known than Cortés, few are in doubt that La Malinche's influence forever transformed South America. Born into the Mexican Nahua clan, La Malinche had been sold into slavery—to the Mayans—after her father's death.[73] It was in the Mayan slave hub—deep in the rainforest—that she first came into contact with Cortés. Arriving by boat, with horses that stunned the locals, Cortés was—as ever—in search of gold.[74] Lacking anything sufficiently shiny, the Mayans placated Cortés with twenty of their slave girls—including La Malinche—and pointed his expedition in the direction of the Aztecs.

Bernal Díaz del Castillo—one of Cortés's band of conquerors, who penned *The True Story of the Conquest of New Spain*—described La Malinche as being a young woman who was 'without embarrassment'. She must have been bright as well as bold, as she quickly acquired a working knowledge of Spanish from Cortés and his band. When Cortés's translator was dumbfounded by one of the local languages, La Malinche stepped in, making deals and asking for directions on his behalf. Indigenous visual accounts of the conquest place La Malinche alongside Cortés.[75] By the conquistadors' own admission, 'with God's will we accomplished much, but only with her help'.[76] Whether a victim or a traitor, La Malinche was, one could imagine, hellbent on using her influence over Cortés to seek her revenge on the Mayans—the people who had enslaved her. By being at his side, she was also in a position to broker alliances between the Spanish and those fighting to free themselves from Aztec oppression. In doing so, La Malinche changed the face of world history.[77]

Spanish conquests brought an end to the civilisations of the Aztecs, the Incas and the Mayans. While the conquistadors claimed to be liberating the indigenous slave populations, they not only re-enslaved them for their own purposes but raided neighbouring areas to take further people captive.[78] Soon, however, the demand for slaves—to sift gold, to grow cotton, tobacco, sugar and cocoa, and to build colonial settlements—outstripped the local supply. Within forty years of European settlement, smallpox and measles decimated the local population to the point that only one in ten people survived.[79] Lacking an indigenous population to exploit, Spain and Portugal instead turned to buying slaves from African slave markets.[80] West Africa was already home to a slave trade, with slaves consisting of people captured during local warfare along with those who had been enslaved by their communities as a punishment for crime, but the insatiability of the demand for slaves from Europe's expanding colonisation of the Americas turned it into a large-scale enterprise.[81] The first ship set sail from West Africa direct for the Americas in 1525 with 404 slaves, of whom only 283 survived the treacherous conditions onboard.[82] Between 1584 and 1600, the number of slaves crossing the Atlantic grew from no more than a thousand a year to twenty thousand a year. They were chained and packed tightly into the underbelly of ships for journeys that typically lasted around three months; the conditions were such that between one in ten and one in five slaves did not survive the journey.[83]

The precious metals that flowed out of South America removed the constraint on Europe's international trade, by providing a ready source of payment for all kinds of imports. Silver mines on Potosí Mountain—in present-day Bolivia—provided sixty percent of the silver produced in Latin America in the latter half of the sixteenth century, making Potosí the world's largest industrial complex at the time.[84] Previously, Europeans hadn't been able to afford to participate fully in international trade as there was a limit to how much of the delicate porcelains, fancy silks and appetising spices they could afford. But with the silver from South America, Spanish merchants found upon returning to Europe that they had something of great value to trade with the Far East. And it wasn't just men who were involved in mining at Potosí. While men mostly worked underground in a system that combined both paid and coerced labour, they were accompanied by their wives and children, who were tasked with sorting, cleaning, crushing and then smelting the ore in wind-blown furnaces built from clay and stone, fuelled by moss, llama dung and shrubbery.[85] Women also provisioned the mines, carrying food, wine and candles up the Potosí mountain, and were active in the selling of silver ore.[86] For three days every week—between Thursday and Saturday—the Plaza del Metal in Potosí was filled with rows of traders, many of whom were women, sitting in neat lines on the floor.[87] Llamas—who carried provisions and ores—would have been a common sight both in the plaza and on the top of the mountain. Logbooks from the Bank of San Carlos reveal that between ten and twenty percent of silver sellers were women.[88]

After being loaded onto ships and passing through Spanish ports, where the Spanish state took a hefty chunk for its treasury, much of the silver was destined for China as payment for its rich produce. China had a thirst for the shiny metal, and as it began to flow eastwards, it eased the nation's coin shortages, providing a boost to China's economy.[89] Europe's brutal conquests of the Americas and its newly flourishing trade with the Far East were therefore inseparable.[90] Paid for by the silver, foreign luxuries from Asia flooded European markets, along with plantation commodities from the Americas such as sugar, tobacco, cocoa, coffee and indigo. As we will see, the greater availability of all kinds of international produce created new opportunities for buying and selling that affected everyone, from pedlars, market stallholders and the owners of shops to those who wanted to invest more directly by funding the voyages that went in search of new produce.[91] But, whilst this was of particular benefit to Spain, where plush palaces and squares were built and paid for with silver, creating a golden age for Spain in the sixteenth century, it was not Spain that went on to lead Europe's economy. Like so many of the golden ages that we have seen in previous chapters, the Spanish Golden Age—based on the conquest of South America—would eventually end in stagnation. So too with Portugal's attempt to grow its wealth through overseas conquest. Exploitation, whether at home or overseas, would not be the recipe for long-run economic growth.

THE MOTHER OF THE MODERN MULTINATIONAL

England came late to global trade. In the sixteenth century, when Spain and Portugal dominated Europe's trade with Asia and the Americas, the English were still struggling to find a place on the world stage. The Queen of England—Elizabeth I—was under pressure to marry into the Spanish throne in order to forge connections with Spain. Had she agreed, Britain would be a very different place today. To start with, I would most likely be writing this book in Spanish rather than English, having had paella rather than a sandwich for lunch. But, perhaps more importantly, it was Elizabeth's insistence on remaining independent of Spain that set the scene for a very different type of economy, one in which merchants had more power than the Crown. It also resulted in a maritime showdown with the Spanish Armada that produced one of the most famous speeches ever delivered by a queen to her troops: 'I know I have the body of a weak and feeble woman; but I have the heart and stomach of a king'. At the end of her speech, Elizabeth I promised that 'we shall shortly have a famous victory over those enemies of my God, of my kingdom, and of my people'. It was a promise she kept and with it, this one woman changed the course of economic history.

The fact that Elizabeth remained the 'virgin queen' of a relatively poor nation meant that English merchants could not, unlike merchants in Spain, rely on the state to do their bidding overseas. The Crown was too poor (especially after battling the Spanish fleet) and so was not in a position to stage its own overseas conquests in an effort to break into lucrative foreign markets. British merchants nevertheless saw what foreign trade could offer and so devised one plan after another in an effort to make their fortunes. Initially this more 'commercial' approach succeeded only in national humiliation. One group of England's 'merchant adventurers' set off in search of a northern passage to Portugal's 'spice islands', hoping to source their own spices, but found themselves colliding with icebergs and being mauled by polar bears.[92] A second group tried setting up trading links through Russia with Persia—forming what became known as the Muscovy Company—but found themselves facing off against the mighty Ottoman military.[93] Another group—comprising ninety men, seventeen women and eleven children, directed by Walter Raleigh—headed to North America, to a place Raleigh christened Virginia, in honour of Queen Elizabeth, and where he hoped to establish a colony from which to conduct trade. But, by the time a second English ship arrived, the settlement was completely deserted and all that remained was skeleton bones.[94] No one knows what happened to the people who had disappeared, never to be heard of again. The only real trading successes that the English had at the time of Queen Elizabeth I were those in the murky field of piracy, which involved scavenging from the boatloads of trade that were in the hands of the Spanish and Portuguese.[95]

Learning from their mistakes and with their sights set on higher goals, England's merchants did not give up hope. In the year 1600, the Earl of Cumberland gathered together 218 investors and approached the Queen with a special request. They explained that they wanted to sail to the 'spice islands' via the southern cape of Africa in order to locate and bring home the exotic produce that could enrich the English palette. Between them, they had secured the funds for a ship—some £68,373—but they knew that their voyage was likely to be treacherous. The combination of stormy seas, pirates and the Portuguese meant that the last time the English had attempted to round the Cape, only one of their four ships returned.[96] There was a distinct chance that this new voyage might suffer the same fate and so, to justify the risk, the investors wanted something from the Queen: a royal charter that granted them monopoly rights over England's trade with Asia, under the title 'The East India Company'. It would become the biggest and longest-lasting company in history, was responsible for turning Britain into a nation of tea drinkers, and, with time, not only made India a colony of the British crown but also commanded close to a half of all the world's trade.[97]

The East India Company's charter prevented the creation of any rival trading companies in England that could undercut the high prices that the Company wanted to charge for any produce that they brought back home from Asia. It also gave them the right—in the name of Elizabeth I—to seize the ships and cargo of anyone else trading in the Indian Ocean, with an agreement that the bounty would be divided equally between the Company and the Crown. To take advantage of the winds blowing east, the investors arranged for their ship—the *Red Dragon*, captained by James Lancaster—to set sail almost immediately in the new year. A year later, in 1602, it landed in Sumatra, returning to England in 1603. Other voyages followed, but their focus soon shifted to India, resulting in chintz—cotton cloth—replacing spices as the company's primary import, with tea later becoming dominant.[98]

There was good reason for the English to set their compass for India. Nestled between the Middle East and China, and with a history of its own that reached back to the ancient Indus River Valley civilisation, it had a lot to offer. At this time, India's Islamic Mughal Emperor—clothed in silk and 'dripping in jewels'—was said to be the wealthiest ruler in the world.[99] India's cities were 'crowded with merchants', whose buying and selling resulted in Indian textiles flooding world markets, as far as Mexico.[100] But the Mughal army was four million strong, and Europeans who overstepped the mark—as the Portuguese had done—found themselves expelled.[101] It took a three-year charm offensive before the East India Company was granted permission by the Emperor to trade with India, through the port of Surat; hopeless attempts at gift giving and conversations which bored the Emperor did not help.[102] Cases of alcohol did not impress a teetotal Muslim court, and neither did the one lonely dog out of an entire pack of mastiffs that survived the journey to India.[103] Once trade between India and England was eventually established, it was monopolised by men. Women were forbidden from the East India Company's Mughal trading hubs—known as factories—and the suggestion that wives might be permitted to travel and live alongside their husbands in India was rejected on three separate occasions by the Company.[104] Despite the blatant obstacles, the fortunes of the East India Company were nevertheless shaped by women.

Mrs Hudson—the friend of a Mrs Maryam Towerson, the wife of an East India Company captain—was the first of a string of English 'she-merchants' to operate in India.[105] With £100 in her purse, she spent eight months at sea onboard the *New Year's Gift*, which set sail from London, bound for Surat, in 1617.[106] After journeying to Agra with the Towersons, she returned home in 1619 with a cargo so large that it cost £7,000 in today's money in freight charges.[107] Her friend and companion Maryam Towerson was equally pivotal. Maryam had been gifted by the Mughal Emperor to an East India Company official named William Hawkins. As part of the attempt to establish 'friendly' relations, and in exchange for gifts from Britain, the Mughal Emperor had insisted that Hawkins marry her.[108] When Hawkins later died at sea, Maryam married Captain Gabriel Towerson—a union that we can only hope was, this time, based on mutual attraction. Maryam's personal connections in the Mughal court no doubt helped her successive English husbands to establish their trading ventures in India.

Beyond the Mughal court, further south in India, it was a Tamil woman—of whom we sadly know very little—who led the East India Company to the site of Madras.[109] While her name is missing from historical records, we know that this woman guided the expedition and negotiation that led to the Company's trading settlement in Madras. In contrast with its 'factories', Madras was the Company's first colonial settlement; it printed its own money and established its own municipal institutions of governance. The company also acquired its next most important settlement—Bombay, present day Mumbai—courtesy of another woman, Catherine of Braganza: the 'island of Bumbye' was part of the Portuguese Princess's dowry when she married King Charles II in 1661.[110] The new Queen was also responsible for introducing the English to the delights of a cup of tea. In fact, when she landed in Portsmouth—ready to travel to London for the royal wedding—a cup of tea was the first thing she requested.[111] She might as well have been on another planet, as the English knew little of the drink, so it was fortunate that she had brought her own tea chest with her. Whilst tea—or 'tay' as it was called—was first sold in London in 1657, it was only once the new Queen's fondness for a brew became widely known that the tea-drinking trend began to develop.[112] Those outside of fashionable circles remained at a loss as to what to do with tea leaves. When one dowager duchess sent a parcel of tea to a relative in Scotland, her cook boiled the leaves, disposed of the water and served it like spinach.[113] The territory of 'Bumbye' similarly perplexed the royal court and so, in an effort to avoid any administrative expense, the King agreed to lease it to the East India Company in perpetuity for the annual sum of £10.[114] This time, the Company welcomed the wives of its officials. Women would, after all, at the very least be a necessary evil if they were to 'populate' the Company's new, more permanent colonial-style settlements. Not only were new company recruits encouraged to travel to India with their wives, single women were also encouraged to make the journey in the hope that they might become the wives of the Company's private army of soldiers. The minutes of the Company's meeting of 30 December 1668 announced a scheme by which 'for one year after their arrival the company are to provide . . . [single women] with food and a set of clothes according to the fashion of the country, during which time they are to be employed in the Company's service'.[115] Soldiers were encouraged to invite young female relatives from back home in England to apply for the scheme, which also made clear that the women were 'not to be permitted to marry any but those of their own nation, or such as are Protestants, and upon marriage they are to be free'.[116] In other words, once they married and settled down in India, they were contributing to the colonial economy by means other than their paid labour.

THE RISE OF THE LOW COUNTRIES

Like the English, the Dutch also set up an East India Company, spurring the development of the Amsterdam Stock Exchange, which traded in its shares. The Netherlands had fought its own particular battle with the Spanish. The 'Low Countries'—consisting of modern-day Belgium and the Netherlands—were officially, and unhappily, part of the Spanish Empire during the sixteenth century. As they entered a lengthy and costly battle for independence, the Spanish Armada was split across two fronts—fighting the Dutch on one side of the North Sea and the English on the other. While Spain managed to maintain its grip on Belgium—where Spanish merchants traded through the cities of Bruges and Antwerp—the Netherlands successfully wrested itself away from Spanish rule. From that point on, the Dutch rise on the world economic stage was magisterial. 'It seems a wonder to the world', wrote Thomas Munn, a seventeenth-century English merchant and economist, remarking that despite being small in terms of population, natural resources and land, the Netherlands had overtaken Spain to become the greatest trading nation the world had ever seen.[117] Dutch artists captured the scene of Amsterdam's canals lined with tall, skinny merchant houses, each as individual as the next, with 'Dutch gable' roofs from which protruded winches that lifted cargo from canal boats, ready to be stored on the top floor. The streets were alive with merchants disappearing into their homes, women doing laundry on canal ramparts and hanging it to dry on nearby bridges—jostling for space with neighbours doing the same—and pedlars with baskets full of apples for sale to passers-by. In the nearby squares, men gathered from all four corners of the globe—dressed in their home fashions—meeting with one another to conduct their business deals.[118] Beyond the busy streets and in a palette of blue, ochre and grey, the painter Vermeer presents us with scenes of domestic bliss: of a woman pouring milk into a jug besides loaves of bread, suggesting that she might have been making a bread pudding, of a woman absorbed in playing the lute, and of another woman sitting quietly writing a letter, in each case lit by the light that streams in from a window on the left-hand side of the canvas. Perhaps the most famous of all of these paintings is the enigmatic *Girl with a Pearl Earring*—her turban as well as her pearls being symbolic of the lucrative Dutch trade with Asia.

While Vermeer presents us with the serene stillness of the inner realm, almost making us feel like we are intruding into people's private lives, women in the Netherlands could also be found in the world beyond the home. Dutch tax registers and the bank-account records of Amsterdam's biggest bank at the time—Wisselbank—help to reveal precisely how many women were directly engaged in international trade. In 1585, eighteen women traders were registered as taxpayers in Amsterdam, and, by 1742, their numbers had grown to 475.[119] While these numbers were dwarfed by those of male merchants, women's presence was growing, from two and a half percent of all merchants to more than ten percent. Bank-account records provide a similar picture. While women represented only one percent of all bank-account holders in the early 1600s, by the eighteenth century they constituted thirteen percent of all account holders at Wisselbank.[120] Sara Chevalier—a merchant and widow—was one of the many women who banked with Wisselbank. Her bank statements reveal that she owned plantations in the Dutch West Indies, had dealings with merchants in London, Bordeaux, Marseille and Genoa, and that she purchased three African slaves—two male and one female.[121] The contribution of women like this to Dutch business life has typically been reduced to two roles: as wives who, through their connections or dowries, were able to inject new funds into a business, and as widows who, later in life, shepherded the family business until their son was old enough to take it on. But while it is their husband's and their son's names that feature much more highly in the historical records, wives contributed much more than they have been given credit for, often having grown up steeped in their own family's business, where they amassed skills and expertise that allowed them to contribute throughout their married life and not just when they became widows.[122] Whether or not women were in the tax or bank-account records, they were contributing to the rise of the economy of northwestern Europe, on both sides of the North Sea.

The presence of poorer women—and those of the 'middling sort'—is even more apparent than that of women from wealthier families. Within the numerous paintings of the Dutch Golden Age we find the interiors of shops, with black-and-white tiled floors and wood-panelled walls. Here we see women behind counters selling cakes or cloth, signalling to us from the canvas that this was—like England—an economy in which women were actively involved.[123] As merchant ships arrived from Asia, filled with tea, coffee, chocolate and cotton cloth, women were at the ready to tempt their customers, not just in Amsterdam but throughout the Netherlands. In towns such as Zwolle, 's-Hertogenbosch and Leiden, between thirty and forty percent of shopkeepers were women.[124] In Leiden, most bakeries, fishmongers and grocery stores were owned and run by women and, while the majority sellers of tobacco, wine and brandy were men, if you wanted to buy tea, coffee or chocolate, it was more often than not a woman that you would be dealing with.[125]

PRIVATE LIVES

It was in women's private lives—not just in their work as shopkeepers, dairymaids and brewers—that the freedom of ordinary women in northwestern Europe is most apparent. From the love letters being written in Vermeer's paintings to the stories in Jane Austen's novels, popular culture was gripped by romance. Rather than being married off by their families at a young age, here it was normal for young women to venture beyond their family home in an effort to find work, earning a wage that gave them control over how they lived their lives. This meant that daughters were able to stand up to any father who tried to marry them off to someone who was not of their own choosing. After all, they had a clear escape route: they could move out, get a job and support themselves. This financial independence allowed women to take charge of marriage: to decide for themselves whether, who and when to marry. The result is visible in the marriage records contained in the dusty archives of churches across northwestern Europe, which reveal two rather striking facts: women typically did not marry until they were around twenty-six years of age and somewhere between ten and twenty percent of women never married.[126] Northwestern Europe was, in other words, surprisingly modern. By contrast, in Italy and much of the rest of southern and eastern Europe it remained common for women to marry in their late teens, often to men who were in their twenties, thirties or even older.[127] In the Middle East, virtually every woman married and did so while she was a girl, normally soon after puberty.[128] Cousin marriage was common in the Arab world, leaving many young women with very few options when it came to husbands, and while in practice most men had only one wife, polygamy was legal.[129] In China, girls similarly married between the ages of fourteen and eighteen and daughters-in-law were expected to be deferential and obedient to their new in-laws, in whose home they would reside.[130] In a Chinese wedding, the girl was transported to her new home, where she and her groom would bow at his family's ancestral altar, dedicating themselves to keeping their spirits alive. Marriage was about submission to the family patriarch.[131] Girls born into the poorest homes were sometimes given away while they were still toddlers, to be raised in the home of their prospective parents-in-law, leaving them with no control over how they lived their lives.[132] In India, Akbar—the sixteenth-century emperor—had three hundred wives.[133] Not only was child marriage common in India then, it remains so today.[134] While women worked just as hard in these other parts of the world, their lack of freedom to venture beyond the home meant that they had much less control over their private lives. Families, as a result, remained highly patriarchal.

Unlike in China, India and the Middle East, married women in northwestern Europe resided in their own marital home, independently of their parents-in-law. Just as they were able to resist being married off to another family, they were also able to resist the practice of being absorbed into their parents-in-laws' home. The result was a shift away from 'extended' families towards more 'nuclear' families. Women saved up and waited to establish their own independent family home with their partner, away from the watchful eyes of their parents-in-law.[135] Whilst this meant delaying marriage, it also allowed women far greater economic agency, as they were not beholden to their husband's family. This further helps to explain why young couples in northwestern Europe typically did not marry until their mid-twenties: they had to work and save until they had enough money to cover the costs of their own family home. In an era before birth control, this meant avoiding sexual relations until they could afford to 'settle down'. Of course, the fact that people had to resist intimate relations with their partner created an added pressure to work hard and to save so that they could marry as soon as they feasibly could.

The sociologist Max Weber has famously argued that a 'Protestant work ethic' gripped northwestern Europe, thereby creating conditions for the rise of the West.[136] In Weber's view, it was the Reformation—a process in which Protestantism challenged the power of the Catholic Church in the course of the sixteenth and seventeenth centuries—that gave birth to this more business-friendly spirit. Protestants, Weber argued, reinterpreted the Bible in a way that encouraged, rather than condemned, making money. Rather than 'blessed are you who are poor' (Luke vi. 20–21), 'Seest thou a man diligent in his business? He shall stand before kings' (Prov. xxii. 29) became the mantra of northwestern Europe. But this 'capitalist spirit'—working hard, being entrepreneurial and saving for the future—could instead be seen as a response to the changes taking place in women's private lives. Women's freedom had shifted family life away from arranged marriage and multigeneration households, which meant that they (and their partner of choice) had to make their own way in the world. The quid pro quo of individual freedom was that your family would not provide for you: you had to work and save in order to create your own future. The ability to have a private life—a partner and children of your own—depended almost entirely on your own efforts: on whether you yourself were doing well enough at work and how much of your own income you had managed to save, rather than the efforts of your parents. Unless you earned enough to support a family, you simply could not afford one. In a world before reliable birth control, marriage meant children—children that no one other than you and your partner would pay to feed and clothe. Tough love ruled, creating an acute incentive for individual effort and aspiration. The fact that young women *had* to financially support themselves was a benefit as well as a curse—for the economy as well as themselves. Protestantism wasn't to thank for the rise of 'capitalism' in Europe; women's economic freedom was the real underlying cause.

With the more 'capitalist' economy also came a more consumerist economy.[137] As people threw themselves into paid work, shopping became part of everyday life. Lacking spare time to knit jumpers, bake their own bread and make their own clay pots, women used the money they earned to buy on the market what they might have previously produced for themselves at home. With it, the idea of fashion emerged and businesses had an incentive to cater to changing individual tastes. Moreover, since women in northwestern Europe had more power within their married home—unlike women who were absorbed into their parents-in-laws' home—their power to spend continued beyond marriage. While they no doubt faced constraints imposed by their husband, they did at least get to choose that husband and did not have to defer to their parents-in-law within the home. Compared with women elsewhere, women in northwestern

Europe were therefore better able to make their own choices about what to eat, what to wear, how and where to work, and had more of a say in how to spend their household's money. Not only did they have greater scope for making their own choices; they also had more money in their pocket. The fact that young couples formed their own self-supporting nuclear households helped to create a higher-wage economy. It did so by enabling fertility and the economy to move in synch: when the economy improved, people could afford to get married sooner, in response to which more babies were born, allowing population to grow in line with the economy's needs; whereas if the economy began to tumble, people inevitably had to postpone marriage until times were better, as a result of which fewer babies were born, helping alleviate the pressure on economic resources, allowing the economy to recover and not be overwhelmed by too many people. The result was that population growth became self-regulating, which helped to maintain the higher wages—and with it the higher standard of living—that came after the Black Death. That, as we will see later in the book, was not the case everywhere.

While this wasn't yet the age of the Industrial Revolution, it was the age in which the 'Industrious Revolution' and the 'Consumer Revolution' emerged.[138] And it was the expanding freedoms of the dairymaids, brewers, sex workers, laundresses, pedlars and shopkeepers—not Protestantism—that lay behind this. The burgeoning financial independence of ordinary young women—their freedom to go out to work, to earn their own livings, to make their own marriage decisions and to be the mistresses of their own homes—put Europe on a new path.

WHILE EUROPE MIGHT HAVE APPEARED TO HAVE BEEN COPYING the recipe for economic growth used by the world's leading civilisations for millennia (that of conquest and empire-building), on its northwestern reaches it was developing foundations based not on exploitation but on liberation. Despite their attempt at world domination, it wasn't South America–looting Spain or Portugal that would prosper in the centuries ahead. It was instead northwestern Europe, where young women were fashioning a more entrepreneurial and more consumerist economy. And, as we will see in the next chapter, women were also at the heart of the political, scientific and literary revolutions that followed—revolutions that pushed northwestern Europe further up the world's economic rankings.

CHAPTER 8

SCIENTISTS, BANKERS AND WRITERS

THE WOMEN OF THE CREATIVE AGE

IN THE SEVENTEENTH CENTURY, EUROPE WAS TORN APART BY religious wars. Protestantism and Catholicism were in open conflict. The damage wasn't only restricted to the battlefield; it also created an ecclesiastical backlash against increasingly free societies. Until then, the Church had, to a degree, tolerated consumerism. It had even made money from brothels, albeit regulating where and on what days of the year sex workers could practise their trade.[1] But as the Catholic Church was challenged by new sects of Christianity, critical of what they saw as the hypocrisy and opulence of religious authorities, it had to prove that it practised what it preached. Christians on both sides of the religious divide began to compete on the grounds of who could be the most pure. Consumerism was deemed sinful and women were seen as the driving force. Catholic and Protestant preachers alike preached that society was out of control and that women were to blame. Parties, theatre and alcohol were banned, low-cut dresses were 'filled in' with big white collars, bright-coloured clothes were placed off-limits, married women were told to cover their hair with a white linen cap, abortion was made illegal, brothels were closed down, single mothers were whipped and witchcraft trials became all the rage. Of the more than 100,000 people tried for witchcraft in Europe, eighty percent were women.[2] Women's freedom was under attack and it was sucking the energy—as well as the fun—out of the economy. But at the outer reaches of Europe, unlike elsewhere, this backlash did not last. By the second half of the century, the English had booted out the religious zealots and were instead on their way to establishing more democratic institutions that constrained the power of whoever ran the country.

As religious warfare and zealotry waned, the very same printing presses that had been used to disseminate religious pamphlets, the Bible and books on how to identify witches were finding new (more economically productive) purposes. Europe not only came alive with intellectual debate, but art and entertainment boomed like never before. Change was visible all around as a break was made from puritanism. This was the era in which Tudor buildings were encased in new classically designed architecture, delicate porcelain replaced pewterware, chintz replaced tapestries, Sheraton furniture replaced heavy carved oak, and floaty, pastel-coloured muslin gowns, cut low around the bosom, with matching bonnets, displaced plain and dark puritan styles. In this 'age of elegance', science usurped superstition, kingship was challenged by democracy and the creative industries were born. This chapter examines how these scientific, political and creative revolutions paved the way for a freer and fairer economy—and how women, invisibly as well as visibly, led the way.

AN ENLIGHTENED AGE

Throughout history, emperors, monarchs and religious leaders wielded their power in a way that impinged on the lives of ordinary people. Those at the top of society were free to trample on the rights and freedoms of everyone else, forcing them to perform unpaid labour service for weeks at a time, commandeering an unfair share of the grain they grew and the cloth they produced, and turning on and expelling minority groups while confiscating the property and possessions they left behind. Even the most intimate aspects of our lives were policed by the despotic duo that was the state and the Church. Sumptuary laws prevented ordinary people from wearing particular cuts and colours of clothing preserved for the clergy and the aristocracy; Church laws dictated when you could or could not be intimate with your spouse—who of course had to be of the opposite sex—and penalised anyone who engaged in sexual activity outside of marriage; usury laws prevented lenders from charging interest on loans, inhibiting the development of financial markets; Statutes of Labourers controlled the wages of workers and limited their geographic and occupational mobility; and a system of licensing and royal charters limited who could engage in buying and selling, whether at the local marketplace or in foreign lands. But, as the feudal way of life gave way to commercialism—and as the Church showed that all it had to offer was bloodshed and misery—it created a push for change.[3] People wanted to keep the rewards of their own hard work without worrying about whether the state would take away their homes, businesses and livelihoods. And they wanted to rid themselves of the religious zealots who, in response to rising consumerism, had been clamping down on their ability to spend their hard-earned money on fashion and entertainment. This in turn required questioning God-given authority and replacing it with something more democratic. It meant having a government that worked in the best interests of wider society—and where average people could have a say in what that meant. In Britain, it culminated not just in the overthrow of Puritan rule but in increasing constraints being placed on the monarchy that was restored to the throne thereafter. In 1688, King James II was overthrown and, in his place, parliament invited his Protestant sister, Mary, and her Dutch husband, Prince William of Orange, to the English throne, on the condition that their rule was more restrained than their predecessors. It is known to historians as the Glorious Revolution—one that happened a century ahead of the French and the American revolutions. The God-given right to rule was replaced with the 'best person for the job' and, for the first time, merit began to trump status.

Political change was not independent of the changes taking place in women's lives: autocracy and patriarchy were two sides of the same coin.[4] Authoritarian political institutions are rooted in patriarchal family forms: rather conveniently, by giving everyday men some power within the home, patriarchy placates those who might otherwise rise up and challenge their rulers. The traditionalists—or cavaliers—who defended the absolute power of monarchs argued that the rule of a king was equivalent to the rule of a father and, as such, was sanctioned by God and by nature.[5] In northwestern Europe, where women had already challenged patriarchy by achieving a greater degree of equality within the home, reducing the power of the monarchy was, therefore, the next natural step. This in turn meant that saving, building a business, investing and innovating could become a route to riches, rather than a route to attracting the unwanted attention of a state that might confiscate the fruits of your labour.

Not just in politics but in science too this was the start of a new age. History was of course already packed full of human ingenuity: the invention of fire, the creation of the first loom, the mixing together of copper and tin to produce bronze, the development of the compass, the water wheel and the printing press. Strokes of genius had enriched societies across the globe since the Stone Age. But what we today call science—systematic, intellectual enquiry of a kind that enables continued technological change—was a product of the Enlightenment. The 'age of reason' brought something much more valuable for the economy than additional cash or resources; it brought a whole new way of looking at the world: a revolution in our mindset, away from seeing the world as driven by fate, magic and heavenly forces and, instead, towards grounding our thought processes in fact. Rather than accepting and abiding by past teachings, intellectuals dared to think for themselves. Before the Enlightenment, plagues and harvest failures—the two greatest threats to life—were assumed to have been sent from the heavens as punishment for sinful behaviour on Earth. Households spent their savings on religious relics in order to bring blessings that would fend off destitution and disease, while states regularly cracked down on parties, alcohol and theatre—and ghettoised and attacked religious minorities—in order to appease the heavens. The result was that a lot of time, money and energy were spent on things that proved not only fruitless but counterproductive, and unsurprisingly, famines and plagues continued unabated. With the Enlightenment, people instead found solutions to our problems by seeing the world as subject to the laws of science—laws that were for us to discover, to explore, to understand and to harness in an effort to better human lives. And whereas, in the past, poverty and suffering were valorised by the Church—and dying young provided a quicker route to heaven—people started to see longer, richer and less arduous lives in a positive rather than a negative light. Perhaps for the first time, progress became seen not only as possible but also desirable.[6] To tackle disease, we began to develop the field of medicine, eventually understanding how to identify bacteria and viruses in a way that enabled vaccines or treatment, while to reduce the risk of famines, we sought to develop disease-resistant crops and fertilisers. And people continued to do so—and still keep doing so today—resulting in the full-scale transformation of our living standards.

Whereas, before, universities were considered a place for theology, by the eighteenth century they were taking on a new role, as places of science. In northwestern Europe, educational institutions received a particular boost, as land and wealth that had been stripped from the Church was used to endow places of research and learning, including Trinity College, Cambridge, built in part from the stones of a dissolved friary.[7] Rather than sitting by candlelight reading the Bible, intellectuals began to roll up their sleeves, perform experiments and travel the world in an effort to push forward the frontier of knowledge. This was a world of telescopes, maps, globes, compasses and 'cabinets of curiosity' filled with neatly arranged and categorised shells, fossils and botanical specimens. From the discovery of new chemical elements to the invention of electricity, the intellectual fizz provided an ever-growing pool into which businesses could dive in an effort to develop machines that would transform production processes, raising productivity and thereby creating economic growth. The printing press provided the means through which this knowledge was disseminated and encyclopaedias, dictionaries and scientific treatises were born. Scientific societies which sprung up in most major cities acted as the provincial hubs at which scientists could present their work to wider audiences, including the all-important engineers and mechanics who had the practical skills to turn intellectual ideas into working machines and, of course, the entrepreneurs who could see the profit in developing and making use of new machines. Mechanical devices, the steam engine and—later—electricity were developed and diffused. Scientists, skilled artisans and entrepreneurs came together to create a whole that was more than the sum of its parts.[8]

As Protestant Europe powered forward, China and the Muslim world—until then a hive of intellectual enquiry and home to the world's most educated elites—reversed course. By this time, the Ottoman Empire was at the heart of the Muslim world, in charge of territories that stretched not only across the Middle East from North Africa to Iran, but into Europe as far as Greece and Hungary. Worried that new thinking would challenge their power, as had happened to ruling elites in Europe, Ottoman authorities clamped down on the printing press.[9] Further east, China's emperors ordered an end to foreign explorations and launched their own version of the Spanish Inquisition, resulting in the persecution of China's educated elite to the point that engaging in any form of free intellectual enquiry was foolhardy.[10] In Europe, however, and precisely because the region was much more politically fragmented, no single monarch—even when they tried—had the power to bring Europe's intellectual buzz to a grinding halt.[11] This meant that where freedom prevailed, progress snowballed. Whenever intellectuals or radicals faced persecution, such as in Spain, they boarded a ship bound for London or Amsterdam, providing further skills and knowledge that powered forward the most tolerant and open societies of Europe. Between East and West, and within Europe itself, a great divergence was underway.

WOMEN IN SCIENCE

The scientists and engineers of the Enlightenment continue to be celebrated today: Isaac Newton, whose mechanics were fundamental to machine-building; Robert Boyle and James Watt, who brought us the steam engine; George Stephenson and Isambard Kingdom Brunel, who gave us the railways; Thomas Edison, who invented the light bulb; and numerous chemists whose work led to the creation of better dyes and stronger metals. In contrast with these towering male figures, women are not typically remembered for their contribution to the scientific revolution. And that is in part because women had to fight harder than men in order to be a part of it, something which Émilie du Châtelet—a French mathematician and physicist—knew all too well.

In the middle of the eighteenth century, du Châtelet was on a mission. Dressed in one of her finest silk gowns, with a choker around her neck and freshly powdered bouffant hair, she left her comfortable château to take a carriage ride into Paris, where she attempted to enter a coffeehouse that was known to be the haunt of the French intellectual elite. Europe's coffee shops were the intellectual hubs of the day, where philosophical discussions and scientific exchanges took place over copious cups of coffee, often continuing into the early hours of the morning. Having worked hard translating Newton's *Principia Mathematica*, du Châtelet was eager to speak to a fellow mathematician who frequented Cafe Gradot. But since coffee shops were not open to women, du Châtelet was refused entry.

While initially dismayed, Châtelet was undeterred. She went home, disguised herself in men's clothing, and then returned to the cafe. When the waiter discovered that she was in fact a woman, he insisted on charging her double. She replied: '[In that case] . . . I expect to be served two cups of coffee'.[12]

At this time, women were not only excluded from coffee shops; they were also excluded from universities and scientific societies. Convents had once been home to many learned women. For women who wanted to dedicate themselves to a scholarly life—one that involved living in a community of women rather than committing to a life of childbearing—convents offered opportunities. As well as being home to theologians, they welcomed and furthered the work of female scribes, translators, herbalists, architects and agriculturalists.[13] Within these cloistered walls was a wealth of female talent. But the dissolution of the monasteries during the English Reformation meant that convents were closed down, resulting in two thousand nuns losing their homes and places of work.[14] For the next three hundred years, learned women had few other places in which they could seek refuge. It wasn't until the late nineteenth century that Oxford and Cambridge admitted women, and then solely in female-only colleges at a safe distance from the far more numerous male-only colleges. The British Association for the Advancement of Science debated the possibility of admitting women but decided only to do so for special galas, as a result of which it wasn't until 1853 that the first woman was admitted to this hallowed society.[15] The Royal Society, which had existed since 1660 and counted Isaac Newton amongst its esteemed fellows, only admitted women in 1945.[16] The popular press poked fun at learned women, depicting them as absorbed in their books as their home fell into tatters, with their children left unsupervised and their husband left with a crying babe in arms.

But despite the exclusivity of the scientific boys' club, women were making waves. Wealthy women from some of Europe's most elite families were busily creating structures that supported academic debate and free enquiry. In England, Anne Conway opened her grand country home to the greatest thinkers of the day, supporting their work through an offer of free bed and board and endless evenings discussing the latest ideas over good food and wine.[17] In Paris, 'salons'—weekly gatherings for invited guests in a private home in the form of a dinner party or an afternoon tea—provided an equivalent space for budding scientists to get to know one another and to share ideas. The first such 'salon' was instigated in 1610 by Catherine de Vivonne and over the course of the next century, many more women followed suit.[18] Marie-Anne Paulze Lavoisier—the wife of the man known for discovering oxygen—was one of many aristocratic women who became renowned for their salons. In addition to playing hostess, she taught herself English so that she could read and translate the latest scientific papers from England and she engaged in extensive correspondence with English scientists to discuss the latest ideas.[19] Other female scientists included Ada Lovelace (who lay the groundwork for the modern-day computer), Mary Anning (who discovered dinosaur fossils), Eunice Newton Foote (who discovered the greenhouse effect), and Caroline Herschel (who discovered the comet). But behind many a successful male scientist was a daughter or wife, like Lavoisier, who helped with experiments and discussed ideas without taking any credit. The history of science might be dominated by men, but women were present, if not counted.

A READER'S MARKET

> *'And what are you reading, Miss—?' 'Oh! It is only a novel!' replies the young lady; while she lays down her book with affected indifference, or momentary shame.—'It is only Cecilia, or Camilla, or Belinda;' or, in short, only some work in which the greatest powers of the mind are displayed, in which the most thorough knowledge of human nature, the happiest delineation of its varieties, the liveliest effusions of wit and humour are conveyed to the world in the best chosen language.*[20]

In chapter five of *Northanger Abbey*, with her usual boldness and wit, Jane Austen took it upon herself to defend not only her growing audience of readers but also her literary peers. Locked out of the most hallowed corridors of learning, women of her age pioneered a whole new creative enterprise, writing fiction and non-fiction for a general audience. In the 1790s alone, the work of more than three hundred women writers was published in Britain.[21] Across Protestant parts of Europe, the proportion of writers who were women doubled from one in ten to one in five.[22] While male scientists were busy impressing one another with their scientific treatises, women tapped into a much bigger audience: the mass market. Noticing the gaps in the market left by their male peers, female writers were the pioneers in identifying a growing appetite for both educational material and works of popular entertainment. In doing so they not only spearheaded a new and growing industry—printing, books and entertainment (the original creative industries)—they also spread learning, debate and literacy beyond scholarly circles. While both the printing press and growing literacy have long been seen as powerful contributing factors in Europe's economic rise, the role of women as pioneers and diffusers has escaped recognition.

Before the printing press, the production of books was an expensive art, which meant that few people could afford to buy them and those who could secured their books in their own private library where they sometimes chained their most treasured volumes to the floor. But, as printing became less expensive, people had more of a reason to learn to read and write. In England, male literacy rates rose from around thirty percent in 1650 to around seventy percent by 1850 and, alongside, the proportion of women who could read rose from only fifteen percent to more than fifty percent.[23] The number of books relative to people witnessed a thirtyfold increase between the fifteenth century and the eighteenth century, during which northwestern Europe overtook Italy as Europe's book-production heartland.[24] In both fiction and non-fiction, female writers captured the new audiences. Short-form pamphlets containing the latest political satire and high-society gossip could be sold in taverns and pleasure gardens. In 1746, the real Lady Whistledown—Eliza Haywood—published her subversive weekly periodical, *The Parrot*, which mocked English society and exposed the hypocrisies surrounding gender and race, all as told through the eyes of a caged parrot.[25] Female writers also developed the genre of the novel. Between 1780 and 1830, ten of the twelve most read novelists in Britain were women.[26] Penned in the style of revealing 'true' stories, novels became the entertainment of choice for the growing middle classes. They were also a vehicle through which women could smuggle social and political critique, allowing their novels to appeal to two different audiences: conservatives and radicals alike. Powerfully but subtly, novelists spotlighted the lives of women, made apparent disparities in wealth, and poked fun at social customs. This was subversion—*Sense and Sensibility*–style.

By representing truth in fiction, female novelists were able to hold a mirror up to society, contributing to social and political change in a way that didn't require the kind of formal education that was largely inaccessible to the female readers of their novels. While not today a household name, Frances Burney—the daughter of a composer and historian—was the most successful English woman writer of the eighteenth century, able to build herself a house in Surrey on the back of her earnings.[27] Across her career, Burney published four novels, numerous plays, a pamphlet and memoirs, eventually attracting the attention of Queen Charlotte, to whom she was presented in 1785 and who later granted Burney the title of Keeper of the Queen's Robes.[28] Burney gripped her audiences with her close observations of English society. She was the Charles Dickens of the eighteenth century: her stories were gritty, disturbing and violent but were balanced with elements of comedy, making them palatable and entertaining.[29] Her first published novel—*Evelina*—questioned class and gender divides and 'took London by storm'.[30] Her character, Reverend Villars, warns his charge, the young Evelina, that 'nothing is so delicate as the reputation of a woman'. But, despite being an illegitimate child whose mother 'died in disgrace', Evelina was able to marry a Lord. It is a novel that reveals the social constraints of the time, but also the potential to escape those shackles. Writing opened a door for middle-class women to do the same.

There were three options when it came to monetising literary creations in the eighteenth century.[31] While in theory an author could sell the copyright of their book to a publisher in return for a one-off payment, since this exposed publishers to the risk of not being able to recoup their costs, it made them reluctant to publish unknown writers and resulted in these writers being offered tiny financial sums. Frances Burney received only £20 from her publishers for her first novel, *Evelina*, despite boldly attempting to negotiate a higher fee.[32] This sum amounted to less than £2,000 pounds in today's money—only a fifth of the annual earnings of a carpenter or blacksmith at the time. Since *Evelina* must have taken more than a fifth of a year to write, it seems that Burney received relatively little reward for it.[33] Some authors were instead able to call upon subscribers to support their publishing endeavours. This 'subscription model' of publishing meant that an author needed to find readers who would commit to purchasing their book in advance of its publication, thereby effectively funding the cost of the print run. In return for their advance purchase, subscribers could have their names printed in a list of supporters at the start of the author's book. This model worked well for writers who either had adequate social connections or who were already popular, but less well for new and less privileged writers without a network or following. It also worked less well, somewhat inevitably, for those who chose to hide their identities, either publishing their works under a pseudonym (like George Eliot) or entirely anonymously.[34] So as not to 'imperil the respected Burney name', *Evelina* was published anonymously—not even Burney's father knew that his daughter had written it. After her name was leaked in a satirical pamphlet, Burney wrote to a family friend to express how 'shocked, mortified, grieved & confounded' she was. She went on to say that she 'had always dreaded as a real Evil my

Name's getting into Print . . . I would a thousand Times rather forfeit my character as a *Writer*, than risk ridicule or censure as a *Female*. I have never set my Heart on Fame, & therefore would not if I *could* purchase it at the expense of all my own ideas of propriety'.[35] Nevertheless, her fear proved unfounded: Burney was able to successfully build a strong list of subscribers and be respected for her work.[36]

The commission deal offered the third and final way of monetising writing. It offered particular opportunities for new writers, who inevitably struggled to get published, albeit at some personal risk. Under this model, the authors themselves promised to cover the costs of advertising and printing, meaning that the publisher was guaranteed to recoup their costs if the book did not sell well. If instead sales were strong enough to cover the costs, then in return for taking the risk that their book would not sell, the author received ninety percent of the profits, leaving the publisher with ten percent by way of their commission. The commission deal made writing a high-stakes game, but it was a model through which unknown writers were able to prove themselves—and pocket the rewards. Jane Austen's publisher—Thomas Egerton—agreed to publish her first book on commission.[37] As it turned out, Austen's books were a roaring success, which meant that they more than recouped their costs. Priced at the equivalent of £69 in today's money, and in a print-run of 750 copies, her first book—*Sense and Sensibility*—turned a profit, leaving Austen with the equivalent of about £13,000 in today's money.[38] For her next book—*Pride and Prejudice*—the publisher offered to buy the copyright outright, paying an upfront sum of £110 (around £9,000 in today's money). Rather than take the risk of continuing with her commission deal, Austen chose the lump sum. In retrospect, she should have turned it down: her earnings would have been four times higher—double her father's annual income—had she continued with the original agreement.[39] Her publisher, who clearly did well out of the deal, saw the future: *Pride and Prejudice* remains immensely successful today. At least Austen learned from her mistake and insisted on publishing her next two novels on commission.

Despite her financial success, Jane Austen's name did not appear on any of her books until after her death.[40] The title page of *Sense and Sensibility* read 'By a lady' when it was published in 1811, and her subsequent books were attributed to 'the author of Sense and Sensibility'. However, within London's literary world, Austen was able to take ownership of her work and, as her success grew, she injected clues as to her identity into her novels. In a letter to her brother, Austen asked if she could use the names of the ships on which he had served in her novel *Mansfield Park*. When he expressed concern that this risked revealing her identity, she replied that 'the Secret has spread so far as to be scarcely the Shadow of a secret now' and that she would not 'even attempt to tell Lies about it' and instead 'shall rather try to make all the Money than all the Mystery I can of it . . . People shall pay for their Knowledge if I can make them'.[41] Women were not the only people who appreciated her works. We know from her letters with the Prince Regent's librarian that—in 1815—she was invited to visit the Prince's library and encouraged to dedicate her next book—*Emma*—to the Prince.[42] While Austen herself felt little but contempt for the Prince, it did encourage her publishers to speed along the book's publication.[43] Women's novels became so popular that even some male novelists chose to hide their identify and publish their books as being written 'By a Lady'.[44]

Like Britain, America was also a place in which women were turning writing into a whole new industry, spreading learning and literacy. Around one in three authors in America by the nineteenth century were women and, as in Britain, they captured the mass as opposed to a narrowly academic market.[45] Hannah Adams wrote the first history of New England and Mary Katherine Goddard—who published the Declaration of Independence, on which her name appears in small print—became the first female newspaper publisher in America. The literary careers of Phillis Wheatley and Susanna Haswell Rowson demonstrate the obstacles and opportunities faced by women writers on this other side of the Atlantic.

In 1761, aged only seven, Wheatley was transported from West Africa on a slave ship called the *Phillis*—after which she became named—and sold to a Boston merchant by the name of John Wheatley (hence her surname). Guided by a Protestant conviction that everyone should read the Bible, the Wheatley family taught Phillis to read and write.[46] She must have impressed academically as, like the Wheatley's own children, she was subsequently taught Latin and the classics and, before long, was writing her own poems. In September 1770, not long after the Boston Massacre—when American patriots faced the full force of British colonisers for agitating for independence—the British evangelist George Whitefield passed away while preaching nearby. In honour of his work, Phillis, then in her mid-teens, wrote an elegy that was considered so moving it was published as a single sheet of broadside, not just in Boston but in New York, Philadelphia and London.[47] Thereafter, Wheatley became known for writing poems in honour of the passing of prominent figures and received commissions from the grief-stricken to write elegies for family members, consoling them at a time of loss. Some invited her into their home to read her poems to guests and to 'prove' her credentials as an author to those who were in doubt. The more Wheatley confounded expectations, the more word spread of her talent. 'A WONDER of the Age indeed!', wrote minister Bernard Page, who described her as 'serene & graceful' as well as 'humble'.[48]

In 1772, Wheatley attempted to gather together a list of three hundred subscribers so that she could publish a collection of her poems. While she was considered something of a celebrity, the American public were not willing to offer financial support for the project. Wheatley began writing to London's publishers, from whom she found a more welcome reception, and was offered patronage from the Countess of Huntingdon. As she packed her bags, she penned a 'Farewell to America' poem, which was printed in eight separate newspapers. With her white cap on her head and her white shawl around her shoulders, she sailed to London to help publicise her forthcoming book. On arrival, Wheatley was given the VIP treatment. She was taken on guided tours, introduced to ministers, intellectuals and artists, and showered with gifts—mostly books, of course. And in London, unlike in Boston, Wheatley was a free woman.[49]

Wheatley became known as a symbol of the antislavery movement. In a letter published by the *Connecticut Gazette*, she wrote that 'God has implanted a Principle, which we call Love of Freedom; it is impatient of Oppression, and pants for Deliverance'.[50] Her message for freedom resonated all the more loudly at a time when Bostonians were dumping their imported tea into the harbour in protest at British control. In 1775, Wheatley sent a poem to George Washington praising his 'valour' and 'virtues' and predicting victory in the War of Independence. With her hometown of Boston under siege the following year, and her poem by that point having reached the press, she was invited to meet George and Martha Washington at one of their army encampments.[51] But by the time her prediction of victory had come true, Wheatley's celebrity had begun to fade. She died on 5 December 1784 and was buried in an unmarked grave.[52]

Susannah Haswell Rowson had a different start in life. Born in England in 1762 to a Lieutenant in the Royal Navy, she spent ten years of her childhood growing up in Boston, where her father was stationed. During the American Revolution, the family were taken prisoner and were subsequently sent back to England in 1778 as part of a prisoner exchange.[53] Having had their property and possessions confiscated by the American revolutionaries, life became more of a struggle. With her family unable to support her, Susannah found work as a governess, and published her first novel, *Victoria* by subscription in 1786, with the patronage of the Duchess of Devonshire, to whom she dedicated the book. In 1787, she married William Rowson, a businessman with an interest in the arts. Despite promising the world, William was less a businessman and more a drunkard, which meant that Susannah needed to support herself, for which she turned to the performing arts.[54] In 1793, she boarded a ship bound for America with a company of actors—her husband in tow—en route to the New Theatre in Philadelphia.[55] In addition to appearing in more than a hundred plays, many of which she wrote herself, Rowson built a reputation as a novelist. Her novel *Charlotte: a Tale of Truth,* the story of a young British woman who was seduced by a military officer, whisked off to America and abandoned into a life of poverty, became America's first best-selling book.[56] Running at more than two hundred editions, it was the most popular novel in America until Harriet Beecher Stowe's *Uncle Tom's Cabin* broke all previous sales records. Known more simply as *Charlotte Temple,* so well liked was the main character of Rowson's book that a fan carved her name onto an empty gravestone in New York, which became a focal point for the book's admirers and a way of honouring the many female immigrants who died in poverty. As recently as 1900, the *New York Daily Tribune* reported that the grave received fifty visitors a day.[57] Rowson's theatrical fame proved to be a blessing rather than a mark of shame, enabling her to muster together enough subscribers to print and publish her books.[58] In 1797, she retired from the stage and invested her savings in establishing her own school; within weeks, she was in receipt of school fees from one hundred girls.[59] Rowson even found her way into the great American songbook, with the aptly titled 'America, Commerce and Freedom'.[60]

Whereas women like Rowson were free to take to the stage in America and Britain, in Asia women were increasingly forbidden from doing so. Japan had once been famous for its female performers. It was a female dancer—Okuni—who in 1603 introduced kabuki theatre to Kyoto.[61] From kabuki troupes to Buddhist nuns, women had travelled the Japanese countryside, singing songs, telling stories and giving puppet performances. But from the seventeenth century, as Confucian culture spread across the Far East from China, Japanese authorities began to prohibit women from performing on stage. Theatres were moved to newly established 'pleasure districts', which also became the home of the female geisha, where they were kept under the watchful eye of the authorities.[62] Back in China itself, not only could women not appear on stage, but in Beijing (the historic centre of Chinese opera) they were forbidden from attending the theatre altogether.[63] Poor parents sold their boys to theatre troupes to play the female roles.[64] In a culture that was increasingly obsessed with female chastity, women creatives were shrouded in shame, in turn depriving the economy of talent that could have helped grow the creative industries, and stemming the spread of literacy. In fact, during the creative age, the number of books relative to people in China was less than a twelfth of that in Western Europe.[65] When it came to women's rights, the East and the West were heading in very different directions, which had significant implications for learning and literacy as well as for creative enjoyment.

While women were the ones hidden away in Asia and the Islamic world, in northwestern Europe it was men who secluded themselves in their scientific societies and universities, while women were the ones out in wider society, turning intellectual endeavour into a money-making enterprise, and unleashing the economy's growth potential by spreading literacy and learning to the wider population.

ENLIGHTENED MORALISM

Priscilla Wakefield not only turned writing into a lifelong career, publishing seventeen books across her lifetime; she also transformed the world of banking. Born in the winter of 1750–1, Wakefield was brought up in a middle-class family as the eldest of eight daughters. Her father was a coal merchant, sourcing coal for the hearths of London, and her mother home-schooled Priscilla and her younger sisters.[66] When she was almost twenty-one, Priscilla married Edward Wakefield in the Quaker meeting house in Tottenham, London. Her new husband—a merchant—had a poor instinct for business. He also had a bad temper, which meant that he struggled with failure. In her journals, Priscilla writes of him regularly being in 'a fit of hysterics'.[67] With three small children to feed and unable to depend on her husband, Priscilla had to make her own living. Taking in washing or working behind the counter of a tavern would have raised eyebrows—and would also no doubt have provoked her husband's temper—so she instead turned to writing, which was something she could do while keeping up appearances. Wakefield's first books tapped into the growing market for home-schooling material. Her *An Introduction to Botany* (published in 1796) found markets on both sides of the Atlantic, and was also translated into French.[68] Alongside, she published books on the geography and history of North America, Africa and India.[69] But for Wakefield, spreading knowledge was not enough by itself. She understood that for individuals to make the most of their lives and, in turn, for the economy to grow, ordinary people needed access to physical capital—money—as well as human capital. The problem, as she saw it, was that the banking sector was not doing enough for the wider population, so she decided to fix this.

Financiers weren't exactly standing still. They were busily developing ever more ways to serve wealthy landowners and merchants, with, of course, an eye to making a profit. Alongside the other revolutions of the era, a 'financial revolution' was underway in the eighteenth century. And, as with printing, it was a sector of Europe's economy that was shifting away from its historic home in Italy towards northwestern Europe, including Edinburgh, London and Amsterdam. Thanks to England's Glorious Revolution, a political revolution in part inspired by women, the state found itself able to borrow against future tax revenues by issuing government bonds. This was because the parliamentary system was seen as much more trustworthy in the eyes of investors than the monarchy had been: when kings were in charge they had had something of a reputation for running up debt and refusing to pay it back. The move towards democracy thereby expanded the capacity of the state to borrow by issuing bonds, because investors were more willing to lend. Alongside the development of the market in government bonds, the insurance industry sprung to life, allowing people to insure against fire or death—with their premiums safely invested by insurance companies in government bonds—and banks began to offer more services to their most trusted customers, including mortgages. Relative to the needs of the wealthy, the needs of everyday people were, however, being overlooked. Banks didn't think that they could profit from offering bank accounts to ordinary people, especially women. However, plenty of women wanted to save and to do so in something safer than a pot hidden under their bed. Wakefield spotted the gap in the market and so, in 1798, taking the situation into her own hands, established the first 'Penny Bank' in England, opening up the world of banking to women and children. Her first saver was a fourteen-year-old orphan girl, who made a deposit of two pounds.

From as little as a penny, any woman or child could open a savings account at Wakefield's Tottenham-based bank, receiving interest of around five percent. In order to keep people's money safe, she invested her savers' deposits in government bonds and used the interest she received on those bonds to pay the interest on people's savings. Instead of running her bank from a grand building, Wakefield set up a table in a local school after the children had left for the day, advertising where she could be found in the local press. By avoiding the cost of plush offices, Wakefield was able to pass on all of the interest received on the government bonds back to her savers. Rather than a money-making endeavour, Wakefield's bank was a charitable undertaking, designed to help people to help themselves. In 1804, in response to popular demand, Wakefield extended her bank accounts to men. By 1817, inspired by Wakefield's own bank, savings banks were springing up across the UK, offering banking services to ordinary people all while under the control of boards of well-meaning trustees who ensured that people's money was properly looked after.

In the same year that Wakefield opened her bank, 1798, she also published her feminist treatise *Reflections on the Present Condition of the Female Sex; with Suggestions for its Improvement*, making the case not just for women's education but for women's work. She began by pointing out that all of the work that women undertook in society—paid or not—was useful work. The most famous economist of the day—Adam Smith, widely considered to be the father of modern economics—had, she argued, overlooked women's work in the home, seeing only paid work outside of the home as being a part of the 'economy'. Wakefield made the case that housework and family care were just as 'productive' for the economy as the work undertaken by husbands.[70] She also questioned the contempt towards women's paid work within middle-class circles:

> *Can it be accounted for on any other ground than that of prejudice, in a country like England, where commerce forms one of the principal sinews of national strength, where the character of the merchant is honourable, and no obstacle to a favourable reception in the highest circles, that degradation should attend the female who engages in the concerns of commerce, and that she whose good sense and resolution enable her to support herself, is banished from that line of company, of which she had perhaps previously formed a distinguished ornament? One of the effects of this ill-directed pride, is to deter young men of liberal prospects, from demeaning themselves, as it is erroneously termed, by marrying a girl who has been trained up to any profitable employment.*[71]

It was, in other words, hypocritical for a society that was embracing commerce to look down on women who worked for a living. Wakefield, however, did not approve of *every* kind of work, which led her to tackle head-on the unspeakable realm of the 'fallen women'.

In the eighteenth century, London's streets provided a cauldron within which people from all walks of life could mix, from the top-hatted gentry to merchants, sailors, pedlars, servants and sex workers. From the 'gin alley' in Hogarth's etching of London's St Giles to the red-light district in Covent Garden, city life offered plenty of opportunities for debauchery. Hogarth's artistic depiction of *A Harlot's Progress* would have been familiar to all of Wakefield's readers. Indeed, between 1757 and 1795, any visitor to London could purchase *Harris's List*, a guidebook to 'Covent Garden Ladies'.

Compiled incognito by a waiter and a journalist, it offered sex in the city, operating both as a practical guide for anyone looking for female company and as erotic reading material. Some began to worry that sex workers—and their clients—had the run of the streets, and preached that they were sinners in need of redemption. The Magdalen Hospital, established in 1758, sought to 'save the hoary head' from 'shame, misery, and death'.[72] Wakefield, however, argued that sex work was an economic and not a social problem, one that resulted from a 'dreadful necessity'.[73] In other words, sex workers were not 'sinners' but, instead, victims of economic misfortune. She pointed out that any young woman risked falling into 'prostitution' as a result of being ill-prepared for other forms of work:

> *In the present state of things, if a poor frail unthinking girl yields to the ardent solicitations of the man who has won her affections, and he be so villainous as to abandon her, she is lost without resource, especially if she be qualified for no occupation but [domestic] service; deprived of character, no person will take her into their family; the wants of nature [e.g. hunger] must be satisfied, even at the price which produces utter destruction; and the forlorn deserted one is compelled to betake herself to that course, which presently terminates all hope of restoration to the esteem of others.*[74]

She confronted conservative readers who worried that women's work would risk female morality by turning their argument on its head: she reasoned that women's exclusion from 'proper' paid work was what instead left them vulnerable to 'immorality'. Her *Reflections* went on to propose a detailed plan for women's work, tabulated by class, with associated educational and training recommendations for each class of women. She recommended that poor women be properly trained as hairdressers, cooks or seamstresses so as to avoid falling into harlotry and that men should be discouraged from working in such professions, keeping them 'safe' for women. To put her plan into action, she co-established her own school—the School for Industry—providing practical training for young women. For the handful of women born into families with means, writing and painting were, instead, at the top of Wakefield's list of occupations, as they could be conducted from the safety of the home, away from men. Gender segregation was, she felt, the route to liberation. One of her peers—Mary Wollstonecraft—knew, however, that segregation could never be the route to equality and so put forward a still more radical agenda for both women and the economy.

MARY, MARY, QUITE CONTRARY

Like Wakefield, Wollstonecraft set up her own school and published widely, including novels as well as non-fiction. Unlike Wakefield, she was able to pinpoint the fundamental stumbling block to women's advancement: the obsession with women's virginity. It was the fear of young women being deemed 'damaged goods' that, she argued, drove restrictions on women's travel, their freedom to work alongside men, and their ability to access educational institutions. While, as we have seen, these restrictions had already become deeply entrenched in the more historically developed parts of the world—in the Far East, India and the Middle East—Wollstonecraft was aware that a similar obsession was starting to grip the middle classes closer to home. Even a feminist like Wakefield appeared to be buying into it. And, since the middle classes were expanding with the economy, she knew that if this purity culture went unchecked, it would do untold damage, not just to women's lives but to the economy too. She was determined to do something about it.

Wollstonecraft had experienced first-hand the consequences of purity culture. She was born in 1759—in an era of *Bridgerton*-style dresses—into a comfortable, middle-class household. Her father, a silk weaver in London, had moved the family to rural Yorkshire in order to pursue a 'gentlemanly' life away from the dirt and noise of the capital. Unlike her brothers, Mary was denied a challenging education and a career in the 'professions'. What she occupied was—akin to a pet canary—a gilded cage. While her brothers had the benefit of a challenging education in the local grammar school, she was educated at home, leaving her looking longingly at her brothers as they departed home each morning. The young Mary was bored and frustrated by home-schooling, which focussed on needlework, music and languages rather than philosophy, politics and science. To make matters worse, by the time she was a teenager, Mary's father's attempt at becoming a 'gentleman' had ruined the family's finances. Whatever remained of the family funds following years of extravagance was plunged into paying for her older brother to enter the law.[75] Mary was instead sent to work as a lady's companion in Bath, a spa city that was all the rage in Georgian Britain, with honey-coloured town houses neatly arranged around green garden squares and crescents. While she might have appreciated the architecture, she did not enjoy the 'genteel life' of accompanying a merchant's wife about town, which was, in her own words, filled with 'unmeaning civilities'. Instead, as we know from her memoirs, she looked forward 'with pleasure' to a time when she could 'lay aside all restraint'.[76]

Unhappy in a world in which she was expected to be a paragon of respectability, Mary returned home to care for her sick mother, who, by all accounts, was not the easiest of patients.[77] Still in need of earning a living, but with no desire to return to life as a lady's companion, in 1784, aged only twenty-five, Mary and her two sisters, along with a good friend—Fanny Blood—opened a school in Newington Green, London. Their aim was to fill the gaping hole in the education of young women, and Newington Green was the perfect place to start: it was home to religious dissenters, a community open to new ideas. A new school, based on radical principles, was welcome. Sadly, the finances of running a school for girls didn't stack up. Too many middle-class families preferred to hire governesses rather than to send their daughters to school, which meant that there were too few pupils to cover the costs. With few other options, Wollstonecraft therefore took up a position as governess to an Anglo-Irish family—the Kingsboroughs—in Ireland. While the Kingsboroughs' daughters were fond of Mary, their mother was not: Mary's progressive views on the education of women were not appreciated by someone who favoured a more traditional and 'genteel' approach. Within a year, Mary was unemployed. Her childhood experiences, the school she had established and her work as a governess, did, however, provide her with a new opportunity. In 1787, she published her first book, aptly titled *Thoughts on the Education of Daughters*. Having tried her hand at the only real professions open to middle-class women—being a lady's companion, schoolmistress and governess—Wollstonecraft harnessed the newly emerging career option of becoming a writer.

Wollstonecraft's family's attempt to climb the social ladder framed how she saw the world: through the lens of the section of society that lived a life somewhere between aristocrats and ordinary people. She witnessed the way in which this newly expanding class attempted to distinguish themselves from ordinary people through not only money but morality. And how, by developing what she called this 'insipid decency', they could judge themselves to be 'better' than the libertine aristocracy. This middle-class monopoly on morality had particular implications for women, who were expected to be the virginal angels who set a good example to other women in society. By trumpeting the virtues of female purity, the middle classes wanted to ensure that working-class girls, despite their freedom to earn, would not be able to compete with their own daughters when it came to attracting the wealthiest husbands. By shrouding the paid labour of women in moral shame, this purity culture risked devaluing the contribution that countless ordinary women were making to the economy while turning middle-class women into highly valued, 'precious' commodities. Since work for middle-class women was considered nothing more than a stop-gap and could not be allowed to jeopardise their marriage prospects by causing their virginity to be treated as suspect, 'decency' came at the cost of women's dependence on men. Indeed, the very ability of the middle classes to claim the moral high ground depended on the fact that preserving a young woman's bodily modesty—ensuring that she was untouched by men—came at a price not only to her but her family: her family had to ensure that she was chaperoned at all times, was taught separately to boys, and did not have to work alongside men to support herself financially. It was a cost that better-off families were able to bear, but one that working-class families, by design, found unaffordable. Morality, in other words, cost money. And Wollstonecraft had little time for it.

In the winter of 1792, Wollstonecraft did what unmarried middle-class women were not supposed to do: she journeyed to Paris to join the revolution where, on 14 July 1789, a mob had stormed the Bastille, the French King's fortress of ammunitions. It was a revolution in which ordinary French women played a pivotal role, with the flag-flying allegorical Marianne soon becoming the symbol of the French Republic. Intellectuals in London, Boston and Berlin were gripped by the cries for liberty, fraternity and equality. Despite being in a state of revolution, Paris acquired a gravitational pull, attracting to its coffeehouses and barricades any foreigner who wanted to experience first-hand the fall of the 'Ancien Régime' and to have their own say in how to build a new—more enlightened—society. Wollstonecraft cheered on the publication of Olympe de Gouges's *Declaration of the Rights of Woman,* which insisted that the rights of man be matched by the rights of woman and, in 1792, published her own feminist masterpiece. Titled *A Vindication of the Rights of Woman with Strictures on Moral and Political Subjects,* it argued that women were just as intellectually capable as men and deserved equal access to education and politics. By identifying purity culture as the remaining stumbling block in the road to gender equality, she suggested that 'men have superior judgement' not because they are cleverer but because 'they give a freer scope to the grand passions, and by more frequently going astray enlarge their minds'.[78] Whereas 'the hero is allowed to be mortal', heroines 'are to be born immaculate'. For women, everything was to be lost; for men, everything was for the taking. What she boldly called for was a 'revolution in female manners'.[79]

Surrounded by expatriates from Britain and America, Wollstonecraft was in her element, honing her French, attending salons, and observing in person the trial of King Louis XVI. But within a month of her arrival—while she was still struggling with conversational French—the trial of the King ended with the guillotine.[80] As a 'reign of terror' descended on Paris, rather than finding herself in a utopia, Wollstonecraft was surrounded by death and fear. She considered returning to London but opted to stay, to report on what was going on in France for the English press and perhaps in the vain hope that she could help to steer things in a better direction. She began drafting a plan for the revolution's Education Committee, hoping that she could help get the revolution back on track.[81] There was also a more personal reason for Wollstonecraft to remain: she had fallen head over heels in love with an American in Paris by the name of Gilbert Imlay. But as revolutionaries inflicted death on a grand scale and anyone who dared criticise them was sent to the guillotine, disillusionment began to set in. Having already criticised the revolution for not doing enough for women, Wollstonecraft knew she was herself at risk. Indeed, in the summer of 1793, Olympe de Gouges was arrested and executed. To make matters worse, and while far from the comforts of home, Wollstonecraft found herself pregnant and abandoned by Imlay. As the French Revolution turned into the Revolutionary Wars, England and France became enemies, leaving Wollstonecraft on French soil in fear for her own life and that of her young child. With Imlay's slippers still at her bedroom door, in the hope that he would eventually return, and a new infant by her side, she threw herself into writing *An Historical and Moral View of the Origin and Progress of the French Revolution; and the Effect It Has Produced in Europe.*[82]

Wollstonecraft asked herself: How could the revolution have taken such a bloodthirsty turn? The answer she came up with was that the revolutionaries had failed to confront their feelings—their inner passion, greed and fear—and had thereby allowed those feelings to guide their actions, which resulted in a loss of rationality. To live by 'sensibility' alone—whether as an individual or as a state—would, she knew, be dangerous, but so too would be basing your life and your politics purely on 'rationality', to the neglect of sensibility. After all, we all have feelings, and to try to ignore those feelings would, Wollstonecraft argued, result in our emotions polluting our reason. In the process she revealed an implicit assumption within the scholarly community of men: that men were assumed to be the people of reason (the people of the mind) and women were seen as emotional creatures (the people of the body). This meant that feelings in men—including in the French revolutionaries—were wrongly 'rationalised', and reason in women was ignored, resulting in both sexes being corrupted. Both men and women were, she argued, a combination of sense and sensibility. Men and women were, in other words, the same. And realising that would be the key to making sure that all future revolutions remained on track.

IN THE AGE OF REVOLUTIONS, NORTHWESTERN EUROPE WAS building the foundations for future growth—or, perhaps more accurately, it was women who were doing so. Adding to the progress made in medieval times, women pushed forward democracy, science, literacy and finance. While wealthy and educated men quietly catered for one another behind closed doors, women looked outward towards wider society, creating a politics, a culture of learning and a system of banking, all of which worked in the interests of the mass of ordinary people. And it was already making a difference to the economy. By the seventeenth century, of the five largest cities in the world, three were European and by 1800, London—once an economic irrelevance—was the largest city in Europe.[83] As we will see in the next chapter, the economic fire was ready to be lit.

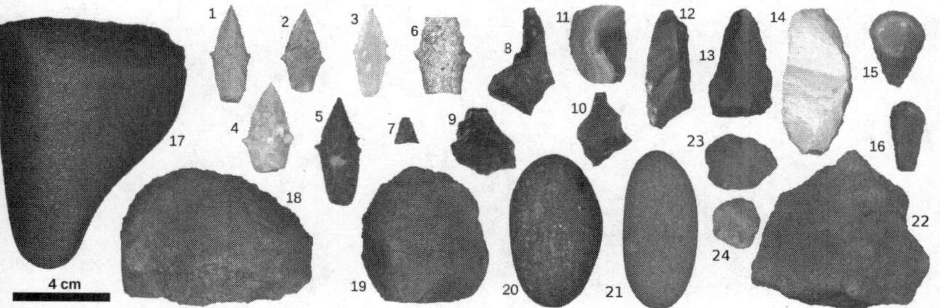

A 9,000-year-old twenty-four-piece hunting toolkit belonging to a female hunter, discovered at the Wilamaya Patjxa archaeological site in Peru in 2018. She is referred to as 'star' by today's local residents—perhaps in part because of all of the media attention that her discovery has attracted. Initially, the young woman was presumed to be male (it has long been standard practice to assume that anyone buried with weapons was male). This and similar such discoveries have fuelled an ongoing debate within the archaeological community on the degree to which hunting was a predominantly male activity.

Terracotta figurine depicting a woman grinding grain (on the right), an activity which typically occupied women for 2–3 hours a day. The figurine, which was discovered in Cyprus and dates to the middle of the first millennium BCE, highlights women's central role as food producers in economic history.

Copy of an ancient Egyptian tomb painting depicting women weaving. The tomb—that of Khnumhotep—dates to c.1897–1878 BCE and the image was copied by Norma de Garis Davies in 1931 as part of the Metropolitan Museum's Egyptian Expedition. Throughout human history, cloth production has been depicted as women's work.

Statue of a wet nurse for an elite household dating to c.1900 BCE. The statue was discovered in the historic region of Anatolia and the wet nurse's name is inscribed as Sitsnefru.

Ancient Greek terracotta vase ('lekythos'), dating t c.550–530 BCE, showing women weaving cloth on vertical loom. While women's economic activity wa heavily circumscribed in ancient Greece, the manufactu of cloth was—as elsewhere—considered women's wo Even in the heavens, women were associated with clo Athena was considered an expert weaver.

Gold coin from the reign of Shajar al-Durr—the slave girl, purchased by the Islamic caliph, who became the first female ruler of Islamic Egypt. Al-Durr played a pivotal role during the Crusades, negotiating a sizeable ransom payment for the release of the captured French king, Louis IX. The coin was produced in 1250 CE.

Painted sarcophagus of an Etruscan woman—Seianti Hanunia Tlesnasa—dating to c.150–140 BCE. Roman women were far less restricted in their economic lives than the women of ancient Greece and were, as a result, far more visible both publicly and in material culture.

Empress Wu—the daughte of a timber merchant whc rose to become the first an only empress of China. Sh reigned from 690–705 CE at the time of the Tang Dynasty, an era that provided the backdrop to China's subsequent 'Golden Age'. The image appears on a hanging scro painting dating to the Min Dynasty (1368–1644).

Handscroll painting of women making silk in their own home, juggling childcare wit cloth manufacture. Silk was the currency of the 'Silk Road', making women's cloth production not only vital for the Chinese economy but also for the global economy. The image was painted by Wang Juzheng in the early eleventh century CE.

Historical depiction of La Malinche with Hernán Cortés from Diego Muñoz Camargo's *History of Tlaxcala* c.1585. Notice that La Malinche is placed at the centre of the image, towering over Cortés, in recognition of her role in the Spanish conquest of the Americas.

Business card ('trade card') of Ann Askew, boot and shoemaker, dated 1735. Note that it dates to a period when buildings were still commonly identified by signs rather than numbers.

'My wife is a woman of mind', satirical print from *The Comic Almanack*, 1847, indicative of the way that learned women were mocked in the media.

Woman working in a coal mine in Halifax, England.

Women at work in a Manchester cotton mill in 1851. Manchester was a heartland of the British Industrial Revolution, during which time Manchester became known as 'cottonopolis'. Women comprised sixty percent of the workforce in Manchester's cotton mills.

Bengali women at work in a cotton ginning factory, preparing raw cotton to make it suitable for spinning, under the supervision of British men.

Ching Shih, the sex worker turned pirate who amassed a fleet of ships that controlled trade in the South China Sea (from the publication *History of Pirates of all Nations*, 1836). By 1805, Shih's fleet outnumbered China's Navy by three boats to one. After reaching an amnesty with China's emperor, the fleet was absorbed by the Chinese state and Shih was made 'Lady by Imperial Decree'.

Efunroye Tinubu (Madam Tinubu), the Nigerian businesswoman who traded tobacco, salt, slaves and ammunitions via the port of Lagos before being exiled by the British. Tinubu was one of the many female traders of West Africa who came face-to-face with European colonialists in the nineteenth century.

Russian Revolutionary Poster which reads: 'Emancipated Woman—Build Socialism!' Women workers—depicted in fields and in factories—featured highly in the propaganda posters commissioned within the USSR.

American World War Two Poster published in New York in 1944 depicting a man and woman in conversation during a lunch break.

Women care workers protesting poor pay and working conditions at a rally in 2015 in New York City for a $15 living minimum wage. Notice the banner and placards which read 'invisible no more'.

CHAPTER 9

FACTORY HANDS, MINERS AND MAIDS

THE WOMEN OF THE INDUSTRIAL AGE

IN THE MIDDLE OF THE EIGHTEENTH CENTURY, ASIA REMAINED the centre of the global economy. While Europe was on the rise, having been behind for millennia it was still far from eclipsing its Eastern rivals. China and India produced over a half of the world's manufactured goods, supplying homes across the globe with everything from delicate porcelain to fine fabrics.[1] By the nineteenth century, however, the British economy had been transformed from rags to riches. Having produced a mere two percent of the world's manufactured goods in 1750, by 1880 it was responsible for a quarter of global industrial output—a major achievement for a small island on the periphery of what had historically been the world's least economically consequential continent.[2] In present-day terms, Britain's achievement could only be matched if Madagascar—an island off the coast of what is today considered the world's poorest continent—became the world's richest nation. Barring this eventuality, Britain's rise from poverty to prosperity will remain the most unlikely economic success story in economic history.

The answer to the question of how Britain performed its economic miracle is easy to find in the history books. It was the famous 'Industrial Revolution': a revolution that shifted production out of homes and workshops and into factories and mills, equipped with new technologies. Powered first by water wheels and later by steam engines, these giant workplaces could produce manufactures on a scale never previously seen. It was the time when Manchester became known for its cotton factories, Sheffield became known for its steel foundries, and Newcastle and Wales became known for their coal mines. It was the time of Queen Victoria and Charles Dickens—when smoky, busy streets were filled with everything from chimney sweeps and girls selling matchsticks to men in top hats and ladies in crinoline gowns. And once Britain had finished industrialising, Industrial Revolutions followed in Europe and the United States. Ever since, Western incomes have travelled along an upward trajectory, albeit with some bumps along the way.

Exactly *why* Britain industrialised and, with it, how Europe and indeed the West became global economic leaders has been pondered by generation on generation of historians. Whilst big debates continue to rage, the different sides are united in one vital failing: their neglect of women. Accounts of the Industrial Revolution consist almost purely of men—of the famous male scientists, engineers and factory owners whose statues, cast in bronze, bask in sunshine in the centre of Britain's biggest cities. This chapter fills the gaping hole in this story, revealing the numerous inconspicuous as well as conspicuous ways in which women powered industry forward. As we will see, it was through the invisible hands of ordinary women—through the numerous individual decisions that women made about work, family and fertility—that the British economy was guided towards the world's first Industrial Revolution. While not deliberately stoking the fire of an economic transformation, women nonetheless provided businesses with the incentives, funds, skills and political backdrop needed for industrialisation to be both possible and profitable. Without the freedom of ordinary women, the Industrial Revolution would, quite simply, never have happened. Britain would still today be one of the world's poorest—as opposed to one of the richest—economies. And it is, equivalently, the lack of women's freedom that similarly explains why so many parts of the world remain poor today.

Why Britain was the first country to have an Industrial Revolution has remained a much-debated mystery for a simple reason: the secret ingredient that is women's freedom has been ignored, and it was this that propelled Britain from economic backwater to industrial giant.

ORDINARY WOMEN

Industry was not new, either to Britain or to this period of history. But industrial production had long depended on manpower—or, in the case of cloth, womanpower. Industry was extremely labour-intensive. This meant that states and empires had grown their industrial base by simply setting more people to work, whether in the home or in workshops. Increasing prosperity came either from using more people or from people working longer and harder, with the rewards typically being captured by those in positions of power. But there was a natural and inevitable limit to how much you could grow an economy in this way. After all, once people were working every waking hour, they could not humanly produce any more. While growing the population, either through conquest or by taking control of women's wombs, gave elites greater numbers of people to exploit, it was not without consequence. And, once again, an economic ceiling was reached once all of the additional people were working at their limits. Of course, occasional developments in technology enabled people to break through this barrier and produce more, as was the case with Huang Dao Po's cotton spinning machine, which spread across China in the thirteenth century, creating a golden age for China's economy. But once everyone had learned to use the new technology, a ceiling was once again reached. Production expanded up to the level made possible by the new technology but then stagnated at that new higher level. For economic growth to be continuous—for production and so incomes to move ever upwards—technological change itself therefore needed to be faster and more continuous.

The shift from superstition to science—a shift that we explored in the last chapter—helped to lay the foundations by creating an ever-growing pool of knowledge that could inspire ongoing technological development. But for industry to develop into a technologically driven powerhouse, this science needed to escape the 'ivory towers' of universities and scientific societies and to make its way into the workplaces where the physical production of everything from cloth to ships took place. New ideas that simply sit on the pages of books do little to affect the world beyond the library. Only once science became of practical use to manufacturers was it, in other words, capable of improving productivity and creating a takeoff in economic growth. For this to happen, producers needed four things: they needed to be able to see the potential profit from developing and using new technologies in the production process; they needed to have access to skilled people who could understand technology and turn ideas into working machines; they needed access to financial funds that could help cover the costs of new machines; and they needed to feel free from the despotic rulers who had long stripped ordinary people of the rewards that came through private enterprise. In Britain, all of these boxes were ticked, and that was, as we will see, in large part thanks to the seeds that had been sown by the relative freedom of everyday women.

While Karl Marx famously saw low wages as the driver of capitalist growth, it is higher—not lower—wages that provide the all-important push for businesses to want to mechanise.[3] After all, why bother building better machines if workers are cheaply and abundantly available to carry out tasks instead? If you can hire a woman to spin cotton by hand for a pittance, why spend money inventing a machine—and the associated water-wheel technology—that does the spinning for you? If paying someone to hand sew a dress is a bargain, why spend time developing the sewing machine? Given that developing machines is inevitably costly, only if workers are relatively expensive does it make sense to look for ways to produce more using something other than bare hands. While people might of course choose to invent for their own amusement—or to impress their friends in the salon—invention only becomes commonplace once businesses can see a profit in mechanising. That is why the Industrial Revolution did not occur in a part of the world where wages were low, but instead in a part of the world where wages—following the devastation of the Black Death—remained at a higher level.[4] In northwestern Europe, the smaller families that resulted from ordinary women going out to work and, in response, marrying later in life—and, indeed, from some women choosing not to marry at all—helped to prevent population growth from spiralling out of control as it recovered from the plague.[5] The result was that in England and Holland, the higher wages that followed the Black Death were not just temporary but were sustained, whereas in both southern Europe and in Asia, the population grew faster and, with it, wages trended continually downwards. The result was that in the eighteenth century, wages in these other parts of the world were only a third of the level they were at in the fifteenth century.[6] That was not, however, the case in Britain, where they remained high. The fortunes of the more historic centres of the global economy were, in other words, undermined by a society in which women had no control over work, marriage and fertility. Ordinary women were instead condemned to a life in which they were married off young, producing one baby after another, with absolutely no choice in the matter.

The fact that men and women in northwestern Europe were earning more than their peers elsewhere in the world—and, with it, had smaller families to feed—also meant that they could better afford to invest in their children's education and to save (including in Priscilla Wakefield's penny bank), which provided the skills and the funds that businesses needed to grow. Vocational skills—of a kind that could be acquired through an apprenticeship—were just as important as the kind of formal education that could be gained at universities, and in fact proved to be instrumental to the development of industrial machinery.[7] Literacy, as we have seen, spread in the centuries running up to the Industrial Revolution, as did the publication of educational books and manuals aimed at a general audience. But none of this was free: families had to pay for their children to learn to read and write and the printed word cost money, as did apprenticeships. The combination of higher wages and smaller families meant that families could, however, better afford this in northwestern Europe compared with elsewhere, thereby providing the workforce with sufficient skill. By 1700, one in four young adult men in England had completed an apprenticeship.[8] And, while in many parts of the world women were locked out of formal apprenticeships, in Britain, the Netherlands and France, young women were also taken on as apprentices, and so could similarly be found hard at work in the 'skilled' trades, working as everything from goldsmiths to glove-makers.[9] Between the 1640s and 1660s, the number of female apprentices in London doubled.[10] As shops were rebuilt and as businesses reopened after the 'Great Fire of London', women as well as men were invited to become tenants and fill the vacancies. Like young men, young women were typically apprenticed between the ages of fourteen and sixteen for a period of between three and seven years, and many moved to London to take up an apprenticeship from rural counties.[11] This would have been unthinkable for young women in China, India and the Middle East. By the eighteenth century, London was home to, amongst others, 250 female printers, 165 female silversmiths and more than 500 female hat-makers.[12] While women were outnumbered by men in the skilled professions, they were nonetheless visible and they were just as capable. Even where women were not contributing *directly* to the skill base of the economy by being apprenticed, it was through the decisions they made about work, family and fertility that families in general were in a strong (and small) enough position to educate or apprentice at least some of their members.

Of course, all of the budding tradespeople and entrepreneurs did not want to live in fear of a government that might unfairly extract the value that they created or regulate against the development and adoption of new technology. If the monarch or the mafia threatens to strip you of your wealth, or takes the side of those who will lose out from the diffusion of new technologies, breaking new ground becomes impossible. It is for understanding the importance of political institutions in this sense that Daron Acemoglu, Simon Johnson, James A. Robinson and Douglass North have won Nobel Prizes in Economics. However, the role of women in creating more democratic and capable political institutions has typically been overlooked. Authoritarian political institutions are, as we noted in the last chapter, rooted in authoritarian family forms. It is within the family that we each have our first taste of life—that we are each 'socialized'. Where families are patriarchal—where women have little voice and where an 'elder' dominates—we learn to respect authority and to keep our mouths shut. Status trumps merit. Where families are more consensual—where men and women are more equal and where young people are allowed a voice—we become socialised into democratic norms from an early age. We get used to having a say, to forming an opinion through discussion and debate and to holding others to account. We speak up rather than shut up. Power and voice within the household act as a model for wider institutions. It means that democratic government only truly thrives where there are democratic family structures that nurture democratic citizens from a young age. It shouldn't be too surprising, therefore, that democracy not only took root but persisted in northwestern Europe, where young women's entry into the paid workforce challenged families, creating a shift away from the kind of patriarchal family structures that were found in Asia and the Middle East.

Whilst women in northwestern Europe were still far from equal to men, it was their *relative* freedom compared with other more distant parts of the world that provided Britain—and its nearby neighbours—with a secret weapon. It created a society in which wages were high enough to incentivise businesses to mechanise; it helped ensure that businesses had the requisite access to savings and skills; and, it kept the democratic transition on track, helping private enterprise to flourish. Women's freedom provided Britain with something that the world's historic economic centres lacked. And that is why Britain found itself in the running for the world's first Industrial Revolution.[13]

HOW WOMEN CUT THEIR CLOTH

'Whoever says Industrial Revolution says cotton'. Those were the words of the historian Eric Hobsbawm.[14] The cotton industry was at the heart of Britain's industrial transformation, leading the way in the modernization of the process of production and the development of new technology. Given the centrality of cloth manufacture to economic history, this shouldn't be all that surprising. In almost every one of history's economic golden ages, the production of cloth—whether silk, linen or cotton—has been of prime importance. The world's leading economies depended on it. In the eighteenth century, Chinese cloth was still the most prized across the world. From exquisite silk curtains to the beautiful gowns that were tended to by an army of domestic servants, Britain's finest country homes were filled with the delicate cloth produced by women across Asia. The Chinese state promoted the motto 'Men plough, women weave', and, in order to keep their daughters metaphorically chained to their spinning wheels, some families—as we have seen—chose to bind their feet.[15] In the Chinese region of Jiangnan, a woman's weaving could generate more money for a family than a man's agricultural exertions.[16] In neighbouring Korea, women made a similarly sizeable contribution to their households; so much so that Korean law forbade men from divorcing wives whose earnings were central to the survival of the family.[17] But, perhaps more than anywhere else in the eighteenth century, India was fast becoming known as the land of 'chintz', producing brightly and tastefully printed cotton cloth to suit all tastes and all budgets.[18] In Nagpur, younger women harvested raw cotton and older women spun it into yarn.[19] Chintz was taking Europe by storm.

English cloth makers had long struggled to compete not just with Asia but with their own European neighbours, including Italy. Britain was better known for farming the sheep that supplied the raw wool used by foreign cloth makers than it was for producing its own high-quality fabric. But by the nineteenth century, the tables had turned: Britain was no longer a covetous importer of foreign cloth; it was clothier to the world. By the 1830s, cotton cloth constituted a half of all of Britain's exports.[20] Quarry Bank Mill, on the outskirts of Manchester in northern England, was one of the cotton mills that helped to lead the way. It was the product of a joint husband and wife team, Samuel and Hannah Greg.

Hannah had benefitted greatly from the educational and literary seeds sown by the women we met in the last chapter. In 1783 she was sent from her family home in Liverpool to boarding school in Stoke Newington, London. Her school was run by two sisters—Elizabeth and Sarah Crisp—and occupied a grand building in the middle of large gardens, which appealed to Hannah's love of nature. Mary Wollstonecraft's own school for girls would have been close by.[21] As a hotbed of intellectual thought, Stoke Newington was well suited to Hannah's academic temperament. While she didn't much enjoy her classes in 'deportment' (which involved learning how to walk like a lady), she was a star pupil when it came to the arts and the sciences.[22]

The same year that Hannah left Liverpool, Samuel Greg—originally from Belfast—was scouring the wet and windy countryside in northern England for a suitable location in which to build a cotton mill.[23] Since the age of eight, Greg had lived with an uncle in Manchester, who ran a cloth-merchant business, importing yarn from Belfast and organising for it to be woven into cloth by cottagers in the farming communities in and around Manchester. Greg inherited the family business after his uncle died, and saw the potential in moving from cottage production to factory production.[24] His inspiration was Richard Arkwright, who had just built a successful cotton-spinning mill equipped with his own patented spinning machine—powered by a water wheel—that transformed raw cotton into spun yarn at a rate never previously seen. With the patent on Arkwright's spinning technology due to lapse, Greg was keen to find a fast-flowing river along which he could build a duplicate mill. On the River Bollin—in a wooded valley just outside Manchester—Greg found a farm up for lease, on whose land he set to work building his cotton mill and offering jobs as spinners to the local farming workforce.[25] It was a doubly good time for Greg to begin his business venture, as the cessation of hostilities with the newly independent 'United States of America' brought an end to the war-related trade embargoes: raw cotton could now be imported into Britain via the port of Liverpool.

Liverpool was Hannah's hometown and, just as Greg's business was starting to turn a profit, and after four years of being away at boarding school, she was returning to the port city, ready to build her life as an independent young woman. Meeting Greg over supper at the home of a mutual friend, Hannah was entranced by his conversation, and in her diary writes of how she 'sat by him all the evening'.[26] Over the weeks and months that followed, they danced, attended musical recitals together and sat side by side to read the latest books on philosophy. Their developing relationship would have been impossible in China, India and the Middle East. In November 1789, a year after their first meeting, they tied the knot.[27] It was, perhaps, a miracle that the wedding festivities took place at all, as Hannah and Samuel had spent the previous weeks arguing over his (lack of) attendance at chapel.[28] Theirs was a spirited relationship. Hannah's diary entries veer between recounting long, happy conversations and 'disputes' about everything from Greek plays to the purpose of charity.[29] Hannah was a humanitarian and believed in using her middle-class privilege to help others—and in bringing Greg onboard with the idea.[30] This was clearly a relationship of equals, one in which Hannah was able to have her voice heard. Not only did the couple connect on an intellectual level, but cloth-making was in the blood of both bride and groom.

Hannah's father—who had died when she was only eleven—came from a family of Scottish cloth merchants who moved to the booming port of Liverpool, where ships were constantly coming and going, creating new opportunities for trade.[31] While Liverpool had ballooned in size in response to Britain's growing involvement in the world economy, nearby Manchester—which Greg had made home—saw itself as the future. Hannah's brothers-in-law had, like Greg, spotted their own opportunities in this budding 'cottonopolis', which gave them plenty to talk about over family dinners. Their marriage brought not only potential business contacts but also a sizeable injection of cash from Hannah's side which allowed Greg's Quarry Bank Mill to transform itself into one of the most profitable cotton-spinning mills in the country.

Standing five-storeys tall, each storey consisting of numerous multipaned Georgian windows, the mill was filled with the thundering sound of the latest spinning machines. Each machine could spin at least fifty threads at a time and the spinning was automated on such a scale that a single spinner could look after two machines at once. This meant that productivity was a hundred times that of traditional spinning, which in Britain as elsewhere consisted of women at their spinning wheels in their own homes. Compared with this 'cottage industry', the cotton mill—built on a scale that could accommodate the sizeable new machines—created a stark separation between work and home. Working life became much less flexible and much more intense. Since the rivers that drove water wheels were faster-flowing in the winter, the working day was—ironically—longest in the dark cold winters. People worked six days a week—for twelve hours a day—leaving one day of rest for attending church, playing sports or gardening.[32] Inside, mills were noisy places—filled with the clunks and clangs of machinery. The noise was so loud that if spinners needed to talk to one another—such as to ask a fellow spinner to look after their machines while they took a toilet break—they had to use sign language. The air was thick with cotton dust and the atmosphere was wet and humid, which had the advantage that it prevented the cotton from splitting.[33] The rain for which the north of England is well-known helps explain why it was in that part of the country that the cotton mills first began to develop.

For many of the workers at the Quarry Bank Mill, home life centred around the nearby village of Styal (which translates as 'the place of the secret' in Anglo-Danish), home to cottages and cobbled streets.[34] Greg's first spinner—about whom we know little aside from her name—was a local woman called Penny Chapman, who had likely spent her former days spinning from her home.[35] By the early nineteenth century, the mill had expanded to the point that it needed a workforce that went beyond local residents. So, to attract workers from further afield, the Gregs converted farm buildings—barns, thatched cottages and farmhouses—into additional homes and built rows of red-brick, two-storey, 'two-up, two-down' terraced houses to house families, with basements below for singles or couples. Each house had its own allotment—enabling every family to grow their own vegetables—and its own outside toilet.[36] The village had its own butcher, baker and brewer, and even its own shoemaker.[37] Situated even closer to the mill itself was a sizeable Apprentice House for child labourers, who constituted a half of the mill's workforce.[38] Some of the children were apprenticed to the mill by an impoverished parent or guardian. Two teenage girls—Elizabeth and Hannah Worrall—were apprenticed after their father, a shoemaker, had passed away. Another three girls—Sarah, Mary and Hannah Bowden—were apprenticed after the death of their mother.[39] Baptismal records reveal that many other children were 'illegitimate', or what were called 'base daughters'.[40]

Most of the child apprentices came not from their families but instead from workhouses—the austere institutions that housed the poorest members of society, known as paupers.[41] At a time when death and disease were commonplace and orphanages and workhouses were overflowing, local authorities paid mill owners to take children aged as young as nine off their hands, to 'train them up' to be productive workers.[42] With contracts that committed them to the mill through to their eighteenth or twenty-first birthday, these orphaned and paupered children were known as 'parish apprentices'. By 1800, ninety child apprentices worked at the mill.[43] Seventy percent of them were girls.[44] In total, the names of almost a thousand children can be found in the record books for Quarry Bank, including in stoppages ledgers (which contain details of any fines imposed on them), wages books (which include any payments for overtime) and the doctors' prescription books (which dealt with any illnesses amongst the children housed at the mill).[45]

Mechanisation leant itself to unskilled child labour. Children were allocated to simple repetitive tasks, including preparing the raw cotton, cleaning under and oiling the machines, changing bobbins and working alongside the spinners as 'piecers', tasked with twisting back together any threads that snapped in the process of being spun, all ideally while the machine continued to run at a fast pace. In return for working late from six in the morning, six days a week, the child apprentices were housed in dormitories and provided with clothing and meals. A breakfast of porridge was served in the mill—in a ten-minute morning break—and the main meal of the day, usually consisting of potatoes, seasonal vegetables and bacon, was served in a half-hour afternoon break.[46] Overtime was paid, at one pence an hour.[47] While Sunday was in theory a day off, it was occupied with lessons in the schoolroom of the Apprentice House, along with two trips to the church in nearby Wilmslow, where the rest of the congregation would have been used to seeing rows of neatly dressed apprentices in their Sunday best: straw bonnets, tied under their chin with green ribbon, and long cloaks that provided protection from the cold.[48] Hannah Greg made herself responsible for the education and medical care of the children, ensuring that a local doctor made regular visits—along with his leeches and laudanum—and that the apprentices were properly schooled on Sundays and after work on a weekday. Hannah tasked her own sons and daughters—starting with her eldest daughter, Bessy—with giving many of the lessons and, by the 1820s, employed two teachers.[49] On Christmas Day, the Gregs held a prize-giving, handing out awards (such as a Bible) for the best schoolwork and best behaviour, which formed the centrepiece of the children's Christmas party.[50]

The child apprentices were drawn not only from nearby northern districts but also from further afield, including from London and the south.[51] In fact, in 1784, Manchester authorities had ordered that no child pauper in their care should be apprenticed to a mill where children were expected to work more than ten hours a day. The workhouses of Liverpool and London were, however, happy to provide children. Many would no doubt have suffered from homesickness, and some walked all the way back to London. The fate of these child runaways—a hundred in total from 1785–1847—features in the records of Quarry Bank.[52] The Day Books of the mill include payments for advertisements for runaway children, along with travel expenses for retrieving them. Once apprehended and brought back to the mill, they were expected to pay for the costs of their own search, which could wipe out many months' worth of overtime earnings.[53] The ledgers also reveal other occasions on which children were fined, including for stealing apples from local orchards, for midwife expenses in the case of one girl who became pregnant, and even for their own funeral expenses, as was the case with Ellen Williams, who died from an infection and was buried on 1 June 1828 aged only fifteen.[54] As an alternative to monetary fines, girls are also known to have had their long hair cut off.[55] For many girls, having their head shaved was the worst form of punishment.

Despite their difficult start in life, many of the child apprentices chose to continue working at Quarry Bank as adults, often transferring from the Apprentice House into the basement apartments in Styal village.[56] Hannah Fluett and James Henshall—who went on to marry—climbed the career ladder to become, respectively, 'spinner' and mill manager.[57] Henshall had come to the attention of the Gregs for excelling during his lessons in the Apprentice House, and they paid for him to undertake additional schooling. He became the Gregs' bookkeeper and, according to his obituary, eventually 'rose to the proud position of Manager'.[58] Two female apprentices—Mary Magin and Sarah Eaton—went on to become 'overlookers', supervising the spinning rooms in the mill. Neither Mary nor Sarah married, perhaps an indication that—unlike Henshall—they faced the choice of a family or a career.[59]

In response to cotton mills like the Gregs', the population of Manchester quadrupled in the last quarter of the eighteenth century, from only 22,500 people to 84,000 people.[60] By 1825, Manchester was home to 104 cotton spinning mills.[61] Women were central to Manchester's cotton industry, constituting sixty percent of the workforce.[62] Cloth-making had—as we have seen in previous chapters—long been the business of women and girls, but before the emergence of cotton mills, it was often a family affair and production mostly took place within the home. As spinning—and then weaving—moved into the mechanised workplace, opportunities for women in the 'cottage' industry sharply collapsed, leaving many in hardship.[63] Through industrialisation, women had been transformed into wage labourers.

THE NEW ENGLAND

In 1790, America was a predominantly rural part of the world. Nineteen of every twenty people lived on farms and the city of New York was home to no more than 33,000 inhabitants, making it smaller than London had been three centuries beforehand.[64] In the decades that followed, the American economy was transformed. Not only did it repeat Britain's industrial success, but it took things a step further, fuelled by the fact that due to shortages of workers, wages were even higher, which pushed mechanisation to the heights of 'mass production'.[65] By the middle of the nineteenth century, cotton mills could be found in abundance on both sides of the Atlantic. Lowell—in New England—became known as the 'Manchester of

America'. From the tender age of ten, a girl by the name of Harriet Robinson worked in one of Lowell's cotton factories, and her autobiography, titled 'Loom and Spindle', gives us a glimpse of her life as a 'mill girl'.[66]

Harriet was fatherless and new to the town of Lowell. A couple of years before, in 1831, her mother had been widowed, and in order to support Harriet and her siblings, she had opened a grocery store in Boston, selling everything from striped candy to kindling wood. Harriet fondly remembered the candy. Sadly, the business failed, and so the family moved—by canal boat—from Boston to Lowell, where Harriet's mother found work as the housekeeper of a boarding house, looking after the numerous factory hands descending on the town. The family's decision to move to Lowell wasn't accidental: Harriet's aunt—also a widow—already ran a boarding house in the town, and it was she who encouraged the family to make the move. Since the Lowell cotton mills employed young women from across the whole of New England, who were therefore in need of a home in the town, boarding houses were big business.[67]

Unlike Harriet, many young women had come to the town after reading adverts or attending a recruitment event in their local hotel: '75 Young Women / From 15 to 35 years of age / Wanted to Work in the Cotton Mills' began one advert, going on to offer a starting salary of a dollar a week plus board and a minimum employment of a year.[68] The Lowell to Boston railroad, which opened soon after the family arrived—in 1835—was one of the first railways in North America, serving those wanting to move into the expanding cotton district, as well as the cotton mill owners who had raw materials and finished cloth to get to and from their factories.[69] Stagecoaches would also have been a familiar sight in the town. While the early workforce were virtually all American-born women, the town increasingly attracted migrants from England and Ireland, many of whom initially arrived to help build the expanding town and lived in shanties.[70]

Records for one of Lowell's mills—the Hamilton Company—reveal that most women entered their employment between the ages of fifteen and nineteen and, as the daughters of farmers, had made the journey from farm to factory.[71] Harriet started work at the younger age of ten. She worked first as a 'little doffer', removing bobbins from spinning machines, and later as a 'drawing-in girl', sitting on a high stool, hook to hand, drawing out the numerous threads ready for the weavers to weave under and over them.[72] Her first weekly pay cheque was two dollars (which was what an overseer could earn in a day), and she worked from five in the morning until seven in the evening, after which she attended evening classes so as to continue her schooling.[73] Only in 1842 did the state limit the hours of work for children to ten hours a day.[74] In her autobiography, Robinson acknowledges the toll this took: 'it has taken nearly a lifetime for me to make up the sleep lost at that early age. But in every other respect it was a pleasant life'.[75] In her own words, 'I wanted to earn money like the other little girls'.[76] This wasn't an exaggeration. Women and girls were vital to the economy of Lowell, so much so that, in 1843, a half of all depositors at the Lowell Institution for Savings were women, contributing a third of all deposits.[77] In the stories they wrote for Lowell's mill girls' magazine—*The Lowell Offering*—young women took pride in their ability to send money home to their families, whether to help widowed mothers or younger siblings.[78] The personal letters of one mill girl—Anna Mason, writing to her family—reveal how much she missed her parents: 'I want to see you all very much but I am making good wages now and if I go home I see no way of earning anything through the spring'. She was earning four dollars a week and, having previously tried a stint as a teacher closer to home, tells her parents that she had decided not to return to teaching as it paid less than her factory work in Lowell.[79] Teaching was, at this time, the profession of choice for young women who wanted to stay close to home, but the proportion of women in New England who taught for a living began to fall as more and more women were pulled into cloth production in the course of the nineteenth century.[80]

The more cotton the Lowell factories spun, the more it in turn created a demand for weaving. Initially, this acted as a spur to traditional 'cottage' cloth production in New England's farming districts, as was also the case in the north of England.[81] New England middlemen such as the firm Jillson's of Richmond purchased machine-spun thread from the factories and arranged for it to be woven into cloth in a 'putting out' system that connected the cotton towns and the surrounding countryside. Anyone with a domestic loom could open an account with Jillson's that supplied them with thread and paid them for the cloth that they wove with it. In the 1820s, forty-two percent of Richmond's residents had at some point woven cloth for Jillson's. Most were farmers or the daughters of farmers. The average person on Jillson's accounts wove 108 yards for them every three months, which would have taken around two or three days a week.[82] What Jillson's—and others like them—offered was therefore a flexible form of work that could be carried out alongside other types of rural work. However, by the 1830s, weaving as well as spinning had been mechanised, creating great hardship for handloom weavers.[83] The earnings of rural weavers plummeted by a third in New England and—on both sides of the Atlantic—women either had to migrate into the towns to take up factory work or find alternative types of 'outwork', which included braiding palm leaves or straw into straw hats, picking up a needle to stitch premade cloth into gloves, shirts or dresses, seaming stockings or 'finishing' lace that had been made on long runs by mechanised machines.[84] Mechanisation created 'winners' and 'losers' on the job front, and required constant adaptation. Key to ensuring that industrialisation did not run out of steam was, therefore, making sure that those who lost out from new technology did not stand in the way of its development and diffusion. In Italy, unlike in Britain and the United States, new spinning and weaving machines were highly regulated, with an accompanying rhetoric of saving traditional manufacture and preserving quality. The more hands-off ('laissez-faire') approach taken by policymakers in Britain and the US made them resilient to the lobbying power of 'traditional' business, which meant that technological progress did not come to a standstill—that everyone in society had to adapt in order to keep up. Women with the least family responsibilities, primarily younger unmarried women, could make the most of the opportunities on offer, as could married men who left their wives and children behind in rural areas while they went in search of new jobs. Sadly, those lumbered with childcare—producing the workforce of the future—were the least mobile and so least able to adapt. Just as today, the unequal distribution of family responsibilities fuelled the inequalities that arose in the process of 'creative destruction'.

SLAVE LABOUR

Along the entire supply chain, from plantation cotton pickers to spinners, weavers and dressmakers, cloth-making was an industry that relied on female labour. Wool had historically been the raw material of choice for British cloth makers; raw cotton, when used, had been imported from India and Egypt, but Samuel Greg pioneered the importation of American-plantation-grown raw cotton, via the port of Liverpool. He also inherited plantations from his uncle. Some of Greg's closest business associates in the cotton industry also owned shares in cotton plantations.[85] American-grown cotton provided the raw material of choice for the Industrial Revolution on both sides of the Atlantic, transforming the southern half of the United States into a cotton kingdom.[86] Between 1790 and 1860, production grew from just 3,000 bales a year to more than four million bales.[87] The majority of this cotton was produced on slave plantations in the American South. While women were more likely to feature amongst the enslaved than amongst plantation owners, Eliza Lucas Pinckney ran a plantation in South Carolina on behalf of her father, and became famous for cultivating and popularising the indigo plant, which supplied cloth makers with indigo dye.[88] By 1865, the slave population amounted to four million people, most of whom had been born into slavery, making them several generations removed from their ancestors who had first crossed the Atlantic in chains.[89] While slaves were permitted to form families—as this conveniently aided the production of the next generation of slaves—a half of all slave families in the Upper South were subsequently torn apart by a spouse—or a child—being sold on to a new master to work in cotton plantations in the Deep South.[90] One in three marriages were forcibly brought to an end in this way.[91] Whether directly through their productive efforts or indirectly through their reproductive labour, slave women supplied the raw material on which the cotton industry was dependent.

Black women were not only central to the production of raw cotton, they were also visible at the opposite end of the industry: turning cloth into the most fashionable dresses of the day. Elizabeth Keckley, born into slavery in Virginia, went on to become the most favoured dressmaker of American high society. When the family to which she was enslaved faced financial difficulty, they planned to hire out her elderly mother—Aggy—as a domestic servant to other white families, pocketing the cash. Elizabeth objected: 'My mother, my poor aged mother, go among strangers to toil for a living! No, a thousand times no!'[92] In her place, she offered—in what little spare time she had—to use her self-taught skills as a seamstress to make gowns for white society. Her dresses were much admired. While the family to whom she was enslaved benefitted greatly from her business acumen, Elizabeth remained enslaved. It was only by borrowing money from society ladies that she was able to purchase her freedom. On 13 November 1855, her Mistress signed the emancipation papers: 'Know all men that I, Anne P. Garland, of the County and City of St. Louis, State of Missouri, for and in consideration of the sum of $1200, to me in hand paid this day in cash, hereby emancipate my negro woman Lizzie, and her son George'.[93] While it took Elizabeth some years to pay off her debt, she was, at last, able to use her talents for her own benefit. But even so, life was harsh; despite being a free woman, she needed to obtain a work permit—and find a white person who could attest that she was no longer enslaved—in order to take her business to Washington. It was here, though, that she took her next big step into high society: at eight a.m., on the day after President Lincoln's inauguration, she was invited to the White House to take the measurements of the First Lady. As Keckley writes in her memoirs, 'I became the regular modiste of Mrs. Lincoln'.[94]

As the American economy expanded, it began to reach out into the wider world. In 1853, the US Navy sent four gunboats to Japan's capital city of Edo (present-day Tokyo), insisting that the country open up to American trade. In response to what was seen as a national humiliation, the shogun—the military dictatorship that had ruled Japan since medieval times—was ousted and imperial leadership restored under Emperor Meiji. This new regime was determined to stand up to Western intrusion, and central to their plan was making a concerted effort to grow the economy, to place it on an equal footing with Britain and America. That in turn meant modernising textile production: shifting away from the traditional home-based production and towards Western-style factory production. Silk was the first sector to mechanise. Silk mills were located in rural regions, where silkworms could be bred and harvested. Cocoons would be dropped into near-boiling water, with girls reaching in—bare handed—to lift them out, peeling off a thread and placing it on a spool, which was rotated by hand. Mechanisation replaced hand rotation with mechanical movement, creating a more even turn and finer silk, but the removal of cocoons from near-boiling water by hand remained. As the industry expanded, recruiters travelled far and wide, scouring the countryside for families with teenage daughters, offering fathers a sign-on bonus; for many families, this 'advance payment' comprised the largest part of their annual cash income. The girls themselves received between five and fifteen cents a day for up to eighteen hours of labour, a large part of which they spent on food.[95]

After silk, cotton spinning was the next trade to industrialise in Japan, and required less skill on the part of the women and girls involved. Once again, fathers would sign recruitment papers which committed their daughters to between one and two years at a time. With little or no say in it themselves, the girls were sent away from their homes to live on site at the mill, where they worked twelve-hour shifts, unable to leave until they had worked off the advance received by their family. To make best use of their machinery, the mills ran twenty-four hours a day. Even the beds were put to maximum use in an effort to keep costs low and profits high: as one group of girls finished their twelve-hour shift, another would rise from their beds, which were occupied afresh by those finishing for the day.[96] This was a system of production that—as elsewhere—depended on cheap female labour: eighty percent of those working in the Japanese textile industry at the close of the nineteenth century were female, and it was women—at the Amamiya silk mill—who held Japan's first industrial strike, demanding better pay and working conditions.[97]

From Britain and America to the Far East, women's hard labours in the textile sector were vital to the survival of their families, along with the wider economy. The mechanisation of the cotton industry ushered in economic growth to a degree never previously experienced. It allowed the West to usurp the world's most historic civilisations and left the Far East in the position of having to run to catch up, starting with Japan. Having been trumped by the new Western cloth producers, the cloth-making industries of China and India were left in ruin, but lacking the high wages, skills, savings and democratic institutions that were characteristic of Britain and, increasingly, the United States, they were not yet in a position to undergo the same industrial transformation. It is, in that sense, of note that Japan led industrialisation in Asia—an island nation where the history of women's freedom was far stronger than on the mainland of Asia, albeit harmed by the spread of Confucianism from China. The associated gap in women's freedom left a significant difference between the mill girls of Britain and America and those of Japan:

while white Western women were able to keep the fruits of their labour, in Japan, the earnings of women were milked by their parents and, subsequently, by the families into which they married. Japan's journey up the international economic league tables was, as a result, far slower; it only caught up with the West towards the end of the twentieth century. The female slaves of America—hard at work in the cotton fields that produced the raw material on which Western cotton factories depended—saw no trace at all of the contribution they made. While the freedom of white women was driving forward the Industrial Revolution, it wasn't a freedom shared with Black women; though the West had in some ways made a break from the economic model of exploitation that had been employed by leading economies since ancient times, it still had a long way to go on the road to liberation. And despite what other historians have argued, this continued exploitation acted as a drag not only on the lives of slave women but also on the economy. Only once *all* women were free to make their own decisions about work and could keep the rewards of their labour would the economy reach its maximum potential.

FROM THE COAL FACE TO HOME FIRES: WOMEN'S WORKING LIVES BEYOND COTTON

> A woman employed . . . at South Biddick (was) riding up one of the pits (when) the other hook, in passing, caught her cloathes [sic]. The weight of the rope forced her out of the loop, and she fell to the bottom of the shaft.[98]

In the eighteenth century, women's names frequently appeared in mining casualty reports, including that above from the northeast of England in 1772. Women had long worked in the mining industry, carrying the coal mined by their husbands up to the surface, whether in baskets or on their backs, and then sorting, breaking and washing the coal. Mining was a system that involved all members of the family, and this was true not only in Britain but also in India and Japan.[99] Living in their own isolated communities, quite separate to the rest of society, those working in the mines had long been seen as ragged, uncivilised and beastly: 'a wilder people I never saw in England', wrote one traveller on a trip to Huddersfield.[100] However, in 1842, Britain's Royal Commission published an investigation into the conditions in the mining industry, containing visualisations of female workers that caused shock and outrage across the country. In the words of one Commissioner, 'chained, belted, harnessed, like dogs in a go-cart, black, saturated with wet, and more than half naked, crawling upon their hands and feet, and dragging their heavy loads behind them—they present an appearance indescribably disgusting and unnatural'.[101]

As demand for coal grew—in large part to fuel the steam engines that increasingly powered the cotton mills in place of their former water wheels—pits became bigger and deeper, and incorporated new technology to bring the coal from the pit face to the surface. Women's involvement in the mining industry was dwindling, but they were not yet absent from the workforce. Of the fifty-six pits in and around Manchester in 1840, where factory jobs were readily available, there were still 365 adult women employed, along with 315 girls aged between thirteen and eighteen, and 114 girls of an even younger age.[102] In Pembrokeshire (Wales), around thirty percent of adult miners were female.[103] Women tended to be in most demand in small pits with narrow passages, along which only the smallest of female figures could—on hands and knees—pull truckloads of coal the equivalent of seventeen miles a day.[104] While many pits took advantage of new technology to cart the coal, some continued—for as long as they could—to use cheap female labour. However, within months of the 1842 report, and by Act of Parliament, women (along with boys under ten) were expelled from work underground, albeit not overground. Some women disguised themselves as men in order to get direct access to the coal face, along with the higher wages that came with it,[105] but the majority were relegated to life as a coal miner's wife, unable to take full advantage of opportunities that were developing in other sectors of the economy (such as cotton) because of their domestic responsibilities. Life in a typical colliery home centred on the kitchen range, which supplied heat and hot water as well as providing cooking facilities. Laundering clothes thick with coal dust would have consumed hours at a time, as would preparing hot, calorie-rich meals for husbands and sons.[106] Damp attracted cockroaches, for which the only solution was to burn candles through the night to keep them at bay.[107] Once married, women had no choice over where they lived: just as their husbands had to follow opportunities from pit to pit, wives had to follow their husbands, packing up their belongings to move into homes that were provided by pit owners, shoddily built at minimum cost, with flagstone floors, draughty roofs, small backyards and open sewers behind.[108] Life as a housewife was neither comfortable nor easy, and rather than earning money, a woman's task became that of saving money on unnecessary expenditure.

Throughout the course of the nineteenth century, rapidly expanding heavy industries like coal mining and iron and steel production increasingly relied on male labour. This was an economy in which sweaty and muscular men with bare arms spent their days banging rivets into steel or shovelling coal into furnaces, just as Thomas Hart Benton later depicted in his 'America Today' murals, which fill a room of their own at the Metropolitan Museum of New York. Ironically, though, many occupations which required little in the way of brute strength were also dominated by men.[109] In Manchester, where women could be found in mines and factories, there was not a single female accountant or auctioneer.[110] Across Britain as a whole, and according to the 1841 census, there were 18,482 doctors, surgeons and chemists, none of whom were women. Similarly, all of the 16,291 barristers, advocates and attorneys in Britain at that time were men.[111] The situation was similar in America. In 1870, Ada Kepley became the first woman in America to receive a law degree—from Northwestern University—but was nevertheless forbidden by state law from becoming a lawyer.[112] The state and male unions colluded with one another to ensure that the best-paid jobs were reserved for men, leaving women in lower-skilled, less well-paid forms of employment.

While workers had previously been banned from unionising, in the nineteenth century the laws against trade unions (or 'combinations' as they were known then) were repealed in Britain. Using their combined power, workers—understandably—began demanding better conditions and higher pay; where a strike risked serious disruption and workers were not easy to replace, employers frequently caved in to their demands. But a common union request, amongst others, was that the employment of women was ended and that men were compensated for the loss of female earnings through being paid higher 'family wages'. In 1808, the hatters of Stockport won their fight to exclude women from hat making, as, two years later, did bookbinders. By 1820, male spinners in the cotton industry of Glasgow and Manchester had followed suit.[113] In Lancashire, male spinners went even further, insisting that no other man be employed unless he was a son, brother or nephew. In 1834, London tailors also went on strike to exclude women from their trade. As one exasperated woman exclaimed in *The Pioneer*: 'surely the men might think of a better method of benefiting themselves than that of driving so many industrious women out of employment. Surely, while they loudly complain of oppression, they will not turn oppressors themselves'.[114]

Having sown the seeds of the Industrial Revolution, women's work was now experiencing a backlash.[115] While a women's pamphlet from the previous century warned that 'none but a fool will take a wife whose bread must be earned solely by his labor and who will contribute nothing toward it herself',[116] women who worked were now increasingly seen as neglecting their families and contributing to the erosion of society's moral fabric. The 'male breadwinner model' of family life was popularised as men were cast in the role of providers and women as caregivers—the 'angels of the house'. In

1865, the managers of a Scottish paper mill announced proudly that they had a policy of not employing married women, 'to prevent the neglect of children'.[117] Whilst it became less common for married middle-class women to work, married working-class women had little choice but to continuing working, but—unlike their husbands—now found themselves working in parts of the economy that were beyond the scope of unions, which were typically more casual and less well paid. Where male breadwinners passed away, went AWOL, or were incapacitated, married women were left seriously exposed to poverty, something which led to high levels of child labour.[118] Young unmarried women of course continued to work, but, since they were increasingly locked out of more lucrative parts of the economy, domestic service provided the only real alternative to the cotton mill. By 1851, according to the English Census, forty percent of women worked as domestic servants.[119] Men, it seems, were happy to accept women working as maids and laundresses, perhaps because this was not a line of work to which they were themselves attracted. And, since it did not appeal to them, men did not consider it to be 'skilled' work, which meant that it was easily taken for granted.

In 1843, an elderly woman named Catherine Anderson, who had been residing with relatives in Scotland for the past six years, demanded retrospective payment for her domestic labours. Her relatives refused, insisting that they had been charitable towards her, and so she took them to court. The court decided in her favour and ruled that 'in all cases of this description, where there is a clear proof of service rendered and no wages paid, wages are due, unless it be made out that there is an agreement that the service is gratuitous'.[120]

By 1900, more American women worked in domestic service than in any other sector. This included twenty-five percent of American-born white women and more than forty percent of African-American and immigrant women.[121] As white middle-class women retreated into the home, they relied on lowly paid female servants to take on the drudgery of their everyday chores.[122]

SILENT INVESTORS

While white middle-class women's participation in the labour market might have been falling, their participation in capital markets was growing. By saving and investing, women were able to contribute to the economy through means other than paid work and to take a share of the proceeds that were created. Women were becoming serious investors, specialising in funding the economy's all-important infrastructure, such as the railways. The steam engine revolutionised industry by providing a new energy source, with the potential to make travel faster and cheaper; this would be of benefit not only to everyday people wishing to take day trips, go on holiday or visit family and friends, but also to businesses. The ability to transport their wares—quickly and across vast distances—transformed trade, enabling businesses to sell to customers far and wide. But first someone had to build the railways, at substantial cost. Railway companies therefore welcomed anyone who wanted to invest in their business, promising a return funded by train ticket sales once the railway lines were finished and in use. Women came to the rescue. While men might have been the ones running the railway companies and looking after the steam locomotives, by the end of the century, a third of railway investors were women.[123] Women, in other words, owned a sizeable share of the railways.

Women's investments also went well beyond railway companies. If we were to add up the value of all stocks and shares in the British stock market in the period from 1870–1902, we would find that a quarter of this wealth was in the hands of women, while a third of the money invested in government bonds also came from women.[124] The majority of female investors were unmarried women or widows. Until the 1880s, when a British woman married, anything she owned had become the property of her husband. These same restrictions had also been imported into America.[125] However, thanks to the Married Women's Property Acts—the outcome of an immense lobbying effort on the part of feminists on both sides of the Atlantic—this began to change; married women now had the right to own and control their own assets.

In America, Hetty Green, whose family owned a whaling business, amassed a fortune on the stock market, proving herself to be a talented investor.[126] She grew up around her elderly grandfather and, since his eyesight was starting to fail, was tasked as a child with reading out to him the prices of stocks and shares from the daily newspaper.[127] At the age of eight, she made her way alone into the nearest town—New Bedford, Massachusetts—where she opened a bank account with the pocket money she had started to save.[128] Priscilla Wakefield would have been proud of her fellow Quaker. This was just the start of Green's financial career: by the time she passed away in the early twentieth century, she was worth $100 million, the equivalent of $2.5 billion in today's money, making her the first female tycoon in the USA.[129] Her investments included New York and Chicago real estate, mines, railroads and government bonds.[130] She knew very well not to put all of her eggs in one basket, and she refused to act impulsively in response to the natural ups and downs of the stock market. But, rather than recognising Green's financial genius, the press disparaged her, nicknaming her the 'Witch of Wall Street'. Despite her wealth, Green lived a relatively austere life, refusing to become a 'socialite', instead enjoying time with her family and her dogs and dressing in plain black clothes.[131] When asked by a reporter what was the source of her success, she replied that it was common sense and hard work: 'I buy when things are low and nobody wants them. I keep them until they go up and people are crazy to get them. This, I believe, is the secret of all successful business'.[132]

Like Wakefield in Britain, women in America turned saving and investment into an everyday activity. In 1903, Maggie Lena Walker—the daughter of an enslaved woman—became the first Black woman to run a bank. Saint Luke Penny Savings Bank was based in Richmond, Virginia, home to what became known after the American Civil War as 'Black Wall Street'. Walker was all too aware of the way that other banks turned their noses up at the African American population, locking them out of important financial services such as insurance and saving. While the world of finance is more commonly assumed to have been dominated by men, women took it on themselves to extend banking from a wealthy minority to the underserved majority.

In the Middle East, the world of finance was also a part of the economy where women could make a difference, albeit from behind closed doors. While compared with Western women, women in the Middle East were less likely to be found taking on apprentices in workshops or serving in shops, they were able to own—and to buy and sell—the government licences (known as *gedik*) that were a requirement for all kinds of occupations. Women might have been invisible, but they were most certainly active. Married women had long owned and controlled their own assets, which typically consisted of a dowry and a half share of any inheritance. On 16 May 1800, Fatma Hanim lodged her will with an Istanbul court, making financial provision for her husband in the event of her death, indicating the types of investments that would deliver sufficient return to cover his care.[133] Women from wealthy households were expected to take a serious interest in their own investments, and many were active in real estate, both as landowners and as landlords of shops and bath houses.[134] Like women in the Middle East, finance provided a means through which women who were becoming increasingly isolated from paid work could—so long as they had the means—help to grow the economy alongside their own financial security.

WOMEN PLAYED THE DECISIVE ROLE IN THE BRITISH INDUSTRIAL Revolution. Not only did they work in cotton factories, on plantations and in mines; behind the scenes they were supplying the domestic labour (paid and unpaid) that enabled men to do their part. But even more consequential than the numerous women workers was the even greater mass of women who—through their choices about work, family and fertility—sowed the initial seeds of the economy's transformation. It was the freedoms won by ordinary women that created an economy with all of the necessary ingredients for an Industrial Revolution. It was only by building on those freedoms that Britain would see its economic growth ratchet up to an even higher level. But, as British high society spread its new ideal of the female housewife, women's economic opportunities became dangerously exposed to the whims and wishes of patriarchs and paternalists. As we will see, this was not just the case within Britain's own shores but even more so across its growing Empire.

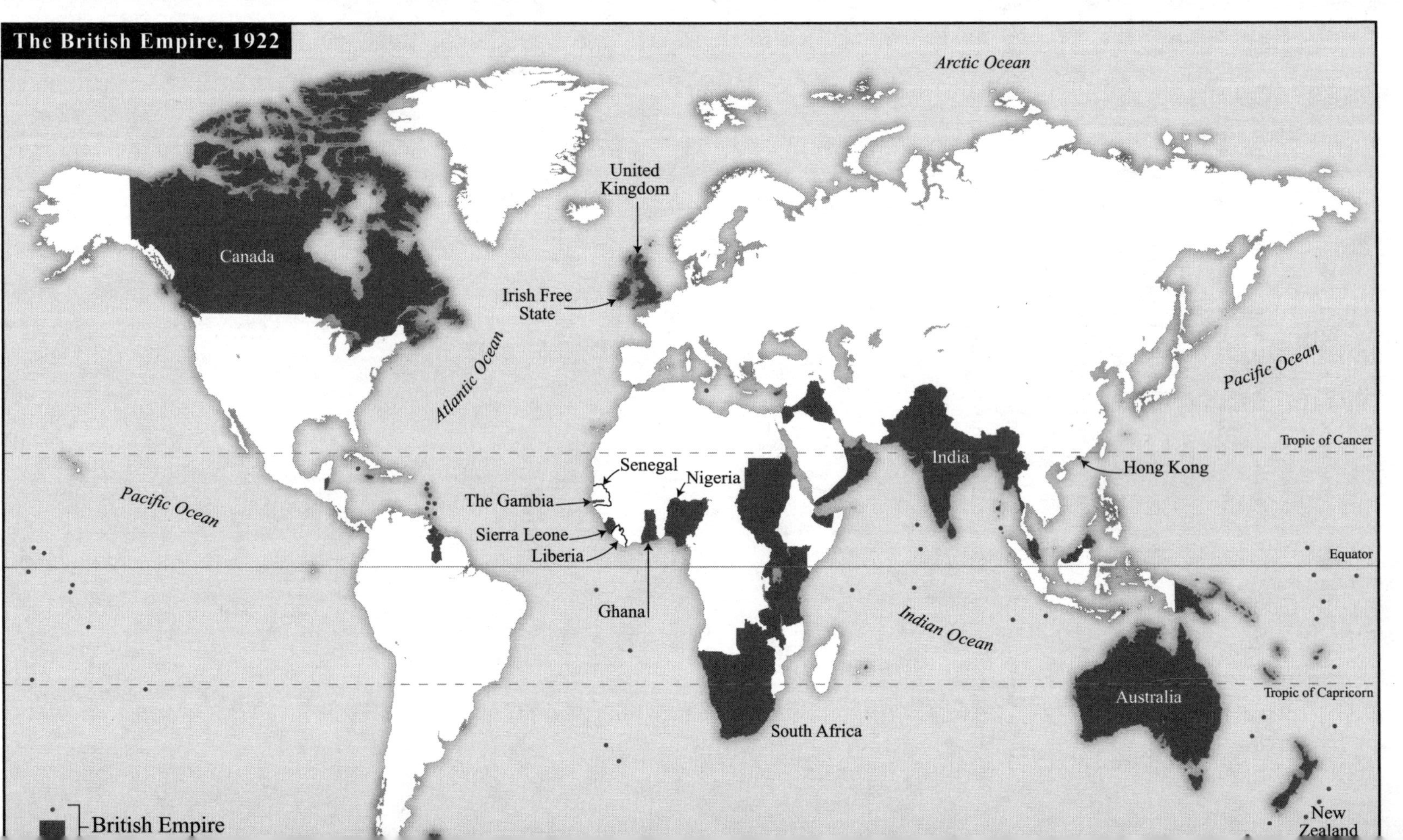

The British Empire, 1922
Arctic Ocean
Canada
United Kingdom
Irish Free State
Atlantic Ocean
Pacific Ocean
Tropic of Cancer
India
Hong Kong
Senegal
Nigeria
The Gambia
Pacific Ocean
Sierra Leone
Liberia
Equator
Ghana
Indian Ocean
Tropic of Capricorn
Australia
South Africa
British Empire
New Zealand

CHAPTER 10

ARMS DEALERS, PIRATES AND SEX WORKERS

WOMEN IN THE ERA OF COLONISATION

As the male breadwinner household became the idealised family form of the nineteenth century, it created a problem: What to do with all the women who were beyond girlhood but hadn't yet found a husband to support them financially? While working-class women went to their local cotton mill or entered domestic service, middle-class women paused for thought. Life as a maid or a cotton spinner looked far too hard and tiring. It also involved mixing with men, which risked gossip that could dent their marriage options. Working as a governess had, historically, provided a respectable form of income, including for the likes of Mary Wollstonecraft, but, as more and more schools were built, governesses increasingly found themselves out of work. It was in response that the Society for Promoting the Employment of Women emerged, to support middle-class women looking for paid work as typists, bookkeepers and printers. There were, however, still too many women chasing too few jobs. When the printer Emily Faithfull—whose *Victoria Press* was appointed printer to the Queen—advertised for an office assistant, she received more than eight hundred applications from women.[1] It was a sign of how many middle-class women were left under-employed in a society that increasingly saw them as wives and mothers.

With a shortage of job opportunities at home, well-connected women devised a solution: to send their unmarried sisters to the colonies. Using the wealth created by the Industrial Revolution, the British were in the process of building an empire, and it was one that depended not just on male colonial officials but on female settlers and missionaries. In more ways than one, the Empire provided an outlet for women who were considered surplus to requirements at home. The Female Middle Class Emigration Society and the Society for the Overseas Settlement of Women arranged overseas postings for educated and respectable ladies. By matching expatriate families in need of a governess with those searching for work, these societies channelled middle-class women to Canada, New Zealand, Australia and Africa. The British justice system did the same with working-class women, sending female convicts to the colonies as a means not only of saving on the expense of imprisoning them at home but also to populate the empire. Alongside the convicts and the governesses were the women missionaries who travelled neither through compulsion nor in search of paid work. Their aim was to 'do good' by spreading Victorian morality under the auspice of doing God's work. Their missions imposed a model of family life that cast women in domestic roles, while forcibly removing the babies of those who refused to toe the line.

While colonisation is more typically associated with men, women were actively involved—and also actively resisted the damage that was done. This chapter tells the story of nineteenth-century empire-building by placing women at its heart: as colonisers, as merchant queens, as pirates and as the people who refused to be squeezed into the Victorian straitjacket.

CONVICTS AND BABY SNATCHERS

On 13 June 1828, a thirty-year-old woman by the name of Elizabeth Coltman stood in the London docks looking up at the ship she was about to board.[2] Her brown hair was blowing in the gentle summer breeze, her face was dotted with moles and she measured just over five foot tall. Despite being in a crowd of ninety-nine women, all of whom were waiting to board the ship, she was lonely and must have feared for her future.[3] The ship—the *Competitor*—was about to embark on a 119-day voyage to the British colony in what is now Australia.[4] After months of sea-sickness, Elizabeth's next stop would be Sydney Harbour—without its modern-day opera house or the sunbeds of Bondi Beach. At that time, Sydney was a settlement comprising just 1773 dwellings, including 176 cottages and 67 wooden tenements.[5] In November 1828—the month after Elizabeth arrived—the colonial authorities took their first census. It gave the total population of New South Wales as being a mere 36,598 people, of which just under half—15,728—were convicts. The indigenous population were unrecorded.

Elizabeth and her fellow female passengers were not setting out on their Antipodean adventure by choice. They were being 'transported' as punishment for their crimes. In Elizabeth's case, it was the crime of theft, for which she was convicted at Coventry County Gaol.[6] The reason that we know so much about her—from her eye colour and complexion to her previous occupation and convictions—is that the British authorities compiled lists of everyone they transported, which the colonial authorities at the receiving end in turn used to identify their new arrivals and to assign them appropriate work. The lists were known as hulk lists. Alongside, the ship's surgeon kept a detailed record of ailments during the long voyage, from which the health of the convicts could be garnered. Through his everyday dealings with the passengers, he was also able to ascertain further details relating to each passenger's educational and occupational background and their general character, which were also properly noted down on paper.[7] Being on a convict ship didn't just come with sea-sickness; it also brought constant examination and judgement. Upon reaching Sydney, the ship had to wait in the harbour—with no one except the surgeon allowed to disembark—until all convicts had been 'minutely' examined by the muster-master and the principal superintendent of prisons.[8]

Decades before, Elizabeth would have found herself being transported to the American East Coast rather than Sydney. In addition to shipping enslaved people across the Atlantic, the British had long transported their criminal class to the American colonies, but, since the War of Independence, Australia had instead become the dumping ground for British felons. Commonly referred to as the 'dregs of society', these convicts have acquired something of a reputation in popular culture. Crime was the scourge of polite society in Victorian Britain, and the British legal system dealt with it swiftly and harshly. But, as their records reveal, convict women were not hardened criminals; they were ordinary women who had had the misfortune of falling on hard times at a point in history when the welfare system was hardly generous. Lacking 'honest' means of support, they had resorted to stealing either food or clothing simply to 'get by'.[9] The vast majority—sixty-five percent—had no prior convictions.[10] And, before turning to crime, most convict women had been employed as maids.[11] Upon arrival in the colony, these convict maids were assigned equivalent work for what was typically a seven-year sentence.[12] In return for grants of Australian land, free settlers—those who arrived by choice rather than by force, to set up their own farms and workshops—were obliged to take on a set number of convict labourers, whom they clothed, housed and fed, thereby eliminating the need for the state to cover the cost of prisoners.[13] Sheep farming created a demand not only for farm labourers but also for domestic staff who could help with cooking, cleaning and laundering for male labourers as well as for the people of the household to which they were assigned. Of the numerous convict women who arrived in the year 1828, we know from the historical records that one Elizabeth Brooks, formerly a domestic servant and nursemaid, was assigned work looking after children; one Hannah Pritchard, a washerwoman, was posted to a laundry; one Jane Dudas was assigned work as a housemaid and, after working off her servitude, continued to work for the same family, being promoted to housekeeper.[14] Of Elizabeth Coltman's own placement, we know tantalisingly little except that she was assigned to an Elizabeth Raine—most likely as a maid.[15] While in theory convict women could return home after their seven-year stint of hard labour, most remained.

Traditionally ignored in the history of Australian economic development, convict women—like female slaves in the American South, ancient Mesopotamia and the Islamic Golden Age—made a significant contribution to the economy.[16] Written-off by male commentators as work-shy and drunken harlots, convict women comprised almost sixty percent of the female labour force of Australia in 1825 and had skills and levels of literacy that rivalled women back home.[17] Only in 1828—the year that Elizabeth arrived—did the 'free' settler population start to outnumber the convict population, in part thanks to the baby-making efforts of the earlier generations of convicts.[18] According to modern-day historians, Australia's only problem may well have been that it didn't have enough women, something which slowed its economic development—specifically its textile industry—relative to Britain and America.[19]

Convicts were carefully selected by the authorities from the prison population, based on their age as well as their health and the nature of their crime.[20] Colonialists wanted women who could make a contribution in more ways than one. Most were aged between fifteen and thirty and so were not only young, fit and able to work but were also of prime childbearing age.[21] Their dual usefulness to the economy of Australia meant that women convicts could make an immediate contribution to the developing economy and then, after serving their time, settle in the territory as free women, helping to grow the population through childbearing.[22] By the 1840s, marriage and motherhood were even more idealised in Australia than in Britain, and were actively encouraged by colonial authorities, who attempted to restrict women's involvement in commerce and retailing—such as by awarding licences to men rather than women—narrowing their opportunities in the world beyond paid and unpaid domestic service.[23]

But as white settler women honed their maternal skills, they stood in judgement over the mothering capabilities of indigenous women. Some saw it as their 'maternalistic duty to rescue indigenous children from . . . a savage background and to raise them instead in a "civilised" environment'.[24] According to the missionary Annie Lock, writing to a fellow female missionary: 'The only thing I can see would [be] to get the children right away from their parents and teach them good moral, clean habits & right from wrong'.[25] The so called 'half-caste' children were the initial target for removal, but by 1911 legislation was in place in every state of Australia (with the exception of Tasmania) to support the forcible removal of indigenous children and their placement in homes and missions. Some of these homes were run by religious organisations and others were run by state governments.[26] The children became known as the 'Stolen Generations'. In America, equivalent practices were in place. Hundreds of thousands of Native American children were removed from their parents to be 'civilised' in dormitories and classrooms, where they were given new names, were punished for speaking their native language and converted to Christianity.[27]

Although indigenous women in both Australia and North America had always provided financially for their families, colonisers now instructed them in the supposed merits of the male breadwinner family. Two British writers described the life of what they referred to as the female 'Australian savage' in 1861:

> *All of the labour devolves on her, and, as no form of agriculture is practiced, this consists principally in the search for the means of life. She collects the daily food, she prepares the camp or the hut at night, she piles fire-wood, draws water, weaves baskets, carries all burdens, and bears the children on her back.*[28]

They went on to paint her as a 'wretched object', who 'when past the prime of life', is 'often deformed and crippled by excessive toil—her body bent, her legs crooked, her ankles swollen'.[29] The lives of indigenous women would, the nineteenth-century reader is led to believe, be more comfortable if they were to adopt Victorian family values. Girls were therefore removed from their mothers to be instructed in domestic service, not only as a means of making them 'useful', but because it would prepare them for carrying out the same duties—this time unpaid—once married. Settlers not only took ownership of land and resources; they dispossessed the people who previously lived upon the land of their own children.

PIRATES AHOY

Whilst Britain was exporting its convicts and missionaries to Australia, it was importing tea from China. The British had become obsessive tea drinkers, and they could afford even more of it with their growing incomes. Unlike cloth and crockery, tea was not something that Britain could produce for itself, which meant that trade with China remained of great value. The difficulty for British merchants was finding something that the Chinese wanted in return for their tea. Since China had its own cloth makers, it was not attracted to Britain's main vehicle of trade—the cloth from its cotton factories. So, the British East India Company came up with a plan: selling opium from the poppies grown in their Indian colonies, turning the British into the most notorious drug dealers in the whole of Asia. Given the addictiveness of opium, the Company was soon turning China into a nation of drug addicts. And since the drugs paid for the tea, money trumped morality.

Guangzhou, at the head of the Pearl River, was China's harbour for international trade. Known to Europeans as Canton, Guangzhou was the capital of Guangdong province—a province which runs along the southern coast of China from Vietnam to Hong Kong. It was a relatively poor region, home to the 'water people' who lived on boats and fished for their livelihood and who were seen as outcasts by land dwellers. As foreign traders flocked to Guangzhou, ocean-bearing ships displaced local fishing vessels, and crates overflowing with tea, porcelain, silk and opium replaced the baskets of fish. And with all of the sailors passing through the hot and humid city also came a profitable trade for brothel keepers. It was out of this 'den of iniquity' that Ching Shih—a sex worker turned pirate—rose to become the thorn in the side of British colonial expansion in the Far East.

Shih was born in Guangdong province around the year 1775, when China's Qing Dynasty was at the height of its power under the Qianlong Emperor.[30] Shih's early life has been described as 'shrouded in mystery and ill repute'.[31] It seems likely that she was born into poverty. China's economy was stumbling not just as a result of Britain's economic rise but, relatedly, because Chinese women lived lives that were much less free. The result was that the population was expanding fast, overwhelming the economy. As land was increasingly subdivided, leading to smaller plots, families struggled to provide for themselves. The associated deforestation—an attempt to source new land—caused flooding that hurt urban centres and harmed the trading links between the town and the country.[32] It was the inevitable consequence of a society in which ordinary women were not free to determine their own destiny: one in which women were married young, resulting in extended families that were growing in size, with few means—other than infanticide—of suppressing population growth. Women's bodies became the tool through which families attempted to overcome poverty, including by selling their daughters to brothel keepers or as concubines to elite men.[33] The social anxieties that these practices created had knock-on consequences for all women, fuelling the notion that a woman's chastity was her most valuable asset and that she therefore needed to be secluded from men. The more women's bodies became the currency of the poor, the more women were deprived of their freedoms. The result was a vicious circle through which the lack of women's freedom provoked an economic situation—one of poverty and the sale of women's bodies—which in turn fed back to support the practices that denied women their freedom in the first place.

Shih was one of the women who worked on the front line of China's growing brothel industry. By her early twenties, she was working at a floating brothel in the port of Guangzhou, where she rose up the ranks to become the brothel madam, responsible for hosting wealthy clients. Amongst her clients were not only international merchants but also local pirates.[34] Notable amongst them was Zheng Yi, who commanded the *Red Flag Fleet* that roamed the South China Sea, preying on international ships. Soon, not only were the couple sailing off into the sunset together; they were leading an explosion in pirate activity, putting fear into the minds of every European sailor en route to China.

Before Shih and Yi formed their romantic partnership, piracy on China's southern coastline was mostly disorganised and amateur, consisting of small groups of fishermen who resorted to looting during the fishing off-season. Piracy seemed so inconsequential that, in 1793, the Emperor had confidently declared that the seas were safe and empty of pirate ships. This overconfidence would leave China's authorities blind and unprepared, and—having discouraged their own merchant shipping—without a proper navy. To make matters worse, the state's heavy-handed approach to trade—which involved merchants having to apply for expensive licences—made smuggling highly profitable, thereby acting as a training ground for budding pirates. And, precisely because of the lack of free-trading opportunities, Western powers happily cooperated with anyone who could help them smuggle precious wares out of China. The stage was set for Shih and Yi.

Shih married her pirate in 1801, becoming joint commander-in-chief of his *Red Flag Fleet*. One of their first adventures was to sail to the rescue of pirates in neighbouring Vietnam, which was launching a crackdown on piracy. As captured pirates were massacred in the thousands, Shih and her husband helped to guide survivors out of

Vietnamese waters into the relative safety of the South China Sea. The loyalty this rescue plan elicited placed Shih and her husband in the perfect position to create a pirate confederacy—the 'Cantonese Pirate Coalition'—laying the foundations for the eruption in piracy in the South China Sea over the course of the decades that followed. By 1804, the coalition fleet already amounted to 400 ships and 70,000 pirates, making it one of the largest pirate confederacies ever seen on the high seas.[35] Shih helped to draw up the formal constitution, which divided pirates into six squadrons, assigned registration numbers to each pirate ship, and made each pirate leader responsible for the medical costs and pensions of their crew.[36] She effectively created her own mini-state—albeit an ocean-going one. By 1805, Shih and Yi's pirate fleet outnumbered the Chinese navy by three boats to one.[37] As the fleet continued to expand, so too did its notoriety.

With a reputation that preceded it, the confederacy was able to make a shift from looting to racketeering. Shih set up an annual passport system, allowing merchants operating in the South China Sea to pay a yearly sum to the pirate coalition in return for a protection slip that granted them safe passage. Any trader who refused to pay for their 'passport' was considered fair game for a full-blown pirate raid. Alongside this, Shih established a 'pay as you sail' system, allowing smaller traders to pay by ship, rather than purchasing a yearly passport that covered more vessels. And, to be fair to the pirates, they were true to their word: if they did board a ship, they would stand down at the sight of a passport; any pirates who did not do so were hunted down and punished by the confederacy, who paid generous compensation to traders by way of an apology. The confederacy even set up its own tax collection office in Guangzhou. The trading infrastructure the pirates provided infuriated the Emperor.

While the pirate confederacy had strength in numbers, one thing that they couldn't control was the weather. In 1807, in a raging storm, Yi was washed overboard, never to be seen again. Shih took full control of the fleet, partnering up with Yi's twenty-one-year-old adopted son, Paou. To consolidate her power, Shih doubled down on the pirate constitution, adding a new code of conduct. It included rules such as not looting coastal villages that were friendly to the pirates, and ensured that four-fifths of all booty was placed in a communal pirate pot, to be equally distributed to all pirates. This was piracy socialist-style. The code of conduct also catered to female captives. The release of women captives was already reasonably common, but their treatment during capture could nevertheless be brutal. Shih tackled this brutality by making rape punishable by death, and ruled that if a pirate married a female captive, he had to be faithful to her. Punishments for pirates under Shih's new constitution included everything from feet being nailed to the deck to being thrown overboard. By imposing her code across the fleet, Shih reduced the power of individual pirate captains, thereby placing herself at the centre of pirate society.

With great reluctance, the Chinese state had eventually to admit that piracy was becoming a problem. In order to tackle it, they began offering arms to landowners who lived along the coastline, inviting them to defend themselves by challenging passing pirates. The plan backfired when Shih's pirates disguised themselves as landed gentry and asked the state for weapons, which the state happily handed over.[38] Without knowing it, the Emperor was arming the very pirates he was hoping to banish. Tired of the embarrassment, the Emperor amassed a war fleet to take on the pirate confederacy directly, but it proved no match for Shih. Her band of pirates defeated the Emperor's fleet and, in the process, sunk more than sixty of his ships. By September 1809, the pirates had taken control of Macao and were making their way to the provincial capital.[39]

It is often said that your enemy's enemy is your best friend. So, having proved incapable of taking on the pirates alone, China turned to Western powers for help. Desperate for military support, the Emperor agreed to pay a handsome sum of money to the Portuguese Navy—as well as to their British rivals—to hunt down and destroy the pirates. In return, Shih took one of the British commanders—Richard Glasspoole—prisoner and turned him into her 'Advisor for Western Affairs'.

Realising that Shih was a force to be reckoned with, the Emperor needed yet another plan of action. He invited Shih's second-in-command—Paou—to talks, perhaps hoping that he would prove to be a less fearsome opponent than Shih herself. When the negotiations began to break down, Shih marched into the imperial office—accompanied by seventeen women and children—and refused to leave until the talks were resolved in her favour. An amnesty was reached by which the pirates were allowed to keep the fortunes that they had amassed over many years and were promised a life of freedom—so long as they agreed to stop looting. To further sweeten the deal, Shih was awarded the title 'Lady by Imperial Decree'.

The pirate confederacy was transformed into China's navy.[40] Through their peace deal, the state acquired 226 pirate ships, 1,315 cannons and almost three thousand other items of weaponry—though Shih was permitted to keep more than twenty ships for her own 'protection'.[41] Paou became a decorated lieutenant-colonel and helped the Chinese navy to break an opium drug-smuggling ring, out of which erupted all-out war between China and Britain. To battle the opium trade, the Emperor ordered the Chinese navy to raid British ships and seize and destroy any opium found onboard. The fact that China resisted the drug dealing was considered an affront to the British government's mantra of 'free trade'. It also risked leaving British tea drinkers going thirsty, as no opium trade meant no tea. By 1839, and in defence of the British East India Company's shipping, Britain had declared war on China.

The Chinese Emperor asked Shih for her advice on how to defeat the British at sea. But, despite her best efforts, China's navy proved no match for Britain's military fleets. By 1842, China had lost the 'Opium War'. Not only did it have to succumb to Britain's demand to freely trade its opium, but it also had to compensate the British East India Company for the opium that had been seized and destroyed.

As part of the peace treaty—the Treaty of Nanjing—Britain was granted control of Hong Kong Island. Chinese resistance to British incursions—along with Britain's growing territorial demands in the region—resulted in a 'Second Opium War' in 1856–60, during which the British captured Beijing in partnership with France. The result was that China had to concede even more territory: the southern part of the Kowloon Peninsula—the part of the coastline just north of Hong Kong Island. The British not only gained complete freedom to trade whatever they liked with China; they now also had their own foothold on Chinese soil.

After her adventurous life at sea, Shih went on to establish a brothel-cum-casino in her old haunt of Guangzhou, where she lived to celebrate her sixty-ninth birthday, passing away—a grandmother—in 1844. Her legacy lives on in the form of the pirate tales still told to Chinese children.

SEXPLOITATION

In 1857, as the Second Opium War was raging in the South China Sea, Indian troops in the employment of the British East India Company mutinied. The cause of the rebellion was a gun known as the Enfield Rifle. The weapon had been newly distributed to the troops of the Company; soldiers were required to bite off the ends of lubricated cartridges before loading their guns. Worried that the lubrication grease was derived from pig and cow meat, Muslims and Hindus alike refused to take up arms as a matter of religious principle. The British responded by imprisoning anyone who refused to fire their rifles. In solidarity with the prisoners, fellow Indian troops in the employ of the Company revolted. In the course of the mutiny, British officers were shot by their troops, and Delhi—which had been taken by the Company—was given back to the Mughal Emperor. Before long, insurrection against the British East India Company was spreading across northern India, resulting in widespread bloodshed on both sides.

The mutiny played into the wider discontent felt by the many thousands of Indians who were being employed by the British East India Company. The Company—which had been chartered by Elizabeth I in 1600—wasn't just a business, it fought for territorial control in order to ensure undisputed access to the rich produce of India. This meant that Indians employed by the Company's private army were expected to fight their own people. By 1803, this private army was 200,000 strong and, as a result of the Company's military endeavours, virtually all of India south of Delhi was 'effectively ruled from a boardroom in the City of London'—the boardroom of the British East India Company.[42] As William Dalrymple writes in his history of the Company, 'It was not the British government that began seizing great chunks of India . . . but a dangerously unregulated private company headquartered in one small office, five windows wide, in London, and managed in India by a violent, utterly ruthless and intermittently unstable corporate predator'.[43] It was in response to the mutiny that the British state took full command of the Company's territories and private army. The associated 1858 'Government of India Act' transferred rule away from the Directors of the Company to a new Secretary of State for India. A Council was established—with members appointed by the Crown—to advise the Secretary of State; the governor-general and provincial governors were made appointable by the British Crown. The British Raj was born—and Queen Victoria was made the Empress of India.[44]

Indian women were left fighting on two fronts: domestic patriarchy and the patriarchy of British imperialism.[45] While the lives of women varied greatly across the different territories of India, arranged marriage and child marriage were far more common than in Britain. The fact that women on average married at a younger age meant that, as in China, wages were relatively low and overall inequality—the gap between rich and poor—was high. While elites could afford an army of poorly paid domestic servants and concubines, workers themselves received little reward for their efforts.

This of course meant that many families had little option but to allow women to work, but that work came with limited choices, low pay and was tinged with shame. The British were not blind to the gender and class (or caste) inequalities. However, they attempted to spin local customs—from female infanticide to female seclusion and widow suicide—as evidence that the country was in need of Britain's 'civilising' influence. Indian women were either cast as victims of Islamic and Hindu traditions or, instead, as sly and cunning prostitutes; in other words, as over-sexed or oppressed, and in either case in need of rescue by British imperialists who, naturally, failed to comprehend their own gender biases. As the historian Philippa Levine notes, '[t]he damning of colonial sites as moral sinks was crucial to the overall picture of their inferiority'.[46] It was what gave the British Empire its supposed legitimacy.

Across the British Empire, women were eroticised by the 'colonial imagination', resulting in the colonies being treated as one giant brothel.[47] In Australia, all Asian and Aboriginal women were assumed to be sexually available, and in both India and Hong Kong, colonial officials commented that prostitution was a routine part of local life.[48] Of course, the reality was that the predominately male population in many colonial encampments—which was comprised largely of soldiers, imperial officials and merchants—fuelled the sex trade, but, naturally, it wasn't the sexual desire of white men that was placed under the spotlight. British imperialists instead saw themselves as moral guardians. Writing in 1861, Henry Mayhew and Bracebridge Hemyng declared:

> *The inhabitants of some islands and the shores of bays and roadsteads, have discovered that in prostituting their women to the crews of trading ships they have a readier means of subsistence than was offered by their former industry. . . . It is for Europeans to repair the evil created by the incontinence of their predecessors.*[49]

It was local inhabitants, not European men, who were seen as the source of 'vice'. Sex workers took on a dual role: as the providers of sexual services for male colonisers and as the excuse the colonial authorities needed to justify their rule—as evidence that the local population were 'primitive'.[50]

Work was central to Victorian respectability, but so too was female chastity, which meant that sex work was certainly not considered work. The census of 1911 thereby included prostitutes in the 'major class of "unproductive labour"', along with beggars, vagrants and thieves.[51] Furthermore, since in Victorian Britain paid work was considered the domain of men—with women expected to dedicate themselves to home-making—women's paid work of whatever kind was open to suspicion. Even 'legitimate' work was seen as a cover for prostitution.[52] Indian women who worked for the public works department in the Punjab as grass cutters or vendors were assumed also to be servicing the sexual needs of soldiers as a side hustle.[53] Indeed, any woman who had contact with the British military stationed in India—including the wives of Indians in the employ of the British East India Company—was considered amenable to sexual advances, which conveniently allowed colonisers to treat them and their husbands as second class.

Venereal disease fanned the flames of moral panic and gave colonial authorities further excuse to treat indigenous populations as in need of moral guidance. Colonial authorities in Australia argued that venereal diseases were wiping out the indigenous population, effectively scapegoating indigenous women for the problems that were instead being caused by the loss of land and habitat to new settlers.[54] Concern was in turn raised that indigenous women were spreading disease to white men. The medical journal *The Lancet* reported that sexually transmitted diseases were the 'most common cause of unfitness for duty' amongst the garrison stationed in Hong Kong. In India, at least thirty percent of white soldiers were estimated to have been hospitalised for STDs in the 1820s and 1830s, resulting in a rallying cry for something to be done.[55] Action came in the form of contagious diseases legislation, which required all sex workers to be formally registered, subjected to regular checks and incarcerated in 'lock hospitals' in the event that infection was identified. The legislation also gave colonial authorities the power to control brothels, limiting them to designated districts—'red light districts'—and subjecting them to controls. Between the 1850s and 1880s, this legislation had been rolled out across the British colonies in China, India, the Caribbean, New Zealand and Australia.[56]

Rather than being seen through an economic lens, sex work was placed under a moral microscope. Poverty and famine were certainly recognised by colonial officials as contributing to the growing numbers of women working in brothels, but were not in any way seen as connected to colonial rule.[57] Wherever famine decimated the countryside, medical officers in nearby towns noted that starving rural women were driven into the hands of urban brothel keepers, forcing down the price of sex and resulting in outbreaks of venereal disease.[58] The claim that women were being sold into prostitution was similarly used in Australia and America to further justify the forcible removal of girls from their mothers.[59] Colonialism was—they argued—saving women from a life of poverty, exploitation and abuse. One of the few white women to acknowledge the adverse effects of colonialism on women was Mary Bennett, who had worked for some years at a mission in Western Australia before becoming an activist for the rights of Aboriginal Australians. Writing to Olive Pink—the botanical illustrator and fellow activist—she appealed to her:

> *NOT to condone or justify taking half-caste children from their aboriginal mothers. The unfortunate mothers are only victims of starvation and to separate parents and children is to destroy both in the most cruel way. . . . The recent Land Act Amendment of W[estern] A[ustralia] takes away from natives the right to hunt over their tribal lands when these are enclosed, and . . . all the native waters are fenced in [by] the [white] squatters . . . Their game is destroyed and their dogs are destroyed and the*

> *only way they can come by a meal is by selling their women. So I say that W[estern] A[ustralia] is deliberately starving their natives to death in their own country.*[60]

As far as colonial authorities were concerned, poverty was the result either of women choosing 'harlotry' over more 'respectable' and 'useful' forms of work, or of women falling victim to indigenous men, who were considered 'careless of women's dignity, happy to trade even their wives for a small consideration'.[61] Racism, sexism and imperialism were intimately connected.

MERCHANT QUEENS

European merchants had been trading in West Africa for almost as long as they had been trading in India and the Far East. But, whereas elsewhere women were associated with brothels, in West Africa women were associated with trade. Markets selling fruit, yams and poultry ran daily in every community and—from Senegal to Nigeria—were considered the domain of women. As one British observer commented on Igboland (in present-day Nigeria), 'Ordinarily no Igbo man takes any part in the actual buying and selling—if an Igbo man be seen buying in the market it is almost an indication that he is either a stranger or a man with no womenfolk to act for him'.[62] Women not only ran their own market stalls; they were also the appointed officials in charge of setting market rules and regulations, from opening times to the prices at which goods were sold. These female officials—the 'mothers of the marketplace'—formed their own police forces and courts to ensure that their rules were obeyed and that any seller who broke them was punished.[63] Buying and selling was in the hands of women—and had been for centuries.

Women operated at all levels when it came to trade: there were those who simply sold their own homegrown produce; there were those who instead specialised in selling produce grown or manufactured by other women; and, on the highest rung of the trading ladder, there were the wealthy 'middlemen'—or, rather, middlewomen—who connected buyers and sellers across long distances.[64] Travelling across the coastal plains, savannahs and uplands of West Africa was no easy task; this acted as a natural barrier that helped to ensure that those who did take the risk were rewarded for their efforts. While the River Niger could be traversed by canoe, trade typically necessitated walking by foot for long periods, stopping to eat and sleep along the way. In order to ensure their safety, women traders travelled in bands of up to thirty.[65] Reluctant to venture too far inland, Europeans initially left markets to indigenous women traders. This meant that as demand for African produce grew—whether in the form of food to feed European traders or in the form of gold to be taken aboard ships—the female 'bourgeoisie' were, at least initially, able to profit from trade with Europe.[66]

Since female entrepreneurs were a common sight in West African ports, it became customary for European trading companies to commission their services and expertise, as a result of which both personal and economic relationships emerged. In eighteenth-century Senegal, colonialists had already created a special title—with associated privileges—for the influential female merchants who married European merchants, officials and soldiers; they were called *signares* ('madam' in Portuguese). The *signares* organised their own inland trading expeditions to source gold and slaves to be sold to their European 'friends'. The descendants of these Senegalese mothers and European fathers became known as the *métis*. Combining their local knowledge with their privileged access to European trading companies, the *métis* were able to amass personal fortunes of a kind that were placed on display in opulent coastal homes looked after by retinues of household slaves. Private riverboats and gold jewellery were also symbols of wealth.[67] Beyond Senegal—in Liberia, Sierra Leone and Ghana—similar elite groups of women traders operated as the brokers between European trading companies and the peoples of West Africa.[68]

Over time, female traders had to adapt to changing global conditions. West Africa had long been famous for its gold—hence why the portion of the Gulf of Guinea that is today Ghana became known as the Gold Coast. During the Islamic Golden Age, Africans traded their gold with Arab traders on the banks of the Falémé River in return for produce from the Far East.[69] European merchants later arrived with cloth, arms, metals, spirits and hardware—anything that could tempt locals into parting with their precious gold. But when gold reserves were uncovered in Brazil at the end of the seventeenth century, demand for African gold collapsed and, in its place, the export of slaves accelerated.[70] Rather than selling gold in exchange for European wares, traders sold slaves, for which European trading companies—venturing across the Atlantic—had a growing demand. These slaves were then taken onboard ships to work in plantations and mines in the Americas, the products of which—from sugar to raw cotton—were sold to Europeans. But, in 1807, after centuries of participation in this 'triangular trade', the British parliament voted to abolish the slave trade. The wealth that was being created by the Industrial Revolution meant that parliament could now afford to take the moral high ground. As British naval ships began patrolling the African coastline in an effort to root out slave traders, trading elites in West Africa had to find other ways of making money. They turned to gum, peanuts and palm oil, organising large-scale plantation production on African soil for export overseas. While this 'legitimate commerce' replaced the export of slaves, it also helped to fuel an internal traffic in slaves destined for domestic agricultural labour.[71]

Ana Joaquina dos Santos e Silva—who was born around the turn of the nineteenth century to an Afro-Portuguese mother and a Portuguese merchant father—was a woman whose wealth was built on the slave trade. While we know little about her childhood, we do know that she married two Portuguese slave traders and, after being twice widowed, continued the practice of trading slaves herself. Around a third of the twelve million slaves transported across the

Atlantic were destined for the Portuguese colony of Brazil, where they worked in mines or on plantations.[72] Many of these slaves boarded ships in Angola—also a colony of Portugal. The Angolan port of Luanda was the hub of this trade, housing slave markets that were famous across the Atlantic. It was here that Silva lived in her Portuguese-style colonial palace, from where she ran her fleet of ships that ferried slaves four thousand miles across the ocean to Brazil. While Britain abolished its slave trade in 1807, the Portuguese continued trading slaves from their West African colonies, which allowed slave traders like Silva to benefit from the ongoing demand for slaves without having to compete with British slave traders. The 1830s and 1840s were, therefore, a boom time for Silva's business. But she also knew that with British political pressure on Portugal to abolish the 'odious commerce', she would eventually need to find ways of diversifying her revenue streams. She turned to land, developing sugar, millet and coffee plantations worked by slave labourers on African soil, and began lending money, which generated streams of interest payments to bolster her finances. She passed away in Lisbon in 1859, having become the wealthiest women in Angola.[73]

At the same time that Silva was developing her business interests in Angola, Madam Efunroye Tinubu was doing the same in Lagos—in present-day Nigeria—where the Portuguese had also developed relations with the local kings (the *obas*). Born in 1805, Tinubu learned her business acumen from her mother and grandmother and, despite relatively humble beginnings, went on marry a Nigerian prince. She was the most respected 'middleman' in the trade which operated between Lagos and the Nigerian interior. Amongst her other trades, which included tobacco, salt and slaves, she also bought and sold ammunitions, becoming the firearms dealer *par excellence* in the region. In 1851, British ships attacked Lagos under the banner of abolishing the slave trade, ousting the Portuguese and the local king. By 1856, Tinubu had been banished from Lagos by the British. She moved to the town of Abeokuta in the southwest of Nigeria, from where she continued trading arms, supplying the region's indigenous military commanders with weapons. For her work as an arms dealer, she was honoured with the title *Iyalode*—the highest-ranking female chieftain. And, despite the British ban on slave trading, Tinubu continued the practice of trading slaves. When she was caught flouting the ban, she is reported to have explained, 'I have a large household and I must feed them well. I need money to do that, that's why'.[74]

British colonisers were moving inland from the coast, attempting to take control of internal trade, helped by their railways. The Royal Niger Company was Britain's trading company in the lower Niger River Valley and was licensed by the British Crown to administer the region, making it the equivalent of the British East India Company. Initially, the company traded through the region's female traders. They included Omu Okwei, who bought items unloaded from British ships—from lamps, gin and matches to pots and plates—and in return supplied palm oil and kernels to the Company. To help grow her business for the long-term, she 'acquired beautiful girls'—some from her debtors to settle their outstanding payments—whom she in turn 'gave [. . .] out as mistresses or wives to influential businessmen'.[75] Okwei's buying and selling enterprise was hugely successful: she owned twenty-four homes, six canoes and one of the first cars in her town. In 1935, in recognition of her trading expertise, she was crowned *Omu*—the market queen—of her hometown. Dressed in a soft velvet gown with regalia that included ivory bracelets and anklets and strings of coral beads, she was escorted to her throne by two female attendants, as African representatives from numerous nearby kingdoms looked on.[76] It was the last time that a woman was crowned market queen in Nigeria, as the British were transferring control away from market queens and towards town councils comprised of local men.[77] The result was not only that female traders began to lose their monopoly over domestic trade, but that trade increasingly became the business of men rather than women.[78] British merchants conspired with local male traders, who acted as their agents, to squeeze women out of the business of buying and selling.

Since women in Britain were increasingly stereotyped as wives, mothers and missionaries rather than breadwinners, British colonisers had little respect for West Africa's history of female merchant activity. With time, the British were not only sidelining indigenous female traders and market officials but were also shifting their attentions to natural resources. Increasingly aware of the profits on offer from 'land pregnant with minerals', European countries entered a scramble for Africa.[79] By the close of the nineteenth century, ten million square miles of the continent had been partitioned and placed in the hands of European rulers, putting more than a hundred million Africans under European rule. The treasures of Africa's own indigenous states and empires—the Ashanti Kingdom of Ghana, the Benin Empire of Nigeria, and the Maqdala of Ethiopia—were looted and their indigenous resistance efforts were brutally suppressed. By 1914, ninety percent of the African continent was under European rule.[80]

In addition to the intrusions of European states, individual Europeans—in search of their fortune—boarded ships and scoured Africa for any sign of gold and diamonds.[81] Where they identified a potential prospect, they negotiated with farmers or tribal chiefs to purchase land, underneath which they constructed diamond and gold mines. From these individual acts of speculation sprung colossal—and highly profitable—European mining companies. And key to their success was denying indigenous people the right to mine their own land.[82] White settler miners were so determined to eliminate Africans from the mining business that they suggested that anyone who bought diamonds from a Black person should face the punishment of having their ears removed or being publicly lashed.[83] The justification used to deny Africans mining licences was that 'the rates at which natives would sell their diamonds' would be too low, because of 'the difference between the general wants, necessities, character, and position of the two races'.[84] South Africa was transformed into an industrial mining complex, run by European men who increasingly stripped Africans of land, rights and opportunities. Before European colonisers arrived, women had been actively involved in the mining business. Women and girls were involved in the centuries-old copper mining industry—bartering the copper they received as their wages for grain and cattle—and were some of the first people to discover and sell diamonds, including a sizeable sixty-one-carat diamond that was sold to a Mr Roos in 1870 by a Khoe woman in return for oxen and a wagon.[85] But, once locked out of running and building their own mining enterprises by Europeans, Africans had to develop other avenues of business. Men formed the Zulu Washermen's Guild, while women specialised in lodging houses.[86] Eleanor Xiniwe—with her husband Paul—built the Temperance Hotel, overlooking the Market Square in King William's Town.[87]

For the majority of men and women, however, life under European colonisation meant poorly paid waged work in mines or domestic service. Men migrated in search of work in mining communities, disrupting the traditional system of family production, leaving women not only looking after the family but in need of finding additional sources of income to supplement their husbands' paltry pay packets. The options women faced in this regard were limited to unskilled and poorly paid casual work, as the education system—in the hand of Christian missionaries—only prepared girls for domesticity.[88] In addition to the denial of labour-market opportunities, women—as the household heads—faced poor housing, high rents, forced removals (as part of programmes to segregate the population along racial lines), and 'pass laws' that limited their freedom of movement by requiring African people to carry and present a pass when travelling and entering towns. But, in response to the oppression, South African women fought back through mass petitions, passive resistance and marches.[89] Their activism continued through the twentieth century.[90]

~

THE FREEDOM OF ORDINARY WOMEN WAS CENTRAL TO BRITAIN'S Industrial Revolution, but British colonisers actively deprived women in the colonies of these same freedoms, justifying their actions as 'saving' them from their 'wretched' lives. British missionaries and officials objected not just to child marriage, widow suicide and seclusion, but also imposed their 'civilising influence' on the female breadwinner. The result was that women suffered not only a loss of land, resources and even their own infants; they also lost their historic role as market queens in West Africa and providers in Australia and North America. The damage that was done to women and their economies was immeasurable.

CHAPTER 11

TYPISTS, TEACHERS AND ENGINEERS

WOMEN IN THE TWENTIETH CENTURY

THE TWENTIETH CENTURY BROUGHT US MOTION PICTURES, space travel and the personal computer, and—in the guises of Hollywood villains, the space race and the computer game Tetris—an economic battle that was unfolding on every screen. It was the battle between capitalism and communism, one that began with the Russian Revolution in 1917 and ended with the fall of the Berlin Wall in 1989. But, despite their stark differences, the two archenemies of the twentieth century shared one thing in common: women were at the heart of their economic transformation.

At the start of the century, running a household was a full-time job, requiring fifty-eight hours of backbreaking labour every week.[1] Hauling water was heavy work and washing clothes involved a scrub-board, wringer and water heated on a stove. Preparing fire grates was a daily chore, soot and smoke made cleaning onerous, and the absence of refrigerators meant that shopping was a daily—as opposed to weekly—task. It is little wonder that only six percent of married women in America worked outside of the home, and that the most affluent homes employed teams of domestic servants to carry the burden, making domestic service—along with farm labour and textile work—the chief occupation of women who were unmarried.[2] By the 1920s, rather than working as servants, women could increasingly be found in factories, producing the home appliances and processed foods that made cooking, washing and cleaning easier than ever before, from refrigerators, vacuum cleaners and washing machines to cake mixes, canned food and infant formula.[3] Daughters were no longer needed to help full-time with the household chores, freeing more of them up to go out to work, not just in factories but in the expanding white-collar sector, where they were in great demand as typists, stenographers and secretaries.[4] World War Two pulled even more women into the workforce and, in the post-war period, marriage bars—which restricted the employment of married women—were lifted, and the expansion in state activity led to the growth of professional occupations such as nursing, teaching and social work. The invention of the contraceptive pill enabled women to remain in education for longer, which meant that more women could pursue a career as well as raising a family. By the end of the century, universities were home to as many female students as male students, and the gender pay gap was—at last—starting to close.

In this chapter we meet the women who supercharged the twentieth century, not just those in the Soviet Union and the West but also those who fought to be free from colonial rule and who increasingly provided the cheap labour for the ever more global economy. As 'free trade' triumphed over imperial relations, factory production spread to parts of the world where labour costs were lowest, with nimble-fingered women providing a cheap and reliable labour pool. Though both China and the Soviet Union resisted being pulled into this 'global capitalist system', they nevertheless saw women as a vital resource for fields and factories and prided themselves on treating men and women on equal terms. But, so long as the communist state was reluctant to grant either sex the freedom to make their own decisions, gender equality could do little for the economy. As a result, the Soviet Union collapsed and the Chinese Communist Party had to turn towards capitalism. The century that had begun with a communist revolution ended with the ascendancy of global capitalism.

REVOLUTIONARY FEVER

Three years into World War One, on International Women's Day in 1917, women workers at Petrograd's textile factories went on strike.[5] The winter had been unusually harsh, freezing transport infrastructure and preventing grain from reaching the city. Worried that their families were on the edge of starvation, women were taking to the streets. Initially, the Russian authorities dismissed the protest, believing that it was just another 'bread riot' that would come to an end once the weather improved and grain started to flow.[6] But, before long, other workers were joining the action.[7] By the next day, more than 150,000 people—men and women—were marching through the city streets.[8] Starting to worry about the prospect of a revolution, the authorities ordered the local military commander to disperse the crowds. Russia's army was, however, already stretched to a breaking point, and there was a feeling amongst the troops that the generals were mismanaging the war effort. Upwards of one million Russian soldiers had already lost their lives after being forcibly conscripted from peasant villages, given little in the way of guns to defend themselves and outfitted in uniforms that fell apart, leaving them barefoot in the hazardous and cold trenches of the Eastern Front.[9] Millions more had been injured. Feeling war-weary, the troops refused to fire; instead, they put down their arms and joined the protestors.[10] Having lost military support, and with no other means of defending himself, the Russian tsar—Nicholas II—had little choice but to step down. The Russian Empire had been brought to its knees by women protestors. A Provisional Government was formed and began to make plans for free democratic elections, promising votes for women as well as men, which made Russia the first major European country to allow women to vote in national elections.[11] The Petrograd Soviet of Workers emerged alongside to represent the political views of Petrograd's workers and revolutionaries. Rather than proclaiming itself as some form of revolutionary government, the Petrograd Soviet initially accepted the Provisional Government and its plans for democratic elections, albeit hoping that socialism would triumph at the ballot box. However, rather than presenting themselves to the public as a united front, a number of competing socialist parties emerged and took to the election trail. Lenin—who had been in exile in Switzerland—was offered safe passage and a financial contribution to his political campaign by the Germans.[12] They knew very well that there was no political agitator greater than Lenin, and that returning him home would set the proverbial cat amongst the pigeons. Chaos in Russia was, after all, in the best interests of the Germans, who were struggling to fight a war that was raging on multiple fronts.

From his first step back on Russian soil in April 1917, Lenin began sowing the seeds of another revolution—what would become the October Revolution, culminating in a full-scale Civil War. Standing on the platform of the railway station after disembarking from his train, Lenin called upon the Russian people to overthrow the Provincial Government and reject their plans for liberal democracy. He promised land and liberty for peasants, food and factories for the workers, and peace for the military.[13] While his political party—the Bolshevik Party—was one of the smallest political groupings, his promises succeeded in attracting between a fifth and a quarter of votes in Russia's first democratic elections. Democracy was, however, not enough for Lenin. He believed that only by annihilating the bourgeoisie and the aristocracy could Russia wipe its slate clean, make a break from its tsarist past, and push ahead to become a just and free nation.[14] This was class warfare, or, more accurately, class genocide.[15] On 25 October 1917, the Bolsheviks stormed the Winter Palace, overthrew the Provisional Government and made Russia the world's first communist state.

While Lenin, Stalin and Trotsky are the names we most associate with the Russian Revolution, women played a pivotal role. Not only did women lead the February Revolution, but for decades the daughters of Russian gentry had—despite the potential consequences—been calling for a radical redistribution of wealth and power. In 1878, Vera Zasulich attempted to assassinate the Governor-General of St Petersburg, which made her Russia's first terrorist and an icon amongst revolutionaries. Despite shooting and wounding the general, Zasulich was pardoned and acquitted.[16] Three years later, Vera Figner, a member of a group that called themselves the People's Will, had turned her flat into a bomb-making factory and meeting place. In March 1881, her comrade in arms—Sophia Perovskaya—gave the final signal that resulted in the assassination of Tsar Alexander II.[17] While Perovskaya faced execution and Figner faced life imprisonment, Zasulich decided to part company with her fellow female radicals. Having read Karl Marx's revolutionary writings, she had decided that only once Russia had advanced from a peasant to an industrial society would it be ripe enough to successfully transition to communism.[18] In 1883, she cofounded the first Russian Marxist group, the Liberation of Labour, and in 1884, she wrote the foreword for the Russian translation of Friedrich Engels's *Socialism: Utopian and Scientific*.[19]

When it eventually came in 1917, the revolution did not take the direction Zasulich had hoped. She thought that Lenin offered a form of socialism that was too power-hungry—too top-down as opposed to bottom-up. He was turning socialism into something much more extreme, depriving individual workers of control in favour of the state. This new political beast was, of course, communism and Zasulich worried that by centralising power, rather than allowing individual peasant communes and factories to self-govern, it would result in corruption and coercion. What she wanted was the original promise of power for the people, not a socialist dictatorship that was in her view little better than the tsarist dictatorship.[20] She wasn't the only female thinker to believe that the Bolsheviks were betraying socialism. Ekaterina Kuskova had made the case for a more peaceful, gradual and democratic form of socialism, one that built support for socialism through the trade union movement rather than imposing a revolution from above.[21] Zasulich and Kuskova were right to have their doubts. By the end of 1918, the Bolsheviks had abandoned their promise of worker control of factories in place of greater centralisation. Alexandra Kollontai—who had spent the past two decades working alongside Russia's women textile workers, had been imprisoned for her revolutionary speeches, and had been made People's Commissar in Lenin's first government—joined the Workers' Opposition movement, printing and distributing a pamphlet that set out workers' objections to Lenin's new plan. Lenin was 'infuriated': he did not take kindly to being challenged.[22] By the early 1920s, Kollontai had been sent overseas, Zasulich had passed away, and Kuskova was in exile.[23] Despite women's best efforts, the Russian Revolution was taking an unnerving turn.

RUSSIAN REALITY

According to some, the Soviets created a veritable female utopia, freeing women from domestic enslavement. They certainly talked the talk in terms of gender equality. They legalised birth control and abortion, permitted divorce and encouraged women's work outside of the home.[24] In place of household drudgery, they promised workplace nurseries and communal dining halls, and set up a Women's Bureau (the *Zhenotdel*) to help make Russia the most equal country in the world. The faces of strong, purposeful and happy women workers—hair neatly tied back under scarves as they tended in overalls to machines, crops and engines—appeared on Soviet postage stamps and propaganda posters.[25] 'Out of All the Countries in the World—Only in the USSR' read one poster from 1931, replete with images of women and accompanied by a quote from Lenin, claiming to have 'cut the roots of oppression'.[26] By 1935, forty-two percent of Russia's industrial workforce were female.[27] And whereas in the past women had been concentrated in the textile sector, they were now also working in mining, metallurgy, the chemical industry and electrical engineering.[28] When it came to white-collar as opposed to manual work, nowhere else in Europe produced as many female scientists, professors, lawyers, artists and state administrators as Soviet Russia.[29] And it was Russian feminist revolutionaries who, using the Soviet Union as a model, helped convince the League of Nations to begin an enquiry into the legal status of women throughout the world.[30] From these bare facts and figures, it would seem that the communist revolution transformed women's lives for the better.

Beneath the headlines, however, life for women was far from utopian. While the feminist theories of the revolutionaries preached that the family was a vehicle for patriarchy, many men took advantage of the associated relaxation in divorce laws by abandoning their wives and children, leaving women without financial support. Almost fourteen percent of marriages were dissolved in the early 1920s—twice as many as in Germany and three times as many as in France.[31] Women were not impressed. In the words of one working-class woman, 'To marry, bear children and to be enslaved by the kitchen and then to be thrown aside by your husband—this is very painful for women'. In the words of another: 'I can't forgive a man who lives with a woman twenty years, has five kids, and then decides his wife no longer pleases him. Why did she please him before, but now she doesn't? Shame on you, comrade men!'[32] Unemployment and homelessness amongst women soared in the 1920s. When a poor peasant woman called Zaminskaia arrived at a labour exchange in search of work to support herself and her two children, she was told that she was neither eligible for work nor benefits.[33] Only those who had previously worked for wages were considered the true 'working-class'; alongside, servants, seamstresses and washerwomen were told that they lacked appropriate experience to be eligible for jobs in industry.[34] Women who had managed to find work in factories were then unceremoniously dismissed in order to create jobs for the four million Russian soldiers returning home from World War One.[35] Women had been deserted not only by their husbands but also by the revolution. By 1929, the head of the Women's Bureau—Aleksandra Artyukhina—told the Party that they needed to make fewer speeches and take more action when it came to women's lives.[36] A year later, her Bureau was closed down on the basis that the Party's new economic plan would (apparently) solve all of women's problems.

The first Five Year Plan—adopted under Stalin's leadership in 1929—aimed for radical change through a programme of 'Collectivisation' of farming and the rapid growth of heavy industry. In the countryside, land and livestock were forcibly removed from peasants and the most successful peasant farmers were deported as enemies of the people. The remainder of the peasant population were tasked with working on newly created collective farms, but without the modern equipment that was making large-scale farming economical in America. Believing that collective farms would be more productive, state economists calculated that the countryside could afford to lose ten million people to industry.[37] Since men were more likely to be sent to the cities to work in the factories, peasant women formed the majority of the agricultural workforce that was left behind.[38] They spent their days planting, weeding and harvesting collective fields, as well as looking after the collectively owned livestock, working from five in the morning until late into the evening.[39] In order to meet their production targets, women needed to bring their children into the fields to work alongside them, which led to high absentee rates in rural schools.[40] For their efforts, women received little reward, with virtually all of the food they consumed coming from the tiny individual plots of allotment-style land that they had been allowed to keep as part of the transition to collective farming.[41] Some wrote to the state to complain that their farm managers were drunkards who regularly stole from the farm while they themselves were left starving and unpaid.[42] As corruption and mismanagement grew and the state continued to demand ever larger amounts of grain to feed the growing industrial workforce, there was all too little left to feed the very people who produced food for everyone else.

Women did not take their situation lightly. More than a third of demonstrations in Russia in the early 1930s consisted of groups of women using pitchforks, knives and stakes to attack government offices and carts of procured grain, and to free those who had been arrested as enemies of the state.[43] On one occasion, a group of more than three hundred women removed two horses and a cow from their local collective farm, returned the horses to their former owners and gifted the cow to a women whose husband had been executed for counterrevolutionary activity. But the state persisted with the process of Collectivisation, with devastating consequences. By 1932–3, the bread basket of the Soviet Union—Ukraine—was left starving. Between five million and seven million people died of hunger as grain was loaded onto railway carts destined for Russian cities.[44] Through their suffering in the countryside, female peasants and their families paid—often with their lives—for the industrialisation of Soviet Russia.[45]

While famine ravaged the countryside, cities were becoming increasingly squalid. As the state shipped people out of the countryside and into urban factories—and many others started to join them in an attempt to escape the catastrophe that was Collectivisation—overcrowding grew to intolerable levels. Since the state lacked the funds needed to expand the urban housing stock, it became normal for a whole family to occupy one room, with multiple families sharing the same kitchen.[46] Given the limited supplies of food, women wasted hours queuing in order to buy basic necessities.[47] And the promised nurseries, after-school clubs and communal dining and laundry facilities were slow to materialise, which meant that women found themselves working two shifts: one in the factory and one at home.[48]

Not only was Stalin's economic programme of Collectivisation catastrophic; his social programme reversed some of the earlier revolutionary gains. Given the widespread poverty, abortion had become so popular amongst women in some cities that it outnumbered live births, resulting in the birth rate plummeting.[49] When the 1937 census revealed that the population was between fourteen and fifteen million lower than expected, the statisticians were shot.[50] New population estimates were drawn up and, in order to ensure that reality matched up to them, contraceptives were withdrawn and abortion was rendered illegal.[51] Women were tasked with producing the next generation of workers, which meant that their individual choice came second to the needs of the state.

In 1937, a peasant woman asked a meeting of her fellow female comrades: 'why are you sitting and saying nothing? After all, you're cold and hungry and you're forced to work day and night; they drink your blood and you're silent; you need to speak the truth!' She was reported and arrested.[52] During Stalin's reign of terror a total of one million people were executed and ten million more were deported to work camps after being labelled enemies of the people.[53] While Soviet Russia claimed to be the most just, democratic and free country in the world, a new constitution—passed in 1936—had made individual rights and freedoms conditional on whatever was considered 'in the interests of the working classes and for the purpose of strengthening the socialist system', which was of course left to the state to judge.[54] Even socialists themselves were not protected from the terror, especially if they had contacts abroad: more German communists were killed by Stalin than by Hitler.[55]

From the beginning, Ariadna Tyrkova-Williams had objected to the violent tactics of the Bolsheviks. Tyrkova-Williams was a political journalist who had worked for newspapers in Moscow and St Petersburg, and after the February Revolution of 1917 she had been elected to the Petrograd Council, where she was an advocate for the Cadet Party. Unlike the Bolshevik Party, the Cadet Party believed in 'improving the lot of the workers within the framework of the capitalist system'.[56] What Tyrkova-Williams wanted was a market economy—with respect for private property—but supplemented with the right to form unions, a maximum eight-hour working day, arbitration of labour disputes and insurance against sickness, accident and old age. After escaping Russia to seek exile in Britain, she published the first narrative of the Russian Revolution in the West, *From Liberty to Brest-Litovsk*, providing English speakers with a critical account of the Revolution. Until her death in 1962, Tyrkova-Williams was an ardent critic of the Soviet dictatorship.[57]

While the Soviet Union revealed the ugly side of communism, the Great Depression did the same for capitalism.

UPS AND DOWNS

In December 1928, in his State of the Union Address, President Calvin Coolidge was filled with optimism about the state of the American economy:

> *No Congress of the United States ever assembled, on surveying the state of the Union, has met with a more pleasing prospect than that which appears at the present time. In the domestic field there is tranquility and contentment, harmonious relations between management and wage earner, freedom from industrial strife, and the highest record of years of prosperity . . . The requirements of existence have passed beyond the standard of necessity into the region of luxury. Enlarging production is consumed by an increasing demand at home and an expanding commerce abroad. The country can regard the present with satisfaction and anticipate the future with optimism.*[58]

America had overtaken Britain to become the richest country in the world and its corporate giants—Ford, General Motors, Woolworth's and Coca-Cola—were fast becoming household names.[59] Not only had industry been transformed by the advent of mass production, but a whirlwind of modernisation had swept through offices, which were now freshly equipped with typewriters, duplicating machines, telephones, dictaphones and electric lighting. Skyscrapers were starting to grace the skylines of New York City and Chicago, while in Florida property developers were turning uninhabited swampland into an 'art deco' landscape of crisp white buildings embellished with colourful detailing.[60] Everywhere, streets were alive with the sound of jazz, motor cars and high heels. Speakeasies flouted the ban on alcohol, cars were rolling off the production line at a rate of four million a year and a growing number of women worked as typists, stenographers and secretaries.[61] Hire-purchase (which allowed people to buy on credit) fuelled the new consumerism while internationally the world economy was becoming precariously dependent on American lending, channelled through government borrowing and stock markets.

In 1929, the bubble began to burst. As interest rates rose, the American stock market started to tumble. In September, the Dow Jones Industrial Average share price peaked at 381.2; by the close of market on 24 October it had dropped to 299.5; and by 13 November it had fallen to 199. Rather than recovering from its losses, the index continued its downward trajectory for years to come. By 1932, the Dow Jones registered at less than a hundred points, meaning that stocks had, on average, plummeted to the point where they had lost three-quarters of their value.[62] For the lucky few, it was of course a good time to buy. Having sold her cosmetics business to Lehman Brothers in 1928 for $7.3 million, Helena Rubinstein was able to buy it back for less than $1 million.[63] Since millions of people had lost their life savings, not everyone was able to take advantage of the buying opportunity. And the stock market wasn't the only thing that crashed; the global economy likewise collapsed. No one was buying, either at home or abroad. As business failures and job losses mounted, the situation snowballed. With nothing to fall back on and little in the way of welfare, the typical family could no longer afford to spend on clothes, eating out or child care and had to cancel magazine subscriptions, club memberships and telephone lines. As local shops and diners lost customers and cleaners and childminders lost clients, the economy fell like a pack of cards. And to make matters worse, as American households and foreign countries alike proved unable to service their debts and savers drew down their savings, the banking system began to falter. As one bank after another closed its doors, more life savings turned to dust. By 1933, more than nine thousand American banks had failed and a quarter of American workers were unemployed.[64] And this wasn't just an American problem; it was global.

Some blamed women for this 'Great Depression', arguing that they had 'taken men's jobs'.[65] Women's growing presence in the world of work was undeniable, which served to make them an easy target. In the nineteenth century, offices had been filled with men who scribbled away in leather-bound ledgers while sitting on tall stools at high desks, but the invention of the telegraph and the typewriter had given birth to telegraphists and typists, an increasing number of whom were women.[66] During World War One, in order to release male clerks for the war effort, tens of thousands of women 'in all the glory of paint and powder, short skirts, high cloth boots, transparent blouses' had been recruited into the British civil service.[67] 'I have heard tell of men, formerly confirmed misogynists, who now sit surrounded by a bevy of beauty and find the official day all too short' remarked one civil servant.[68] By the late 1920s, clerical work was expanding and the number of women in American offices had begun to exceed the number of men.[69] The spread of department stores—temples to the new consumerism—created opportunities for those who could charm customers into parting with their cash. And the shift away from coal mining and steel manufacture to lighter forms of industry that focused on producing consumer goods—from lamps to radios—was driving a 'feminisation' of manufacturing.[70] But the reality was that unemployment was highest in parts of the economy where men still dominated, and lowest in the expanding white-collar sector, which had been responsible for eighty-five percent of the growth in women's jobs since 1890.[71] Despite this, once recession turned into depression, women were actively encouraged to withdraw from the labour force in order to create jobs for men. The American Federation of Labor urged employers to discriminate against 'married women whose husbands have permanent positions', with a poll of Americans conducted by Gallup in 1936 revealing that eighty-two percent of people approved of such discrimination.[72] In both the public and the private sector, marriage bars—once common in the late nineteenth century—were reintroduced, locking married women out of the workplace once more.[73] By the late 1930s, eighty-seven percent of American school districts refused to hire married women, and seventy percent made unmarried teachers unemployed once they married.[74] Marriage bars also affected a half of all women in insurance, banking, publishing and utilities.[75] In addition, Federal Order 213, passed in 1932, made it mandatory for the Federal Government to fire one or other of a spouse where both worked for the Government, which typically meant that the wife lost her job.[76] With narrowing labour-market opportunities, and with one in four men out of work at the peak of the Great Depression, women had to find other ways of supporting themselves and their families.

Self-sufficiency became the strategy for survival. Goods and services that were previously purchased through the market were instead substituted for with women's unpaid labour, or were carried out on a more casual basis. Women had to spend more time cooking from scratch, making clothes for their family instead of buying them, and caring for children and sick relatives rather than relying on paid help. Sewing classes were one of the few things to benefit from the Great Depression, as more women enrolled and went to night school to hone their homemaking skills in order to save money on anything that could be brought in-house. Alongside, purchases of canned food collapsed and, in their place, glass-jar sales—suitable for home canning—took off.[77] In an effort to make a few extra cents, women offered to take in ironing, laundry, mending and boarders, and they baked cakes and jarred pickles to sell from their front yard. As the economy tanked, women were, in other words, left picking up the slack.[78] And, where they possibly could find work, they increasingly became the main breadwinners of their families, creating a reversal of roles within the home. Sadly, it was a situation that created resentment rather than improving the status of women.[79]

As Western countries rearmed in response to the Nazi threat, industry received a much-needed boost. In order to make sure it was prepared for the threat of Hitler, the military needed more tanks, guns, ships and soldiers' uniforms, all of which got factories whirring once more and the economy moving. As men were mobilised to fight, women were tasked with taking on 'men only' jobs in shipyards, aircraft plants, arsenals, munitions and steel mills.[80] 'Rosie the Riveter' captured the public imagination and punched glamour and femininity into heavy industry. The American government issued a pamphlet—*When You Hire Women*—addressed to those unfamiliar with employing women and drawing on the experiences of those who had already become accustomed to women workers.[81] 'We didn't want women, but now they're here we've found they are just as fast and just as capable as the men. They are all right', remarked one such employer.[82] The pamphlet went on to advise that '[s]ometimes foremen and fellow workers need to be shown that women can do the job before they will cooperate'.[83] One such foreman went on to exclaim: 'Where have I been all these years? Why, these women are easier to train than men and can do finer work'.[84]

Six million women were pulled into paid employment in America alone, increasing women's labour-force participation rate by fifty percent. In the UK, the conscription of women into war industries resulted in eighty percent of married women joining the workforce.[85] In America, more than a half of the newly employed women were married women, albeit mostly those with older children, as the employment of those with children under fourteen was 'strong[ly] opposed' by the American government.[86] A survey conducted by the Women's Bureau suggested that three out of four working women wanted to remain in the workforce after the war.[87] While the war didn't instigate the upward march in women's employment, it catalysed a trend that had been underway since the start of the century and opened up areas of employment that had previously been designated 'men only'. In Britain, the proportion of women workers who were employed in the engineering trades doubled between 1931 and 1951, from six percent of all working women to twelve percent.[88] During this same time period, the number of women working in vehicle manufacture doubled, while employment in textile manufacture went into decline and the number of women working in domestic service dropped to only a seventh of the number employed in 1931.[89] The currents of women's work were to shift even faster in the latter half of the twentieth century.[90]

THE POST-WAR CONSENSUS

After the misery of the Great Depression, followed by the rise of fascism, Western democracies were under pressure to make sure that such global catastrophes would never happen again. Since both communism and capitalism had been shown wanting, governments aimed for a 'mixed economy' that was intended to combine the best of both worlds. The economist John Maynard Keynes—who helped to create the international architecture for the post-war global economy, including the World Bank and the International Monetary Fund—was a regular in policy circles and argued that government tax and spending power could be employed to keep the capitalist economy on an even keel. The building of government capacities during the war—a necessity for wartime planning—enabled Keynes's intellectual blueprint to be put into practice. Across the West, liberal democracies began to 'manage' their economies in a way that not only delivered jobs but that bridged the gap between rich and poor. Trade unions were welcomed into government departments and management suites, the rich were subjected to higher taxes, and, through the creation of the National Health Service in Britain, healthcare was made available based on need rather than ability to pay. William Beveridge—who years before had worked as an assistant for the economist and social reformer Beatrice Webb—put forward a plan for a comprehensive national insurance system, through which every worker would make automatic contributions from their pay packet to create a safety net for periods of unemployment, illness, maternity and old age. While Europe led the way with this 'welfare state', by the 'swinging sixties' the American President Lyndon B. Johnson was announcing a war on poverty and racial injustice through his 'Great Society' program.

Before the twentieth-century, government spending had been small and focused almost entirely on the military, but now the state was branching out into education, healthcare, pensions and infrastructure, forming a bigger part of the economy. In 1900, government was responsible for only around ten percent of spending in the UK and no more than three percent of spending in the USA. By 1936, this had already grown to twenty percent in the UK and ten percent in the USA, but by 1975, government represented almost a half of the economy in the UK and a third in the USA.[91] Across the Western world, government was bigger and was doing much more than ever before.

For women, the expansion in the state had its upsides and its downsides. Feminists criticised the welfare state for treating women as dependents. The system of national insurance—the tax that was introduced on workers' pay to fund the welfare state—treated men and women differently. This was a problem, because an individual's entitlement to benefits (from sick pay to pensions) was linked to their individual contributions, which meant that the less someone contributed, the less they were building a nest egg against future adversity, such as sickness, unemployment and old age. In Britain, the National Council of Women had called for equal contributions and equal benefits for men and women, but this had fallen on deaf ears.[92] Married women who worked were, unlike men, given the option of 'opting out' of paying the full rate of national insurance, on the basis that their husband's wages and contributions would provide them with adequate support in the event of adversity. This meant that they paid only half the contribution that would have been expected had they been male and, with it, were entitled to substantially lower benefits. The presumption was that women didn't need to make their own separate financial provision—that husbands would look after their wives—something which women themselves couldn't take for granted and which left all too many women exposed to poverty later in life.[93] Women whose families were struggling financially felt under particular pressure to 'opt out' as a means of reducing their household's outgoings. Katherine Bompas and Elizabeth Abbott calculated that the British welfare state locked nine million women out of national insurance. But while an opportunity was missed on the equality front, many women welcomed the fact that the welfare state did at least recognise the work that women undertook within the home with the payment of family allowances, something which proved to be extremely popular at the ballot box.[94] Family allowances of five shillings a week for each child beyond the first were paid directly to the mother. Of course, the presumption was that women were the caregivers. But more schools, hospitals, care homes and libraries—along with an associated growth in the civil service—also brought an expansion in public-sector jobs, which created more opportunities for women working as civil servants, teachers, doctors, nurses and librarians. The fastest-growing sectors were education and healthcare—two of the most female-dominated parts of the economy.[95] Already by 1961, 800,000 people worked in Britain's state-education system and 600,000 people worked in the NHS, but by the late 1970s their combined workforce was closer to three million people.[96]

Whether it was a result of state intervention or of a more vibrant private sector, the post-war economy was a world apart from the Great Depression years. Throughout the 1950s and the 1960s, unemployment remained low, inflation was under control, and trade and investment were booming. The economy was getting bigger and it was also becoming more equal. 'You've never had it so good' became the rhetoric of politicians. 'Jobs for life' became the norm, as did pay rises, while shopping, eating out and an occasional holiday came within the reach of most families. Even owning a family car became more of a reality than an aspiration. This was the 'Mad Men' age of mass consumerism, and while men dominated big companies, female entrepreneurs also made their mark: Helen Walton, with her husband Sam Walton, turned a nickel and dime store into the world's largest retailer, Walmart; 'Cookie Queen' Debbi Fields turned her love of making cookies into a multi-million-dollar retail business, Mrs. Fields Cookies; Barbara Holdridge cofounded the first audiobook business, Caedmon Records, whose first recording was *A Child's Christmas in Wales* by Dylan Thomas;[97] and Lillian Vernon created her catalog business, which went on to become the first female-owned company to list on the American stock exchange.[98]

Women astutely identified and tapped into the growing market of female consumers—a market that was being underserved by male executives.[99] In the early twentieth century, Annie Minerva Turnbo Malone and Madam C. J. Walker had already become America's first Black female millionaires by selling haircare products, from hair-growth serum to straighteners, door-to-door through chains of commissioned agents and by mail order.[100] Along similar lines, Elizabeth Arden—who dropped out of nursing college and became a bookkeeper at a pharmaceutical company—established a makeup business that developed its own products and recruited travelling saleswomen and demonstrators, as well as opening its own worldwide salons. It became the first beauty company to sell eye makeup to American women.[101] Mary Kay Ash—whom Lifetime Television declared 'the most outstanding woman in business in the twentieth century' and who rewarded her best saleswomen with pink Cadillacs—built her successful cosmetic brand with the motto 'God first, family second, career third'.[102] Brownie Wise created the 'party plan' model of selling that brought Tupperware to every kitchen, and Ruth Handler revolutionised the toy market with a doll that appealed to the aspirations of American girls, cofounding the company Mattel.[103]

While women were proving themselves to be just as capable as men, films, magazines and television promoted a model of the family in which happy housewives tended to their husbands, children and communities. The immediate post-war period appeared to bring a return to 'traditional' family life: young women were marrying in their early as opposed to mid-twenties and the 'baby boom' was set in motion. When combined with the lower birth rates of the Great Depression—resulting in a smaller cohort of young women after the war—this meant that businesses struggled to find enough young single women to recruit.[104] In response, they relaxed marriage bars and turned to older married women who could be tempted back into the workforce having already raised their family.[105] By 1960, thirty-one percent of married women in America—just over a half of all working women—were in paid employment, up from twelve percent thirty years beforehand.[106] In Britain, a government survey noted that 'it has been apparent for some years that the only major source of potential recruits to the labour force . . . consists of married women'.[107] The proportion of married women in Britain who worked outside the home had risen from less than ten percent in 1931 to forty percent in 1971.[108] Rather than staying at home, mothers increasingly opted to return to the workplace after raising their family, preferring to earn money to purchase ready-made clothes and cooked meals than to spend their time creating home-made equivalents, and allowing them to tap into the expanding range of exciting consumer goods, from televisions to the latest furniture trends.[109] By 1980, married women were returning to the workforce even more quickly after having children, which meant that instead of taking 'dead-end jobs' once their children had left home, women could instead build long-term careers. By this point, almost a half of American women with children under six years of age were in paid work, compared with only one in five such women twenty years earlier.[110] But, despite women's growing presence in the workforce, the gender pay gap remained stubbornly high: in America, women earned sixty-four percent of men's hourly earnings and in Britain around seventy percent.[111] It was time to change that.

EQUAL RIGHTS

Black women led the way in fighting for equality.[112] The legacy of slavery meant that there was no history of Black women being 'housewives' and, since the Black community faced discrimination in jobs and education, women's income was necessary to help support the household.[113] The typical Black family—unlike white, middle-class families—could not afford to live off the income of a single breadwinner. As a result, in 1890, the proportion of Black married women who worked was ten times the proportion of white married women who worked, with more than ninety percent of Black women working in agriculture or as domestic servants for white women. In 1930, by which point white married women were being drawn into the labour force, there remained a three times difference, and, by 1970, the gap had narrowed further to the point that it was a difference of 1.3 times.[114] In Britain, Black women also participated more highly than white women in the labour market. While sixty-one percent of white married women aged between forty-five and fifty-nine were in employment by the late 1970s, the equivalent number for women of African Caribbean origin was eighty-five percent and they were much more likely to be in full-time—as opposed to part-time—employment.[115] But, despite their high and long-standing labour-force participation, minority women faced discrimination on two fronts: gender and race.

In America, Black women faced segregation in almost every aspect of their lives, from the counters of restaurants to seats on the buses. On 1 December 1955, Rosa Parks had been arrested for refusing to give up her bus seat to a white person, an act of protest which helped to ignite the civil rights movement that culminated in Martin Luther King's 'March on Washington' and the Civil Rights Act of

1964. It was thanks to the last-minute addition to the Civil Rights Acts that women of all colours—including white women—were able to achieve their subsequent victories in the fight against discrimination in the workplace. Just a day before the Civil Rights Act was passed into law, the word 'sex' was smuggled into the act alongside the word 'race'.[116] The result was that in 1964, employment discrimination on the basis of either race or sex became illegal, something which created the foundations for further legal change.

Title VII of the Civil Rights Act forbade both racial and gender stereotyping, which meant that women could—in legal terms—no longer be discriminated against on the basis that they might have children. When the case of *Meritor Savings Bank v. Vinson* was brought to the Supreme Court in 1986, sexual harassment was also recognised as a violation of Title VII, allowing women for the first time to stand up to 'hostile environments'.[117] The Civil Rights Act that provided the basis for this case had been further supplemented by the Civil Rights Act of 1968 (also known as the Fair Housing Act), which prohibited racial discrimination when it came to the sale and rental of housing, providing 'the basis for homeownership on a wide scale'.[118]

In the same year that the Civil Rights Act of 1968 passed in the United States, 187 women sewing machinists from the Ford Motor Company plant in Dagenham, England, walked out of the factory and went on strike.[119] The Company had ruled that the women's work was unskilled, meaning that they were being paid only eighty-five percent of the wage earned for equivalent work undertaken by men.[120] In the words of one machinist, called Vera, 'The money came into it, but it was the fact that they wouldn't class us as skilled—That's what we fought for'.[121] As Sheila, another machinist at the factory, noted: 'It was a skilled job. I mean you had to have two years machining experience before Ford would even consider taking you on [. . .] and there's a man going around with a broom getting B grade same as us. We could get up and use his broom, but he couldn't sit down and use our machine, so we felt we was skilled!'[122] After four weeks on strike—during which time the cars produced by the

Ford plant were left without seat covers—the women were offered a pay deal equivalent to ninety-two percent of male pay. Despite agreeing to return to work their activism continued.[123] Their strike would go on to make history in the form of the Equal Pay Act of 1970, which, for the first time in Britain, made it illegal to pay and treat men and women differently for carrying out the same work.

In America, the campaign for an 'Equal Rights Act'—which first began in 1923, was eventually passed by the Senate in 1972 and then failed ratification after being blocked at the level of individual states—is still ongoing. The weaker Equal Pay Act had successfully passed in 1963, in large part because it had less teeth and so received much wider support. Trade unions liked the way that 'equal pay for equal work' prevented companies from using cheaper female labour to undercut male workers, and since the act only applied to cases in which men and women were doing exactly the same work, it didn't ruffle too many feathers amongst those who wanted to maintain laws that supposedly 'protected' women (e.g. forbidding them from working certain kinds of jobs, or long hours, or night-shifts, as many states chose to do).[124]

Discrimination in the workplace wasn't the only inequality that women faced. As the sounds of the Beatles and the Beach Boys blasted across the airwaves, an American woman with a well-paid job, savings account and strong references applied to open an account at a metropolitan department store. When the credit manager refused her application and was asked why, he replied, 'She could get pregnant tomorrow'.[125] Store credit was not easy to come by for even the most financially stable of women. The same problem also applied to mortgages. When approving these, banks took the husband's earnings into account but only a portion—if any—of the wife's earnings. Despite the fact that more than forty percent of women earned a wage, creditors were reluctant to lend to them, on the expectation that they might drop out of the labour force.[126] Difficulty accessing credit was a serious obstacle for female entrepreneurs. In 1973, of the 33,948 business loans granted by the Small

Business Administration in the USA, only 123 went to women.[127] A male cosignatory was a common requirement for a business loan.[128] In 1974, the Senate passed the Equal Credit Opportunity Act (ECOA), which prohibited discrimination on the basis of sex when it came to granting loans. In 1976—not before time—the act was amended to include race.[129] The fight for equal rights on the basis of sex and race were tightly bound, something which was similarly clear in the global push for decolonisation.

DECOLONISATION AND GLOBALISATION

In the twentieth century, the battle to unseat colonial rule came to a head. During each of the century's economic milestones, from the Great Depression to the civil rights movement, colonialism was placed in the dock. In 1929, a group of Nigerian Igbo women, tired of economic hardship and imperial rule, pulled up their skirts and exposed their bottoms to British imperialists. Known as the 1929 'Women's War', this was a show of collective resistance that led British officials to draw comparisons with the suffragette movement.[130] In a joyous show of sisterly solidarity, women danced and sang outside government buildings, peacefully but vocally protesting colonial rule. A year later, on 12 March 1930, Mahatma Gandhi began his campaign of civil disobedience in India with a 'Salt March'. He set out on foot—with a few dozen supporters—from his religious retreat in the Indian state of Gujarat to walk 385 kilometres to the town of Dandi on the Indian coast. Along the way, he stopped to rest at a different village every night, gathering an increasing number of followers. Once the march reached the sea, Gandhi and his followers—by then numbering in the hundreds—scooped up handfuls of salt, breaking the law that regulated salt production. At the time, the production and distribution of salt was under the control of the British colonial overlords, who imposed a hefty tax on the foodstuff, generating tax revenue for the British government. Indians who attempted to source and sell their own salt, thereby evading the tax, faced a prison sentence. When Gandhi was imprisoned for encouraging people to source their own salt from the shore at Dandi, thousands of his supporters marched on the British saltworks at Dharasana. They were led by the poet Sarojini Naidu—the female Mahatma Gandhi.

Naidu was a child genius. She had entered the University of Madras aged only twelve, after which she studied at King's College, London and at Girton College, Cambridge. She travelled the British colonies campaigning for independence, cofounded the Women's Indian Association, and in 1925 became the first Indian woman to lead the National Congress, the political party that pushed for independence. Naidu accompanied Gandhi to London to meet with the British government—meetings which no doubt left them feeling frustrated and unheard—and worked alongside him on the campaign for civil disobedience. She believed that independence would only be successful if women were actively involved and that the liberation of India and the liberation of women were inextricably linked. She encouraged the people of India to spin and weave their own cloth in resistance to British imports and to support the local village economy, something which she saw as a feminist as well as an anti-imperialist act. She electrified crowds during her numerous speeches, at which she would point to her own sari, noting that in 'every inch spun of this stuff there is the benediction of a woman who knows that her hands are buying bread for her little children'.[131] Known as 'the Nightingale of India', Naidu was imprisoned on several occasions for her peaceful resistance to British rule.

At this time, around a quarter of the global population lived within the bounds of the British Empire. While the fight for independence had been stewing since the first imperialist set foot on foreign soil, independence movements in Africa and Asia gathered steam after World War One. In 1947, India and Pakistan became separate and independent nations. In 1957, the Gold Coast—which became known as Ghana—was the first sub-Saharan African colony to achieve independence. Other territories followed, with Nigeria and Senegal—a colony of France—achieving independence in 1960. It was in that same year that the United Nations, in what became known as its 'Declaration on Decolonization', committed to 'bringing colonialism in all its forms and manifestations to a speedy and unconditional end, and in this context, declared, inter alia, that all people had a right to self-determination'.[132]

Colonisation had facilitated a division of labour within the global economy that placed colonies in a situation of dependency and relegated them to producing lower-value items with limited growth potential. Colonies exported the primary products and raw materials that fed and fuelled their colonisers and, in turn, colonisers processed those raw materials and exported the finished manufactured goods back to the people of the colonies, who were encouraged to 'Buy British' as opposed to developing their own industries.[133] After achieving independence, many former colonies therefore made a concerted effort to advance economically by building their own modern manufacturing base, using tariffs to protect their infant industries from Western imports and competition. By the 1970s, some of these 'developing countries' were starting to look outward rather than inwards, with the aim of exporting their manufactures to Western countries. International trade was booming, transportation costs were falling, Western investors were looking for new places to invest, and rising costs of production in the West made outsourcing production to former colonies increasingly attractive.[134] In 1970, manufactured goods represented only a fifth of exports from 'developing countries'—which still mostly consisted of agricultural items and raw materials—but by 1990, manufacturing had grown to represent sixty percent of exports.[135]

As manufacturing jobs relocated to parts of the world where labour was more plentiful and where trade unions lacked power, cotton factories in Manchester and New England could not compete. 'Made in Bangladesh', 'Made in Macao' and 'Made in Honduras' became a regular sight on our clothing labels. The spread of international garment production created new job openings for women and the female share of employment in manufacturing began to climb.[136] Women workers were seen as low-cost, hardworking, flexible and easy to discipline.[137] By the turn of the century, women formed the majority of workers in 'export processing zones' in the 'Global South'.[138] Women were central to the growth taking place not only in the West but in the world beyond.

By the end of the century, and in what the World Bank referred to as an 'Economic Miracle', the Far East was biting at the heels of the Western economy. After opening themselves to global markets, Hong Kong, Indonesia, Japan, Malaysia, Singapore, South Korea, Taiwan and Thailand had focused on investing in people—including by sponsoring their brightest students to study abroad—in an effort to advance beyond low-wage, labour-intensive manufacturing and towards more technologically advanced, higher-wage sectors. A consensus began to develop in global policy circles that free markets and globalisation—so long as they were combined with investment in education—would place all economies on the path to prosperity, as came to be demonstrated by one country more than any other: China.

CHINA TRANSFORMED

For most of the twentieth century, China was closed to the world. Western colonialism, and the losses it inflicted on China during the Opium Wars, had humiliated the Emperor in front of his own people, which led to growing tensions, eventually culminating in a communist revolution. The new ruling elite had no appetite for a relationship with the West and treated international economic organisations with suspicion. They did not aspire to trade and consumerism and instead valorised the simple life of peasant farming. Under communism, China became a country without shops and restaurants, where everyone was expected to wear the same grey uniform.[139] While China was poor, it was relatively gender equal. From the beginning, the Chinese Communist Party had championed the 'liberation' of women, including from the practices of foot-binding and arranged marriage.[140] It understood that the failings of the previous centuries were a product of the mistreatment of women and distinguished itself from the imperial past with a drive to treat women as equals. 'Women hold up half the sky', said Mao Zedong, adding that '[w]hatever men comrades can accomplish, women comrades can too'.[141] So that they could work outside the home, mothers were given instructions on how to tie their babies to the bed such that they wouldn't roll off while their mothers were out at work: 'attach a wooden stake or an iron rod, use a belt to attach it there, and tie the end around the baby's waist'.[142] Being a housewife was not an option in communist China.

But while women might have been treated as equals in China, by limiting the individual decision-making capacity of its citizens, the Communist Party left no room for individual initiative and enterprise. Like Soviet Russia's programme of Collectivisation, China's 'Great Leap Forward'—a programme which aimed to boost production in the countryside—brought starvation and famine that cost between fifteen and thirty million lives.[143] The result of its failing economy was that China became home to more poor people than anywhere else in the world. But, unlike Soviet Russia, by the 1970s the Chinese Communist Party was facing up to its policy errors. In 1978, China introduced a series of economic reforms that attempted to combine the best of what communism and capitalism had to offer by opening a second track for its economy that could operate alongside its state-run businesses: it allowed people to form their own private enterprises and started to welcome foreign investment, in partnership with China's own business sector.

Shortly after the reforms, Zhang Xin, a fifteen-year-old girl who had grown up in the Chinese countryside, migrated from the mainland to Hong Kong (a colony of Britain until 1997), where she spent the next five years working in factories.[144] Although she worked long hours on monotonous production lines, the fact that she could earn her own money created a rush of freedom: 'I could buy anything I wanted to buy. I could eat anything I wanted to eat. And I could wear anything I wanted to wear,' she later explained.[145] In 1985, she moved to the UK to study economics.[146] England was at first a culture shock. On the first night, she sat on her suitcase and cried.[147] She knew no one and still needed to develop her English language skills. She found work in a fish and chip shop—run by a Chinese family—where she was placed in charge of asking customers whether they wanted salt and vinegar. Having honed her English, by 1992, Zhang had graduated from the University of Cambridge with a Master's degree in Development Economics.[148] For the next couple of years she worked for Goldman Sachs, where she gained experience as an investor, learning to spot investment opportunities and bring them to fruition. In 1995, Zhang and her husband—Pan Shiyi—set up their own real estate company and in 1998 they developed SOHO New Town, a residential and commercial district next to China's World Trade Center.[149] Their company became the first to win a bid for land in Beijing's business district, for which she has become known as 'the woman who built Beijing'.[150]

China—still technically a communist country—has become the poster child for free markets. Since opening up its economy, its economic growth rate has averaged around nine percent a year, average incomes have risen eightfold and 800 million people have been pulled out of poverty.[151] But it isn't market reforms alone that have enabled this rapid transformation; it is the combination of market reforms and gender equality, something which has delivered the greatest economic miracle since Britain's Industrial Revolution.

MARKET MANIA

While Zhang Xin was studying in England, she became familiar with the face of one particular woman on her television screen. It was Margaret Thatcher. 'I remember I was in awe watching her and thinking: "How could she speak so well? How is that possible that she was debating with this roomful of hundreds of men?" She was so brave and she was so good. And I just had her . . . as my role model', explains Zhang.[152] Like Zhang, Thatcher had risen from humble beginnings. She was born in Grantham, Lincolnshire, where she grew up in her parents' grocery shop. After attending her local grammar school, she was awarded a place at Oxford University, where she became president of the student Conservative Association. After climbing to the top of the Conservative Party and becoming Britain's first female Prime Minister in 1979, Thatcher made it her mission to transform the British economy. In the nineteenth century, Britain had been the richest economy in the world, but by the 1970s it had fallen behind European peers such as Germany and France and, of course, America.[153] During the post-war period, large swathes of British industry had been brought into state ownership—from aviation, railways and shipbuilding to coal mining, gas and telecoms—and became plagued by poor management and fractious relations between management and the workforce. Poor performance appeared to be rewarded with ever-greater government subsidies.[154] A lack of competition meant that quality was low and prices were high, strike activity regularly brought production to a standstill, electricity supply was so unreliable that households were frequently plunged into darkness and in 1976 the government had to ask the International Monetary Fund (IMF) for a bailout. As medicine for the failing economy, Thatcher promised the electorate a reversal of the policy framework that had guided government in the post-war era. She rolled back the state and deregulated the economy in order to 'set markets free'. Her hope was that greater competition—in place of government control—would improve economic efficiency, create new opportunities for economic growth and produce a better deal for consumers who were tired of pricey and shoddy goods. State-owned industries were privatised, trade unions were tamed, taxes were reduced and capital markets were liberalised. In order to subject the economy to greater foreign competition, Britain joined the European Single Market, which made trade cheaper and easier.[155] Across the Atlantic, Ronald Reagan became Thatcher's political and economic soul mate, championing private-sector enterprise and limited government. From China to America, capitalism was gripping governments—and the internet was about to turn the dial towards hyper-capitalism.

A BYTE OF THE CAKE

By the 1990s, the computer revolution—the biggest technological change since the steam engine—was transforming both the American and the British economies.[156] The internet connected financial markets across the world as computer power revolutionised the buying and selling of shares and enabled deeper analysis of global investment trends. Markets were better connected than ever before. While Bill Gates, Steve Jobs and Tim Berners-Lee are the names most associated with computing, women had been advancing the industry from the beginning. Indeed women were themselves the first computers, charged with doing the repetitive and laborious calculations in many an office, as we have already seen. Since the earliest computer programs were considered akin to such work, programming was similarly left to women, who were self-taught, treated as low-skilled and paid a pittance. Twentieth-century computing pioneers included Mary Coombs—the first female commercial computer programmer in Britain—who worked on a computerised stock-control system for Lyons tearooms, designed to ensure that they never ran out of tea and cake. The Lyons computer—nicknamed LEO I—was the world's first business computer: it was so large that it occupied an entire room. Once debugged by Coombs and her fellow programmers, it was so efficient—not just in terms of managing stock control but also in terms of speeding up payroll—that Lyons diversified away from selling afternoon teas to selling its technology to other businesses around the world. Working at the same time as Coombs, Dina St Johnston founded the first independent software company in the UK, having previously developed classified programs for the Royal Navy, along with the first computerised program for local government administration.[157] On the other side of the Atlantic, Mary Winston Jackson, who had joined the racially segregated Langley Memorial Aeronautical Laboratory's Computing section in 1951, went on to become NASA's first Black female engineer, as memorialised in the film *Hidden Figures*;[158] Sandy Lerner cofounded Cisco Systems, who made the first routers, in turn enabling the development of the internet;[159] Meg Whitman became CEO of eBay, where she oversaw the explosive growth in internet shopping;[160] and Carly Fiorina became President and CEO of Hewlett-Packard—the first woman to lead a Fortune 50 company.[161]

As Silicon Valley developed, so too did the financial sector. Having been liberated from government regulations, London and New York transformed themselves into global cities. As financiers and tech entrepreneurs reaped the rewards of new growth opportunities, wages elsewhere in the economy stagnated, resulting in a growing gap between rich and poor. Some blamed the cheap foreign imports from the Global South while others pointed to the way that new technologies—such as 'computer-aided design' and robotics—were creating production lines devoid of workers. As jobs were shed in industry, new jobs opened up in retail, hospitality and care, but without the same pay and promotion prospects; the result was the hollowing out of traditional, middle-income, skilled jobs, leaving a two-tier economy of highly paid tech and finance roles for some and low-paid service work for the rest. Inequality in America returned to levels not seen since the nineteenth century.[162]

In this new economy, education was more important than ever before: brainpower had replaced brawn as the quality most valued by employers. Handsomely paid jobs were on offer only for those with the appropriate degrees. For young women, the contraceptive pill was key to taking advantage of these new economic opportunities, enabling the most academically minded to spend more time in education and thereby pursue careers that brought higher pay packets.[163] By the end of the century, and for the first time ever, more American women were graduating from college than American men.[164] The result was that while income inequality was growing, the gender pay gap was closing. By 2000, women in Britain and America earned three-quarters of men's earnings, compared with a mere sixty percent thirty years beforehand.[165] Not only had the employment of women grown considerably since the start of the century, but women themselves were starting to reap greater rewards for their efforts.

'Education, education, education' was adopted as a campaign slogan of the Labour Party in Britain, who refashioned themselves as 'New Labour' under Tony Blair. At the 1997 polls, Labour managed to oust the Conservatives by rejecting its own socialist past and embracing Thatcher's belief in markets. The antidote to inequality offered to the electorate—whether in terms of gender or in terms of income—was therefore more education, not less capitalism. As China's newly liberalised economy went from strength to strength and the Soviet Union collapsed, Francis Fukuyama declared 'the end of history'.[166] The battle between communism and capitalism appeared to have been won, the world seemed more peaceful and better connected than ever before, and it looked as if the march towards the equality of the sexes was nearing completion.

~

IN THE TWENTY-FIRST CENTURY, OPTIMISM GAVE WAY TO PESSIMISM as both peace and prosperity were abruptly disturbed. In 2001, New York's World Trade Centre crumbled following a vicious terrorist attack and by 2008 the financial system was in crisis and the global economy was entering the 'Great Recession'. In academic circles, global capitalism was placed on trial, charged with being exploitative as opposed to liberating, while around the dinner table and in the press, questions were raised about whether women really could 'have it all'. In the next chapter we will identify where today's working women can be found, spotlight the female pioneers who are hard at work creating the economy of the future and consider how much further women have to go on the path to equality.

CHAPTER 12

CREATIVES, CARERS AND CLEAN-TECH INNOVATORS

WOMEN IN THE TWENTY-FIRST CENTURY

In the last three decades, the global economy has transformed beyond all recognition. If you were to compare a list of the ten biggest companies in the world today with an equivalent list from the end of the last century, you would find little overlap: companies such as General Motors and Citigroup—big players in the twentieth century—have lost their top spots to the likes of Apple and Amazon.[1] Technological advances in computing, science and medicine have given birth to entirely new areas of the economy while shaking the foundations of long-established sectors. China and India have opened their economies to global trade, becoming giants on the world stage. Back-office services—for businesses including banks, utilities and delivery companies—have been outsourced from

Europe and the United States to middle-income countries, creating new jobs for the growing number of university graduates in the Global South. The global workforce has become increasingly mobile, leading millions to cross borders in search of a better life, including to work in the care homes and hospitals that tend to the West's ageing population. And, on the academic front, Singapore, South Korea, China and Japan have joined Europe and America as hotspots for scientific research.[2]

As the resultant economic growth has spread across the world, it has pulled a billion people out of poverty worldwide and, for the first time in history, most of the world can now be categorised as middle-class.[3] Not only has the gap between the 'developed' and the 'developing' world begun to close, so too has the gap between men and women. Globally, one in two women are now engaged in paid work. In the US and Britain, the gender pay gap—the gap in earnings between men and women—has halved since 1970, falling from just under forty percent to just under twenty percent, and equal pay legislation now exists in ninety-eight countries.[4] But despite all the good news, serious challenges remain. In 2008, the world economy faced the biggest shock since the Great Depression—the Global Financial Crisis. Alongside, climate crises and global pandemics—including Covid-19—have served to underline the vulnerabilities inherent in this modern, interconnected global economic system.

In this chapter we consider how the economic developments of the twenty-first century are impacting women, and how women are both harnessing opportunities and responding to challenges. As we will see, while men dominate in the much-hyped technology sector, women are far better represented in biotech and the creative industries. Moreover, in healthcare and social care—arguably the sector with the greatest growth potential but also the poorest pay—women comprise the vast majority of the workforce. As the economy continues to evolve in the years ahead, the outcomes for women will be a mixture of possibility and precarity.

ON THE MONEY

At the start of the twenty-first century, economists were feeling optimistic. In 2003, Robert Lucas—the Nobel Prize–winning economist—boldly announced to the American Economic Association that the 'central problem of depression-prevention had been solved'.[5] The Great Depression would, in other words, never happen again. Three years later, *The Economist* magazine reported that 'having grown at an annual rate of 3.2% per head since 2000, the world economy is over halfway towards notching up its best decade ever . . . Market capitalism, the engine that runs most of the world economy, seems to be doing its job well'.[6] If you were leaving school at the time, planning how to find the highest-paying career, your best option would have been to get a degree in economics and to set your sights on a job in finance. After all, property markets were booming and stock markets were growing, creating business opportunities for a growing army of portfolio managers, stock brokers and investment bankers. As the financial sector flourished, London and New York attracted not only financial types but also a profusion of people who could service their every need. With bankers came baristas and, within a stone's throw of Wall Street, top restaurateurs ready to serve up their Wagyu steak dinners. New York's competitor—the square mile known as the City of London—was spilling out into the old West India docklands in London's East End, turning Canary Wharf from a 'wasteland of derelict wharves' into a miniature version of its international rival, one which houses a half of Britain's tallest buildings and whose tenants came to include Barclays, HSBC and Citigroup.[7]

The expansion in financial services was understandable. Finance lubricates the wider economy. Without the development of banks and stock markets, most businesses would be unable to access the funds they need to grow—only the rich would be able to start their own companies, limiting the potential of the economy to expand. However, benefits do not come without costs. Whilst finance allows our economy to grow, it also creates a roller-coaster ride along the way. The reason for this turbulence is simple: the future is completely unpredictable, which makes investing very difficult. Investment decisions inevitably involve making predictions about the future. In other words, we have to consider questions such as how much property prices are likely to rise, whether stocks will do better than bonds, which parts of the world are likely to be the next economic hotspots, which sectors will provide the greatest growth potential and what the next consumer fads will be. Finance and fortune-telling therefore have rather more in common than most financial professionals would probably like to admit. And, precisely because the future is unknowable, it is impossible to answer any investment question with complete certainty, in turn meaning that we cannot calculate the 'true' value of any stock, property or other asset. As a result, financial markets lack an anchor—instead, asset prices can blow with the wind; with whatever people—in aggregate—have come to 'think' will happen. For want of a crystal ball, people have a tendency to follow the crowd; after all, if other people are ploughing their money into a particular stock, property, sector or market, that very action will be pushing up its value. Herd behaviour takes over and the resultant waves of optimism and pessimism translate into serious fluctuations.

The more we can borrow money to purchase shares or property, the more prices are pushed upwards in a boom, and in turn tumble in a bust. But, fortunately or not, the amount of lending that banks are willing to offer us isn't endless; it depends on a careful calculation: weighing up the profit that the banks can make from the interest we pay on our loans with the potential risk that we default on them, potentially leaving the banks seriously out of pocket. It is this 'default risk' that prevents lending from getting completely out of control; it explains why banks have historically been very conservative. However, at the start of the twenty-first century, and in competition with other banks to make profits—profits that satisfied the growing number of shareholders who could easily jump ship—banking institutions began to lend like never before. It wasn't that they had entirely forgotten about default risk; it was that they felt that they had devised a magical new way of reaping the benefits of additional lending—all of those extra interest-payment streams—while reducing the associated risk. Their scheme involved packaging together high-risk investments—particularly sub-prime mortgages—thinking that by putting multiple such loans together, they could make them less risky: that, in other words, to lend to lots of sub-prime borrowers was better than lending to just one, as while one homeowner might default on their loan, not all would. Hence, by grouping high-risk loans together—and then selling slices of these loan packages off to investors—banks believed that they were turning high-risk loans into lower-risk loans. With it, sub-prime lending boomed and everyone seemed happy: aspiring homeowners who had traditionally been locked out of mainstream lending were able to get onto the housing ladder; existing homeowners were pleased that property prices were rising; banks were happily granting more loans; and financial institutions were buying up slices of the packaged-together loans, believing that they were a good investment for their clients. While homeowners were becoming increasingly leveraged—with mortgages that were large relative to their incomes—the obvious danger appeared to be masked by the fact that the rise in the value of property seemed to justify the bigger mortgages. And, if the bank was happy to lend to you, surely—people thought—they couldn't be doing anything that wasn't sensible. But once rumours started to develop that this situation was unsustainable, the pack of cards began to tumble. Loan offers were withdrawn, which meant fewer buyers for properties—and fewer investors wanting to purchase the packaged-together mortgage products—leading to asset prices plunging, further credit contraction and further property price falls. Homeowners suddenly found that they were much more indebted than they had anticipated and financiers who had bought packages of mortgage debt began to realise that it wasn't as low-risk as they had thought. Lehman Brothers—a giant in the financial world who had underwritten millions of the sub-prime mortgage packages in the hope of benefitting from the interest streams—collapsed, putting thousands of financiers out of work and sending shock waves through Wall Street. Other financial giants—who had similarly invested in the wave of sub-prime lending—faced similar difficulties. Banks suddenly switched from being overly exuberant to instead being overly cautious. Even their long-standing customers couldn't convince them to lend them money, resulting in a worldwide credit crunch. With businesses and households unable to access credit, the tremors spread across the whole economy. Just as extra lending had helped to generate a boom, the contraction in lending generated a global bust.

Some have blamed toxic masculinity for the financial crisis, believing that greed and arrogance led financiers to think that they could perform their magic trick—or to brazenly ignore the associated risks. Christine Lagarde, then France's finance minister and later IMF Chief, famously suggested that if Lehman Brothers had been Lehman Sisters, the 2008 financial crisis might not have occurred. To be fair, the upper echelons of the financial industry were—and still are—dominated by men. Since 1980, the major British banks had employed more women than they did men, but the vast majority of their female recruits worked in lower-grade administrative and clerical positions that offered few promotion prospects: women who worked in banks were typically recruited at the age of sixteen, fresh out of school, while men were recruited with more advanced qualifications, into 'careers' as opposed to 'jobs'.[8] At the start of the twenty-first century, only ten percent of senior managers in British banks were female and only 1.7 percent of bank CEOs were women.[9] Still today, the vast majority of senior managers and CEOs in the financial sector are men. In 2020, there were four times as many male senior managers in British banks than there were female ones, and the proportion of bank CEOs that were women had risen to a mere 9.7 percent.[10] Estimates suggest that, at the current rates of progress, it will take eighty-eight years until the banking industry is truly equal.[11]

So, does the lack of gender balance matter and was this really what caused the financial crisis? Bank of England researchers have found that banks with a higher proportion of women in senior roles performed better—both in terms of risk and return—than those where men were more dominant. Wider studies of European banks revealed that banks with more diversified boards were less likely to need public bailouts and faced fewer fines from regulators.[12] Doubtless the 'macho' culture in finance did not help the stability of the financial system, but it would be foolish to draw the conclusion that if more bankers were women, financial crises would be avoidable. The reality is that women are unlikely somehow to be better able to predict the future than men and that women can become equally caught up in 'irrational exuberance', believing that 'this time is different'—that, for example, higher property prices are justifiable and aren't about to crash. What matters, therefore, isn't whether a financier is male or female, but that there is enough diversity—enough people challenging one another—to avoid groupthink. In that sense, recent attempts to open up the world of finance to a broader range of talent can only be a good thing. And, as we will see, this new generation of investors will have plenty of investment opportunities to choose from—from technology giants, biotech and clean-tech startups to creative industries, hospitals and care homes.

EYES ON TECH

Thanks to the Global Financial Crisis, finance has lost much of its lustre. The owners of Canary Wharf—the people who own the land on which the financial towers have been erected—now look to tech companies rather than banks as potential tenants and, when it comes to the most lucrative degrees, computer science and engineering have overtaken economics as the qualifications that offer the best long-term pay prospects.[13] Comparing the salaries of recent graduates five years after they've left college reveals that computer science and engineering graduates now command the highest salaries, averaging more than $70,000 a year, just ahead of economics at $65,000 and close to double the earnings of liberal arts majors.[14] Even those with PhDs in Economics—people who would previously have made a career in finance—are starting to eschew banks in favour of tech companies.[15]

Mira Murati is one of the women leading the way in the development of Artificial Intelligence (AI), including through the creation of ChatGPT. As a child, Murati was passionate about maths, spending her days solving mathematical problem sets and attending Olympiads.[16] She grew up in Albania, at a time when the economic system was transitioning from communism to capitalism. The fact that maths could offer complete and certain answers gave it a gravitational pull in a period of political flux. Moreover, as Murati explained in an interview with Kevin Scott, the Chief Technology Officer for Microsoft: 'In the first years of my childhood, Albania was incredibly isolated, like North Korea is today. And so, there wasn't much inflow of entertainment or anything really besides books'.[17] When she was sixteen, Murati was offered a scholarship to complete her schooling in Vancouver, Canada. She wanted to use knowledge to solve 'really hard problems' that make 'our lives better', and so decided to study mechanical engineering at college; having spent her senior year at Dartmouth College building a hybrid race car, she then went to work at Tesla. It was while working on Auto Pilot—self-driving technology—for the Model X car at Tesla that Murati became particularly interested in AI. She saw how AI could create cars that were intelligent enough to take on the role of the driver, but she didn't want to just 'become a car person'. She wanted to take AI out of the realm of being applied to narrow or specific problems to see how it could be used more widely.[18] She joined OpenAI, which had been founded as a nonprofit organisation in 2015 with a mission 'to ensure that artificial general intelligence benefits all of humanity'.[19] In November 2022, it took the world by storm when its newly released AI chatbot—ChatGPT—went viral.[20] Within weeks of its release, my colleagues and I—along with numerous other academics across the world—were being called into university meetings to discuss how the chatbot was changing the face of learning and, in particular, what we were going to do about all of the students who were using it to write their essays.

When asked at a recent event what AI is good for, Murati replied, 'Everything! Everything will be impacted by it'.[21] AI is now used by radiographers when inspecting scans to search for evidence of tumours, by climate scientists to generate more accurate weather forecasts, by delivery companies when planning routes, by customer-service teams when chatting with customers online, and by search engines, websites and media platforms that want to learn from our searches, clicks and purchases so as to give us more of what we want. Like the machines of the Industrial Revolution, the intelligence that AI has to offer has the power to automate the more repetitive aspects of our jobs—from performing linguistic translations to carrying out basic research or answering routine customer-service enquiries—allowing us to spend time on more demanding tasks. In addition to 'amplifying our intelligence', it can also expand our creativity. While you might not want AI to write a complete script, score, article or essay for you, you might want to use it to suggest—say—a hundred possible endings, providing inspiration that can fire your creative juices.

Like finance, tech is a sector dominated by men. Since over three-quarters of people working in AI and Data Science across the world are men, Murati is the exception rather than the rule. This has created concerns that there is a lack of female input in AI development, potentially resulting in human biases—such as sexism—featuring in things like chatbots, virtual reality and advertising, articles and videos that surface on our internet feeds with the help of AI.[22] The scarcity of women in tech also means that the sector's expansion will benefit men more than it will women. As the Alan

Turing Institute notes: 'As AI becomes ubiquitous in everyday life, closing the gender gap in the data science and AI workforce matters'.[23]

At Google, 32.5 percent of the global workforce are female, but looking more deeply at their workforce demographics reveals that only a quarter of their technology employees are women, compared with 46.4 percent of their non-technology employees (such as those working in HR or accountancy).[24] At Meta—the parent company of Facebook, Instagram and WhatsApp—women comprise thirty-seven percent of the total workforce but only 25.8 percent of their technology employees.[25] At Apple, thirty-five percent of the workforce are female, but—as with Google and Meta—only a quarter of their technology employees are women, compared with forty-five percent of the non-technology part of their workforce.[26] At Microsoft, women similarly comprise 33.1 percent of the global workforce, but only 26.6 percent of those women work in technology roles in the core part of the business.[27]

The gender gap in technology starts at school. In the European Union, only seventeen percent of those studying IT in upper secondary school or college are girls.[28] In the United States, fewer than a quarter of IT graduates are women and in the UK only one in five.[29] While sixty-one percent of male students in the UK say that they would consider a career in technology, only twenty-seven percent of female students say likewise.[30] But this is not the case everywhere in the world. There is significant variation in women's representation in IT, suggesting that the gender gap is neither natural nor inevitable. In India, Algeria, Saudi Arabia, Thailand, Malaysia, the Philippines and Peru, women represent almost a half of students who study IT upon leaving school, while in Oman, Myanmar, Syria, Tunisia, the UAE, Benin and Qatar, women represent more than a half of ICT graduates.[31] It is, perhaps, beyond the West where we might find the female technology leaders of the future. And, increasingly, they will be in a white coat in a laboratory rather than behind a computer, as tech is revolutionising biological sciences.

THE SCIENCE OF LIFE

We all dream of living longer and healthier lives—a dream that leads pharmaceutical companies to imagine big dollar signs. But medical research is expensive: it can take years to pay off, if it pays off at all. Curing cancer, solving infertility and alleviating pain are goals that have motivated scientists for decades if not centuries and, where pharmaceutical companies see a potential profit in developing associated drugs, they are happy to fund the research, offering handsome salaries in order to attract the top science graduates. But, in addition to the pharmaceutical giants, a whole host of smaller 'biotech' companies have sprung to life in recent years, researching avenues that they believe are being overlooked by 'big pharma'. Where these startups are able to turn their research into potentially profitable treatments or drugs, the pharmaceutical giants seek to bring them in-house, resulting in merger and acquisition (M&A) deals that can create big windfalls for biotech founders. In 2023, more than a hundred such deals took place, with a total value of around $200 billion.[32] While there are clearly big sums to be made in biotech, however, there are also big sums to be lost. Where research leads to dead ends, biotech companies can, of course, lose everything, making the industry a high-stakes game. As noted by one of biotech's 'fiercest women', Bari Kowal, the female Head of Development Operations who oversees clinical trials at the New York–based drugmaker Regeneron, 'You have to have a thick skin'.[33]

The most lucrative biotech deal in 2023 was Pfizer's forty-three-billion-dollar acquisition of Seagen, a twenty-five-year-old biotech company focused on developing cancer medicines that aim to kill cancer cells while minimising damage to other parts of the body. The acquisition doubled Pfizer's oncology research and drug pipeline, leading their Chief Oncology Officer to announce that it was 'a great day for Pfizer, and, more importantly, for people living with cancer'.[34] Seagen was a company that scored highly not only on fighting cancer—with 147,000 cancer patients having been treated with Seagen medications worldwide—but also on gender diversity:

its global workforce was more than fifty percent female and its leadership—at executive director level and above—was forty-one percent female.[35]

In the UK, US and Europe, between forty and fifty percent of people working at biotech companies are women, and women dominate the pipeline of new entrants in the industry. But not all biotechs are as female-friendly at the top of the business as they are at the bottom. On average, only one in three senior executive roles are filled by women, along with only twenty percent of C-suite positions (CEO, CFO, etc.), and only one in four US biotech startups was founded by a woman.[36] Biotech also intersects with the much more male-dominated world of technology. Artificial intelligence is growing in importance when it comes to medical research, for example by allowing scientists to create proteins with the properties needed for their experiments, but, as a field, AI is short on female talent.[37] In addition, those who hold the purse strings—the venture capitalists from the financial world who help to fund new startups—are, typically, men. This means that while women may be relatively well represented in biotech, they are ultimately pitching their scientific ideas to teams of men. In order to help address the resultant biases that can arise, in 2022 a group of fifty-three female biotech CEOs got together for a three-day summit and founded the 'Biotech Sisterhood', a network that connects women executives with potential investors.[38] And, sensing that female startups with growth potential were being overlooked, some 'angel' investors are now actively searching to invest in female-founded businesses.[39] If this continues, biotech—more than tech—has the potential to be an area of growth that helps to close, rather than widen, the gender gap in the years ahead.

CREATIVE ENERGY

On 28 March 2024, a cryptic video of a woman typing on an old-style typewriter appeared on Spotify, along with a two-week countdown clock. On clicking play, the words '[e]ven statues crumble if they're made to wait' were spelled out on a sheet of paper by the typewriter keys.[40] The author of the video—and indeed the woman with her fingers on the keys—was Taylor Swift. As the accompanying clock counted down, the world sat waiting in anticipation of Swift's new album: *The Tortured Poets Department*. Less than twelve hours after its release, the album broke the record for the most streams in a day, totalling more than 300 million.[41] By the end of its first week, the number of streams exceeded one billion. Swift's 'Eras' tour—which began in March 2023—had already set another record, as the highest-grossing music tour ever, with revenues that surpassed those of the previous record holder, Elton John (from his 'Farewell Yellow Brick Road' tour). As Swift toured the world with her trusty guitar—dressed in glittering gowns and body suits and with hair that flowed naturally over her shoulders—she announced to the crowds: 'No group of people this big has ever gotten together for one thing'.[42]

In October 2023, *Forbes* magazine declared that Swift had made her way onto their list of global billionaires, making her the first person in history to become a billionaire through musical talent alone.[43] While musicians have always drawn in crowds, the creative industry—which encompasses music, theatre, film, television, fashion, advertising, handicrafts, design and computer games—is growing in scale. Global exports of what are defined as 'cultural goods and services' doubled in the period between 2005 and 2019 and Netflix, Bollywood, K-pop and Amazon Prime have become household names.[44] Britain has become a global creative hub. Over the last decade, the creative industries in the UK have grown at more than one and a half times the rate of the wider economy.[45] Job creation in Britain's creative sector has been five times higher than in the rest of the economy, and estimates suggest that one million more people in Britain will be working in the creative sector by 2030—on top of the two million people already in the industry.[46] Creative industries are also expanding outside of the West, with India now the world's largest film producer.[47] Economists predict a forty percent growth in the creative sector worldwide over the next seven years, meaning that it could soon be responsible for ten percent of the global economy.[48]

Not only are the arts rivalling the sciences; they are harnessing the latest scientific tools—AI, virtual reality, digital editing, digital payment, CGI and online streaming—to maximise audiences and, with them, revenues. Music streaming, for example, now accounts for over a half of global music-industry revenues.[49] Just as nineteenth-century theatres used electricity and advertising to draw in the crowds and twentieth-century film studios employed the latest camera and sound-recording technologies to bring us motion pictures in full technicolour, today's entrepreneurially minded creatives are turning to modern-day technology to grow their businesses. The creative industries are not competitors for the tech industry—they are where technology and human creativity intersect.

Women like Phiona Okumu are globalising the creative sector. Having worked in music journalism and public relations across Africa, she was determined to bring African bands to global audiences. After joining Apple Music, one of her first successes was getting the Nigerian singer Mr Eazi on a Hollywood Boulevard billboard.[50] She went on to become Spotify's Head of Music for sub-Saharan Africa, where—under their RADAR programme—she has been guiding musicians, including the South African R&R singer Elaine, towards big record deals.[51]

In total, women represent around a half of workers in the creative sector, placing them in a strong position to benefit from future growth.[52] According to the United Nations, women are naturals when it comes to the production of cultural goods and services more generally: '[I]n communities across the world, rich cultural value and traditional designs have been protected and nurtured by women through creative industries'.[53] The only stumbling block is that while women dominate in those parts of the industry that have historically been considered feminine—for example in wardrobe, hair and makeup in the film industry—they are underrepresented in the most lucrative parts of the creative world and in senior roles.[54] In 2023, women comprised only fifteen percent of American film directors, thirty-two percent of leading roles and twenty-five percent of scriptwriters.[55] In the 2023–4 classical concert season, women conducted around twenty percent of concert performances in America—this was higher than previous years but still a tiny minority of performances.[56] Across the world, men also dominate when it comes to recipients of film awards and national art prizes.[57] While the continued expansion in the creative industries is set to create an equal number of additional job opportunities for men and women, this may not alone be enough to close the gender gap.

WHO CARES?

None of us is getting any younger and, at some point, most of us will need to be looked after. Since 1900, average life expectancy across the globe has more than doubled, from thirty-two years to seventy-one years.[58] Alongside this, the average number of children born to women has fallen from five in the 1960s to just over two today.[59] The year 2018 marked a global crossover point where—for the first time in human history—there were more people aged sixty-five or older than there were children aged five or under.[60] The future is one of more elderly people in need of care and fewer family members available to perform such duties, making health and care one of the fastest-growing parts of the economy. Around ten percent of the workforce in high-income countries already work in the health and care sector.[61] Unlike garment production and call centres—both of which have relocated overseas—care is a sector that cannot relocate, which means that growing demand for care in the West is being translated directly into job growth in the domestic care sector. After all, while you can import your wardrobe favourites from overseas and speak to your utility company or bank long-distance, if you live in London or New York, you're not realistically able to drop your children off at a nursery in Lagos and then drop in to see your elderly parents at a care home in Lima on your way home in the evening.

In other words, if you need live-in help, a nursery for your children, a care home for your parents or immediate medical attention, it will be people in your local area who provide these services. But while the sector cannot easily move across borders, workers certainly can.

In the same way that wealthy families in Britain and America once sourced domestic help from amongst communities of young immigrant women, families today are looking to migrant women to meet their domestic needs. Live-in nannies and carers have become popular amongst those with the financial means to pay for tailor-made help, with nurseries and care homes providing the same services on a larger—and typically more efficient—scale. In Britain, one in five care workers are from overseas.[62] In the US, a quarter of long-term care workers are from abroad—even more if on-site housekeeping and maintenance staff in care homes are included.[63] The Brookings Institution—an American economic think-tank—notes that America is facing an 'unprecedented shortfall in the necessary supply of caregivers', making care increasingly unaffordable. Expanding the number of immigrant caregivers can, it notes, help to make 'long-term care more accessible, effective, and affordable for older Americans'.[64] Hospitals are also turning to overseas workers to fill vacancies. One third of doctors and nurses recruited in the UK now come from overseas.[65] Dr Sumaira Babar, a consultant radiologist, moved to the UK from Pakistan to work in the NHS. Babar says that she has relished the opportunity to work overseas, not just for herself but for her young children, who, she says are able to experience a 'new culture'.[66] Africa is also helping to meet the West's labour needs. Over a six-month period in 2023, twenty nurses from the intensive care unit at Greater Accra Regional Hospital in Ghana migrated to Britain and America. One nurse at the hospital told the BBC that around a half of the people she graduated with had moved to work overseas, and that she was planning to join them. According to the nursing lead at the hospital, the exodus is harming patients.[67] The International Council of Nurses has warned that the 'brain drain' of health professionals from poorer to richer countries is exacerbating local staff shortages and hurting health-care provision.[68] But the 'pull factor' is understandable: nurses from Ghana can earn a salary that is seven times higher in the UK than at home.[69]

Health and care is not only the sector estimated to have the most job creation potential; it is also—unlike tech—a sector dominated by women.[70] In low and middle-income countries, sixty-three percent of health and care workers are women. In high-income countries, it is even higher: three-quarters of the workforce are women.[71] But, alongside this, it is also a sector that pays relatively poorly. In the UK, forty-three percent of workers in adult social care earn below the living wage—the minimum income required to meet basic needs. As one care worker explains:

> *I get to serve others through simple acts of kindness. A kind word, a cup of tea, a listening ear to those who need it. Given how meaningful the work is I'm angry that my employers and other care providers don't give us a fair wage. For me, it means I sometimes have to work a triple shift. That's a day followed by a night shift followed by another day. It's exhausting. I've just got married and as I look forward to the possibility of family, how can I stay in this job I love so much?*[72]

In order to meet their basic needs, it is normal for care workers to work multiple shifts. As Nkem Okoli—also a care worker in the UK—explains:

> *I went into care because I am an empathetic person. I always try to put myself in other people's shoes. I would love to see my passion for my work reflected in my pay. I have poured my heart and soul into my work, taking every opportunity to improve my skills; doing many overtime shifts to add to my income. Taking care of someone else's family is rewarding,*

but I also need to take care of my own. A real living wage would mean I could spend more time with my children and feel less guilty. I could work the right number of hours and give my all to my job.[73]

In March 2024, home care workers in New York went on a hunger strike to protest their twenty-four-hour shifts. Wrapped in warm clothes to brave the winter weather, they gathered with placards outside City Hall, where they remained for five days—many of them immigrant women of colour. Lai Yea Chan, sixty-nine, speaking through a translator, told CBS News that she was taking part in the strike to improve conditions for the next generation. Councilman Christopher Mare, who supported the strikers and has put a bill to end the twenty-four-hour shifts before the City Council, noted that his own mother worked twenty-four-hour shifts and that he sometimes wouldn't see her for three days at a time. Not only are twenty-four-hour shifts common practice in New York, but those who work them are paid for only thirteen of the twenty-four hours.[74]

Domestic workers—those who work in private homes—are exposed not only to poor pay and long hours but also to mistreatment. Labour codes that apply to workers in other sectors of the economy have historically overlooked domestic workers, leading to fewer rights and protections and with that greater levels of abuse.[75] This is especially the case for those far away from their own family support systems and whose legal status leaves them afraid of the authorities. In 2007, a contractor working on a luxury development in New York was eating a box of doughnuts in his truck when a malnourished-looking woman approached him, urgently pointing to her stomach. Unable to speak much English, she was begging him for a doughnut. Originally from Indonesia, it turned out that—along with another immigrant woman—she was working for a wealthy married couple who were treating her like a slave. When the couple were eventually brought to court, the two women described how they had been unable to leave the house, had to sleep on the floor and had been beaten with rolling pins and scalded with hot water. Their isolation and their lack of legal status had meant that they had been unable to escape or seek help.[76] As the trial of the couple was in progress, Domestic Workers United—who represent care workers, cleaners and nannies—demonstrated outside the courthouse, drawing attention to the fact that mistreatment was an all-too-common occurrence in the sector.

Domestic workers in America have been organising since the 1960s in an effort to fight for more rights. At that time, one third of Black women worked as domestics, mostly under the thumb of white, middle-class women: a power imbalance that reflected the broader racial inequalities within American society.[77] It was Black women who therefore led the way in the US in campaigning for more rights, with minority women continuing that fight today. The same organisational efforts have been repeated in other parts of the world, including in Latin America, where around thirty percent of households are involved in paid domestic work, whether as workers or as employers. In 2011, the domestic workers' movement in Brazil succeeded in securing an international 'Domestic Workers Convention', placing governments across the world under pressure to roll out rights and protections to domestic workers.[78] The Convention states:

> [D]omestic work continues to be undervalued and invisible and is mainly carried out by women and girls, many of whom are migrants or members of disadvantaged communities and who are particularly vulnerable to discrimination in respect of conditions of employment and of work, and to other abuses of human rights. . . . [I]n developing countries with historically scarce opportunities for formal employment, domestic workers constitute a significant proportion of the national workforce and remain among the most marginalized.[79]

Continuing to address exploitative conditions and poor pay in the years ahead—whether in a domestic or more institutional setting—will be key to ensuring that the growth of the health and care sector does not exacerbate existing labour market inequalities.

The situation within the health and care sector itself also has knock-on consequences for the wider economy. Despite the continued growth in the sector, demand is outstripping supply, resulting in a 'crisis in care'.[80] Shortages of hospital beds, care homes and nursery places are placing pressure on families—and, particularly, women. Globally, women shoulder three-quarters of unpaid care, which means that shortages in care services impact women working elsewhere in the economy, who have to juggle careers with taking care of family members.[81] According to the International Labour Organization, this unpaid care work is the 'main barrier to women's labour force participation'.[82] Worldwide, seventy percent of women express a preference for being in paid work, but, in practice, only a half of women are in the workforce.[83] When working women in 142 countries were recently asked about the challenges they face, work-family balance and a lack of affordable care ranked ahead of unfair treatment and unequal pay.[84]

Difficulties finding and accessing care for loved ones has resulted in women's labour-force expansion coming to a standstill across the West, well before we have reached a point at which men and women have equal participation.[85] Alongside this stalled progress in their labour-force participation, women are still less likely than men to be found in senior positions. The proportion of management positions held by women—which is twenty-eight percent worldwide—has barely increased since the end of the last century.[86] Difficulties juggling work and unpaid care are at the heart of this gender gap. If greater gender equality is to be achieved, then either care services will need to expand or men and women will need to share caring responsibilities more evenly.[87] While men today spend more time looking after children than their grandfathers' generation, when asked how couples with children should ideally arrange their work and family responsibilities, the male breadwinner model—or a variant in which women work part-time—remains the ideal for seventy percent of people surveyed in high- and middle-income countries.[88] Interestingly, surveys reveal that while women with and without children express a similar desire for paid work, once men have children, they are—on average—less supportive of their partner's work outside of the home.[89] In other words, while women have entered the world of work, men are not—to an equivalent degree—entering the realm of unpaid care.

The first half of the gender revolution—sharing paid work—was the achievement of the twentieth century. The second half of this revolution—sharing unpaid care—needs to be the achievement of the twenty-first century.

SAVING THE PLANET

Like the 'crisis in care', environmental damage and climate change has the power to place the brakes on global economic growth. Increased pollution and extreme weather disrupt cities and wreak havoc for transport systems and trade, while making us less healthy and less productive. In 2022, wildfires disrupted numerous US cities, including Detroit and Minneapolis, and in California they have become a yearly phenomenon. Flooding has affected countries on both sides of the Atlantic. But, compared with the rest of the world, the West is escaping relatively unscathed. Asia is home to every one of the world's top one hundred most polluted cities; eighty-three of them are in India, where 1.3 billion people—ninety-six percent of the population—face pollution levels that are seven times higher than the World Health Organisation's minimum standards for air quality. In March 2024, pollution shut down Thailand's capital—Bangkok—after the government ordered people to work from home so as to avoid the smog on the city's streets. In the world's most polluted countries, people are expected to lose between three and six years of life as a result of the higher levels of respiratory illness, asthma and heart and lung disease resulting from pollution.[90] Over the last two decades, climate change has cost the most exposed countries—those known as the Vulnerable Twenty—twenty percent of the value of their economies.[91] It is a sign of the costs that other countries could have to bear if sufficient action is not taken. China—like India—used to rank as one of the most polluted countries in the world, but by adopting clean air policies it has managed to climb down the global rankings, showing the potential for progress.

Across the globe, there is growing public pressure to address the spectre of climate change. Fossil fuel companies are having to change tack, ploughing investment into clean-energy generation as a means of diversifying their income streams. Entrepreneurially minded scientists have also been busy setting up their own businesses, using scientific knowledge to develop solutions to the climate crisis that avoid or repair the damage done by traditional manufacturing processes. Over the course of the next five years, more than a half of the tipping points required to make green technologies commercially viable will have been met.[92] We have already reached the point where the cost of generating solar and wind power has fallen below the equivalent price of gas and coal. By 2021, three-quarters of new additions to global energy capacity comprised either solar or wind. Battery technology represents another tipping point. Based on current trends, by 2025–6 technology should have progressed to the point that the cost of electric vehicles is equal to—rather than above—the cost of traditional vehicles. Our ability to make green ammonia in a cost-efficient way—which would render it a financially viable replacement for traditional fertiliser—is also within sight. In addition to this, AI has the potential to help in the battle against climate change, from better managing energy demand to improving climate-alert systems. Overall, global investment will need to rise by between two and three percent of global incomes if the clean energy and digital transformation is to be achieved, equating to $5–7 trillion a year, making for 'the greatest investment opportunity since the Industrial Revolution'.[93] Those who are best positioned to understand these clean technologies ('clean-tech') will be best able to reap the financial rewards when the ensuing growth comes.

Businesses have been competing to be at the forefront of this clean-tech revolution, racing to develop technologies that can be sold across the world. But through their energy policies and regulations, governments can also—for better or worse—affect the direction of travel. China has had its Five-Year Plan, the EU has had its Green Deal, India has had its Energy Access and Green Hydrogen policies, and the US has had policies to both discourage and promote fossil fuels.[94] The fact that the transition to cleaner technologies can create job losses as well as opportunities explains why policies can change course, sometimes dramatically. Up to five million jobs could be lost in fossil fuels alone, including in areas such as mining and oil extraction.[95] Since this is a sector that is more than eighty percent male, those job losses are set to impact men more than women.[96] But so too are the immediate benefits. While the clean-tech industry is a growth hotspot, like the wider tech industry it is dominated by men. But since renewable energy is less male dominated than fossil fuels—sixty-eight percent male as opposed to eighty percent male—a transition to cleaner energy could be seen as benefitting women at the expense of men.[97] That's despite women still being in a clear minority in clean-tech.

Carolyn Hicks—who cofounded Brill Power, a company developing smart batteries—notes that she often finds herself in meetings, conference and workplaces 'where it's difficult to even find one woman'.[98] She developed her battery research company while studying for an MBA at the University of Oxford, having completed her undergraduate and Master's degrees in Engineering. Her cofounders—both fellow students—were in the process of completing their Engineering PhDs.[99] In 2024, Brill Power partnered with Fellten—a battery manufacturer that produces batteries for electric vehicles—turning the startup's research into reality. Like many tech startups, it was a business that grew directly out of cutting-edge university research. When asked what obstacles stop women from pursuing engineering, Hicks notes that 'there is a perception that you have to be "one of the guys" and get your hands dirty constantly. And while you can choose to do that, it's often not the bulk of many engineering careers'.[100] She adds:

> We're not going to change the gender imbalance right away—although progress is being made, it will take a generation. A good focus would be to emphasise that it's okay to be in a minority and feel comfortable with it. If you are the only woman in the room, then embrace it and want to make a difference.[101]

If the world transitions to cleaner technologies, there will be an opportunity to address one of the world's most fundamental but overlooked disparities—one that affects many more women than those who actually work in the energy sector. Across the globe, 770 million people—most of them in Asia or Africa—have no access to electricity, while more than two billion people lack access to clean cooking fuel, relying instead on wood, coal, kerosene or solid biomass.[102] Whether in the form of the extra domestic toil that is involved in a home that lacks electricity—and with it a vacuum cleaner and a washing machine—or in the form of the amount of time it takes to collect firewood, it is women who bear the brunt. Clean technologies that (perhaps more as a byproduct than an intention) help to spread electricity to parts of the world that are currently 'off grid' have the potential to reduce the traditional domestic burden that is placed on the world's women—one that, as we have seen, still represents the biggest obstacle to women's paid work across the world today.

~

ONE BILLION PEOPLE ACROSS THE WORLD HAVE BEEN LIFTED OUT of poverty since the end of the twentieth century. By 2030 the world is predicted to reach the point where a half of its inhabitants are officially middle-class—able to afford luxuries on top of basic necessities.[103] Women's contributions to this remarkable progress should not go unnoticed. As we have seen in the course of the last two chapters, women's efforts are not only keeping themselves fed but transforming their communities and indeed the entire world. Whether it is in the tech sector, care, the creative industries, finance, agriculture, manufacturing or retail, women are making their mark: one in two of the world's working-age women are now in receipt of a pay cheque and one in three of the world's businesses are owned by women.[104] But, just as in history, not all women are receiving the full rewards of their labour and many women are still denied the freedom to make their own choices about work, family and fertility: the gender pay gap remains stubborn at just over twenty-percent; in India, Egypt and the Middle East, which together with China once dominated the world economy, women are today more likely to be secluded than was ever the case in history; women continue to carry the weight of domestic responsibilities; and not only are a half of women in developing countries denied the freedom to control their own fertility, but this can also now be said of women in close to a half of the states in the US.[105] The end result of this extensive gender inequality is that women in aggregate earn only fifty-seven percent of what men across the world earn each year.[106] Taken together with the even more significant gap in wealth, this leaves women financially dependent on men and at far greater risk of poverty. The twenty-first century is providing women with a mix of precarity and possibility—which of those will weigh more heavily will depend on the outcome of women's continued efforts to resist the types of backlash that they have repeatedly faced through the course of economic history. And so too will the future of the global economy.

CONCLUSION

HUMANS ARE ACQUISITIVE CREATURES. ASIDE FROM MEETing our daily needs, we have a thirst for beautiful objects, for possessions that express our personality and for items that can provide comfort. In addition to food, clothing, and pots and pans, we fill our homes with furniture, trinkets and televisions. The effort to produce more and better versions of our worldly goods, and the never-ending drive to find something new and exciting, are what gives rise to economic growth. And, as we have seen throughout this book, from the time human beings were hunting and building their first homes, women have been at the forefront of economic activity, pioneering new sectors of the economy, whether in the form of cloth-making and ceramics or publishing and computing. Ancient artefacts, historic tax registers, dusty court records and paintings on gallery walls all help to reveal the myriad of ways in which women have contributed to our economies over time. But, despite the wealth of evidence, men are commonly seen as the wizards of business, money and trade, meaning that women's involvement in the economy has either been overlooked or treated as a sideshow. And this is in large part because history has been written by men, for men and about men.

By restoring women to their rightful place in global economic history, this book attempts to remove the blinders that have been placed on the story of how the world grew rich. As we have seen, it's not only well-known male figures like Genghis Khan, Hernán Cortés, J. P. Morgan and Karl Marx who should be seen as the movers and shakers of global economic history, but equally significant women like Huang Dao Po, La Malinche, Priscilla Wakefield, Ching Shih, Maggie Lena Walker and Sarojini Naidu. Rather than being the passive beneficiaries—or victims—of the wealth created by men, women have always been cocreators. Whether it's ancient Egypt, the Roman Empire, the Islamic (and Chinese) Golden Age or the Industrial Revolution, we cannot understand the creation of economic prosperity—and the rise and fall of civilisations—without including women.

But while women have always been at the heart of the economy, the type of work they have undertaken, the extent to which they have been rewarded for their work, the freedom with which they have been able to make their own choices and the extent to which their work has been shrouded in shame has varied considerably across time and place. It is these factors that spell the difference between an economy that simply features in the history books—one that has withered with time—and one which continues to flourish in the present day.

But for me, researching economic history isn't simply about fashioning a more accurate understanding of the creation of prosperity. History also provides a vast pool from which we can draw lessons to help us navigate our way to the future. Comparing and contrasting the great array of societies that have featured in this book allows us to draw ten particular lessons of significance; lessons that not only inform the present by placing women's work and the gender pay gap in historical perspective, but that provide the keys to a more prosperous and equal future for everyone.

WOMEN'S FREEDOM TO WORK AND TO EARN DRIVES ECONOMIC SUCCESS

From the beginning, societies understood that their wealth depended on women. Whether it was women's special ability to create new life or the cloth, food and manufactures they produced to meet more immediate needs, women were considered the most vital economic resource. This meant that in some societies, women were the ones in control—in the heavens as well as on Earth. From the Indus River to the plains of North America, women were worshipped as 'mother goddesses' and it was men—not women—who moved between families upon marriage. Since women were the anchors of family and community, they formed tight, lifelong networks and took charge of land and property. Other societies, however, saw enslaving women as a means to 'get rich quick'. Women's inherent worth meant that women were understood as property before the idea of property even existed.[1]

During the Stone Age, it wasn't just jade, flint and obsidian that were traded; it was also women. Then, as empires developed in China, the Middle East and India, so too did harems of enslaved women acquired through conquest or diplomatic gift giving.[2] Aside from sexually gratifying male rulers, slave women also formed the basis of economic growth, producing additional people for the state as well as the cloth that formed the currency of the premodern world. Men weren't the only ones benefitting from this exploitation. From Mesopotamia to the Inca Empire, elite women could often be found running workshops filled with slave women.

Whilst exploiting women might have presented an easy path to prosperity, it also created a ceiling beyond which the economy could not expand: exploitative practices and unfair treatment rarely get the best out of people. Only when we are free to make our own choices and can keep the associated rewards do we truly excel. And, in turn, only when we excel as individuals do we, at an overall level, create a dynamic and flourishing economy. It was by failing to grasp this fact that so many of history's 'greatest' civilisations sealed their fate. In Egypt, Iran and India, women have yet to retrieve the ground that they lost.

The subjugation of women was at the heart of why many of the world's first economic hotspots were unable to sustain their economic growth. It was instead the Western world—a place that was peripheral to the global economy—that gave birth to an

Industrial Revolution and opened the doors to much more substantial prosperity. This rags-to-riches story—one that began with Britain—is one that has been told time and time again, but women have always been the missing ingredient. The result is that historians continue to scratch their heads as to how this economic miracle could have occurred. By implicitly focusing on men, they fail to acknowledge the significant difference in Western women's lives from those in the East. While women's freedom was by no means perfect and was certainly not shared by all women in society, economics is a relative as well as absolute game. Relative freedom is what mattered for climbing to the top of the world economy and, in those terms, it is undeniable that the freedoms that ordinary women had won in Britain far exceeded those of women in China, India and the Middle East.

The path to freedom was not, however, a seamless onward march. Like numerous societies before them, Western societies had long pursued an economic model of exploitation: one in which the value women (and men) created was extracted by elites. Slavery certainly did not end with the Roman Empire: as the Vikings marauded across the continent in the centuries after it fell, they enslaved European women and put them to work in 'sunken-floored weaving huts' to produce the cloth that was the currency of their trade;[3] in an effort to build their presence in the global economy, Europeans also traded young women—even more so than young men—across the Mediterranean.[4] In both senses, the exploitation of women helped to drag Europe out of the 'Dark Ages', allowing the elite to build castles, palaces and estates on the back of the wealth women created. Then, as the Spanish reached out across the Atlantic, they put women as well as men to work in silver mines, providing the precious currency that enabled the globalisation of the world economy. Three centuries later, enslaved women were picking cotton on American plantations alongside men, creating wealth for the American South and providing Britain's industrialists with cheap raw materials. And while *single* white European women were free to work and to take control of their lives, until 1848 in New York state and 1882 in Britain, once a woman got married, her husband took control of any property and assets she owned.[5] Freedom didn't apply equally to all women—it depended on marital status, class, ethnicity and race. And what some might have described as freedom, others would have instead described as economic necessity. Women also faced a constant steam of backlash as men attempted to monopolise the most lucrative jobs, precisely because women were an economic threat. But the more that the West embraced liberation over exploitation, the more the centre of economic gravity shifted in its direction. We cannot understand the rise of the Western world—or modern economic growth—without placing women's freedom at the heart of our story. Chinese revolutionaries and policymakers are some of the few to appreciate this fact and it is by doing so that China has been able to perform the greatest economic miracle since the British Industrial Revolution, along with a small handful of its close neighbours.

History has seen dramatic shifts in terms of which parts of the world have dominated the global economy. These reveal that it is not simply whether women are 'working' or are recognised as valuable that drives long-term prosperity but, instead, whether women are free to make their own choices about work and to keep the rewards of their hard labour. It is in this sense that the lack of basic freedoms for women will ultimately prove the limiting factor for regions that—alongside China—are today attempting to climb back up the global economic rankings.

WOMEN HAVE ALWAYS BEEN THE HIDDEN FORCE BEHIND FAMILY BUSINESSES

Historically, the home was at the heart of the economy—it was the place where wants and needs emerged and where work to satisfy them took place. Homes were workplaces and families were businesses. In the Old Testament, the ideal wife was described as an industrious multitasker:

> *She seeketh wool, and flax, and worketh willingly with her hands. She is like the merchants' ships; she bringeth foods from afar. She riseth also while it is yet night, and giveth meat to her household, and a portion to her maidens. She considereth a field, and buyeth it: with the fruit of her hands she planteth a vineyard . . . She layeth her hands to the spindle, and her hands hold the distaff . . . She maketh fine linen, and selleth it; and delivereth girdles unto the merchant.*[6]

In ancient Greece, women ran the home-based workshops that provided the financial wherewithal to support their husbands' military, political and artistic endeavours.[7] Fast forward to the British Industrial Revolution, and wives like Hannah Greg were instrumental to the success of their husbands' industrial enterprises, including in the all-important cotton industry.[8] Across the Atlantic, Benjamin Franklin wrote in his autobiography of how his wife, Deborah, worked 'cheerfully in my business, folding and stitching pamphlets, tending shop, purchasing old linen rags for the papermakers'.[9] In Germany, Bertha Benz—the wife of Karl Benz, who in 1886 patented the gasoline motor car—not only used her inheritance to finance his 'tinkering', but she also performed the world's first test drive.

On a fine summer morning in 1888, while her husband was fast asleep, Bertha Benz quietly steered her husband's prototype vehicle out of the workshop and, with her two boys beside her, set out on a twelve-hour, 106-kilometre journey to her parents' home.[10] Karl had forbidden the test drive, believing that his vehicle wasn't sufficiently roadworthy, but Bertha—who often rolled up her sleeves and joined Karl in his workshop—had greater faith.[11] She was keen to demonstrate to the world the potential of the 'Motorwagen' and to use her long-distance journey as a practical way of identifying and addressing design faults. On her dash though the German countryside—overtaking horse-drawn carriages and leaving many a farm labourer stunned at the sight of a vehicle that could move as if by magic—she faced clogged valves, had trouble with the brakes and ignition, and ran out of petrol. But, on each occasion, she was able to diagnose and resolve the faults with her own bare hands: she removed her garter to insulate a spark plug, asked a cobbler to make a leather pad to help with the brakes and purchased cleaning solvent from a pharmacist to top up her fuel tank.[12] In the words of Mercedes-Benz USA, '[s]he drove more than a car, she drove an industry'.[13]

For centuries, women have been performing 'hidden labour', supporting their husbands' and fathers' enterprises by managing staff, dealing with correspondence, keeping on top of the accounts and carefully curating social networks in an effort to generate extra clients.[14] But at the very same time that Bertha Benz was in the driving seat, government statisticians—who were then attempting to devise proper measures of the economy—decided not to count women's work where it consisted of working in family businesses or on family farms or of taking in boarders (effectively running a B&B)—all of which were common activities for married women.[15] Instead, women like Bertha were classified as economic dependents—a burden to their male relatives and to the economy.

The fact that, across history, widows have successfully steered the businesses of their deceased husbands further serves to demonstrate how involved women have been behind the scenes. These widows include Rebecca Lukens, whose father founded an iron mill making barrel hoops and nails in Pennsylvania.[16] When Lukens married, her husband took over her father's business, but in 1825, with the business almost bankrupt and Rebecca pregnant with her sixth child, he passed away. Under her subsequent leadership, the business—Brandywine Iron Works and Nail Factory—became a mainstay on the New York Stock Exchange. At the height of America's industrial age, Brandywine was the largest producer of boilerplates for steam engines and steam trains. The fact that it was normal for widows in Europe and America to assume the businesses of their deceased husbands can also be evidenced by business directories. A detailed look at Philadelphia's directories from 1796—comparing entries with those from 1794 and 1791—reveals that many of the women boarding-house keepers, grocers and shopkeepers had been widowed by husbands who, years before, had been running the same enterprise.[17]

Family businesses are not just consigned to the past; they are also a feature of the modern-day economy. Across the world, more than a half of businesses are owned and run by families, employing around sixty percent of the global workforce and creating around seventy percent of everything we buy in our daily lives.[18] While most of these businesses are, on paper, owned by men, if history is anything to go by, wives and daughters continue to be the 'silent partners' of the business world.

LAW, BANKING AND NETWORKS HAVE CONSPIRED TO INHIBIT WOMEN'S ENTREPRENEURSHIP

The reality that most businesses in history have been owned by men is difficult to deny. In fact, in the business directories that circulated in Britain's major cities during the Industrial Revolution, men outnumber women at a rate of ten to one.[19] There were, as we have seen, notable female entrepreneurs, including Julia Felix in Roman Pompeii. Whether on ancient seals and stone tablets or on the kinds of bank documents and business cards available from more recent history, we can and do find the names of female business owners once we start to look. But while women entrepreneurs certainly existed, the reality was that many more men than women owned their own business, and this continues to be the case today.

Despite the extensive support that women offered to businesses officially owned and run by men, history has conspired against the self-made 'shepreneur'. Examples of women who rose from poverty to prosperity by nurturing their own business are—sadly—few and far between. One of the reasons for the scarcity of self-made businesswomen is that accessing credit has always been more difficult for women than for men, meaning that women-founded businesses have been unable to grow to the same extent as male-owned businesses and so have tended to remain small. In addition to their exclusion from the banking system and laws that treated married women as the property of their husbands, their lack of contacts within the wider business community did not help. Guilds, coffeehouses, universities and gentlemen's clubs that barred women from entering necessarily deprived female entrepreneurs of the networks through which business deals could be done and capital could be tapped. The result was that, compared with men, women were historically more likely to be running smaller rather than larger businesses.[20]

This situation remains the case today. While women own around thirty-nine percent of all private businesses in the United States, they employ no more than nine percent of the private-sector workforce.[21] When it comes to seed capital, only around two percent of venture-capital funding in Europe and America goes to businesses founded solely by women.[22] Not only are most venture capitalists men, but, according to a study published in the *Harvard Business Review,* the questions venture capitalists ask of female entrepreneurs stack the odds against them: while two-thirds of the questions posed to male startups focus on long-term growth potential, two-thirds of the questions posed to female startups focus instead on potential losses.[23] It is little surprise that whilst businesswomen who own large and successful companies certainly exist, they are still considered something of a novelty, so exceptional that their achievements are trumpeted—including in books like this.

Interestingly, female entrepreneurship is relatively more popular in poorer as opposed to wealthier parts of the world. In low-income countries, women are more likely than men to be self-employed and are nine times more likely to be self-employed than Western women. An incredible eighty-eight percent of working women in low-income countries are self-employed, compared with ten percent of women in high-income countries.[24] And while one in three businesses across the world are now owned by women, in East Asia and South America it is one in two.[25] But, despite their ubiquitous presence, the challenges faced by these female entrepreneurs are on a par with those in the West a century or more ago.

Violeta Pacheco Mejía—a female entrepreneur from Peru who today runs a successful eco-friendly alpaca and cotton clothing company employing fourteen women—had to ask her husband to borrow on her behalf in order to expand her business. Banks refused to lend to Violeta simply because she was a woman, which meant that without her husband acting as signatory she would have been unable to access loans to purchase factory premises, equipment and raw materials.[26] This type of financial exclusion remains common. In some countries, women are still barred from even opening a bank account. In fact, a total of 740 million women worldwide, and more than six in ten women in Africa and the Middle East, do not have their own account.[27] Even in countries where women can open accounts, it remains normal practice in some for banks to make decisions about loans on the basis of gender.[28] Across the developing world, female entrepreneurs face a $1.7 trillion deficit in financing compared with their male equivalents.[29]

Whether working behind the scenes in family businesses or as proud owners of their own enterprise, history shows that 'women in business' is not a contradiction in terms. Women's entrepreneurial spirit has the power to supercharge the economy—but for this to happen, women must be treated in exactly the same way as men.

WOMEN HAVE WORKED IN ALL KINDS OF JOBS—UNLESS MEN HAVE STOPPED THEM

The arrival of big business tipped the balance away from home production and towards salaried employment.[30] As a result, people in wealthier countries today are much more likely to be workers in someone else's business than entrepreneurs in their own right. It can, after all, feel safer to take a job working for someone else—perhaps with the aim of one day making it onto a company board—than to start your own enterprise. And for those without access to cash or qualifications, a job might offer the surest form of financial security.

From the beginning, big business has turned to young women as a source of reliable, cheap and pliable wage labour. The cloth workshops of ancient Egypt and Mesopotamia were staffed by large numbers of women, some of whom brought their children to work. Subsequently, and in both Britain and America, the cotton factories that were at the heart of the Industrial Revolution employed a predominantly female workforce, as did their later equivalents in industrialising Japan and Russia, a trend which continues today in the form of the clothing sweatshops of the Global South that supply our high-street chains.[31]

While women workers have long been the mainstay of factory production, men came to dominate other types of jobs, including the lucrative professions. As we have seen, at the peak of Britain's Industrial Revolution, there were a total of 18,482 doctors, surgeons and chemists in Britain, none of whom were women. Similarly, of all 16,291 barristers, advocates and attorneys, not a single one was female.[32] New England's census of 1885 categorised people into seventeen thousand different occupations, of which women could be found in only a third.[33] By the nineteenth century, women's work had become concentrated in just two sectors: cloth manufacture and domestic service.

Before the Industrial Revolution, and as we have noted throughout this book, women could be found in all manner of jobs. They worked as milkmaids, brewers, shopkeepers, miners and on construction sites.[34] And it is precisely because women were considered worthy competitors that men have so often conspired with one another to keep them out of the most lucrative jobs.[35] The field of medicine provides one such example. Women have long been involved in looking after the health and wellbeing of their families and communities. A woman named Peseshet who lived five thousand years ago was the first female physician from history that we know of by name.[36] But as medical associations and medical schools developed, women were pushed out of the medical profession. In ancient Greece, Hippocrates's school of medicine barred women and even as recently as the nineteenth century, most medical schools across the world were still male-only.[37]

The medical profession was not alone. In the nineteenth century, men's desire to exclude women from the top jobs led to marriage bars that forbade the employment of married women.[38] In Britain, women were barred from practising law until the Sex Disqualification (Removal) Act of 1919 and until 1946, female civil servants had to resign from their job if they wanted to marry; in the Foreign Office this continued to be the case until 1973.[39] The marriage bar at Barclays Bank was only removed in 1964, and only after the Sex Discrimination Act of 1975 were employers under the obligation to offer maternity leave and to keep a woman's job open for her to return.[40]

Marriage bars meant that women were forced to choose between having a career and having a family. Of all American women who graduated from college before 1900, three-quarters therefore remained single.[41] Many of these women worked as social reformers, journalists, factory inspectors, teachers and social workers, setting their sights on building a more equal society rather than on creating their own family.[42] Since pursuing marriage and a career was impossible, there was little reason for academically minded young women who did have a serious boyfriend to remain in education, as a result of which drop-out rates were significantly higher for female college graduates than for male college graduates. Only with the relaxation of marriage bars and the invention of the contraceptive pill—which enabled women to actively control their fertility—were women able to even consider combining a career and a family.

But while women's opportunities in most Western countries have expanded, elsewhere they have been in retreat. Today, in Egypt, India and the Middle East, women who in the past would have been going out to work or starting their own business are more likely to be confined to the home. In South Asia, less than a third of women are in paid work, while throughout the Middle East and North Africa an average of only one in five women are in the labour force.[43] In modern-day Afghanistan, women have been banned from the workplace altogether, putting Afghan women on a par with ancient Greek women in terms of the seclusion they are forced to endure. Ironically, some of the most unequal societies today are ones in which women were once relatively equal, meaning that equal opportunities can never be taken for granted: women must be constantly on guard.

Why women have at times been welcomed into lucrative professions while at other times they have been pushed to one side is a question that this book's tour through economic history can help to answer. Where population growth has pushed down wages, creating widespread poverty and competition for jobs, men have been more inclined to see women as a threat. Where, instead, labour shortages have developed, women's economic participation has been encouraged. After the collapse of the Bronze Age—which brought death and destruction to the earliest civilisations—there were shortages of male potters and so women were drawn into Greece's pottery workshops, resulting in pottery designs that mirrored woven cloth, with repeated zig-zag and swirl decoration.[44] After the Black Death in the middle of the fourteenth century, when there was again a shortage of male workers, women were once more in high demand, including on farms, where they were employed to tend cattle, giving birth to the stereotypical image of the milkmaid.[45] In the nineteenth century, the American Civil War created a shortage of male teachers, bringing large numbers of women into the profession.[46] During the First and the Second World Wars, industrialists also famously turned to women, and after World War Two, shortages of young single women—in part because of the post-war baby boom—led businesses to relax their 'marriage bars' and so employ married women.[47]

That throughout history men have sought to lock women out of productive activity—sometimes having only accepted their inclusion at times of labour shortages—shows how much of a threat men have felt women to be to their own employment: in other words, it shows that women represent an equally capable group, with whom men have not wanted to compete.

WORKING FROM HOME LEAVES WOMEN INVISIBLE

While work carried out within the home had once been the norm for both men and women, in the course of history it became gendered—seen as inherently female and not considered 'proper work'.

Once growing numbers of people began to work outside of the home, it created the illusion that the economy was something 'out there'—an ephemeral force that was separate from our own inner sanctums. Instead of being thought of as places of production, homes became seen as places for nurturing loved ones. Married women were told that 'real' work wasn't suited to the 'gentler sex', even though the work they were expected to devote themselves to within the home—cleaning, cooking, laundry and care—was dirty, time-consuming and back-breaking. Wives who laundered their husbands' clothes and provided them with fuel in the form of hot food were classified by government statisticians as both 'economically inactive' and 'economic dependents'. This remains the case today.[48]

This work that happens beyond the 'formal' economy—work that isn't even classified as work and isn't counted as part of our economy—is enormous in scale. Across the world, the amount of unpaid care that takes place in our families and communities (all of the time that we spend looking after our children and loved ones) is the equivalent of two billion people working full-time for nothing.[49] Three-quarters of this care is provided by women.[50] Adding up all of the hours involved and the pay such work would command if it was performed for money rather than for free, feminist economists have calculated that it equates to between twenty and sixty percent of the economic activity (GDP) that *is* being measured in our economies.[51] Based on the higher end of these estimates, this is the equivalent of excluding the US, China and the EU from global GDP calculations. This is not a small omission.

Work from home during Covid-19 began to lift the lid on this hidden world, as people who would normally be in the office realised how much effort it takes to run a household and to keep everyone fed, clean and healthy. While it served to underline the importance of combining family and paid work, the women that society has labelled 'housewives' have long had an appetite for paid work that could be conducted within the home alongside domestic duties. The financial rewards that they have received for this labour have, however, been a pittance. This is because those doling out 'work from home' knew that women with family responsibilities didn't have much of an alternative to it. Being a mother a century or two ago meant working long into the night to make ends meet, making hats, gloves or other small garments from the kitchen table, using raw materials supplied by local merchants or shop owners—often in competition with factory equivalents produced by younger unmarried women. And since this 'handicraft' economy was poorly paid and operated behind closed doors, it was considered peripheral and 'informal'—not part of the real economy.

While working from home has historically offered opportunities for women, it has also allowed families and businesses alike to exploit the value that women create. Today, the flexibility offered by remote working comes at the cost of a lower salary. That means that those who are expected to carry the weight of domestic responsibilities are experiencing less financial reward for their work.[52] Businesses are able to pocket more of the value that their remote employees create, leaving them in a position to better reward those who *can* commit to being in the office—typically male breadwinners. This has lessons for today, giving added impetus to attempts to address the two factors that continue to trap women in the home: cultural systems that favour female seclusion and the 'crisis of care' that is making it increasingly difficult to juggle paid work with caring responsibilities, slowing down women's ability to make further progress in the workplace.[53]

WOMEN STILL NEED TO BE COUNTED— BY HISTORIANS AS WELL AS ECONOMISTS

By failing to recognise the value that women have long created for our economies, we not only get a false impression that economies have been dominated by men; we also get a warped impression of what the economy is. When we 'add women and stir', we must rethink our whole definition of the economy—and who is a part of it.

The labour-force participation rate is the tool economists use to measure the involvement of men and women in the economy. It captures everyone in registered paid employment as well as those actively seeking paid work, together with anyone who is registered as self-employed and running their own business. It is, however, an ahistorical measure, one that overlooks the fact that for much of history the home has been at the heart of the economy and economic activity has often occurred behind closed doors. While people have been hard at work since the beginning of time, venturing out of the home to engage in paid work is a relatively recent phenomenon. Similarly, when, in the modern day, we talk of women's labour-force participation increasing, that doesn't mean that women were—before they 'participated'—making no contribution to the economy. And it shouldn't mean that governments can 'bank' the contribution that those 'newly' participating women are making whilst ignoring the fact that the work they were already doing—work which went uncounted—still needs to be done. It is by failing to acknowledge the enormous amount of work that women outside of the 'labour force' are already undertaking (e.g. unpaid care, informal and unrecognised work, or work for family businesses), that governments have made the mistake of presuming that 'getting more women into work' will provide an easy way of boosting the economy. Indeed, it *will* boost GDP (economists' most favoured measure of the economy), but that's in part because the work women were doing beforehand wasn't, as already noted, counted as part of GDP. This can leave policymakers neglectful of the obstacles that women face when moving into the 'labour force'—such as the lack of childcare and elderly care—as a result of which women are left doing two sets of work (work that is officially counted and work that is taken for granted). Survival has always depended on hard work, but trying to capture it is more of a challenge than economists like to admit.

Compared with economists, who can fall back on their government statistical agencies, historians have naturally had to consider a wider range of evidence when it comes to the economy. But the sources historians have relied on have done a much better job of capturing the participation of men than that of women: stone tools, items made of bronze and iron ploughs have left more of a trace than cloth, which more easily disintegrates; men have been more likely to be registered as holders of family farms and businesses, leaving an impression that women were not making an equal contribution to them; and, as now, the relentless work involved in keeping everyone fed, clean and cared for can easily pass without notice. But, as we have seen throughout this book, if we choose to look, historical evidence of women's contribution to the economy *can* be found.

WOMEN'S ECONOMIC HISTORY IS UNDER-RESEARCHED BUT FILLED WITH POTENTIAL—SO LONG AS WE BREAK OUT OF THE BOX

It is often said that women were the first thing to be traded in history; that was, therefore, where I naturally wanted to start when writing this book. Trying to evidence it was, however, much more difficult than I expected. Research on the matter is sorely lacking. Inanimate and non-perishable items such as amber, pearls and stone axes can of course be found in archaeological digs and so are commonly used to build a picture of how different regions were connected and the types of items that were traded. In the period before bronze collars and iron shackles, wooden yokes and ropes would, in contrast, have soon worn down and disintegrated, leading to a lack of evidence of any trade in people.[54] Recent scientific evidence (using DNA technology) provided at least some clues, though, helping to establish whether men or women—or both equally—were exchanged between communities and, based on skeletal remains and teeth analysis, how well they were treated (indicative of whether their 'exchange' was consensual or not). While more such analysis still needs to be carried out within the archaeological community, providing the potential for exciting new discoveries in the years ahead, what evidence does exist suggests that, from relatively early on, women were often the ones being 'exchanged' between communities. Moreover, as I moved forward in history to the period after the written word developed, examining written documentation on slavery from different parts of the world, one thing more than any other began to stand out: that female slaves have commonly been prized more highly than male slaves. In ancient Greece it was female slaves who were seen as the trophies of conquest;[55] the Rig-Veda—Hinduism's sacred book from around 1500 BCE—contains far more references to female slaves than it does to male slaves;[56] in the Islamic world, around two-thirds of African slave captives were women;[57] and in medieval Europe, female slaves sold for fifty percent more than male slaves.[58] Economic value has, in other words, always rested in women.

Of course, that finding in itself was not enough to write a new global economic history; doing so has required engaging with myriad other sources. Court records and petitions to rulers proved particularly revealing, not only of women's contribution but of those who felt threatened by it. For example, in eighteenth-century Istanbul (formerly Constantinople), twenty-five male weavers complained to Ottoman authorities that women were 'embroidering imitation flower designs of low quality in their homes'. The associated imperial decree tells us that the authorities 'demanded that the women end their activities'.[59] By contrast, in London, petitions reveal that women were much more successful in defending their work. They include a petition to the Lord Mayor of London from 1699 from eight female market traders, objecting to a doubling of fees for their market stalls.[60] As one of the women pointed out in the petition, she had been plying her trade for eighteen years. But, in addition to the more obvious historical records, I also found how important it was to cast the net wide, looking for sources that might be seen as relating more to religious or social history than to economic history. For example, the records of London's Church Courts for the seventeenth and eighteenth centuries—which dealt with cases of marriage, divorce and defamation—have proved to be an unexpected but highly illuminating source. It turned out that while giving their testimony in court cases, men were asked about their occupation and women were asked how they were maintained, all of which was recorded. Over a half of the women declared themselves as being employed, a quarter of them in domestic service, a fifth of them in clothing (whether tailoring or mending), and a tenth of them as laundresses or cleaners.[61] In fact, three-quarters of the unmarried women who appear in the court records declared that they worked for a living, as did a similar proportion of widows, and around a third of wives.[62] Indeed, without women's earnings, many families would have struggled to make ends meet.[63]

While overlooked by those attempting to explain Britain's Industrial Revolution, historical artefacts revealed another significant finding: that women's paid work in Britain was something they could be proud of—not just an economic necessity—indicative of a society where women had much greater equality and opportunity than was the case elsewhere. Records from London's livery companies—the guilds and other such professional associations—reveal, for example, that it was normal for the wives of male professionals to work.[64] While some worked alongside their husbands, many also worked independently, carving out their own businesses.[65] One of the guilds (the Mercers' Company) was the landlord of London's Royal Exchange—home to London's most upmarket shops—and their rental books revealed that close to a half of the retail space at the end of the seventeenth century was rented by women.[66] One of my favourite finds was a little-known collection of women's business cards, held at the British Museum. They include 'Ann Askew, Shoemaker. At the Boot, next door to the Three Tuns and Rummer in Grace Church Street. Sells all sorts of Men's shoes, Boots, and Slippers'.[67] Not only was it normal for women to run their own businesses, but they could do so with pride. That would be difficult to establish with the type of modern-day measures used by economists today, yet social attitudes are key to establishing the degree to which women's economic opportunities are (or are not) limited.

WE CANNOT UNDERSTAND THE WORKINGS OF THE ECONOMY—INCLUDING WHAT MAKES IT PROSPEROUS OR POOR—WITHOUT PLACING SOCIETY ALONGSIDE THE ECONOMY

Social practices reveal much more than economic data alone. For example, characteristic of the way women have long been treated as property, in three-quarters of the world today money still changes hands when a woman marries.[68] In Sub-Saharan Africa, where women historically have busily worked in the fields and been in charge of local markets, potential husbands are expected to financially compensate the bride's parents for the loss of a 'productive' family member by paying a 'bride price'. In China, where historically women have spun cloth to support their families—sometimes with their feet bound—bride price similarly remains common. By contrast, in the Middle East and South Asia, a financial transfer takes place in the opposite direction, in the form of a dowry.[69] Fathers are expected to financially provide for their daughters because the work that women undertake once married is not considered sufficiently valuable. What precludes women's paid work in these parts of the world is a culture in which a woman's worth and her family's honour depend on female bodily purity. Women who go out to work therefore risk bringing shame on their family. As men's earnings have risen, more and more families in South Asia and the Middle East have been able to afford to seclude women, restricting women's freedom to work and to earn. Since it is the reputation of male family members that is boosted when their wives, sisters and daughters are considered 'unpolluted', it is also the men who reap the associated reputational rewards, which include better access to jobs and credit through social networks that depend on a family's reputation. Women and the economy, by contrast, carry the cost. It is the fact that women are not recognised for the work that they nevertheless continue to carry out within the home—or the honour that they create for their families—that explains why the popularity of dowries is growing rather than falling in countries such as India; women are, in other words, expected to bring a dowry into marriage to compensate for being a supposed financial burden.

But while popular culture is sometimes obsessed with dowries, bride price predates them and has also been far more common. This suggests that in most societies, women have indeed been valued for the work that they could carry out, to the point that a husband was expected to 'buy' a woman from her family.[70] Of course the fact that the woman herself was not the one receiving the payment—that she was effectively turned into a commodity—shows starkly that being recognised as a valuable resource is not by itself enough to guarantee rights or freedoms.

Global economic history has long overlooked the value of women. Economists make the same mistake, not only leaving women's work uncounted but failing to identify the social factors that limit women's economic opportunities and what needs to change if we are to attain a more equal and prosperous economy—one where women can reap the value they themselves create.

PAID WORK CAN BE BOTH LIBERATING AND EXPLOITATIVE

According to some commentators, encouraging women's paid work is not the answer to gender inequality. Observing life in Britain during the Industrial Revolution, Karl Marx—the man best known for his critique of capitalism—came to the conclusion that women were in fact better off in the home than in the factory. Long hours, poor working conditions and miserly pay was, he argued, exploitative and, by engaging in paid work, women were, he suggested, competing down the wages that men would otherwise receive—wages that would enable a husband to support a family.[71] The Russian revolutionary Alexandra Kollontai, who visited Russia's newly emerging factories towards the end of the nineteenth century, argued that the plight of 'bourgeois' women was very different to the plight of working-class women.[72] The former, she noted, wanted the right to work, whereas the latter wanted protection from 'the heavy cross of wage labor'.[73]

Although its exploitative potential is clear, paid work nonetheless offers an escape from a form of exploitation that women have always faced: that which occurs within the home. Women's unpaid contributions to their families as wives, mothers, grandmothers, daughters and daughters-in-law are, as we've seen, regularly undervalued. Hence why, despite their hard labours in the home, women in some societies are expected to 'pay their way' through a dowry and also why women who bring larger dowries into marriage are treated better by their husbands and parents-in-law than those with smaller dowries.[74] Whether we like it or not, with money comes power. No matter how much someone is contributing to the family (and wider economy) in a non-financial sense, it does not guarantee fair treatment. Without cash in their pocket and the potential to build an independent life of their own, it is impossible for women to escape the exploitation that can result. This is something that abusers know all too well. Encouraging their spouse to cut back on paid work is a strategy commonly used by male abusers in an effort to assert control over their victims. A recent study reveals that women who cohabit with men who physically abuse them experience a drop in their earnings of the equivalent of nearly $2000 a year.[75] In the words of one survivor of physical abuse: 'The first feature of control was financial.

As soon as I had less economic independence that's when the [violence] started'.[76] 'Escaping' paid work can be a recipe for greater not lesser exploitation.

Throughout history, the argument that paid work is exploitative has been harnessed by those who would prefer that women be confined to the home—not just individual abusers but nation states. As the British middle-classes began to idealise the 'housewife' in the course of the nineteenth century, they looked disapprovingly on parts of the world where women were hard at work in agriculture, arguing that women were being exploited and that paid work should be reserved for men in order to protect women.[77] Whether in the era of colonisation or in modern-day Afghanistan, supposed good intentions—claims of looking after women's best interests—have long been a veil for imposing patriarchal practices. And, sadly, it is one that makes the economic situation worse, not better. After all, just as China experienced in the course of the eighteenth and nineteenth century, where women lack choice, population growth can easily overwhelm the economy, resulting in downward pressure on wages and a tumbling down in the global economic rankings. Exploitation in the world of work cannot be denied; however, the solution is never to reduce women's options but instead to increase them.

THE GENDER PAY GAP MIGHT HAVE IMPROVED, BUT IT'S NOT GOING AWAY ANYTIME SOON

Iran was once a place renowned for its gender equality. In ancient Persia, not only could women work alongside men, but they also received equal pay.[78] Throughout history, equal pay has, however, been the exception and not the rule. In the Sumerian cloth workshops of ancient Mesopotamia, female supervisors earned only a third of the earnings of their male counterparts.[79] Women who instead worked on the land were paid in barley, receiving between thirty and sixty litres a month, compared with men who received between sixty litres (as a bare minimum) and 300 litres.[80] Fast forward to the age when Europeans began colonising the Americas, and in the Potosi silver mines women labourers earned a half of the male wage.[81] During the British Industrial Revolution, a woman painting flowers onto porcelain at Wedgwood's factory earned sixty percent of the wage of her male peers.[82] In the 1920s, in Soviet Russia, which claimed to be at the forefront of equality in all senses of the term, women on average earned a mere sixty-four percent of the male wage.[83] And while progress in closing the gender pay gap has continued in recent decades, women across the world still earn significantly less on average than men: the gender pay gap currently stands at just over twenty percent worldwide.[84]

Today, there are three main reasons why women are on average paid less than men: firstly, because in some countries the economy is dominated by the state or by a private monopoly, meaning that employers don't have to fiercely compete with one another for workers and so can get away with paying women less; secondly, because women are more likely than men to occupy junior positions; and, thirdly, because women tend to be concentrated in what are typically labelled 'female' jobs—in the clerical sector, in education, in care, in retail, or in cleaning and catering—all of which might be considered an extension of the work that women have long been expected to perform within the family.[85] Since such work has traditionally been undervalued when performed by women within the home, it is similarly considered to be deserving of little reward when it is performed for pay outside of it. It is this 'occupational segregation'—the way society sees jobs as either for women or for men—that, combined with the lower rates of career progression of women, explains the persistence of the gender pay gap in economies such as Britain, the United States and the European Union.[86] Addressing women's low pay therefore requires action on a number of fronts: lifting pay in poorly paid parts of the economy, where women are more likely to be found, including in the expanding care sector, which is set to employ even more women in the decades ahead; ensuring that sectors dominated by men—such as engineering, tech and the professions—are welcoming for women; removing barriers that halt women's career progression in all sectors of the economy, which in turn necessitates a more equal division of family responsibilities between men and women; and resisting the concentration of power in the hands of either the state or big business, both of which have a tendency to extract the value that women create in the knowledge that they cannot easily find work elsewhere.

The World Bank has calculated that eliminating the gender gap would double the rate at which the global economy is growing, lifting global incomes by more than twenty percent.[87] As we have seen, history backs this up: whether it's the ancient Etruscans, Industrial Revolution Britain or China in the twenty-first century, the most prosperous economies are those where women are relatively free to make their own decisions about work and can keep the rewards. But based on current rates of progress, it will take until 2158 for women throughout the world to be equal to men.[88] That is five generations from now, meaning that no one alive today will live to see a world that is truly equal. I don't know about you, but I'm certainly not going to sit back and wait that long.

~

IT IS BY CHALLENGING THE IDEA THAT THE ECONOMY IS 'JUST for men' that we can work towards a future in which women's contributions are recognised, respected and valued across the world. That begins by acknowledging not only that women have been at the heart of the most notable economic success stories in history, but, more generally, that all economies have depended on women's hard work—whether they are rich or poor, free or slave-based. A truly flourishing economy, however, relies on women being able to make their own choices about work, giving them the space to make the most of their talents and to be creative and innovative. Sadly, relatively few societies have managed to achieve this (and, just as importantly, to retain it). Not only are women poorer for it, so too are their economies. That a woman should be able to earn her own money, to keep the money she earns, and to do so proudly, sadly cannot be taken for granted. And that is why I have written this book.

But, ultimately, it is not economic historians like me who have the power to change the course of history; it is instead those who follow in the footsteps of the women who have, throughout time, been active on the front line of the economy. Women's insistence on change didn't begin or end with the suffragettes. Their demands were heard loud and clear in the Roman Forum; in the slave revolts of the Islamic world; in the peasant revolts of the fourteenth century; in the French Revolution; in 1885 at Japan's Amamiya silk mill; in 1888 at the Bryant & May matchstick factory in London; in Russia on International Women's Day in 1917; in Nigeria in 1929; and in 1968 at Ford's Dagenham Plant.[89]

As the fight continues, we can be sure that like the past, the future is not something that will happen to women—it will be made by them.

ACKNOWLEDGEMENTS

This book is the product of thousands of academic articles and manuscripts written by generations of economic historians, archaeologists and economists whose work has transformed our vision of the past. Their influence will be apparent throughout the chapters herein. Weaving together the insights of countless researchers to create a global economic history—told through the eyes of women as well as men—has been an honour. Writing a single accessible narrative necessarily, however, means omitting the stories of many women who would be just as worthy of inclusion as those in this book, and to them—or their descendants—I apologise.

Over the past quarter of a century, the universities of Oxford and Cambridge have provided a fertile and supportive backdrop for my academic research and explorations. Within the academic community, I am particularly indebted to Bob Allen and Avner Offer for their undoubted influence and unwavering academic support and encouragement over the last twenty years. Their approach to economic history has greatly shaped the way I think about the past and has given me enough confidence to break out of silos and span time and place. Deborah Oxley, Sara Horrell, Jane Humphries, Alan Fersht, David Secher, Amy Erickson, Philippa Levine, Clive Lawson, Michelle Baddeley, Julia Shvets, Martin Daunton, Paul Cartledge and David Abulafia have provided much appreciated friendship, inspiration and collegiality. I am grateful to each and every one. I have also benefitted from not only the published work but the camaraderie of Bina Agarwal, Ruth Scurr, Kate Lister, Lucy Delap, Emma Rees, Carolina Alves, Karenjit Clare, Bronwen Everill, Deirdre McCloskey and Erin Hengel. To all of my academic friends and peers from whom I have learned so much—and also to my sister Stephanie—thank you.

Hachette's Martin Redfern—who first suggested that I write this book—deserves an especially big thanks. This book would not have existed without his idea and encouragement. Holly Purdham (at Headline Press) and Emily Taber (at Seal Press) have, along with Martin, expertly guided the manuscript. I cannot thank them enough for their support and advice. The wider team at Headline Publishing and Seal Press are a pleasure to work with. At Headline, Grace McCrum, Ruth Case-Green and Katie Green provided expert help along with the fabulous marketing team (including Alara Delfosse, Rosie Margesson, Lucy Howkins and Caitlin Raynor). At Seal Press, Lara Heimert, Brian Distelberg, Liz Wetzel, Jessica Breen, Annie Chatham, Angela Messina, Meghan Roberts, Liz Morris, Lori Lewis and Gillian Sutliff deserve particular thanks. Martin Lubikowski has provided expert help with historical maps. I would also especially like to thank the British Museum's Lucia Rinolfi along with my agent, Hannah Weatherill at Watson, Little Ltd.

My greatest debt is to James, my husband of twenty years, for his unfailing love and support. I count myself extraordinarily fortunate to have a husband who considers me an equal in every way and who gives me the space and freedom to pursue my own goals (and who is always willing to pore over my latest drafts). This book is dedicated to him.

IMAGE CREDITS

Page 1

Hunting toolkit: Randall Haas, University of Wyoming, Creative Commons Attribution-Share Alike 4.0 International license

Terracotta figurine: The Metropolitan Museum of Art, New York, Object Number 74.51.1643

Page 2

Tomb painting: The Metropolitan Museum of Art, New York, Object Number 33.8.16

Sitsnefru statue: The Metropolitan Museum of Art, New York, Object Number 18.2.2

Ancient Greek vase: The Metropolitan Museum of Art, New York, Object Number 31.11.10

Page 3

Gold coin: Copyright The Trustees of the British Museum, Object number 1849,1121.294

Sarcophagus of Seianti Hanunia Tlesnasa: Copyright The Trustees of the British Museum, Object number 1887,0402.1

Page 4

Empress Wu: Copyright CPA Media Pte Ltd via Alamy Stock Photo

Home silk making: Copyright CPA Media Pte Ltd via Alamy Stock Photo

Page 5

La Malinche: Copyright World History Archive via Alamy Stock Photo

Ann Askew business card: Copyright The Trustees of the British Museum, Asset number 1307958001

'My wife is a woman of mind': Copyright The Trustees of the British Museum, Object reference 1978,U.2847

Page 6

Woman in coal mine: Copyright Chronicle via Alamy Stock Photo

Manchester cotton mill: Copyright Pictorial Press Ltd via Alamy Stock Photo

Page 7

Cotton ginning factory: Copyright British Library Images (via Bridgeman Images), Shelfmark Photo 703/(22)

Ching Shih: Copyright IanDagnall Computing via Alamy Stock Photo

Efunroye Tinubu: Copyright The History Collection via Alamy Stock Photo

Page 8

Russian Revolutionary Poster: Copyright Shawshots via Alamy Stock Photo—original poster art by Adolf Strakhov

American World War Two Poster: Copyright incamerastock via Alamy Stock Photo—originally published by Bressler Editorial Cartoons, Inc.

Care workers protesting: David Grossman via Alamy Stock Photo

BIBLIOGRAPHY

Abbott, N. (1942) 'Women and the State in Early Islam', *Journal of Near Eastern Studies*, 1(3), pp. 106–126. doi:10.1086/370650.

Abraham, K. N. and Woolf, J. (2022) *Black Victorians: Hidden in History*. London: Duckworth.

Abram, A. (1916) 'Women Traders in Medieval London', *The Economic Journal*, 26(102). doi:10.2307/2222473.

Acemoglu, D., Johnson, S. and Robinson, J. (2002) 'The Rise of Europe: Atlantic Trade, Institutional Change and Economic Growth', NBER Working Paper 9378. doi:10.3386/w9378.

Achebe, N. (2020) *Female Monarchs and Merchant Queens in Africa*. Athens, OH: Ohio University Press.

Adams, A., Huttunen, K., Nix, E. and Zhang, N. (2024) 'The Dynamics of Abusive Relationships', *The Quarterly Journal of Economics*, 139(4), pp. 2135–2180.

Adams, C. (2018) 'Nile River Transport Under the Romans', in A. Wilson and A. K. Bowman (eds.) *Trade, Commerce, and the State in the Roman World*. Oxford: Oxford University Press.

Adams, D. W. (1995) *Education for Extinction: American Indians and the Boarding School Experience, 1875–1928*. Lawrence, KS: University Press of Kansas.

Agarwal, B. (1994) *A Field of One's Own: Gender and Land Rights in South Asia*. Cambridge: Cambridge University Press.

Agarwal, B. (2016) *Gender Challenges. Volume 2: Property, Family, and the State*. New Delhi, India: Oxford University Press.

Agencia Peruana De Noticias (2016) 'High Status Female Found Buried at Aspero Archaeological Site in Peru, Andina'. Available at: https://andina.pe/ingles/noticia.aspx?id=609012.aspx (Accessed: 6 May 2024).

Ahmed, L. (1992) *Women and Gender in Islam: Historical Roots of a Modern Debate*. New Haven: Yale University Press.

Albanesi, S. and Olivetti, C. (2007) 'Gender Roles and Technological Progress'. doi:10.3386/w13179.

Alesina, A., Giuliano, P. and Nunn, N. (2013) 'On the Origins of Gender Roles: Women and the Plough', *The Quarterly Journal of Economics*, 128(2), pp. 469–530. doi:10.1093/qje/qjt005.

Alford, K. (1984) *Production or Reproduction?: An Economic History of Women in Australia, 1788–1850*. Melbourne: Oxford University Press.

Alford, K. (1986) 'Colonial Women's Employment as Seen by Nineteenth-Century Statisticians and Twentieth-Century Economic Historians', *Labour History*, (51), p. 1. doi:10.2307/27508793.

BIBLIOGRAPHY

Alger, I. et al. (2020) 'Paternal Provisioning Results from Ecological Change', *Proceedings of the National Academy of Sciences*, 117(20), pp. 10746–10754. doi:10.1073/pnas.1917166117.

Allam, S. (1989) 'Women as Owners of Immovables in Pharaonic Egypt', in B. S. Lesko (ed.) *Women's Earliest Records: From Ancient Egypt and Western Asia*. Atlanta, GA: Scholars' Press, pp. 123–135.

Allen, R. C. (2009) *The British Industrial Revolution in Global Perspective*. Cambridge: Cambridge University Press.

Allen, R. C. (2017a) 'Lessons from History for the Future of Work', *Nature*, 550(7676), pp. 321–324. doi:10.1038/550321a.

Allen, R. C. (2017b) *The Industrial Revolution*. Oxford: Oxford University Press.

Allen, R. C. (2018) 'The Hand-Loom Weaver and the Power Loom: A Schumpeterian Perspective', *European Review of Economic History*, 22(4), pp. 381–402. doi:10.1093/ereh/hex030.

Allen, R. C. and Heldring, L. (2022) 'The Collapse of Civilization in Southern Mesopotamia', *Cliometrica*, 16(2), pp. 369–404. doi:10.1007/s11698-021-00229-2.

Amott, T. L. and Matthaei, J. A. (1991) *Race, Gender and Work: A Multi-Cultural Economic History of Women in the United States*. Montreal: Black Rose Books.

Anderson, A. et al. (2023) 'The Myth of Man the Hunter: Women's Contribution to the Hunt Across Ethnographic Contexts', *PLOS ONE*, 18(6). doi:10.1371/journal.pone.0287101.

Andrews, M. and Lomas, J. (2018) *A History of Women in 100 Objects*. Gloucestershire: History Press.

Anyanwu, J. C. (1992) 'Women's Access to Credit Facilities from Commercial Banks in Nigeria', *Savings and Development*, 16(4), pp. 421–440.

Apple (2024) 'Inclusion & Diversity', https://www.apple.com/diversity/.

Arnaboldi, F. et al. (2021) 'Gender Diversity and Bank Misconduct', *Journal of Corporate Finance*, 71, p. 101834. doi:10.1016/j.jcorpfin.2020.101834.

Asher, C. B. and Talbot, C. (2023) *India Before Europe*. Cambridge: Cambridge University Press.

Ashmolean Museum (no date) 'Ancient Greek Coins—Notes for Teachers'. Oxford: Ashmolean Museum.

Athey, S. and Luca, M. (2019) 'Why Tech Companies Hire So Many Economists', *Harvard Business Review*.

Atwood, R. (2005) 'A Monumental Feud', *Archaeology*, 58(4), pp. 18–25.

Auriol, E. et al. (2022) 'Women in Economics: Europe and the World', Toulouse School of Economics Working Papers, No. 1288.

Backhouse, R. E. (2002) *The Penguin History of Economics*. London: Penguin Books.

Badawi, Z. (2024) *An African History of Africa: From the Dawn of Civilisation to Independence*. London: W. H. Allen.

Baer, S. (2023) '2023–2024 Season: By the Numbers', *Women's Philharmonic Advocacy*, 12 June. Available at: https://wophil.org/2023-2024-season-by-the-numbers/?doing_wp_cron=1734510881.9240601062774658203125#.

Baral, S. (2024) 'How Life Sciences Can Make the Right Deals in a Time of Change', EY Health Sciences and Wellness.

Baraniuk, C. (2023) 'The Women Tackling the "Woeful" Diversity in Plumbing', BBC. Available at: https://www.bbc.co.uk/news/business-65808712.

Barber, E. W. (1995) *Women's Work: The First 20,000 Years*. New York: W. W. Norton.

BIBLIOGRAPHY

Barker, H. (2006) *The Business of Women*. Oxford: Oxford University Press.

Barker, H. (2023) 'Slavery in the Black Sea Region', in D. A. Pargas (ed.) *The Palgrave Handbook of Global Slavery Throughout History*. Palgrave, pp. 159–178.

Barrero, J. M., Bloom, N., Davis, S. J., Meyer, B. H. and Mihaylov, E. (2022) 'The Shift to Remote Work Lessens Wage-Growth Pressures', NBER Working Paper 30197. doi:10.3386/w30197.

Barron, C. M. (1989) 'The "Golden Age" of Women in Medieval London', *Reading Medieval Studies*, XV, pp. 35–58.

Barrow, R. J. (2018) *Gender, Identity and the Body in Greek and Roman Sculpture*. New York: Cambridge University Press.

Bartoloni, G. and Pitzalis, F. (2016) 'Etruscan Marriage', in S. L. Budin and J. M. Turfa (eds.) *Women in Antiquity: Real Women Across the Ancient World*. Abingdon, Oxon: Routledge.

Bateman, V. N. (2019) *The Sex Factor: How Women Made the West Rich*. Cambridge, UK: Polity Press.

Bateman, V. N. (2023) *Naked Feminism: Breaking the Cult of Female Modesty*. Cambridge, UK: Polity Press.

Baumeister, R. F. and Twenge, J. M. (2002) 'Cultural Suppression of Female Sexuality', *Review of General Psychology*, 6(2), pp. 166–203. doi:10.1037/1089-2680.6.2.166.

Bawden, C. R. (2025) 'Kublai Khan', *Encyclopaedia Britannica*. Available at: https://www.britannica.com/biography/Kublai-Khan (Accessed: 9 January 2025).

Becker, A. (2019) 'On the Economic Origins of Restrictions on Women's Sexuality', *SSRN Electronic Journal*. doi:10.2139/ssrn.3432818.

Becker, H. (2016) 'Roman Women in the Urban Economy', in S. L. Budin and J. M. Turfa (eds.) *Women in Antiquity: Real Women Across the Ancient World*. Abingdon, Oxon: Routledge, pp. 915–931.

Beckett, G. W. (2013) *A Population History of Colonial New South Wales*. Gatton, Qld: Colonial Press.

Beevor, A. (2022) *Russia: Revolution and Civil War 1917–1921*. London: Weidenfeld & Nicolson.

Beevor, A. and Rogers, J. (2023) 'Antony Beevor Breaks Down the Russian Revolution of 1917', *History Hit*. Available at: https://www.youtube.com/watch?v=p52KiKFkLRM (Accessed: 21 August 2024).

Beneria, L. (2007) 'Gender and the Social Construction of Markets', in I. van Staveren et al. (eds.) *The Feminist Economics of Trade*. Oxford: Routledge.

Benn, C. D. (2002) *China's Golden Age: Everyday Life in the Tang Dynasty*. Oxford: Oxford University Press.

Bennett, J. M. (1996) *Ale, Beer and Brewsters in England: Women's Work in a Changing World, 1300–1600*. New York: Oxford University Press.

Bennett, J. M. (2010) 'Compulsory Service in Late Medieval England', *Past and Present*, 209(1), pp. 7–51. doi:10.1093/pastj/gtq032.

Beresford-Jones, D. et al. (2017) 'Refining the Maritime Foundations of Andean Civilization: How Plant Fiber Technology Drove Social Complexity During the Preceramic Period', *Journal of Archaeological Method and Theory*, 25(2), pp. 393–425. doi:10.1007/s10816-017-9341-3.

Berg, M. (1993) 'What Difference Did Women's Work Make to the Industrial Revolution?', *History Workshop Journal*, 35(1), pp. 22–44. doi:10.1093/hwj/35.1.22.

BIBLIOGRAPHY

Bergeron, M. E. (2011) 'Death, Gender, and Sea Shells in Carthage', *Pallas*, (86), pp. 169–189. doi:10.4000/pallas.2143.

Bernstein, W. J. (2009) *A Splendid Exchange: How Trade Shaped the World*. London: Atlantic Books.

Bessard, F. (2020) *Caliphs and Merchants: Cities and Economies of Power in the Near East (700–950)*. Oxford: Oxford University Press.

Bharat, S. (2019) 'Indian Women's Agency Through Indian Women's Literature', in R. W. Dimand and K. Madden (eds.) *The Routledge Handbook of the History of Women's Economic Thought*. Oxford: Routledge, pp. 13–32.

Bierman, H. (2008) 'The 1929 Stock Market Crash', *EH.Net Encyclopedia*. Edited by R. Whaples. Economic History Association.

Birge, B. (2002) *Women, Property, and Confucian Reaction in Sung and Yüan China (960–1368)*. Cambridge: Cambridge University Press.

Black, J. (2011) *A Brief History of Slavery: A New Global History*. London: Robinson.

Blackburn, J. (2024) 'AI Everywhere: Transforming Our World, Empowering Humanity—a Conversation with Mira Murati', Dartmouth Engineering. Dartmouth College.

Blackburn, S. (1995) 'How Useful Are Feminist Theories of the Welfare State?', *Women's History Review*, 4(3), pp. 369–394. doi:10.1080/09612029500200174.

Blau, F. D., Winkler, A. E. and Ferber, M. A. (2016) *The Economics of Women, Men, and Work*. New York: Oxford University Press.

Blofield, M. and Jokela, M. (2018) 'Paid Domestic Work and the Struggles of Care Workers in Latin America', *Current Sociology*, 66(4), pp. 531–546. doi:10.1177/0011392118765259.

Bogachev, I. (2023) 'How the Growing Creative Economy Will Soon Devour the Real Economy', *Forbes*, 16 May.

Bonfante, L. (2016) 'Motherhood in Etruria', in S. L. Budin and J. M. Turfa (eds.) *Women in Antiquity: Real Women Across the Ancient World*. Abingdon, Oxon: Routledge.

Bosker, M., Buringh, E. and van Zanden, J. L. (2013) 'From Baghdad to London: Unraveling Urban Development in Europe, the Middle East, and North Africa, 800–1800', *The Review of Economics and Statistics*, 95(4), pp. 1418–1437. doi:10.1162/rest_a_00284.

Bouras, C. (2002) 'Aspects of the Byzantine City, Eighth–Fifteenth Centuries', in A. E. Laiou (ed.) *The Economic History of Byzantium: From the Seventh Through the Fifteenth Century*. Washington, D.C.: Dumbarton Oaks Research Library and Collection.

Boustan, L. P. and Collins, W. (2013) 'The Origins and Persistence of Black-White Differences in Women's Labor Force Participation', NBER Working Paper 19040. doi:10.3386/w19040.

Bowman, A. (2018) 'The State and the Economy: Fiscality and Taxation', in A. Wilson and A. Bowman (eds.) *Trade, Commerce, and the State in the Roman World*. Oxford: Oxford University Press, pp. 27–52.

Bray, F. (1995) 'Textile Production and Gender Roles in China, 1000–1700', *East Asian Science, Technology, and Medicine*, 12(1), pp. 115–137. doi:10.1163/26669323-01201009.

Bresson, A. (2016) *The Making of the Ancient Greek Economy*. Princeton, NJ: Princeton University Press.

BIBLIOGRAPHY

Brixi, H., Porter Peschka, M. and Qiang, C. Z. (2023) 'She Can Too: Upskilling Girls Today for the Digital Jobs of Tomorrow', *World Bank*. Available at: https://blogs.worldbank.org/en/digital-development/she-can-too-upskilling-girls-today-digital-jobs-tomorrow.

Broadberry, S. et al. (2015) *British Economic Growth, 1270–1870*. Cambridge: Cambridge University Press.

Brock, R. (1994) 'The Labour of Women in Classical Athens', *The Classical Quarterly*, 44(2), pp. 336–346. doi:10.1017/s0009838800043809.

Brodman, J. (2017) *Sex Rules!: Astonishing Sexual Practices and Gender Roles Around the World*. Coral Gables, FL: Mango.

Brosius, M. (2016) 'No Reason to Hide', in S. L. Budin and J. M. Turfa (eds.) *Women in Antiquity: Real Women Across the Ancient World*. Abingdon, Oxon: Routledge.

Brown, J. K. (1970) 'A Note on the Division of Labor by Sex', *American Anthropologist*, 72(5), pp. 1073–1078. doi:10.1525/aa.1970.72.5.02a00070.

Brown, M. and Satterthwaite-Phillips, D. (2018) 'Economic Correlates of Footbinding: Implications for the Importance of Chinese Daughters' Labor', *PLOS ONE*, 13(9). doi:10.1371/journal.pone.0201337.

Bryson, V. (2016) *Feminist Political Theory*. London: Palgrave.

Buckholtz, A. (2021) 'The Creative Economy Takes Center Stage', *International Finance Corporation*. World Bank Group. Available at: https://www.ifc.org/en/stories/2021/the-creative-economy-takes-center-stage.

Budin, S. L. (2016) 'Female Sexuality in Mesopotamia', in S. L. Budin and J. M. Turfa (eds.) *Women in Antiquity: Real Women Across the Ancient World*. Abingdon, Oxon: Routledge.

Budin, S. L. and Turfa, J. M. (2016) *Women in Antiquity: Real Women Across the Ancient World*. Abingdon, Oxon: Routledge.

Buringh, E. and van Zanden, J. L. (2009), 'Charting the Rise of the West': Manuscripts and Printed Books in Europe, a Long-Term Perspective from the Sixth Through Eighteenth Centuries', *The Journal of Economic History*, 69(2), pp. 409–445.

Burnard, T. (2022) 'A Global History of Slavery in the Medieval Millennium', *Slavery & Abolition: A Journal of Slave and Post-Slave Studies*, 43(4), pp. 819–826. doi:10.1080/0144039x.2022.2101296.

Burnette, J. (2008a) *Gender, Work and Wages in Industrial Revolution Britain*. Cambridge: Cambridge University Press.

Burnette, J. (2008b) 'Women Workers in the British Industrial Revolution', *EH.Net Encyclopedia*. Edited by R. Whaples. Economic History Association. Available at: https://eh.net/encyclopedia/women-workers-in-the-british-industrial-revolution/.

Caldwell, L. (2021) 'From Household to Workshop: Women, Weaving, and the Peculium', in B. Longfellow and M. Swetnam-Burland (eds.) *Women's Lives, Women's Voices: Roman Material Culture and Female Agency in the Bay of Naples*. Austin, TX: University of Texas Press, pp. 51–65.

Callow, E. (1899) *Old London Taverns: Historical, Descriptive and Reminiscent*. London: Downey & Co.

Calvi, R. and Keskar, A. (2021) 'Dowries, Resource Allocation, and Poverty', *Journal of Economic Behavior and Organization*, 192, pp. 268–304.

Cameron, C. M. (2023) 'Injection: An Archaeological Approach to Slavery', in D. A. Pargas and J. Schiel (eds.) *The Palgrave Handbook of Global Slavery Throughout History*. London: Palgrave Macmillan.

Campbell, G. (2005) 'Columbus', in G. Campbell, *The Oxford Dictionary of the Renaissance*. Oxford University Press.

Card, E. (1980) 'Women, Housing Access, and Mortgage Credit', *Signs: Journal of Women in Culture and Society*, 5(S3). doi:10.1086/495720.

Cardillo, G., Onali, E. and Torluccio, G. (2020) 'Does Gender Diversity on Banks' Boards Matter? Evidence from Public Bailouts', *Journal of Corporate Finance*, 71, p. 101560. doi:10.1016/j.jcorpfin.2020.101560.

Carlin, D. (2024) 'Hunger Strike to End 24-Hour Home Health Aide Shifts Ends After 5 Days', *CBS News*.

Carlin, M. (2008) '"What Say You to a Piece of Beef and Mustard?": The Evolution of Public Dining in Medieval and Tudor London', *Huntington Library Quarterly*, 71(1), pp. 199–217. doi:10.1525/hlq.2008.71.1.199.

Carswell, G. (2016) 'Struggles over Work Take Place at Home: Women's Decisions, Choices and Constraints in the Tiruppur Textile Industry, India', *Geoforum*, 77, pp. 134–145. doi:10.1016/j.geoforum.2016.10.009.

Cassidy, L. M. et al. (2025) 'Continental Influx and Pervasive Matrilocality in Iron Age Britain', *Nature*, 15 January. doi.org/10.1038/s41586-024-08409-6.

Castagnetti, S. and Haines, E. (2023) 'Ogu Umunwanyi, Ekong Iban, Women's War: A Story of Protest by Nigerian Women', *National Archives—Records and Research*. National Archives, 30 March. Available at: https://blog.nationalarchives.gov.uk/ogu-umunwanyi-ekong-iban-womens-war-a-story-of-protest-by-nigerian-women/.

Cevherli, F. (2022) 'As a Commercial Genius Khadija bint Khuwaylid (RA) and Her Mudarabah Partnership with Prophet Muhammad (SAW)', *International Journal of Islamic Economics and Finance Studies*, pp. 299–310. doi:10.54427/ijisef.1191298.

Chapman, J. R. (1975) 'Women's Access to Credit', *Challenge*, 17(6), pp. 40–45.

Charlesworth, A. and Johnson, P. (eds.) (2018) 'Securing the Future: Funding Health and Social Care to the 2030s', *Joint Report of the IFS and the Health Foundation in Association with the NHS Confederation*.

Chatelard, A. (2016) 'Women as Legal Minors and Their Citizenship in Republican Rome', *Clio. Women, Gender, History*, 43, pp. 24–47.

Chowdhury, B. (2018) 'Scheherazade: The Story of a Storyteller', *Art UK*, 23 January. Available at: https://artuk.org/discover/stories/scheherazade-the-story-of-a-storyteller (Accessed: 22 February 2024).

Christian, M. A. (2013) 'Phoenician Maritime Religion: Sailors, Goddess Worship, and the Grotta Regina', *Die Welt des Orients*, 43(2), pp. 179–205. doi:10.13109/wdor.2013.43.2.179.

Cirotteau, T., Kerner, J. and Pincas, E. (2022) *Lady Sapiens: Breaking Stereotypes About Prehistoric Women*. London, England: Hero.

Clark, A. (1919) *Working Life of Women in the Seventeenth Century*. New York: Dutton.

Clark, S. R. (2003) 'Representing the Indus Body: Sex, Gender, Sexuality, and the Anthropomorphic Terracotta Figurines from Harappa', *Asian Perspectives*, 42(2), pp. 304–328. doi:10.1353/asi.2003.0036.

Clean Energy Research Centre UBC (2017) 'Women and Innovation: The Bertha Benz Story', Clean Energy Research Centre UBC. Available at: https://www.youtube.com/watch?v=vK1dwvtTlcM (Accessed: 21 August 2024).

Cline, E. H. (2021) *1177 B.C.: The Year Civilisation Collapsed*. Princeton, NJ: Princeton University Press.

Cock, J. (1980) *Maids and Madams: A Study in the Politics of Exploitation.* Johannesburg: Raven Press.

Cohen, E. E. (2016) 'The Athenian Businesswoman', in S. L. Budin and J. M. Turfa (eds.) *Women in Antiquity: Real Women Across the Ancient World.* London: Routledge, pp. 714–725.

Collins, P. (2021) *The Sumerians: Lost Civilizations.* London: Reaktion.

Collinson, D. L. (1987) 'Banking on Women: Selection Practices in the Finance Sector', *Personnel Review*, 16(5), pp. 12–20. doi:10.1108/eb055575.

Connor, C. L. (2004) *Women of Byzantium.* New Haven: Yale University Press.

Conteh, M. (2021) 'Spotify's Sub-Saharan Africa Head of Music Phiona Okumu—Future 25', *Rolling Stone.* 'Future of Music' issue, 15 June.

Cooper, J. S. (1989) 'Third Millennium Mesopotamia', in B. S. Lesko (ed.) *Women's Earliest Records: From Ancient Egypt and Western Asia.* Atlanta, GA: Scholars' Press, pp. 47–52.

Costin, C. (2013) 'Gender and Textile Production in Prehistory', in D. Bolger (ed.) *A Companion to Gender Prehistory.* Oxford: Wiley & Sons, pp. 180–202.

Costin, C. L. (1993) 'Textiles, Women, and Political Economy in Late Prehispanic Peru', *Research in Economic Anthropology*, 14(3), pp. 3–28.

Crafts, N. (2018) *Forging Ahead, Falling Behind and Fighting Back: British Economic Growth from the Industrial Revolution to the Financial Crisis.* Cambridge: Cambridge University Press.

Crawford, P. and Gowing, L. (2000) *Women's Worlds in Seventeenth-Century England.* London: Routledge.

Creamer, W., Haas, J. and Castillo, H. M. (2017) 'A Culturescape Built over 5,000 Years, Archaeology, and Vichama Raymi in the Forge of History', in F. Armstrong-Fumero and J. H. Gutierrez (eds.) *Archaeology, Ethnohistory, and the Politics of Cultural Continuity in the Americas.* University Press of Colorado, pp. 189–207.

Creel, H. (1965) 'The Role of the Horse in Chinese History', *The American Historical Review*, 70(3), pp. 647–672. doi:10.1086/ahr/70.3.647.

Cribb, J., Disney, R. and Sibieta, L. (2014) 'The Public Sector Workforce: Past, Present and Future', IFS Briefing Note BN145.

Culham, P. (1982) 'The "Lex Oppia"', *Litmus*, 41(4), pp. 786–793.

D'Ambra, E. (2021) 'Real Estate for Profit: Julia Felix's Property and the Forum Frieze', in B. Longfellow and M. Swetnam-Burland (eds.) *Women's Lives, Women's Voices: Roman Material Culture and Female Agency in the Bay of Naples.* Austin, TX: University of Texas Press, pp. 85–105.

Dabhoiwala, F. (2012) *The Origins of Sex: A History of the First Sexual Revolution.* London: Penguin Books.

Dagron, G. (2002) 'The Urban Economy, Seventh–Twelfth Centuries', in A. E. Laiou (ed.) *The Economic History of Byzantium: From the Seventh Through the Fifteenth Century.* Washington D.C.: Dumbarton Oaks Research Library and Collection, pp. 385–453.

Dale, M. K. (1933) 'The London Silkwomen of the Fifteenth Century', *The Economic History Review*, 4(3), pp. 324–335. doi:10.2307/2590651.

Dallas, K. (1946) 'Transportation and colonial income', *Historical Studies: Australia and New Zealand*, 3(12), pp. 297–312. doi:10.1080/10314614608594869.

Dalrymple, W. (2020) *The Anarchy: The Relentless Rise of the East India Company.* London: Bloomsbury.

BIBLIOGRAPHY

Dattani, S. et al. (2023) 'Life Expectancy', OurWorldInData.org. Available at: https://ourworldindata.org/life-expectancy.

Dauphin, C., Ben Jeddou, M. and Castex, J.-M. (2015) 'To Mecca on Pilgrimage on Foot and Camel-Back: The Jordanian *Darb Al-Hajj*', *Bulletin for the Council for British Research in the Levant*, 10(1), pp. 23–36. doi:10.1179/1752726015z.00000000029.

David, R. (2016) 'Understanding the Lives of Ancient Egyptian Women', in S. L. Budin and J. M. Turfa (eds.) *Women in Antiquity: Real Women Across the Ancient World*. London: Routledge, pp. 181–193.

Davis-Kimball, J. and Behan, M. (2003) *Warrior Women: An Archaeologist's Search for History's Hidden Heroines*. New York, London: Warner; Time Warner.

de Beaune, S. A. (2019) 'A Critical Analysis of the Evidence for Sexual Division of Tasks in the European Upper Paleolithic', in K. A. Overmann and F. L. Coolidge (eds.) *Squeezing Minds from Stones: Cognitive Archaeology and the Evolution of the Human Mind*. New York: Oxford University Press.

De Moor, T. and van Zanden, J. L. (2009) 'Girl Power: The European Marriage Pattern and Labour Markets in the North Sea Region in the Late Medieval and Early Modern Period', *The Economic History Review*, 63(1), pp. 1–33. doi:10.1111/j.1468-0289.2009.00483.x.

De Vries, J. (2009) *The Industrious Revolution: Consumer Behavior and the Household Economy, 1650 to the Present*. Cambridge: Cambridge University Press.

Deere, C. D. and Doss, C. R. (2006) 'The Gender Asset Gap: What Do We Know and Why Does It Matter?', *Feminist Economics*, 12(1–2), pp. 1–50. doi:10.1080/13545700500508056.

Demosthenes (1989) *Orations, Volume VI*. Translated by A. T. Murray. Loeb Classical Library.

Deng, K. and Shengmin, S. (2019) 'China's Extraordinary Population Expansion and Its Determinants During the Qing Period, 1644–1911', *Population Review*, 58(1), pp. 20–77. doi:10.1353/prv.2019.0001.

Deng, K. and Zheng, L. (2015) 'Economic Restructuring and Demographic Growth: Demystifying Growth and Development in Northern Song China, 960–1127', *The Economic History Review*, 68(4), pp. 1107–1131. doi:10.1111/ehr.12100.

Denisova, L. (2018) 'The Daily Life of Russian Peasant Women', in M. Ilic (ed.) *The Palgrave Handbook of Women and Gender in Twentieth-Century Russia and the Soviet Union*. London: Palgrave Macmillan, pp. 149–165.

Department for Culture, Media and Sport (2023) 'Ambitious Plans to Grow the Economy and Boost Creative Industries', Press Release: Department for Culture, Media and Sport, 13 June.

Desilver, D. (2023) 'Most US Bank Failures Have Come in a Few Big Waves', Pew Research Center.

Devonshire, J. (2024) 'The Only Woman in the Room: Brill Power's Carolyn Hicks on Getting More Females into STEM', *The Manufacturer*.

Diamond, J. (2005) *Guns, Germs and Steel: A Short History of Everybody for the Last 13,000 Years*. London: Vintage Books.

Dolan, E. W. (2024) 'Scientists Say Media Storm Around "Myth of Man the Hunter" Study Was Unjustified and Misleading', *PsyPost*.

Dollinger, P. (1999) *The German Hansa*. London: Routledge.

Domar, E. D. (1970) 'The Causes of Slavery or Serfdom: A Hypothesis', *The Journal of Economic History*, 30(1), pp. 18–32. doi:10.1017/s0022050700078566.

Domínguez, E. et al. (2010) 'Women Workers in the Maquiladoras and the Debate on Global Labor Standards', *Feminist Economics*, 16(4), pp. 185–209. doi:10.1080/13545701.2010.530603.

Doody, M. A. (2010) *Frances Burney: The Life in the Works*. Cambridge: Cambridge University Press. Originally published in 1988.

Dossani, K. (2013) 'Virtue and Veiling: Perspective from Ancient to Abbasid Times'. MA Thesis, San Jose State University.

Downing, M. (1985) 'Prehistoric Goddesses: The Cretan Challenge', *Journal of Feminist Studies in Religion*, 1(1), pp. 7–11.

Downs, K. (2008) 'Mirrored Archetypes: The Contrasting Cultural Roles of La Malinche and Pocahontas', *Western Folklore*, 67(4), pp. 397–414.

Dublin, T. (1994) *Transforming Women's Work: New England Lives in the Industrial Revolution*. Ithaca, NY: Cornell University Press.

Dyer, C. (2005) *An Age of Transition? Economy and Society in England in the Later Middle Ages*. Oxford: Oxford University Press.

Earle, P. (1989) 'The Female Labour Market in London in the Late Seventeenth and Early Eighteenth Centuries', *The Economic History Review*, 42(3), p. 328. doi:10.2307/2596437.

Eberle, R. (2001) *Chastity, Transgression & Women's Writings 1792–1897: Interrupting the Harlot's Progress*. Basingstoke, UK: Palgrave Macmillan.

Ebrey, P. B. (1993) *The Inner Quarters: Marriage and the Lives of Chinese Women in the Sung Period*. Berkeley: University of California Press.

Ebrey, P. B. (2002) *Women and the Family in Chinese History*. London: Routledge.

Ebrey, P. B. (2023) *The Cambridge Illustrated History of China*. Cambridge: Cambridge University Press.

Edlund, J. and Öun, I. (2023) 'Equal Sharing or Not at All Caring? Ideals About Fathers' Family Involvement and the Prevalence of the Second Half of the Gender Revolution in 27 Societies', *Journal of Family Studies*, 29(6), pp. 2576–2599. doi:10.1080/13229400.2023.2179531.

Ekejiuba, F. (1967) 'Omu Okwei, the Merchant Queen of Ossomari: A Biographical Sketch', *Journal of the Historical Society of Nigeria*, 3(4), pp. 633–646.

El-Azhari, T. (2021) *Queens, Eunuchs and Concubines in Islamic History, 661–1257*. Edinburgh: Edinburgh University Press.

El-Badawi, E. I. (2022) *Queens and Prophets: How Arabian Noblewomen and Holy Men Shaped Paganism, Christianity and Islam*. London: Oneworld Academic.

El-Cheikh, N. M. (1997) 'Describing the Other to Get at the Self: Byzantine Women in Arabic Sources (8th–11th Centuries)', *Journal of the Economic and Social History of the Orient*, 40(2), pp. 239–250. doi:10.1163/1568520972600766.

Elbirlik, L. K. (2021) 'Ottoman Women Investors as Caretakers of the Family: The Purchase of Esame and Gedik Licences by Women in Istanbul', Women, Money and Markets Conference Paper.

Elson, D. and Pearson, R. (1981) 'The Subordination of Women and the Internationalisation of Factory Production', in K. Young, C. Wolkowitz and R. McCullagh (eds.) *Of Marriage and the Market*. Abingdon, Oxon: Routledge.

Elvin, M. (1998) 'The Environmental Legacy of Imperial China', *The China Quarterly*, 156, pp. 733–756. doi:10.1017/s0305741000051328.

Elvin, M. (2004) *Retreat of the Elephants—an Environmental History of China*. New Haven: Yale University Press.

Encyclopaedia Britannica (2007) 'Hortensia', *Encyclopaedia Britannica*. Available at: https://www.britannica.com/biography/Hortensia (Accessed: 22 January 2024).

Encyclopaedia Britannica (2016) 'Panathenaea', *Encyclopaedia Britannica*. Available at: https://www.britannica.com/topic/Panathenaea (Accessed: 7 August 2024).

Encyclopaedia Britannica (2018) 'Caravan', *Encyclopaedia Britannica*. Available at: https://www.britannica.com/topic/caravan-desert-transport (Accessed: 22 January 2024).

Encyclopaedia Britannica (2018a) 'Dido', *Encyclopaedia Britannica*. Available at: https://www.britannica.com/topic/Dido (Accessed: 22 January 2024).

Encyclopaedia Britannica (2019) 'St. Helena', *Encyclopaedia Britannica*. Available at: https://www.britannica.com/biography/Saint-Helena (Accessed: 22 January 2024).

Encyclopaedia Britannica (2023) 'Battle of Badr', *Encyclopaedia Britannica*. Available at: https://www.britannica.com/event/Battle-of-Badr (Accessed: 25 January 2024).

Encyclopaedia Britannica (2023a) 'Mongol Empire', *Encyclopaedia Britannica*. Available at: https://www.britannica.com/place/Mongol-empire (Accessed: 5 February 2024).

Encyclopaedia Britannica (2024) 'Abu al-Abbas al-Saffah', *Encyclopaedia Britannica*. Available at: https://www.britannica.com/biography/Abu-al-Abbas-al-Saffah (Accessed: 22 February 2024).

Encyclopaedia Britannica (2024a) 'Battle of Salamis', *Encyclopaedia Britannica*. Available at: https://www.britannica.com/event/Battle-of-Salamis (Accessed: 7 August 2024).

Encyclopaedia Britannica (2024b) 'Susanna Rowson', *Encyclopaedia Britannica*. Available at: https://www.britannica.com/biography/Susanna-Rowson (Accessed: 26 June 2024).

Encyclopaedia Britannica (2024c) 'Frances Burney', *Encyclopaedia Britannica*. Available at: https://www.britannica.com/biography/Fanny-Burney (Accessed: 26 June 2024).

Engel, B. A. (2004) *Women in Russia, 1700–2000*. Cambridge: Cambridge University Press.

Engels, F. (1884) *The Origin of the Family, Private Property and the State*. Hottingen-Zurich.

Entman, L. (2017) 'Dark Side of the Mound: Vanderbilt Researchers Unearth Clues to a Mysterious Peruvian Archaeological Site', *Vanderbilt Magazine*. Available at: https://news.vanderbilt.edu/2017/05/29/dark-side-of-the-mound-vanderbilt-researchers-have-unearthed-clues-to-a-mysterious-peruvian-archaeological-site-14-millennia-in-the-making/ (Accessed: 6 May 2024).

Erickson, A. L. (2008) 'Married Women's Occupations in Eighteenth-Century London', *Continuity and Change*, 23(2), pp. 267–307. doi:10.1017/s0268416008006772.

Erickson, A. L. (2022) 'Wealthy Businesswomen, Marriage and Succession in Eighteenth-Century London', *Business History*, 66(1), pp. 29–58. doi:10.1080/00076791.2022.2036131.

ESPAS (2019), 'Global Trends to 2030: Challenges and Choices for Europe', European Union.

Esping-Anderson, G. (2009) *The Incomplete Revolution: Adapting to Women's New Roles*. Cambridge: Polity.

Eswaran, M. (2014) *Why Gender Matters in Economics*. Princeton, NJ: Princeton University Press.

European Commission et al. (2008) 'System of National Accounts', Joint Statistical Framework for National Accounts.

Eurostat (2020) 'Girls and Women Among ICT Students: What Do we Know?', European Union.

Evans, M. (2020) *Making Respectable Women: Changing Moralities, Changing Times*. London: Palgrave Macmillan.

Everill, B. (2024) *Africonomics: A History of Western Ignorance*. London: William Collins.

Fan, X. and Wu, L. (2023) 'The Shaping of a Gender Norm: Marriage, Labor, and Foot-Binding in Historical China', *International Economic Review*, 64(4), pp. 1819–1850. doi:10.1111/iere.12663.

Fara, P. (2016) 'The Lost Women of Enlightenment Science', *New Scientist*, 26 May.

Federal Reserve (2024) 'The Labor Market for Recent College Graduates', Federal Reserve Bank of New York. Available at: https://nyfed.org/collegelabor.

Federico, S. (2001) 'The Imaginary Society: Women in 1381', *Journal of British Studies*, 40(2), pp. 159–183. doi:10.1086/386239.

Felder, D. G. (2020) *The American Women's Almanac: 500 Years of Making History*. Detroit: Visible Ink.

Ferguson, D. (2024) 'How Bridgerton's Real Life Lady Whistledown Scandalised 18th-Century Society', *Observer*, 19 May.

Filbee, M. (1980) *A Woman's Place: An Illustrated History of Women at Home*. London: Ebury Press.

Firkus, A. (2021) *America's Early Women Celebrities: The Famous and Scorned from Martha Washington to Silent Film Star Mary Fuller*. Jefferson, NC: McFarland & Company, Inc., Publishers.

Fischer, H. G. (1989) 'Women in the Old Kingdom and the Haracleopolitan', in B. S. Lesko (ed.) *Women's Earliest Records: From Ancient Egypt and Western Asia*. Atlanta, GA: Scholars' Press, pp. 5–25.

Fletcher, E. (2024) 'How We Can Support Female Entrepreneurs to Thrive in Biotech', insider.co.uk.

Ford, T. (2013) 'A Woman's Battle to Inherit Land in Ivory Coast', *BBC News*.

Foreman-Peck, J. (2011) 'The Western European Marriage Pattern and Economic Development', *Explorations in Economic History*, 48(2), pp. 292–309. doi:10.1016/j.eeh.2011.01.002.

Foster, B. R. (1989) 'Western Asia in the Second Millennium', in B. S. Lesko (ed.) *Women's Earliest Records: From Ancient Egypt and Western Asia*. Atlanta, GA: Scholars' Press, pp. 141–144.

Frank, R. I. (1975) 'Augustus' Legislation on Marriage and Children', *California Studies in Classical Antiquity*, 8, pp. 41–52. doi:10.2307/25010681.

Frankopan, P. (2016) *The Silk Roads: A New History of the World*. London: Bloomsbury.

French, M. (2008) *From Eve to Dawn: A History of Women, Volume I*. New York: Feminist Press at the City University of New York.

Fukuyama, F. (1989) 'The End of History?', *The National Interest*, 16, pp. 3–18.

Fulghum, M. M. (2001) 'Under Wraps: Byzantine Textiles as Major and Minor Arts', *Studies in the Decorative Arts*, 9(1), pp. 13–33. doi:10.1086/studdecoarts.9.1.40662797.

Galbraith, J. K. (2021) *The Great Crash*, 1929. London: Penguin Classics.

Galt, C. M. (1931) 'Veiled Ladies', *American Journal of Archaeology*, 35(4), pp. 373–393. doi:10.2307/498098.

Geldard, R. (2024) 'Gender Gap: This Is the State of Work for Women in 2024', World Economic Forum, 27 June. Available at: https://www.weforum.org/agenda/2024/06/women-work-gender-gap-2024/.

Geraghty, R. M. (2007) 'The Impact of Globalization in the Roman Empire, 200 BC–AD 100', *The Journal of Economic History*, 67(4), pp. 1036–1061. doi:10.1017/s0022050707000484.

German, S. (2007) 'Dance in Bronze Age Greece', *Dance Research Journal*, 39(2), pp. 23–42. doi:10.1017/s0149767700000206.

Gilligan, I. (2019) *Climate, Clothing, and Agriculture in Prehistory: Linking Evidence, Causes, and Effects*. Cambridge: Cambridge University Press.

Glahn, R. V. (2016) *The Economic History of China: From Antiquity to the Nineteenth Century*. Cambridge: Cambridge University Press.

Glassner, J.-J. (1989) 'Women, Hospitality, and the Honor', in *Women's Earliest Records: From Ancient Egypt and Western Asia*. Atlanta, GA: Scholars' Press, pp. 71–90.

Glazebrook, A. (2011) 'Porneion', in A. Glazebrook and M. M. Henry (eds.) *Greek Prostitutes in the Ancient Mediterranean, 800 BCE–200 CE*. Madison, WI: University of Wisconsin Press.

Glazebrook, A. (2016) 'Prostitutes, Women, and Gender in Ancient Greece', in S. L. Budin and J. M. Turfa (eds.) *Women in Antiquity: Real Women Across the Ancient World*. London: Routledge, pp. 703–713.

Gleba, M. (2016) 'Women and Textile Production in Pre-Roman Italy', in S. L. Budin and J. M. Turfa (eds.) *Women in Antiquity: Real Women Across the Ancient World*. Abingdon, Oxon: Routledge.

Global Entrepreneurship Monitor (2023) 'Global Entrepreneurship Monitor 2022/23 Women's Entrepreneurship Report', Global Entrepreneurship Monitor (GEM)—Global Entrepreneurship Research Association.

Glucksmann, M. (1990) *Women Assemble: Women Workers and the New Industries in Inter-War Britain*. London: Routledge.

Goldin, C. (1990) *Understanding the Gender Gap: An Economic History of American Women*. New York: Oxford University Press.

Goldin, C. (2023) '2023 Prize Lecture in Economic Sciences: Claudia Goldin', Nobel Prize.

Goldman, W. Z. (2011) *Women at the Gates: Gender and Industry in Stalin's Russia*. Cambridge: Cambridge University Press.

Goody, J. (1976) *Production and Reproduction: A Comparative Study of the Domestic Domain*. Cambridge: Cambridge University Press.

Google (2021) 'We're Listening, Learning, and Taking Action', 2021 Diversity Annual Report.

Gordon, M. S. and Hain, K. A. (2017), *Concubines and Courtesans: Women and Slavery in Islamic History*. Oxford: Oxford University Press.

Gowing, L. (2016) 'Girls on Forms: Apprenticing Young Women in Seventeenth-Century London', *Journal of British Studies*, 55(3), pp. 447–473. doi:10.1017/jbr.2016.54.

Gowing, L. (2022) *Ingenious Trade: Women and Work in Seventeenth-Century London*. Cambridge: Cambridge University Press.

Graf, D. F. (2018) 'The Silk Road Between Syria and China', in A. Wilson and A. K. Bowman (eds.) *Trade, Commerce, and the State in the Roman World*. Oxford: Oxford University Press.

Green, A. S. (2020) 'Killing the Priest-King: Addressing Egalitarianism in the Indus Civilization', *Journal of Archaeological Research*, 29(2), pp. 153–202. doi:10.1007/s10814-020-09147-9.

Green, P. (2017) 'When Things Got Tough', *London Review of Books*, 7 September.

Greenhalgh, S. (1977) 'Bound Feet, Hobbled Lives: Women in Old China', *Frontiers: A Journal of Women Studies*, 2(1), p. 7. doi:10.2307/3346103.

Greenspan, A. (2007) *The Age of Turbulence: Adventures in a New World*. New York: Penguin Press.

Gregory, P. (2023) *Normal Women: 900 Years of Making History*. London: William Collins.

Grimley, N. and Horrox, C. (2023) 'Ghana Patients in Danger as Nurses Head for NHS in UK—Medics', *BBC News*, Accra. Available at: https://www.bbc.co.uk/news/world-africa-65808660.

Guha, S. (1989) 'The Handloom Industry of Central India: 1825–1950', *The Indian Economic and Social History Review*, 26(3).

Haas, J. and Creamer, W. (2006) 'Crucible of Andean Civilization: The Peruvian Coast from 3000 to 1800 BC', *Current Anthropology*, 47(5), pp. 745–775. doi:10.1086/506281.

Haas, J., Creamer, W. and Ruiz, A. (2004) 'Power and the Emergence of Complex Polities in the Peruvian Preceramic', *Archaeological Papers of the American Anthropological Association*, 14(1), pp. 37–52. doi:10.1525/ap3a.2004.14.037.

Haas, R. et al. (2020) 'Female Hunters of the Early Americas', *Science Advances*, 6(45), November. doi:10.1126/sciadv.abd0310.

Hafford, W. B. (2018) 'A Spectacular Discovery: Burials Simple and Splendid', *Expedition Magazine*, 60(1), pp. 58–65.

Hagen, R.-M. and Hagen, R. (2010) *Masterpieces in Detail*. Köln: Taschen.

Halim, D. (2020) 'Women Entrepreneurs Needed—Stat!', *World Bank Blogs*. World Bank, 5 March. Available at: https://blogs.worldbank.org/en/opendata/women-entrepreneurs-needed-stat.

Handley, L. (2017) 'Zhang Xin: The Woman Who Built Beijing', CNBC: *The Brave Ones*.

Hansen, V. (1996) 'The Mystery of the Qingming Scroll and Its Subject: The Case Against Kaifeng', *Journal of Sung-Yuan Studies*, 26, pp. 183–200.

Hansen, V. (2003) 'The Astonishing Finds from the Turfan Oasis: What They Reveal About the History of the Silk Road', in *The Glory of the Silk Road*. Dayton Art Institute.

Hansen, V. (2005) 'How Business Was Conducted on the Chinese Silk Road During the Tang Dynasty, 618–907', in W. N. Goetzmann and K. G. Rouwenhorst (eds.) *The Origins of Value: The Financial Innovations That Created Modern Capital Markets*. New York: Oxford University Press.

Hansen, V. (2011) 'The Place of Coins and Their Alternatives in the Silk Road Trade', in *Proceedings of the Symposium on Ancient Coins and the Culture of the Silk Road*. Shanghai.

Hardy, B. L. et al. (2013) 'Impossible Neanderthals? Making String, Throwing Projectiles and Catching Small Game During Marine Isotope Stage 4 (Abri du Maras, France)', *Quaternary Science Reviews*, 82, pp. 23–40. doi:10.1016/j.quascirev.2013.09.028.

Hardy, B. L. et al. (2020) 'Direct Evidence of Neanderthal Fibre Technology and Its Cognitive and Behavioral Implications', *Scientific Reports*, 10(1). doi:10.1038/s41598-020-61839-w.

Harris, B. (2017) 'What the Pay Gap Between Men and Women Really Looks Like', World Economic Forum. Available at: https://www.weforum.org/agenda/2017/11/pay-equality-men-women-gender-gap-report-2017/.

Harris, B. H. and Marshall, L. (2024) 'Immigration to Address the Caregiving Shortfall', Brookings Institution—Commentary. Brookings Institution, 2 April. Available at: https://www.brookings.edu/articles/immigration-to-address-the-caregiving-shortfall/.

Harris, C. and McKenna, C. (2021) 'Ching Shih and the Pirates of the South China Coast: Shifting Alliances, Strategy, and Reputational Racketeering at the Start of the 19th Century', *Global History of Capitalism Project*, Oxford Centre for Global History, 20.

Harris, R. (1989) 'Independent Women in Ancient Mesopotamia?', in B. S. Lesko (ed.) *Women's Earliest Records: From Ancient Egypt and Western Asia*. Atlanta, GA: Scholars' Press, pp. 145–156.

Hasell, J. (2023) 'How Has Income Inequality Within Countries Evolved over the Past Century?', *Our World in Data*, 6 July. Available at: https://ourworldindata.org/how-has-income-inequality-within-countries-evolved-over-the-past-century.

Häußler, S. (2004) 'Kyubang Kasa', in Y.-K. Kim-Renaud (ed.) *Creative Women of Korea: The Fifteenth Through the Twentieth Centuries*. New York: Routledge.

Hawass, Z. (1997) 'Tombs of the Pyramid Builders', *Archaeology*, 50(1), pp. 39–43.

Hawass, Z. A. (2024) *Mountains of the Pharaohs: The Untold Story of the Pyramid Builders*. New York: The American University in Cairo Press.

Head, B. V. (1880) 'On the Chronological Sequence of the Coins of Ephesus', *The Numismatic Chronicle and Journal of the Numismatic Society*, 20, pp. 85–173.

Headrick, D. R. (2009) *Technology: A World History*. New York: Oxford University Press.

Health Foundation (2021) 'Over a Million More Health and Care Staff Needed in the Next Decade to Meet Growing Demand for Care', Health Foundation.

Heckman, J. and Killingsworth, M. (1986) 'Female Labor Supply: A Survey', in O. Ashenfelter and R. Layard (eds.) *Handbook of Labor Economics*. Elsevier Science.

Hedley, M. (2019) *Women of the Durham Coalfield: Hannah's Story*. Chicago: History Press.

Hemelrijk, E. (2016) 'Women's Daily Life in the Roman West', in S. L. Budin and J. M. Turfa (eds.) *Women in Antiquity: Real Women Across the Ancient World*. Abingdon, Oxon: Routledge, pp. 895–904.

Heuvel, D. van den (2007) *Women and Entrepreneurship: Female Traders in the Northern Netherlands, c.1580–1815*. Amsterdam: Aksant.

Hickman, K. (2019) *She-Merchants, Buccaneers and Gentlewomen: British Women in India*. London: Virago.

Hinchliffe, E. (2023) 'Women CEOs Run More Than 10% of Fortune 500 Companies for the First Time in History', *Fortune*.

Hinds, M. (1972) 'The Murder of the Caliph 'Uthmân', *International Journal of Middle East Studies*, 3(4), pp. 450–469. doi:10.1017/s0020743800025216.

Hinsch, B. (2021) *Women in Song and Yuan China*. Lanham: Rowman & Littlefield Publishers.

Hobbes, T. (1651) *The Leviathan*. London: Andrew Crooke.

Hobsbawm, E. J. (1968) *Industry and Empire*. Weidenfeld & Nicolson.

Hoel, B. (1982) 'Contemporary Clothing "Sweatshops", Asian Female Labour and Collective Organisation', in J. West (ed.) *Work, Women and the Labour Market*. London: Routledge & Kegan Paul, pp. 80–98.

Hoffman, J., Farquharson, K. and Venkataraman, V. V. (2021) 'The Ecological and Social Context of Women's Hunting in Small-Scale Societies', *Hunter Gatherer Research*, 7(1–2), pp. 1–31. doi:10.3828/hgr.2023.8.

Hogenboom, M. (2012) 'Peasants' Revolt: The Time When Women Took Up Arms', *BBC News*, 14 June. Available at: https://www.bbc.co.uk/news/magazine-18373149.

Homer, A. (2022) 'Growth in NHS Recruits from Abroad Prompts Concern About Over-Reliance', *BBC News*. Available at: https://www.bbc.co.uk/news/uk-61230287.

Homestead, M. J. and Hansen, C. (2010) 'Susanna Rowson's Transatlantic Career', *Early American Literature*, 45(3), pp. 619–654. doi:10.1353/eal.2010.0031.

Hong Fincher, L. (2023) *Leftover Women: The Resurgence of Gender Inequality in China*. London: Bloomsbury Academic.

Hopkins, K. (1980) 'Taxes and Trade in the Roman Empire (200 B.C.–A.D. 400)', *Journal of Roman Studies*, 70, pp. 101–125. doi:10.2307/299558.

Hopkins, K. (2002) 'Rome, Taxes, Rents and Trade', in W. Scheidel and S. Von Reden (eds.) *The Ancient Economy*. Edinburgh: Edinburgh University Press, pp. 190–230.

Horrell, S. and Humphries, J. (1995) 'Women's Labour Force Participation and the Transition to the Male-Breadwinner Family, 1790–1865', *The Economic History Review*, 48(1), pp. 89–117. doi:10.2307/2597872.

Horrell, S. and Humphries, J. (1997) 'The Origins and Expansion of the Male Breadwinner Family: The Case of Nineteenth-Century Britain', *International Review of Social History*, 42(S5), pp. 25–64. doi:10.1017/s0020859000114786.

Horrell, S., Humphries, J. and Weisdorf, J. (2020) 'Malthus's Missing Women and Children: Demography and Wages in Historical Perspective, England 1280–1850', *European Economic Review*, 129, p. 103534. doi:10.1016/j.euroecorev.2020.103534.

Horrell, S., Humphries, J. and Weisdorf, J. (2021) 'Beyond the Male Breadwinner: Life-Cycle Living Standards of Intact and Disrupted English Working Families, 1260–1850', *The Economic History Review*, 75(2), pp. 530–560. doi:10.1111/ehr.13105.

Hoteit, L. et al. (2024) 'The Next 50 Years of Work', *Boston Consulting Group*.

Hruby, J. (2018) 'Building a Statistical Model to Evaluate the Sexes of Ancient Greek Fingerprints', Conference Paper, SAA Annual Meeting.

Hu, Z. and Khan, M. (1997) 'Why Is China Growing So Fast?', *Economic Issues No. 8*, International Monetary Fund.

Hudson, V. M., Bowen, D. L. and Nielsen, P. L. (2020) *The First Political Order: How Sex Shapes Governance and National Security Worldwide*. S.l.: Columbia University Press.

Humphries, J. (2024) 'RES 2024 Annual Public Lecture: Do Economists Care?', Royal Economic Society. Available at: https://www.youtube.com/watch?v=vOB6tMhRuWk&t=2s (Accessed: 21 August 2024).

Humphries, J. and Schneider, B. (2018) 'Spinning the Industrial Revolution', *The Economic History Review*, 72(1), pp. 126–155. doi:10.1111/ehr.12693.

Humphries, J. and Weisdorf, J. (2015) 'The Wages of Women in England, 1260–1850', *The Journal of Economic History*, 75(2), pp. 405–447. doi:10.1017/s0022050715000662.

Hunt, V. et al. (2020) 'Diversity Wins: How Inclusion Matters', McKinsey & Company.

Hutton, D. (1985) 'Women in Fourteenth Century Shrewsbury', in L. Charles and L. Duffin (eds) *Women and Work in Pre-Industrial England*. Abingdon, Oxon: Routledge, pp. 83–99.

Iglikowski, V. (2015) '"A Perfect Nuisance": The History of Women in the Civil Service', History of Government. GOV.UK, 26 May. Available at: https://history.blog.gov.uk/2015/05/26/a-perfect-nuisance-the-history-of-women-in-the-civil-service/.

Iglikowski-Broad, V. (2021) 'Just a Pill: 60 Years of the Contraceptive Pill on the NHS', National Archives, 4 December. Available at: https://blog.nationalarchives.gov.uk/just-a-pill-60-years-of-the-contraceptive-pill-on-the-nhs/ (Accessed: 15 August 2024).

Ilic, M. (2018) '"Equal Pay for Equal Work": Women's Wages in Soviet Russia', in M. Ilic (ed.) *The Palgrave Handbook of Women and Gender in Twentieth-Century Russia and the Soviet Union*. London: Palgrave Macmillan, pp. 101–115.

International Energy Agency (2023a) 'Putting Gender Equality at the Heart of the Clean Energy Transition'. International Energy Agency, 8 March. Available at: https://www.youtube.com/watch?v=5MSRyvhsz6A.

International Energy Agency (2023b) 'World Energy Outlook 2023'. Paris: International Energy Agency.

International Finance Corporation (2017) 'MSME Finance Gap'. Washington, D.C.: International Finance Corporation.

International Labour Organization (2016) 'Women at Work'. Geneva: International Labour Organization.

International Labour Organization (2018) 'Care Work and Care Jobs for the Future of Decent Work'. Geneva: International Labour Organization.

International Labour Organization (2022) 'Global Estimates of Modern Slavery: Forced Labour and Forced Marriage'. Geneva: International Labour Organization.

International Labour Organization and World Health Organisation (2022) 'The Gender Pay Gap in the Health and Care Sector: A Global Analysis in the Time of COVID-19'. Geneva: Labour Organization and the World Health Organization.

Irvine, G., Johnson, S. and Spacey, B. (2024) 'The Real Living Wage in Social Care', Policy Paper of Living Wage Foundation with IIPR.

Irvine, R. (2005) *Jane Austen*. Abingdon, Oxon: Routledge.

Ischinsky, E. and Tisch, D. (2023) 'Women in the Global Super Rich, an Analysis of the Forbes World's Billionaires List, 2010–2023', *Australian Feminist Studies*, 37(114), pp. 458–474. doi:10.1080/08164649.2023.2243649.

Israel, J. I. (1989) *Dutch Primacy in World Trade, 1585–1740*. Oxford: Clarendon Press.

Jacobs, M. D. (2005) 'Maternal Colonialism: White Women and Indigenous Child Removal in the American West and Australia, 1880–1940', *The Western Historical Quarterly*, 36(4), pp. 453–476. doi:10.2307/25443236.

Jain, C. et al. (2023) 'Women's Land Ownership in India: Evidence from Digital Land Records', *Land Use Policy*, 133, p. 106835. doi:10.1016/j.landusepol.2023.106835.

Jenkins, R. (1866) 'Report on the Territories of the Rajah of Nagpore', Submitted to the Supreme Government of India. Calcutta: Gazette Press.

Jones, H. (2013) *The Métis of Senegal: Urban Life and Politics in French West Africa*. Bloomington: Indiana University Press.

Jordan, A. (2009) 'I Am No Man: A Study of Warrior Women in the Archaeological Record', *Field Notes: A Journal of Collegiate Anthropology*, 1(7), pp. 94–111.

Joshel, S. R. (2010) *Slavery in the Roman World*. New York: Cambridge University Press.

Justel, J. J. (2016) 'Women, Gender and Law at the Dawn of History', in S. L. Budin and J. M. Turfa (eds.) *Women in Antiquity: Real Women Across the Ancient World*. Abingdon, Oxon: Routledge, pp. 77–100.

Kabeer, N. (2004) 'Globalization, Labor Standards, and Women's Rights: Dilemmas of Collective (in)Action in an Interdependent World', *Feminist Economics*, 10(1), pp. 3–35. doi:10.1080/1354570042000198227.

Kabeer, N. (2011) 'Between Affiliation and Autonomy: Navigating Pathways of Women's Empowerment and Gender Justice in Rural Bangladesh', *Development and Change*, 42(2), pp. 499–528. doi:10.1111/j.1467-7660.2011.01703.x.

Kanze, D. et al. (2017) 'Male and Female Entrepreneurs Get Asked Different Questions by VCs—and It Affects How Much Funding They Get', *Harvard Business Review*.

Karras, R. M. (1996) *Common Women: Prostitution and Sexuality in Medieval England*. New York: Oxford University Press.

Karras, R. M. (2023) 'Injection: A Gender Perspective on Domestic Slavery', in J. Schiel and D. A. Pargas (eds.) *The Palgrave Handbook of Global Slavery Throughout History*. London: Palgrave Macmillan, pp. 215–224.

Kay, G. and Jackson, S. (2024) 'The History of OpenAI, from the Early Days with Elon Musk to the ChatGPT Maker Being Put on Blast by Scarlett Johansson', *Business Insider*, 22 May.

Kazhdan, A. P. (1998) 'Women at Home', *Dumbarton Oaks Papers*, 52, p. 1. doi:10.2307/1291775.

Keckley, E. (1868) *Behind the Scenes: Or, Thirty Years a Slave and Four Years in the White House*. London: Partridge and Oakley.

Keddie, N. R. (1990) 'The Past and Present of Women in the Muslim World', *Journal of World History*, 1(1), pp. 77–108.

Keddie, N. R. (2007) *Women in the Middle East: Past and Present*. Princeton: Princeton University Press.

Kellaway, L. (2013) 'The Arrival of Women in the Office', BBC Radio 4—*History of Office Life*, 25 July. Available at: https://www.bbc.co.uk/news/magazine-23432653 (Accessed: 22 August 2024).

Kelly-Buccellati, M. (2016) 'Women's Power and Work in Ancient Urkesh', in S. L. Budin and J. M. Turfa (eds.) *Women in Antiquity: Real Women Across the Ancient World*. Abingdon, Oxon: Routledge, pp. 48–63.

Kelly, G. (1992) *Revolutionary Feminism: The Mind and Career of Mary Wolstonecraft*. New York: St Martin's Press.

Kenez, P. (2017) *A History of the Soviet Union from the Beginning to Its Legacy*. New York: Cambridge University Press.

Kennan, C. (2019) 'On the Threshold? The Role of Women in Lincolnshire's Late Medieval Parish Guilds', in V. Blud, D. Heath and E. Klafter (eds.) *Gender in Medieval Places, Spaces and Thresholds*. London: University of London Press, pp. 61–74. doi:10.2307/j.ctv9b2tw8.11.

Kenoyer, J. M. (2004) 'Ancient Textiles of the Indus Valley Region', in N. Bilgrami (ed.) *Tana Bana: The Woven Soul of Pakistan*. Karachi: Koel Publications, pp. 18–31.

Kessler-Harris, A. (2003) *Out to Work: A History of America's Wage-Earning Women*. New York: Oxford University Press.

Kharas, H. J. (2023) *The Rise of the Global Middle Class: How the Search for the Good Life Can Change the World*. Washington, D.C.: Brookings Institution Press.

Kimble, J. and Unterhalter, E. (1982) '"We Opened the Road for You, You Must Go Forward": ANC Women's Struggles, 1912–1982', *Feminist Review*, (12), p. 11. doi: 10.2307/1394879.

King, D. (2012) *Russian Revolutionary Posters: From Civil War to Socialist Realism, from Bolshevism to the End of Stalin: From the David King Collection at Tate Modern.* Millbank, London: Tate Publishing.

King, H. (2024) 'Women in Banking and Finance: How Has It Transformed in Twenty Years?', Freshminds. Available at: https://www.freshminds.co.uk/blog/2024/02/women-in-banking-and-finance?source=google.com.

Kishtainy, N. (2017) *A Little History of Economics.* New Haven: Yale University Press.

Klimina, A. (2019) 'Contextualising Women's Economic Thought in Late Imperial Russia and in the Early Years of Revolution, 1870–1920', in K. Madden and R. W. Dimand (eds.) *The Routledge Handbook of the History of Women's Economic Thought.* Oxford: Routledge.

Kloss, M. M. (2023) 'Slavery in Medieval Arabia', in D. A. Pargas and J. Schiel (eds.) *The Palgrave Handbook of Global Slavery Throughout History.* London: Palgrave Macmillan, pp. 139–158.

Ko, D. (1994) *Teachers of the Inner Chambers.* Stanford: Stanford University Press.

Kok, J. (2017) 'Women's Agency in Historical Family Systems', in J. L. van Zanden, A. Rijpma and J. Kok (eds.) *Agency, Gender and Economic Development.* Abingdon, Oxon: Routledge.

Krugman, P. (2009) 'How Did Economists Get It So Wrong?', *New York Times,* 2 September.

Krzanich, A. (2021) 'Waged Worker or Unpaid Family Member? Female Domestic Labour and the Presumption of Remuneration in Scots Law, 1800–1850', Women, Money and Markets Conference Paper.

Kuhn, D. (1984) 'Tracing a Chinese Legend: In Search of the Identity of the "First Sericulturalist"', *T'oung Pao,* 70(4), pp. 213–245. doi:10.1163/156853284x00099.

Kuhrt, A. (1989) 'Non-Royal Women in the Late Babylonian Period: A Survey', in B. S. Lesko (ed.) *Women's Earliest Records: From Ancient Egypt and Western Asia.* Atlanta, GA: Scholars' Press, pp. 215–239.

Kumar, L. (2017) 'Ching Shih', in L. Kumar (ed.) *Encyclopedia of World Biography.* Gale.

Kussmaul, A. (1981) *Servants in Husbandry in Early Modern England.* Cambridge: Cambridge University Press.

Laiou, A. (1981) 'The Role of Women in Byzantine Society', *Jahrbuch der Österreichischen Byzantinistik,* 31(1), pp. 233–260.

Laiou, A. (2001) 'Women in the Marketplace of Constantinople (10th–14th Centuries)', in N. Necipoğlu (ed.) *Byzantine Constantinople Monuments, Topography and Everyday Life.* Leiden: Brill, pp. 263–271.

Laiou, A. and Morrisson, C. (2007) *The Byzantine Economy.* Cambridge: Cambridge University Press.

Laiou-Thomadakis, A. E. (1980) 'The Byzantine Economy in the Mediterranean Trade System; Thirteenth–Fifteenth Centuries', Dumbarton Oaks Papers, 34, pp. 177–222. doi:10.2307/1291451.

Langlois, A.-I. (2016) 'The Female Tavern-Keeper in Mesopotamia', in S. L. Budin and J. M. Turfa (eds.) *Women in Antiquity: Real Women Across the Ancient World.* Abingdon, Oxon: Routledge, pp. 113–125.

Law, R. W. (2011) 'Inter-Regional Interaction and Urbanism in the Ancient Indus Valley'. Indus Project.

Lazarus, D. (2014) 'Canary Wharf Boss Sees Future in Creative Campus', *Financial News.*

Lee, R. B. and DeVore, I. (1968) *Man the Hunter: The First Intensive Survey of a Single, Crucial Stage of Human Development—Man's Once Universal Hunting Way of Life*. Transaction Publishers.

Lee, T. B. (2014) '40 Maps That Explain the Roman Empire', *Vox*, 19 August. Available at: https://www.vox.com/world/2018/6/19/17469176/roman-empire-maps-history-explained.

Leke, A. et al. (2023) 'The Secrets of Outperforming Family-Owned Businesses', McKinsey & Company.

Lesko, B. S. (1989) *Women's Earliest Records: From Ancient Egypt and Western Asia*. Atlanta, GA: Scholars' Press.

Levine, P. (2003) *Prostitution, Race, and Politics: Policing Venereal Disease in the British Empire*. London: Routledge.

Lewis, J. (2010) *Work-Family Balance, Gender and Policy*. Cheltenham, UK: Edward Elgar.

Liddle, J. and Joshi, R. (1985) 'Gender and Imperialism in British India', *South Asia Research*, 5(2), pp. 147–164. doi:10.1177/026272808500500206.

Lim, L. Y. C. (1990) 'Women's Work in Export Factories: The Politics of a Cause', in I. Tinker (ed.) *Persistent Inequalities: Women and World Development*. New York: Oxford University Press.

Lister, K. (2021) *Harlots, Whores & Hackabouts: A History of Sex for Sale*. London: Thames & Hudson.

Livshits, V. (2008) 'The Sogdian "Ancient Letters" (I, III)', *Iran and the Caucasus*, 12(2), pp. 289–293. doi:10.1163/157338408x406065.

Lopez, R. S. (1964) 'Market Expansion: The case of Genoa', *The Journal of Economic History*, 24(4), pp. 445–464. doi:10.1017/s0022050700061179.

Lovén, L. L. (2020) 'Women, Trade, and Production in the Urban Centres of Roman Italy', in *Urban Craftsmen and Traders in the Roman World*. Oxford University Press (Oxford Studies on the Roman Economy), pp. 200–221.

Lücker, K. and Daenschel, U. (2019) *History of the World with the Women Put Back In*. New York: History Press.

MacGregor, N. (2010) *A History of the World in 100 Objects*. London: Allen Lane.

Malanima, P. (2009) *Pre-Modern European Economy: One Thousand Years*. Boston: Brill.

Marcar, A. (2004) 'Aegean Costume and the Dating of the Knossian Frescoes', *British School at Athens Studies*, 12, pp. 225–238.

Mark, J. J. (2012) 'Herodotus: On the Customs of the Persians', *World History Encyclopedia*, 18 January. Available at: https://www.worldhistory.org/article/149/herodotus-on-the-customs-of-the-persians/#google_vignette.

Mark, J. J. (2014) 'Artemisia I of Caria', *World History Encyclopedia*, 12 March. Available at: https://www.worldhistory.org/Artemisia_I_of_Caria/.

Mark, J. J. (2017) 'Women's Work in Ancient Egypt', *World History Encyclopedia*. worldhistory.org. Available at: https://www.worldhistory.org/article/1058/womens-work-in-ancient-egypt/ (Accessed: 23 May 2024).

Mark, J. J. (2020) 'Inventions & Innovations of Ancient Persia', *World History Encyclopedia*. Available at: https://www.worldhistory.org/article/1505/inventions-innovations-of-ancient-persia/.

Mark, J. J. (2021) 'Sappho of Lesbos', *World History Encyclopedia*. worldhistory.org. Available at: https://www.worldhistory.org/Sappho_of_Lesbos/ (Accessed: 23 May 2024).

Marshall, J. H. (1931) *Mohenjo-Daro and the Indus Civilization*. London: Arthur Probsthain.

Marsot, A. L. al-Sayyid (2007) *A History of Egypt: From the Arab Conquest to the Present.* Cambridge: Cambridge University Press.

Martin, D. S. (2024) 'The World's Celebrity Billionaires 2024', *Forbes*, 3 April.

Marx, K. (1890) *Capital, Volume 1*. London: Penguin Classics (1990 ed.).

Masterson, V. (2024) 'Women Founders and Venture Capital—Some 2023 Snapshots', Forum Agenda, World Economic Forum.

Matschke, K.-P. (2002) 'The Late Byzantine Urban Economy, Thirteenth–Fifteenth Centuries', in A. Laiou (ed.) *The Economic History of Byzantium: From the Seventh Through the Fifteenth Century*. Washington, D.C.: Dumbarton Oaks Research Library and Collection.

Maxtone Graham, Y. (2023) *Jobs for the Girls: How We Set Out to Work in the Typewriter Age*. London: Abacus.

Mayhew, H. and Hemyng, B. (1861) 'Prostitutes', in H. Mayhew (ed.) *London Labour and the London Poor*. London: Frank Cass & Co., pp. 35–273.

Mayor, A. (2016) 'Warrior Women: The Archaeology of Amazons', in S. L. Budin and J. M. Turfa (eds.) *Women in Antiquity: Real Women Across the Ancient World*. Abingdon, Oxen: Routledge, pp. 969–985.

McCarthy, A. (2016) 'Businesswomen and Their Seals in Early Mesopotamia', in S. L. Budin and J. M. Turfa (eds.) *Women in Antiquity: Real Women Across the Ancient World*. Abingdon, Oxon: Routledge, pp. 101–112.

McClintock, A. (1995) *Imperial Leather: Race, Gender, and Sexuality in the Colonial Conquest*. New York: Routledge.

McCloskey, D. N. (2021) *Bourgeois Equality: How Ideas, Not Capital or Institutions, Enriched the World*. Chicago: University of Chicago Press.

McCormick, M. (2001) *The Origins of the European Economy: Communications and Commerce, c.700–c.900*. Cambridge: Cambridge University Press.

McCormick, M. et al. (2012) 'Climate Change During and After the Roman Empire', *Journal of Interdisciplinary History*, 43(2). doi:10.1162/JINH_a_00379.

McGinn, K. L., Ruiz Castro, M. and Lingo, E. L. (2018) 'Learning from Mum: Cross-national Evidence Linking Maternal Employment and Adult Children's Outcomes', *Work, Employment and Society*, 33(3). doi:10.1177/0950017018760167.

McIntosh, J. (2008) *The Ancient Indus Valley: New Perspectives*. Santa Barbara, CA: ABC-CLIO.

McIntosh, M. K. (2005) 'The Benefits and Drawbacks of Femme Sole Status in England, 1300–1630', *Journal of British Studies*, 44(3), pp. 410–438. doi:10.1086/429708.

McKee, S. (2004) 'Inherited Status and Slavery in Late Medieval Italy and Venetian Crete', *Past & Present*, 182(1), pp. 31–53. doi:10.1093/past/182.1.31.

Megalommati, N. (2017) 'Women and Family Law in Byzantium', *Historical Reflections / Réflexions Historiques*, 43(1). doi:10.3167/hrrh.2017.430103.

Mercedes-Benz (2019) 'Bertha Benz: The Journey That Changed Everything', Mercedes-Benz. Available at: https://www.youtube.com/watch?v=vsGrFYD5Nfs (Accessed: 21 August 2024).

Mercedes-Benz USA (2018) 'Bertha Benz: The First Driver', Mercedes-Benz USA. Available at: https://www.youtube.com/watch?v=JBL_G-C51Dk&t=136s (Accessed: 21 August 2024).

Mercer, C. (2018) 'The Philosophical Roots of Western Misogyny', *Philosophical Topics*, 46(2), pp. 183–208. doi:10.5840/philtopics201846218.

Mercier, L. and Gier, J. (2006) *Mining Women: Gender in the Development of a Global Industry*. New York: Palgrave Macmillian.

Mernissi, F. (1994) *The Forgotten Queens of Islam*. Cambridge: Polity Press.

Meta (2022) 'Embracing Change Through Inclusion', Meta's 2022 Diversity Report.

Meyer-Fong, T. (2007) 'The Printed World: Books, Publishing Culture, and Society in Late Imperial China', *The Journal of Asian Studies*, 66(3), pp. 787–817. doi:10.1017/s0021911807000964.

Meyers, C. (2016) 'Women's Daily Life (Iron Age Israel)', in S. L. Budin and J. M. Turfa (eds.) *Women in Antiquity: Real Women Across the Ancient World*. Abingdon, Oxon: Routledge, pp. 488–500.

Michalopoulos, S., Naghavi, A. and Prarolo, G. (2017) 'Trade and Geography in the Spread of Islam', *The Economic Journal*, 128(616), pp. 3210–3241. doi:10.1111/ecoj.12557.

Microsoft (2023) 'Global Diversity & Inclusion Report 2023', Microsoft—Global Diversity & Inclusion.

Middleton, G. D. (2023) *Women in the Ancient Mediterranean World: From the Palaeolithic to the Byzantines*. Cambridge: Cambridge University Press.

Mieroop, M. V. de (1989) 'Women in the Economy of Sumer', in B. S. Lesko (ed.) *Women's Earliest Records: From Ancient Egypt and Western Asia*. Atlanta, GA: Scholars' Press, pp. 53–69.

Mieroop, M. V. de (2021) *A History of Ancient Egypt*. Chichester, West Sussex: Wiley-Blackwell.

Milkman, R. (2016) *On Gender, Labor and Inequality*. Chicago: University of Illinois Press.

Milks, A. (2020) 'Did Prehistoric Women Hunt? New Research Suggests So', *The Conversation*, 4 November.

Milton, A. (2023) 'The Incredible Story of the African Prints That Made the "Mama Benzes" Rich', *EL PAÍS*, 6 April.

Modelski, G. (2003) *World Cities*. Faros 2000.

Mokyr, J. (1990) *The Lever of Riches: Technological Creativity and Economic Progress*. New York: Oxford University Press.

Mokyr, J. (2009) *The Enlightened Economy: An Economic History of Britain, 1700–1850*. London: Yale University Press.

Mokyr, J. (2017) *A Culture of Growth: The Origins of the Modern Economy*. London: Princeton University Press.

Molony, B., Theiss, J. M. and Choi, H. (2016) *Gender in Modern East Asia: An Integrated History*. Boulder: Westview Press.

Moore, K. and Lewis, D. (1998) 'The First Multinationals: Assyria Circa 2000 B.C.', *Management International Review*, 38(2), pp. 95–107.

Morris, I. (2010) *Why the West Rules—for Now: The Patterns of History and What They Reveal About the Future*. London: Profile Books.

Morrow, B. (2024) 'All the Records Taylor Swift Has Broken', *The Week*, 10 May.

Mortimer, R. (2018) 'Fatima al-Fihri: Founder of the World's First University', Manchester University Press, 8 March. Available at: https://manchesteruniversitypress.co.uk/blog/2018/03/08/fatima-al-fihri-founder-worlds-first-university/ (Accessed: 22 February 2024).

Moss, J. (2015) '"We Didn't Realise How Brave We Were at the Time": The 1968 Ford Sewing Machinists' Strike in Public and Personal Memory', *Oral History*, 43(1).

Muckerheide, M. (2023) 'The Finance Gap for Women Entrepreneurs Is $1.7 Trillion. Here's How to Close It', World Economic Forum, 26 October. Available at: https:

//www.weforum.org/agenda/2023/10/women-entrepreneurs-finance-banking / (Accessed: 22 August 2024).

Muhly, J. D. (1973) 'Tin Trade Routes of the Bronze Age: New Evidence and New Techniques Aid in the Study of Metal Sources of the Ancient World', *American Scientist*, pp. 404–413.

Muhly, J. D. (1985) 'Sources of Tin and the Beginnings of Bronze Metallurgy', *American Journal of Archaeology*, 89(2), pp. 275–291. doi:10.2307/504330.

Muldrew, C. (2011) '"Th'ancient Distaff" and "Whirling Spindle": Measuring the Contribution of Spinning to Household Earnings and the National Economy in England, 1550–1770', *The Economic History Review*, 65(2), pp. 498–526. doi:10.1111/j.1468-0289.2010.00588.x.

Muncaster, J. (2003) '"Six Foote of Shop Roome": Women as Subjects in the Records of the Royal Exchange in the 1690s'. Master's dissertation. Birkbeck, University of London.

Murray, S. C., Chorghay, I. and MacPherson, J. (2020) 'The Dipylon Mistress: Social and Economic Complexity, the Gendering of Craft Production, and Early Greek Ceramic Material Culture', *American Journal of Archaeology*, 124(2), pp. 215–244. doi:10.3764/aja.124.2.0215.

Nadasen, P. (2015) *Household Workers Unite: The Untold Story of African American Women Who Built a Movement*. Boston: Beacon Press.

Nadwi, M. A. (2016) *Al-Muhaddithat: The Women Scholars in Islam*. Oxford: Interface Publications.

Nappo, D. (2018) 'Money and Flows of Coinage in the Red Sea Trade', in A. Wilson and A. K. Bowman (eds.) *Trade, Commerce, and the State in the Roman World*. Oxford: Oxford University Press.

National Trust (2007) *Quarry Bank*. Swindon: Park Lane Press.

Nature Biotechnology (2023a) 'Generating "Smarter" Biotechnology', *Nature Biotechnology*, 41, 157. doi:10.1038/s41587-023-01695-x.

Nature Biotechnology (2023b) 'Women Build Strength in Numbers', *Nature Biotechnology*, 41, 301. doi:10.1038/s41587-023-01727-6.

Nature Biotechnology (2024) 'Growing Community Across the C-suite', *Nature Biotechnology*, 42, 345. doi:10.1038/s41587-024-02192-5.

Ndzamela, P. (2021) *Native Merchants: The Building of the Black Business Class in South Africa*. Cape Town: Tafelberg.

Neal, L. and Cameron, R. E. (2003) *A Concise Economic History of the World: From Paleolithic Times to the Present*. New York: Oxford University Press.

Nekoei, A. and Sinn, F. (2021) 'Herstory: The Rise of Self-Made Women', CEPR Discussion Paper. doi:10.2139/ssrn.3741332.

New York Daily Tribune (1900) 'Charlotte Temple's Grave', *New York Daily Tribune*, 9 June.

Nicholas, S. (1989) *Convict Workers: Reinterpreting Australia's Past*. Cambridge: Cambridge University Press.

Nielson, L. (2012) 'Gender and the Politics of Music in the Early Islamic Courts', *Early Music History*, 31, pp. 235–261. doi:10.1017/s0261127912000010.

Nifosi, A. (2019) *Becoming a Woman and Mother in Greco-Roman Egypt: Women's Bodies, Society and Domestic Space*. Oxford: Routledge.

NMAI (2009) 'Haudenosaunee Guide for Educators', *National Museum of the American Indian Education Office*.

Novikova, N. and Ghodsee, K. (2023) 'Alexandra Kollontai (1872–1952): Communism as the Only Way Toward Women's Liberation', in F. de Haan (ed.) *The Palgrave Handbook of Communist Women Activists Around the World*. London: Palgrave Macmillan.

Nyyssölä, M. (2022) 'Bride Price or Dowry?', *UNU-WIDER Blog*: https://www.wider.unu.edu/publication/bride-price-or-dowry#:~:text=The%20bride%20price%20tradition%20is,dowry%20tradition%20is%20still%20strong.

Ó Gráda, C. (2016) 'Did Science Cause the Industrial Revolution?', *Journal of Economic Literature*, 54(1), pp. 224–239. doi:10.1257/jel.54.1.224.

O'Faolain, J. and Martines, L. (1979) *Not in God's Image: Women in History from the Greeks to the Victorians*. London: Virago.

O'Rourke, K. H. and Williamson, J. G. (2002) 'After Columbus: Explaining Europe's Overseas Trade Boom', *The Journal of Economic History*, 62(2), pp. 417–456.

Oakeshott, W. (1936) *Commerce and Society: A Short History of Trade and Its Effects on Civilization*. Oxford: Clarendon Press.

Obina, O. E. (1996) 'Women's Access to Credit and Finance in the 1990s', *The African Review*, 23(1/2), pp. 33–45.

Ogilvie, S. C. (2019) *The European Guilds: An Economic Analysis*. Princeton, NJ: Princeton University Press.

Olabarria, L. (2020) *Kinship and Family in Ancient Egypt: Archaeology and Anthropology in Dialogue*. Cambridge: Cambridge University Press.

Ortiz-Ospina, E. and Roser, M. (2023) 'Government Spending', *Our World in Data*, March. Available at: https://ourworldindata.org/government-spending.

Ortiz-Ospina, E., Tzvetkova, S. and Roser, M. (2024) 'Women's Employment', *Our World in Data*, March. Available at: https://ourworldindata.org/female-labor-supply.

Oxley, D. (1996) *Convict Maids: The Forced Migration of Women to Australia*. Cambridge: Cambridge University Press.

Pamuk, Ş. and Shatzmiller, M. (2014) 'Plagues, Wages, and Economic Change in the Islamic Middle East, 700–1500', *The Journal of Economic History*, 74(1), pp. 196–229. doi:10.1017/s0022050714000072.

Papagianni, E. (2002a) 'Byzantine Legislation on Economic Activity Relative to Social Class', in A. E. Laiou (ed.) *The Economic History of Byzantium: From the Seventh Through the Fifteenth Century*. Washington, D.C.: Dumbarton Oaks Research Library and Collection, pp. 1060–1070.

Papagianni, E. (2002b) 'Legal Institutions and Practice in Matters of Ecclesiastical Property', in A. E. Laiou (ed.) *The Economic History of Byzantium: From the Seventh Through the Fifteenth Century*. Washington, D.C.: Dumbarton Oaks Research Library and Collection, pp. 1037–1047.

Pare, S. (2023) 'Egypt Had an Unusually Powerful "Female King" 5,000 Years Ago, Lavish Tomb Suggests', *Live Science*.

Pargas, D. A. (2023) 'Slavery in the US South', in D. A. Pargas and J. Schiel (eds.) *The Palgrave Handbook of Global Slavery Throughout History*. London: Palgrave Macmillan, pp. 441–457.

Park, A. (2023) '2023's Fiercest Women in Life Sciences', *FIERCE Pharma*.

Parker, A. J. (1992) *Ancient Shipwrecks of the Mediterranean and the Roman Provinces*. Oxford: BAR Publishing.

Parker, G. (2002) 'Ex Oriente Luxuria: Indian Commodities and Roman Experience', *Journal of the Economic and Social History of the Orient*, 45(1), pp. 40–95. doi: 10.1163/156852002320123055.

Parker, J. and Rathbone, R. (2007) *African History: A Very Short Introduction*. Oxford: Oxford University Press.

Paul, C. K. (1876) *William Godwin, His Friends and Contemporaries: Volume 1*. London: Henry S. King & Co.

Perry, C., Eltis, D., Engerman, S. L. and Richardson, D. (2021), *The Cambridge World History of Slavery, Volume 2: AD 500–AD 1420*. Cambridge: Cambridge University Press.

Persson, K. G. (2010) *An Economic History of Europe: Knowledge, Institutions and Growth, 600 to the Present*. Cambridge: Cambridge University Press.

Peterson, J. (2002) *Sexual Revolutions: Gender and Labor at the Dawn of Agriculture*. Walnut Creek, CA: Altamira Press.

Pfizer (2023) 'Pfizer Completes Acquisition of Seagen', Pfizer press release.

Phillips, D. D. (2009) 'Hypereides 3 and the Athenian Law of Contracts', *Transactions of the American Philological Association*, 139(1), pp. 89–122. doi:10.1353/apa.0.0026.

Phillips, T. (2017) 'In China Women "Hold Up Half the Sky" but Can't Touch the Political Glass Ceiling', *Guardian*, 13 October.

Phizacklea, A. (1982) 'Migrant Women and Wage Labour: The Case of West Indian Women in Britain', in J. West (ed.) *Work, Women and the Labour Market*. London: Routledge & Kegan Paul, pp. 99–116.

Picton, J. (2016) 'Living and Working in a New Kingdom "Harem Town"', in S. L. Budin and J. M. Turfa (eds.) *Women in Antiquity: Real Women Across the Ancient World*. Abingdon, Oxon: Routledge, pp. 229–242.

Pinchbeck, I. (1977) *Women Workers and the Industrial Revolution*. Abingdon, Oxon: Routledge. First published in 1930.

Pink, E. E. (2006) 'Frances Burney's Camilla: "To Print My Grand Work . . . by Subscription"', *Eighteenth-Century Studies*, 40(1), pp. 51–68. doi:10.1353/ecs.2006.0046.

Platt, L. (2018) 'Beatrice Webb, William Beveridge, Poverty, and the Minority Report on the Poor Law', *London School of Economics Blog*. London School of Economics, 23 February. Available at: https://blogs.lse.ac.uk/lsehistory/2018/02/23/beatrice-webb-william-beveridge-poverty-and-the-minority-report-on-the-poor-law/.

Pomeroy, S. B. (1975) *Goddesses, Whores, Wives, and Slaves*. New York: Schocken Books.

Potter, D. (2015) *Theodora: Actress, Empress, Saint*. Oxford: Oxford University Press.

Price, M. (2018) 'Master Female Artisan Broke the Male-Dominated Mold in Ancient Greece', *Science*, 7 September.

Price, N. et al. (2019) 'Viking Warrior Women? Reassessing Birka Chamber Grave BJ.581', *Antiquity*, 93(367), pp. 181–198. doi:10.15184/aqy.2018.258.

Price, N. S. (2022) *The Children of Ash and Elm: A History of the Vikings*. London: Penguin Books.

PwC (2017) 'Women in Tech: Time to Close the Gender Gap', A PwC UK research report.

Quinn, J. (2024) *How the World Made the West: A 4,000-Year History*. London, UK: Bloomsbury.

Raffield, B. (2019) 'The Slave Markets of the Viking World: Comparative Perspectives on an 'Invisible Archaeology'', *Slavery & Abolition*, 40(4), pp. 682–705. doi:10.1080/0144039x.2019.1592976.

Raman, A. (2022) 'Indian Cotton Textiles and British Industrialization: Evidence of Comparative Learning in the British Cotton Industry in the Eighteenth and Nineteenth Centuries', *The Economic History Review*, 75(2), pp. 447–474. doi:10.1111/ehr.13143.

Ramirez, J. (2022) *Femina: A New History of the Middle Ages, Through the Women Written Out of It*. London: W. H. Allen.

Regan, H. (2024) 'The World's 100 Worst Polluted Cities Are in Asia—and 83 of Them Are in Just One Country', CNN.

Reid, J. N. (2014) 'Slavery in Early Mesopotamia from Late Uruk Until the Fall of Babylon in the *Longue Durée*', D.Phil thesis, University of Oxford.

Ridgway, D. (2016) 'Demaratus (1), of Corinth, Legendary Father of Tarquinius Priscus', *Oxford Classical Dictionary*. Available at: https://oxfordre.com/classics/view/10.1093/acrefore/9780199381135.001.0001/acrefore-9780199381135-e-2083 (Accessed: 22 January 2024).

Ritchie, H. and Roser, M. (2024) 'Age Structure', Ourworldindata.org. Available at: https://ourworldindata.org/age-structure.

Rivollat, M. et al. (2023) 'Extensive Pedigrees Reveal the Social Organization of a Neolithic Community', *Nature*, 620(7974), pp. 600–606. doi:10.1038/s41586-023-06350-8.

Robertson, R. (2021) *The Enlightenment: The Pursuit of Happiness*. New York: HarperCollins.

Robins, R. G. (1989) 'Some Images of Women in New Kingdom Art and Literature', in B. S. Lesko (ed.) *Women's Earliest Records: From Ancient Egypt and Western Asia*. Atlanta, GA: Scholars' Press, pp. 105–116.

Robinson, A. (2021) *The Indus: Lost Civilizations*. London: Reaktion Books.

Robinson, H. H. (2020) *Loom and Spindle: Or, Life Among the Early Mill Girls*. Milton Keynes: Alpha Editions. Originally published in 1898.

Robinson, K. (1996) *What Became of the Quarry Bank Mill Apprentices?* Wilmslow, Cheshire: Quarry Bank Mill.

Roffet-Salque, M. et al. (2018) 'Evidence for the Impact of the 8.2-KYBP Climate Event on Near Eastern Early Farmers', *Proceedings of the National Academy of Sciences*, 115(35), pp. 8705–8709. doi:10.1073/pnas.1803607115.

Romano, R. B. (2020) 'Women in the Silver Mines of Potosí: Rethinking the History of "Informality" and "Precarity" (Sixteenth to Eighteenth Centuries)', *International Review of Social History*, 65(2), pp. 289–314. doi:10.1017/s0020859019000555.

Rose, R. B. (1995) 'Feminism, Women and the French Revolution', *Historical Reflections*, 40(s1), pp. 187–205. doi:10.1111/j.1467-8497.1994.tb00879.x.

Rose, S. O. (1993) *Limited Livelihoods: Gender and Class in Nineteenth-Century England*. Los Angeles: University of California Press.

Roser, M. (2024) 'Fertility Rate', OurWorldInData.org. Available at: https://ourworldindata.org/fertility-rate.

Rostek, J. (2021) *Women's Economic Thought in the Romantic Age*. Abingdon, Oxon: Routledge.

Rowlandson, J. (ed.) (1998) *Women and Society in Greek and Roman Egypt: A Sourcebook*. Cambridge: Cambridge University Press.

Royle, O. R. (2023) 'Facebook Parent Meta Still Pays Women in the U.K. and Ireland Less Than Men and Gives Them Much Smaller Bonuses—Despite Previous Commitments for Gender Parity by 2023', *Fortune*.

Rubin, J. (2017) *Rulers, Religion and Riches: Why the West Got Rich and the Middle East Did Not*. Cambridge: Cambridge University Press.

Rutterford, J. et al. (2011) 'Who Comprised the Nation of Shareholders? Gender and Investment in Great Britain, c. 1870–1935', *The Economic History Review*, 64(1), pp. 157–187. doi:10.1111/j.1468-0289.2010.00539.x.

Ryan, C. and Jethá, C. (2011) *Sex at Dawn: How We Mate, Why We Stray, and What It Means for Modern Relationships*. New York: HarperCollins.

Saberi, H. (2013) *Tea: A Global History*. London: Reaktion.

Saini, A. (2024) *The Patriarchs: How Men Came to Rule*. London: 4th Estate.

Sara-Lafosse, R. V.-C. (2007) 'Construction, Labor Organization, and Feasting During the Late Archaic Period in the Central Andes', *Journal of Anthropological Archaeology*, 26(2), pp. 150–171. doi:10.1016/j.jaa.2006.07.002.

Scheidel, W. (2017) *The Great Leveler: Violence and the History of Inequality from the Stone Age to the Twenty-First Century*. Princeton, NJ: Princeton University Press.

Scheidel, W. and Friesen, S. J. (2009) 'The Size of the Economy and the Distribution of Income in the Roman Empire', *Journal of Roman Studies*, 99, pp. 61–91. doi:10.3815/007543509789745223.

Schiel, J. (2023) 'Slavery in the Western Mediterranean', in D. A. Pargas and J. Schiel (eds.) *The Palgrave Handbook of Global Slavery Throughout History*. London: Palgrave Macmillan, pp. 179–193.

Schlegel, A. (1991) 'Status, Property, and the Value on Virginity', *American Ethnologist*, 18(4), pp. 719–734. doi:10.1525/ae.1991.18.4.02a00050.

Science Museum (2020) 'Women in Computing', Science Museum: Objects and Stories. Science Museum, 31 May. Available at: https://www.sciencemuseum.org.uk/objects-and-stories/women-computing.

Scott, K. (2023) 'Behind the Tech with Kevin Scott: Mira Murati, Chief Technology Officer, OpenAI', Microsoft—Behind the Tech. Microsoft.

Seagen (2022) 'Who We Are: Corporate Responsibility at Seagen', Seagen.com.

Secretary-General, United Nations (2024) 'Progress Towards the Sustainable Development Goals Report of the Secretary-General', High-Level Political Forum on Sustainable Development, Convened Under the Auspices of the Economic and Social Council.

Sekers, D. (2013) *A Lady of Cotton: Hannah Greg, Mistress of Quarry Bank Mill*. Stroud, Gloucestershire, England: History Press.

Seyrig, H. (1950) 'Palmyra and the East', *Journal of Roman Studies*, 40(1–2), pp. 1–7. doi:10.2307/298497.

Shatzmiller, M. (1994) *Labour in the Medieval Islamic World*. Leiden: Brill.

Shatzmiller, M. (1997) 'Women and Wage Labour in the Medieval Islamic West: Legal Issues in an Economic Context', *Journal of the Economic and Social History of the Orient*, 40(2), pp. 174–206. doi:10.1163/1568520972600748.

Shatzmiller, M. (2007) *Her Day in Court: Women's Property Rights in Fifteenth-Century Granada*. Cambridge, MA: Harvard University Press.

Shatzmiller, M. (2011) 'Economic Performance and Economic Growth in the Early Islamic World', *Journal of the Economic and Social History of the Orient*, 54(2), pp. 132–184. doi:10.1163/156852011x586831.

Shelmerdine, C. W., Budin, S. L. and Turfa, J. M. (2016) 'Women in the Mycenaean Economy', in S. L. Budin and J. M. Turfa (eds.) *Women in Antiquity: Real Women Across the Ancient World*. Abingdon, Oxon: Routledge, pp. 618–634.

Shenk, M. K. et al. (2010) 'Intergenerational Wealth Transmission Among Agriculturalists', *Current Anthropology*, 51(1), pp. 65–83. doi:10.1086/648658.

Shenk, M. K. et al. (2019) 'When Does Matriliny Fail? The Frequencies and Causes of Transitions to and from Matriliny Estimated from a de Novo Coding of a Cross-Cultural Sample', *Philosophical Transactions of the Royal Society B: Biological Sciences*, 374(1780), p. 20190006. doi:10.1098/rstb.2019.0006.

Shetterly, M. L. (no date) 'Mary W. Jackson', *NASA: People*. NASA. Available at: https://www.nasa.gov/people/mary-w-jackson-biography/.

Shoemaker, R. B. (1998) *Gender in English Society, 1650–1850*. New York: Longman.

Shoshan, B. (1981) 'Fāṭimid Grain Policy and the Post of the Muḥtasib', *International Journal of Middle East Studies*, 13(2), pp. 181–189. doi:10.1017/s0020743800055288.

Silano, S. (2023) 'Women Founders Get 2% of Venture Capital Funding in US', *Morning Star*.

Silver, M. (2011) 'Finding the Roman Empire's Disappeared Deposit Bankers', *Historia*, 60(3), pp. 301–327. doi:10.25162/historia-2011-0013.

Sinn, F. and Nekoei, A. (2021) 'The Origin of the Gender Gap', *VoxEU*. CEPR, 27 May. Available at: https://cepr.org/voxeu/columns/origin-gender-gap (Accessed: 26 June 2024).

Sirry, M. (2011) 'The Public Role of Dhimmīs During ʿAbbāsid Times', *Bulletin of the School of Oriental and African Studies*, 74(2), pp. 187–204. doi:10.1017/s0041977x11000024.

Skaff, J. K. (2003) 'The Sogdian Trade Diaspora in East Turkestan During the Seventh and Eighth Centuries', *Journal of the Economic and Social History of the Orient*, 46(4), pp. 475–524. doi:10.1163/156852003772914866.

Skills for Care (2023) 'The State of the Adult Social Care Sector and Workforce in England', Report published by Skills for Care.

Slater, E. (2006) 'Caffa: Early Western Expansion in the Late Medieval World, 1261–1475', *Review (Fernand Braudel Center)*, 29(3), pp. 271–283.

Smith, A. (1776) *An Inquiry into the Nature and Causes of the Wealth of Nations*. London: W. Strahan and T. Cadell.

Smith, J. C. (2021) *Black Firsts: 500 Years of Trailblazing Achievements and Ground-Breaking Events*. Canton, MI: Visible Ink Press.

Smith, J. I. (1985) 'Women, Religion and Social Change in Early Islam', in Y. Y. Haddad and E. B. Findly (eds.) *Women, Religion, and Social Change*. Albany: State University of New York Press.

Smith, R. D. (2015) 'Calamity and Transition: Re-imagining Italian Trade in the Eleventh-Century Mediterranean', *Past & Present*, 228(1), pp. 15–56. doi:10.1093/pastj/gtv022.

Smuts, B. (1995) 'The Evolutionary Origins of Patriarchy', *Human Nature*, 6(1), pp. 1–32. doi:10.1007/bf02734133.

Snow, P. and Dorling Kindersley (2018) *History of the World Map by Map*. London: Dorling Kindersley Limited.

Sommer, M. H. (2000) *Sex, Law, and Society in Late Imperial China*. Stanford: Stanford University Press.

Sommer, M. H. (2015) *Polyandry and Wife-Selling in Qing Dynasty China: Survival Strategies and Judicial Interventions*. Oakland, CA: University of California Press.

Splitstoser, J. C. et al. (2016) 'Early Pre-Hispanic Use of Indigo Blue in Peru', *Science Advances*, 2(9). doi:10.1126/sciadv.1501623.

Spufford, P. (1988) *Money and Its Use in Medieval Europe*. Cambridge: Cambridge University Press.

Stafford, P. (1989) 'Women in Domesday', *Reading Medieval Studies*, XV.

Stafford, W. (2002) *English Feminists and Their Opponents*. Manchester: Manchester University Press.

Standing, G. (1989) 'Global Feminization Through Flexible Labor', *World Development*, 17(7), pp. 1077–1095. doi:10.1016/0305-750x(89)90170-8.

Stanley, M. (no date) 'Women in the Civil Service—History', https://www.civilservant.org.uk. Available at: https://www.civilservant.org.uk/women-history.html.

Statista (2024) 'Distribution of Movie Directors in the United States from 2011 to 2023, by Gender', Statista Research Department. Available at: https://www.statista.com/statistics/696871/movie-director-gender/#:~:text=In%202023%2C%20for%20example%2C%20women,terms%20of%20on%2Dscreen%20employment.

Stenton, F. M. (1969) *The Free Peasantry of the Northern Danelaw*. Oxford: Oxford University Press.

Stern, N. and Romani, M. (2023) 'The Global Growth Story of the 21st Century: Driven by Investment and Innovation in Green Technologies and Artificial Intelligence', Policy Insight: Grantham Research Institute on Climate Change and the Environment, London School of Economics and Political Science and Systemiq.

Suss, J., Angeli, M. and Eckley, P. (2021) 'Gender, Age and Nationality Diversity in UK Banks', Bank of England Staff Working Paper No. 929.

Svärd, S. (2016) 'Neo-Assyrian Elite Women', in S. L. Budin and J. M. Turfa (eds.) *Women in Antiquity: Real Women Across the Ancient World*. Abingdon, Oxon: Routledge, pp. 126–137.

Swaddling, J. (2016) 'Seianti Hanunia Tlesnasa: An Etruscan Aristocrat', in S. L. Budin and J. M. Turfa (eds.) *Women in Antiquity: Real Women Across the Ancient World*. Abingdon, Oxon: Routledge, pp. 769–780.

Sweeney, D. (2016) 'Women at Deir al-Medina', in J. M. Turfa and S. L. Budin (eds.) *Women in Antiquity: Real Women Across the Ancient World*. Abingdon, Oxon: Routledge, pp. 243–254.

Swetnam-Burland, M. (2021) 'Women's Work? Investors, Money-Handlers, and Dealers', in B. Longfellow and M. Swetnam-Burland (eds.) *Women's Lives, Women's Voices: Roman Material Culture and Female Agency in the Bay of Naples*. Austin, TX: University of Texas Press, pp. 29–22.

Syme, R. (1939) *The Roman Revolution*. Oxford: Clarendon Press.

Tauseef, K. (2022) 'Shajara al-Durr', *World History Encyclopaedia*, 4 July. Available at: https://www.worldhistory.org/Shajara_al-Durr/ (Accessed: 22 February 2024).

Tchernia, A. (2016) *The Romans and Trade*. Oxford: Oxford University Press.

Tenney, J. S. (2017) 'Babylonian Populations, Servility, and Cuneiform Records', *Journal of the Economic and Social History of the Orient*, 60(96), pp. 715–787. doi:10.1163/15685209-12341440.

Terborg-Penn, R. (1990) 'Black Women Freedom Fighters in South Africa and in the United States: A Comparative Analysis', *Dialectical Anthropology*, 15(2–3), pp. 151–157. doi:10.1007/bf00264650.

Terki-Mignot, A. (2016) *Changing Patterns of Female Employment in Westmorland, 1787–1851*. B.A. Dissertation. University of Cambridge.

The Engineer (2024) 'Q&A: Carolyn Hicks, CFO/COO and Co-Founder at Brill Power', *The Engineer*.

The London Sustainable Development Commission (2018) 'Women in Cleantech', Greater London Authority.

The Royal Society (no date) 'History of the Royal Society', The Royal Society. Available at: https://royalsociety.org/about-us/who-we-are/history/ (Accessed: 26 June 2024).

The Trans-Atlantic Slave Trade Database (2024) 'Slave Voyages', Slave Voyages—timeline. Available at: https://www.slavevoyages.org/assessment/estimates.

Thomas, C., McNeil, C. and Gandon, A. (2023) 'Finding Hope: The Final Report of the IPPR Health and Care Workforce Assembly', *IPPR*.

Thomas, C. G. (1973) 'Matriarchy in Early Greece: The Bronze and Dark Ages', *Arethusa*, 6(2), pp. 173–195.

Thompson, G. et al. (2012) 'Olympic Britain', House of Commons Library.

Torkington, S. (2023) 'These Are the World's Leading Science and Technology Hotspots', World Economic Forum, 16 October. Available at: https://www.weforum.org/agenda/2023/10/innovation-technology-wipo-countries-ranking/.

Treggiari, S. (1975) 'Jobs in the Household of Livia', *Papers of the British School at Rome*.

Trigger, B. G. (2007) *Understanding Early Civilizations: A Comparative Study*. Cambridge: Cambridge University Press.

Trinity College (no date) 'Brief History of the College', Trinity College, University of Cambridge. Available at: https://www.trin.cam.ac.uk/about/historical-overview/in-brief/ (Accessed: 26 June 2024).

Tu, L. (2023) 'What's the World's Oldest Language?', *Scientific American*, 24 August. Available at: https://www.scientificamerican.com/article/whats-the-worlds-oldest-language1.

TUC (no date) 'How Ford's Striking Women Drove the Equal Pay Act', Trades Union Congress. TUC. Available at: https://www.tuc.org.uk/workplace-guidance/case-studies/how-fords-striking-women-drove-equal-pay-act.

Tuckniss, W. and Mayhew, H. (1861) 'Introduction', in H. Mayhew (ed.) *London Labour and the London Poor*. London: Cass & Company, pp. xi–xl.

Turfa, J. M. (2016) 'Health and Medicine for Etruscan Women', in S. L. Budin and J. M. Turfa (eds.) *Women in Antiquity: Real Women Across the Ancient World*. Abingdon, Oxon: Routledge.

Turner, B. (2021) 'Scientists Solve the Mystery of the Etruscans Origins', *Live Science*, 28 September. Available at: https://www.livescience.com/origins-of-etruscans-discovered.

Tyldesley, J. (2011) 'The Private Lives of the Pyramid-Builders', BBC History, 17 February. Available at: https://www.bbc.co.uk/history/ancient/egyptians/pyramid_builders_01.shtml (Accessed: 12 May 2024).

UK Bioindustry Association (2023) 'Diversity and Inclusion in UK Biotech', UK Bioindustry Association.

UK Parliament (no date a) 'East India Company and Raj 1785–1858', UK Parliament. Available at: https://www.parliament.uk/about/living-heritage/evolutionofparliament/legislativescrutiny/parliament-and-empire/parliament-and-the-american-colonies-before-1765/east-india-company-and-raj-1785–1858/.

UK Parliament (no date b) 'Ford Strike Report', UK Parliament. Available at: https://www.parliament.uk/about/living-heritage/transformingsociety/tradeindustry/industrycommunity/collections/equal-pay/ford-strike/.

Umri, S. J. and Umri, J. U. (2008) 'Economic Role of Women: The Islamic Approach', *Policy Perspectives*, 5(1), pp. 115–126.

UNESCO (2021) 'Gender & Creativity: Progress on the Precipice'. Paris: UNESCO.

UNESCO (2022) 'Re|shaping Policies for Creativity: Addressing Culture as a Global Public Good'. Paris: UNESCO.

UNESCO (no date a) 'City of Potosí' World Heritage List. Paris: UNESCO. Available at: https://whc.unesco.org/en/list/420/.

UNESCO (no date b) 'The Belitung Shipwreck', UNESCO Silk Roads Programme. Available at: https://en.unesco.org/silkroad/silk-road-themes/underwater-heritage/belitung-shipwreck.

UNFPA (2021) 'My Body Is My Own', Report of UNFPA.

UNIDO (2013) 'Women in Creative Industries', UNIDO Gender Newsletter, 4.

United Nations (2019) 'Guidelines for Producing Statistics on Asset Ownership from a Gender Perspective', United Nations Department of Economic and Social Affairs Statistical Division.

United Nations (2020) 'The World's Women 2020: Trends and Statistics', United Nations.

United Nations (no date) 'United Nations and Decolonization', United Nations. Available at: https://www.un.org/dppa/decolonization/en/about.

Unterhalter, E. (1987) *Forced Removal: The Division, Segregation and Control of the People of South Africa*. London: Canon Collins House.

US Department of Labor (1944) 'When You Hire Women'. Women's Bureau, Special Bulletin No. 14.

Van Bavel, B., Campopiano, M. and Dijkman, J. (2014) 'Factor Markets in Early Islamic Iraq, c. 600–1100 AD', *Journal of the Economic and Social History of the Orient*, 57(2), pp. 262–289. doi:10.1163/15685209-12341349.

Van Casteren, A. et al. (2022) 'The Cost of Chewing: The Energetics and Evolutionary Significance of Mastication in Humans', *Science Advances*, 8(33). doi:10.1126/sciadv.abn8351.

Van Staveren, I. et al. (2007) *The Feminist Economics of Trade*. Oxford: Routledge.

Vicente, M. et al. (2021) 'Male-Biased Migration from East Africa Introduced Pastoralism into Southern Africa', *BMC Biology*, 19(1). doi:10.1186/s12915-021-01193-z.

Voigtländer, N. and Voth, H.-J. (2013) 'How the West "Invented" Fertility Restriction', *American Economic Review*, 103(6), pp. 2227–2264. doi:10.1257/aer.103.6.2227.

Walbank, F. W. (2024) 'Alexander the Great', *Encyclopaedia Britannica*, December 2024. Available at: https://www.britannica.com/biography/Alexander-the-Great.

Wallach, J. (2012) *The Richest Woman in America: Hetty Green in the Gilded Age*. New York: Anchor Books.

Wang, H. (2013) 'Textiles as Money on the Silk Road?', *Journal of the Royal Asiatic Society of Great Britain & Ireland*, 23(2), pp. 165–174. doi:10.1017/s135618631300014x.

Ward-Perkins, B. (2006) *The Fall of Rome: And the End of Civilization*. Oxford: Oxford University Press.

Ward, W. A. (1989) 'Non-Royal Women and Their Occupations in the Middle Kingdom', in B. S. Lesko (ed.) *Women's Earliest Records: From Ancient Egypt and Western Asia*. Atlanta, GA: Scholars' Press, pp. 33–43.

Watt, W. M. (1977) 'Muhammad', in P. M. Holt, A. K. S. Lambton and B. Lewis (eds.) *The Cambridge History of Islam*. Cambridge: Cambridge University Press.

Webb, D. A. (2023) 'Commanding the Respect of All Who Knew Her: Recovering the Marginalised History of Eleanor Xiniwe and the Challenges of the Colonial Archive', *Social Dynamics*, 49(3), pp. 435–449. doi:10.1080/02533952.2023.2267778.

Weber, M. (1930) *Protestant Ethic and the Spirit of Capitalism*. London: George Allen & Unwin.

Weisser, S. O. (2001) *Women and Romance: A Reader*. New York: New York University Press.

Wells, J. (1983a) 'The Day the Town Stood Still: Women in Resistance in Potchefstroom, 1912–30', in B. Bozzoli (ed.) *Town and Countryside in the Transvaal*. Johannesburg: Ravan Press.

Wells, J. C. (1983b) 'Why Women Rebel: A Comparative Study of South African Women's Resistance in Bloemfontein (1913) and Johannesburg (1958)', *Journal of Southern African Studies*, 10(1), pp. 55–70. doi:10.1080/03057078308708067.

Wenghofer, R. (2014) 'Sexual Promiscuity of Non-Greeks in Herodotus' Histories', *Classical World*, 107(4), pp. 515–534. doi:10.1353/clw.2014.0044.

Westall, R. (1994) *Wilmslow and Alderley Edge: A Pictorial History*. Guildford: Phillimore.

Wheeler, D. (2011) 'Santos e Silva, Ana Joaquina dos', in H. L. Gates, E. Akyeampong and S. J. Niven (eds.) *The Dictionary of African Biography*. Oxford: Oxford University Press.

Wickman, C. (2005) *Framing the Early Middle Ages: Europe and the Mediterranean, 400–800*. Oxford: Oxford University Press.

Wiesner-Hanks, M. (2019) *A Concise History of the World*. Cambridge: Cambridge University Press.

Wiesner-Hanks, M. E. (2015) *Women and Gender in Early Modern Europe*. Cambridge: Cambridge University Press.

Wilding, A. (2022). Explore the Ancient Greek Festival of the Panathenaia. Open University. Available at: https://www.youtube.com/watch?v=nQLyd2rKgd8.

Wilson, A. and Bowman, A. (2018) 'Introduction', in A. Wilson and A. Bowman (eds.) *Trade, Commerce, and the State in the Roman World*. Oxford: Oxford University Press, pp. 1–26.

Winterer, C. (2010) 'Model Empire, Lost City: Ancient Carthage and the Science of Politics in Revolutionary America', *The William and Mary Quarterly*, 67(1), pp. 3–30.

Wollstonecraft, M. (1988) *A Vindication of the Rights of Woman*. Edited by C. Poston. New York: W. W. Norton. Originally published in 1792.

Wood, A. (1991) 'North-South Trade and Female Labour in Manufacturing: An Asymmetry', *Journal of Development Studies*, 27(2), pp. 168–189. doi:10.1080/00220389108422191.

World Bank (2022) 'Four Decades of Poverty Reduction in China', The World Bank and the Development Research Center of the State Council, P.R.C.

World Bank (2024) 'Women, Business and the Law, 2024', International Bank for Reconstruction and Development, The World Bank.

Wright, K. I. (2014) 'Domestication and Inequality? Households, Corporate Groups and Food Processing Tools at Neolithic Çatalhöyük', *Journal of Anthropological Archaeology*, 33, pp. 1–33. doi:10.1016/j.jaa.2013.09.007.

Wright, R. P. (2010) *The Ancient Indus: Urbanism, Economy, and Society*. New York: Cambridge University Press.

Wu, N. (2024) 'The World's Richest Self-Made Women in 2024', *Forbes*, 3 April.

www.priscillawakefield.uk (no date) 'Family, Priscilla Wakefield—Tottenham Activist'. Available at: https://www.priscillawakefield.uk/family.html (Accessed: 26 June 2024).

Xiang, W. and Pang-White, A. A. (2018) *The Confucian Four Books for Women (NÜ Sishu)*. New York: Oxford University Press.

Xue, M. M. (2021) 'High-Value Work and the Rise of Women: The Cotton Revolution and Gender Equality in China', Working Paper.

Xue, M. M. and Koyama, M. (2018) 'Autocratic Rule and Social Capital: Evidence from Imperial China', *SSRN Electronic Journal*. doi:10.2139/ssrn.2856803.

Yazigi, M. (2005) 'Some Accounts of Women Delegates to Caliph Mu'āwiya: Political Significance', *Arabica*, 52(3), pp. 437–449. doi:10.1163/1570058054191824.

Yellen, J. (2017) 'So We All Can Succeed: 125 Years of Women's Participation in the Economy', 125 Years of Women at Brown Conference, Brown University.

Yemitan, Ọladipọ (1987) *Madame Tinubu: Merchant and King-Maker*. Ibadan: University Press.

Young, E., Wajcman, J. and Sprejer, L. (2021) 'Where Are the Women? Mapping the Gender Job Gap in AI; Policy Briefing Summary', The Alan Turing Institute.

Zanden, J. L. van (2012) *The Long Road to the Industrial Revolution*. Leiden: Brill.

Zarinebaf-Shahr, F. (2001) 'The Role of Women in the Urban Economy of Istanbul, 1700–1850', *International Labor and Working-Class History*, 60, pp. 141–152. doi:10.1017/s0147547901004495.

Zeng, T. C., Aw, A. J. and Feldman, M. W. (2018) 'Cultural Hitchhiking and Competition Between Patrilineal Kin Groups Explain the Post-Neolithic Y-chromosome Bottleneck', *Nature Communications*, 9(1). doi:10.1038/s41467-018-04375-6.

Zeuske, M. (2023) 'The Rise of Atlantic Slavery in the Americas', in D. A. Pargas and J. Schiel (eds.) *The Palgrave Handbook of Global Slavery Throughout History*. London: Palgrave Macmillan, pp. 379–393.

Zucchi, K. (2024) 'Top Women Entrepreneurs', *Investopedia*, 6 March. Available at: https://www.investopedia.com/articles/personal-finance/040515/10-most-successful-women-entrepreneurs-decade.asp.

NOTES

INTRODUCTION

1. Albanesi and Olivetti, 2007
2. Ischinsky and Tisch, 2023; Wu, 2024
3. Hobbes, 1651
4. Zucchi, 2024
5. Auriol et al., 2022
6. International Labour Organization, 2016, p. 6
7. International Labour Organization, 2016, p. 28; World Bank, 2024, p. ix
8. World Bank, 2024, p. xv; Hinchliffe, 2023
9. International Labour Organization, 2018
10. World Bank, 2024; International Labour Organization, 2018
11. UNFPA, 2021, p. 31
12. Harris, 2017
13. Jain et al., 2023
14. Only 13 percent of the 2,781 global billionaires are women (Ischinsky and Tisch, 2023).
15. Barber, 1995, p. 181
16. Allam, 1989, pp. 128–35

CHAPTER 1: HUNTERS, FARMERS AND CLOTHIERS

1. Alger et al., 2020
2. Wiesner-Hanks, 2019, p. 20
3. Wiesner-Hanks, 2019, p. 30
4. de Beaune, 2019, p. 378
5. Milks, 2020
6. Haas et al., 2020; Anderson et al., 2023
7. Cirotteau et al., 2022, pp. 138–9
8. Cirotteau et al., 2022, p. 139; on the question of gender-based roles, also see Hoffman et al., 2021, and Dolan, 2024
9. Wiesner-Hanks, 2019, p. 32
10. Wiesner-Hanks, 2019, p. 19; van Casteren et al., 2022
11. Wiesner-Hanks, 2019, pp. 19, 33; Andrews and Lomas, 2018, p. 56
12. Wiesner-Hanks, 2019, p. 50
13. Cirotteau et al., 2022, p. 157
14. Hardy et al., 2013; Hardy et al., 2020; Barber, 1995, p. 53
15. Hardy et al., 2020; Barber, 1995, p. 78; Cirotteau et al., 2022, p. 159
16. Cirotteau et al., 2022, pp. 164–5
17. Barber, 1995, p. 94
18. Cirotteau et al., 2022, p. 161

19. Cirotteau et al., 2022, pp. 161–4
20. Neal and Cameron, 2003, p. 26
21. French, 2008, p. 75; Cirotteau et al., 2022, p. 151
22. Wiesner-Hanks, 2019, pp. 51–2
23. Diamond, 2005, p. 117
24. Cirotteau et al., 2022, p. 151
25. Cirotteau et al., 2022, p. 147
26. Meyers, 2016, p. 490
27. Roffet-Salque et al., 2018; Gilligan, 2019, p. 38
28. Wiesner-Hanks, 2019, p. 32
29. Gilligan, 2019, pp. 130–58; Headrick, 2009, p. 28
30. Headrick, 2009, pp. 22–4
31. Gilligan, 2019, p. 135
32. Gilligan, 2019, p. 136
33. Gilligan, 2019, p. 146; Headrick, 2009, p. 28
34. Gilligan, 2019, pp. 146, 163
35. Gilligan, 2019, pp. 130–80
36. Gilligan, 2019, pp. 130–60
37. Barber, 1995, pp. 180–7
38. Barber, 1995, p. 93; Ebrey, 2023, p. 18
39. Costin, 2013
40. Meyers, 2016, p. 497
41. Shenk et al., 2019
42. French, 2008, pp. 38–9
43. NMAI, 2009
44. French, 2008, pp. 38–9
45. Cassidy et al., 2025
46. Saini, 2024, p. 21
47. Wiesner-Hanks, 2019, pp. 37, 56–7
48. Rivollat et al., 2023
49. Wiesner-Hanks, 2019, p. 23; Neal and Cameron, 2003, p. 21
50. Wiesner-Hanks, 2019, p. 36; Neal and Cameron, 2003, p. 21
51. Wiesner-Hanks, 2019, p. 61
52. Roser, 2024
53. Pomeroy, 1975, pp. 14–5; Wiesner-Hanks, 2019, p. 37
54. Shenk et al., 2019
55. Saini, 2024, p. 21
56. Wiesner-Hanks, 2019, p. 52
57. Wiesner-Hanks, 2019, pp. 53–4
58. Goody, 1976; Peterson, 2002
59. Wright, 2014
60. Alesina, Giuliano and Nunn, 2013
61. Wiesner-Hanks, 2019, p. 53
62. Becker, 2019
63. Engels, 1884
64. Zeng et al., 2018; Hudson et al., 2020, p. 22
65. French, 2008, p. 10

NOTES TO CHAPTER 2

CHAPTER 2: DOCTORS, SCRIBES AND INNKEEPERS

1. Neal and Cameron, 2003, p. 27
2. French, 2008, p. 9; Scheidel, 2017, p. 39
3. Saini, 2024
4. Barber, 1995, p. 167
5. Barber, 1995, p. 167
6. Scheidel, 2017, p. 39
7. Trigger, 2007, pp. 46–8
8. Hawass, 1997; Sweeney, 2016
9. Tyldesley, 2011
10. Tyldesley, 2011
11. Hawass, 1997, p. 43
12. Tyldesley, 2011
13. Hawass, 1997, p. 43
14. Tyldesley, 2011; Hawass, 1997, p. 43
15. Sweeney, 2016
16. Olabarria, 2020, pp. 138–41
17. Sweeney, 2016
18. Sweeney, 2016
19. Sweeney, 2016, p. 246
20. Barber, 1995, p. 202
21. Lesko, 1989, p. 25; Barber, 1995, chapter 8
22. Sweeney, 2016, p. 250
23. Sweeney, 2016, p. 250
24. Nekoei and Sinn, 2021
25. Lesko, 1989, p. 3; Fischer, 1989, p. 23; Mark, 2017
26. Mark, 2017
27. David, 2016
28. David, 2016
29. Hawass, 1997
30. Neal and Cameron, 2003, p. 28
31. French, 2008, p. 93; Scheidel, 2017, p. 53; Trigger, 2007, p. 330
32. French, 2008, p. 94
33. Scheidel, 2017, pp. 53–4
34. Scheidel, 2017, p. 54
35. Neal and Cameron, 2003, p. 29
36. Scheidel, 2017, p. 54; Reid, 2014, pp. 17–29
37. Justel, 2016, pp. 83–8; Reid, 2014, pp.17–29; Tenney, 2017, p. 736
38. Kuhrt, 1989, p. 230. Estimates vary greatly, with some suggesting an even higher figure (Neal and Cameron, 2003, p. 30) and others noting that the extent of slavery and servitude is highly debated and near-impossible to quantify (Reid, 2014).
39. Tu, 2023
40. Neal and Cameron, 2003, p. 28
41. Muhly, 1985
42. Muhly, 1973
43. Cooper, 1989, pp. 47–8
44. Mieroop, 1989, pp. 54–5, 62

45. Svärd, 2016, p. 132; Lücker and Daenschel, 2019, p. 33
46. Justel, 2016, pp. 83–6
47. Barber, 1995, pp. 170–4; Moore and Lewis, 1998, p. 102
48. Mieroop, 1989, p. 64; Modelski, 2003
49. Barber, 1995, p. 176
50. Barber, 1995, p. 179
51. Barber, 1995, p. 181
52. Trigger, 2007, p. 159
53. Langlois, 2016
54. Glassner, 1989, p. 81; Harris, 1989, p. 146
55. Kelly-Buccellati, 2016
56. McCarthy, 2016
57. Law, 2011, p. 486
58. McIntosh, 2008; Wright, 2010; Robinson, 2021
59. McIntosh, 2008; Wright, 2010; Robinson, 2021; Marshall, 1931
60. Green, 2020
61. Wright, 2010, p. 329
62. Wright, 2010, p. 232
63. McIntosh, 2008, pp. 183–4, 394; Wright, 2010, pp. 162, 223–4
64. Wright, 2010, pp. 264–7
65. Wright, 2010, pp. 279–80
66. Clark, 2003, p. 322
67. Ebrey, 2023, p. 15
68. Ebrey, 2023, p. 16
69. Ebrey, 2023, p. 12
70. Ebrey, 2023, pp. 17–20
71. Kuhn, 1984, p. 216
72. Kuhn, 1984, pp. 217, 222
73. Kuhn, 1984, p. 221
74. Kuhn, 1984, pp. 215, 236
75. Gilligan, 2019, pp. 158–9
76. Bray, 1995, pp. 118–9
77. Hafford, 2018; Collins, 2021; Ebrey, 2023; Pare, 2023
78. Picton, 2016; Barber, 1995, p. 179
79. Bray, 1995, pp. 118–22; Hansen, 2011; Wang, 2013
80. Atwood, 2005
81. Creamer et al., 2017
82. Creamer et al., 2017
83. Haas et al., 2004
84. Haas and Creamer, 2006; Beresford-Jones et al., 2017
85. Entman, 2017; Splitstoser et al., 2016
86. Splitstoser et al., 2016
87. Entman, 2017
88. Haas and Creamer, 2006
89. Atwood, 2005; Haas and Creamer, 2006; Haas et al., 2004
90. Agencia Peruana De Noticias, 2016
91. Costin, 2013; Costin, 1993

92. Costin, 2013
93. Costin, 2013
94. Foster, 1989, p. 141
95. Harris, 1989, p. 148
96. Kuhrt, 1989, p. 228
97. Harris, 1989, pp. 155–7
98. Dossani, 2013
99. Dossani, 2013
100. Wright, 2010, p. 313
101. Becker, 2019
102. Ward, 1989, p. 37; Trigger, 2007, pp. 184–6
103. Fischer, 1989, p. 25
104. Ward, 1989, p. 43
105. Robins, 1989, p. 115
106. Allam, 1989, pp. 128–35
107. Picton, 2016, pp. 238–9
108. Picton, 2016, p. 232
109. Lücker and Daenschel, 2019, pp. 48–9
110. Ebrey, 2023, p. 81
111. Ebrey, 2023, p. 29
112. Trigger, 2007, p. 190
113. Lücker and Daenschel, 2019, pp. 50–1
114. Quoted in Greenhalgh, 1977
115. Greenhalgh, 1977, p. 12
116. Molony et al., 2016, p. 10
117. Quoted in Greenhalgh, 1977, p. 11
118. Trigger, 2007, p. 191
119. Trigger, 2007, p. 190
120. Trigger, 2007, p. 189
121. Trigger, 2007, p. 191
122. Trigger, 2007, p. 191
123. Trigger, 2007, p. 190
124. Trigger, 2007, p. 190
125. Schlegel, 1991, p. 724
126. Bateman, 2023, chapter 2
127. Trigger, 2007, p. 190

CHAPTER 3: COURTESANS, POETS AND POTTERS

1. Cline, 2021
2. Mieroop, 2021
3. MacGregor, 2010, p. 159
4. Head, 1880
5. MacGregor, 2010, p. 161
6. Oakeshott, 1936, pp. 5, 8
7. MacGregor, 2010, p. 160
8. MacGregor, 2010, p. 161
9. Oakeshott, 1936, p. 5

10. Wenghofer, 2014, p. 516
11. Budin and Turfa, 2016, p. 439
12. Bergeron, 2011, p. 181
13. Snow and Dorling Kindersley, 2018, p. 55
14. Christian, 2013
15. Oakeshott, 1936, p. 5
16. Oakeshott, 1936, p. 5
17. Ashmolean Museum, n.d.
18. Mark, 2020
19. MacGregor, 2010, p. 162
20. Mark, 2020
21. MacGregor, 2010, p. 165
22. MacGregor, 2010, p. 166
23. MacGregor, 2010, p. 166
24. Green, 2017
25. Mark, 2014; Encyclopaedia Britannica, 2024a
26. Jordan, 2009; Davis-Kimball and Behan, 2003; Mayor, 2016
27. Pomeroy, 1975, p. 2
28. Pomeroy, 1975, p. 8
29. Pomeroy, 1975, pp. 2–5
30. Pomeroy, 1975, pp. 25–30
31. Pomeroy, 1975, pp. 52–6
32. Pomeroy, 1975, p. 57; Glazebrook, 2011
33. Pomeroy, 1975, p. 57
34. O'Faolain and Martines, 1979, p. 46
35. Glazebrook, 2016
36. Lister, 2021, pp. 29–30
37. Lister, 2021, pp. 29–30
38. Galt, 1931
39. Barrow, 2018, chapter 3
40. Marcar, 2004, p. 226; Murray et al., 2020
41. Murray et al., 2020
42. Barber, 1995, p. 213
43. Barber, 1995, p. 244
44. Cohen, 2016, p. 722
45. Barber, 1995, pp. 281–2
46. Wilding, 2022
47. Encyclopaedia Britannica, 2016
48. Encyclopaedia Britannica, 2016
49. Encyclopaedia Britannica, 2016
50. Barber, 1995, p. 282
51. Barber, 1995, pp. 282–3
52. Cohen, 2016, p. 721
53. Brock, 1994, p. 338
54. Cohen, 2016
55. Barber, 1995, p. 87
56. Cohen, 2016, p. 722

57. Barber, 1995, pp. 276, 284
58. Barber, 1995, chapter 10
59. Cohen, 2016, p. 715
60. Cohen, 2016, p. 715
61. Backhouse, 2002, p. 20; Kishtainy, 2017, p. 9
62. Backhouse, 2002, p. 22; Kishtainy, 2017, p. 11
63. Kishtainy, 2017, p. 12
64. Pomeroy, 1975, p. 48
65. Pomeroy, 1975, pp. 50–1
66. Quoted in Pomeroy, 1975, p. 51
67. Cohen, 2016, p. 716
68. Backhouse, 2002, p. 16
69. Backhouse, 2002, p. 23
70. Kishtainy, 2017, p. 11
71. Demosthenes, Oration 57, 1989, p. 230
72. Demosthenes, Oration 57, 1989, pp. 230–1
73. Brock, 1994, p. 336
74. Brock, 1994, p. 336
75. Brock, 1994, p. 341
76. Pomeroy, 1975, p. 141
77. Lister, 2021, pp. 29–30
78. Cohen, 2016, pp. 718–9
79. Phillips, 2009, p. 99
80. Phillips, 2009, pp. 110–1
81. Phillips, 2009, p. 118
82. Cohen, 2016, p. 719
83. Pomeroy, 1975, p. 37
84. Pomeroy, 1975, p. 36
85. Pomeroy, 1975, p. 38
86. Pomeroy, 1975, p. 38; Bresson, 2016, p. 154
87. Barber, 1995, p. 119
88. Barber, 1995, pp. 116–7
89. German, 2007, p. 23
90. German, 2007
91. French, 2008, p. 9
92. Marcar, 2004
93. Pomeroy, 1975, pp. 39–40; Thomas, 1973, p. 178
94. Thomas, 1973; Pomeroy, 1975, p. 13; Downing, 1985
95. Pomeroy, 1975, p. 13; Downing, 1985
96. Hruby, 2018; Price, 2018
97. Price, 2018
98. Hruby, 2018
99. Pomeroy, 1975, pp. 52–3
100. Pomeroy, 1975, p. 54; Mark, 2021
101. Pomeroy, 1975, p. 53
102. Mark, 2021
103. Pomeroy, 1975, p. 54; Mark, 2021

104. Mark, 2021
105. Pomeroy, 1975, pp. 52–5
106. Walbank, 2024
107. Lister, 2021, pp. 29–30
108. Lücker and Daenschel, 2019, p. 71
109. Rowlandson, 1998, p. 4
110. Olabarria, 2020, pp. 138–41
111. Nifosi, 2019, p. 7
112. Walbank, 2024
113. Nifosi, 2019, pp. 8–9, 235
114. Nifosi, 2019, p. 27
115. Nifosi, 2019, p. 27
116. Nifosi, 2019, chapters 1 and 6
117. Turfa, 2016, p. 798

CHAPTER 4: MERCHANTS, PROPERTY DEVELOPERS AND MONEYLENDERS

1. MacGregor, 2010, p. 163
2. Quinn, 2024, p. 180
3. Lee, 2014
4. Becker, 2016, p. 925
5. Becker, 2016, p. 925; Baraniuk, 2023
6. Turner, 2021
7. Swaddling, 2016
8. Swaddling, 2016, p. 776
9. Bonfante, 2016
10. Turfa, 2016, p. 799
11. Bonfante, 2016
12. Bartoloni and Pitzalis, 2016
13. Turfa, 2016, p. 798
14. Gleba, 2016; Bartoloni and Pitzalis, 2016
15. Ridgway, 2016
16. Budin and Turfa, 2016, p. 439
17. Encyclopaedia Britannica, 2018a
18. Winterer, 2010, p. 15
19. Snow and Dorling Kindersley, 2018, p. 66
20. Culham, 1982
21. Winterer, 2010, p. 15
22. Culham, 1982
23. Chatelard, 2016
24. Winterer, 2010, p. 14
25. Encyclopaedia Britannica, 2007
26. Chatelard, 2016, pp. 33–4
27. Chatelard, 2016, p. 27
28. Chatelard, 2016, p. 37
29. Chatelard, 2016, p. 37
30. Chatelard, 2016, p. 37

31. Hopkins 1980; Hopkins, 2002
32. Geraghty, 2007, p. 1045; Parker, 1992
33. Bowman, 2018
34. Snow and Dorling Kindersley, 2018, pp. 60–1
35. Oakeshott, 1936, p. 32; Nappo, 2018
36. Oakeshott, 1936, p. 32; Nappo, 2018
37. Ebrey, 2023, p. 71
38. Frankopan, 2016, p. 3
39. Ebrey, 2023, p. 73
40. Ebrey, 2023, p. 73
41. Ebrey, 2023, p. 74; Frankopan, 2016, p. 8
42. Hansen, 2005, p. 49; Bray 1995, p. 123
43. Graf, 2018
44. Graf, 2018
45. Livshits, 2008
46. Livshits, 2008
47. Nappo, 2018, p. 558
48. Parker, 2002
49. Wilson and Bowman, 2018, p. 14
50. Wilson and Bowman, 2018, p. 14
51. Hemelrijk, 2016, p. 896
52. Adams, 2018
53. Becker, 2016, p. 926
54. Becker, 2016, p. 927
55. Becker, 2016, p. 926
56. Becker, 2016, p. 922
57. D'Ambra, 2021, p. 88
58. D'Ambra, 2021, p. 89
59. D'Ambra, 2021, p. 89
60. Swetnam-Burland, 2021, p. 40
61. D'Ambra, 2021, pp. 90, 103
62. Swetnam-Burland, 2021
63. Lovén, 2020
64. Swetnam-Burland, 2021, p. 37
65. Lovén, 2020
66. Lovén, 2020, p. 216
67. Swetnam-Burland, 2021, p. 30
68. Frank, 1975, p. 49
69. Silver, 2011, p. 304
70. Swetnam-Burland, 2021, p. 36
71. Swetnam-Burland, 2021, p. 37
72. Swetnam-Burland, 2021, p. 39
73. Treggiari, 1975
74. Treggiari, 1975, p. 58
75. Geraghty, 2007, p. 1043; Joshel, 2010
76. Caldwell, 2021, p. 57
77. Caldwell, 2021, pp. 57–8

78. Caldwell, 2021, p. 54
79. Caldwell, 2021, p. 61
80. Caldwell, 2021, p. 61
81. Geraghty, 2007, pp. 1041–51; Scheidel, 2017, p. 72
82. Scheidel, 2017, p. 75
83. Frank, 1975, pp. 44–5
84. Frank, 1975, p. 48
85. Frank, 1975, p. 47
86. Becker, 2016, p. 922
87. Chatelard, 2016, p. 29
88. Chatelard, 2016, pp. 29–30
89. Lovén, 2020, p. 891
90. Swetnam-Burland, 2021, p. 35
91. Becker, 2016, p. 926
92. Becker, 2016, p. 916
93. Lovén, 2020
94. Tchernia, 2016, chapters 5 and 19
95. Geraghty, 2007, p. 1045
96. Silver, 2011
97. Wilson and Bowman, 2018, p. 9; Parker, 1992; Tchernia, 2016, pp. 118–9; Silver, 2011. On climate, see McCormick et al., 2012.

CHAPTER 5: BROKERS, CONCUBINES AND WET-NURSES

1. Bosker et al., 2013
2. Keddie, 2007, p. 24
3. Watt, 1977, p. 33
4. Encyclopaedia Britannica, 2018
5. Encyclopaedia Britannica, 2018
6. Dauphin et al., 2015
7. Watt, 1977, p. 34
8. Cevherli, 2022
9. Cevherli, 2022
10. Abbott, 1942, p. 123
11. Watt, 1977, p. 38
12. Watt, 1977, p. 39
13. Watt, 1977, p. 41
14. Encyclopaedia Britannica, 2023
15. El-Badawi, 2022, p. 263
16. Abbott, 1942
17. Nadwi, 2016
18. Abbott, 1942, p. 109
19. Abbott, 1942
20. Smith, 1985, p. 24
21. El-Badawi, 2022, p. 220
22. Abbott, 1942, p. 123
23. Abbott, 1942, pp. 114, 124; El-Badawi, 2022, p. 220
24. Keddie, 2007, pp. 22–3

25. Ahmed, 1992, p. 61; El-Badawi, 2022, p. 65; Keddie, 2007, p. 26
26. Abbott, 1942, p. 114
27. Keddie, 2007, pp. 26–7; Abbott, 1942, p. 114
28. Abbott, 1942, p. 115
29. Hinds, 1972, p. 450
30. Keddie, 2007, pp. 26–7
31. Keddie, 2007, p. 29; Bessard, 2020, pp. 18–9
32. Bessard, 2020, p. 18; Sirry, 2011, p. 191
33. Michalopoulos et al., 2017
34. Shatzmiller, 2011, p. 174
35. Shatzmiller, 1994
36. Shatzmiller, 2011, p. 171
37. Bessard, 2020, p. 188
38. Bessard, 2020, pp. 189–91
39. Shatzmiller, 2011, p. 172
40. Yazigi, 2005, pp. 441–3
41. On the former, Bessard, 2020, p. 239
42. El-Azhari, 2021, p. 65
43. Lücker and Daenschel, 2019, p. 149
44. Encyclopaedia Britannica, 2024
45. Bosker et al., 2013, p. 1419
46. Shatzmiller, 1994, p. 350
47. Shatzmiller, 1994, pp. 348–50; Shatzmiller, 2011, p. 164; Bessard, 2020, p. 238
48. Shatzmiller, 1994, pp. 348–50; Shatzmiller, 2011, p. 164; Bessard, 2020, p. 238
49. Bessard, 2020, p. 236
50. Shatzmiller, 1997, p. 177
51. Shatzmiller, 1994
52. Bosker et al., 2013, p. 1423
53. Van Bavel et al., 2014, p. 264
54. Pamuk and Shatzmiller, 2014, p. 217
55. Silver, 2011; Van Bavel et al., 2014
56. Bessard, 2020, pp. 212–3
57. Bessard, 2020, p. 209
58. Chowdhury, 2018
59. Lücker and Daenschel, 2019, pp. 150–1
60. Lücker and Daenschel, 2019, pp. 150–1
61. Mernissi, 1994, p. 53
62. Mernissi, 1994, p. 62
63. Mernissi, 1994, p. 51
64. Lücker and Daenschel, 2019, pp. 150–1
65. El-Azhari, 2021, pp. 93–4
66. Mernissi, 1994, p. 55
67. Shatzmiller, 2011, p. 153
68. Mernissi, 1994, p. 38
69. Mernissi, 1994, p. 38
70. Pamuk and Shatzmiller, 2014, p. 217; Bessard, 2020, pp. 228, 240; Shatzmiller, 2007, p. 150

71. Pamuk and Shatzmiller, 2014, pp. 207–8, 212
72. Pamuk and Shatzmiller, 2014, pp. 216–8; Bessard, 2020, pp. 192, 269
73. Shatzmiller, 2011, p. 174
74. Shatzmiller, 2007, pp. 149–50
75. Shatzmiller, 2007, p. 150
76. Mernissi, 1994, p. 45
77. Shatzmiller, 2011, p. 160
78. Shatzmiller, 2011, pp. 159–60
79. Lücker and Daenschel, 2019, p. 172; Mortimer, 2018
80. Shatzmiller, 1994, p. 347
81. Shatzmiller, 1994, chapter 7
82. These words were—perhaps falsely—attributed to Muhammad by a witness (Lücker and Daenschel, 2019, p. 148).
83. Lücker and Daenschel, 2019, p. 148
84. Quran (2:228; 4:34); Umri and Umri, 2008, p. 121
85. Shatzmiller, 2007, p. 115
86. Shatzmiller, 1997, pp. 179–87
87. Shatzmiller, 2007, p. 95
88. Pamuk and Shatzmiller, 2014, pp. 215–6; Shatzmiller, 1994, pp. 64–5
89. Shatzmiller, 2007, p. 98
90. Keddie, 1990, pp. 87–90
91. Umri and Umri, 2008, p. 120
92. Keddie, 1990
93. Keddie, 1990, p. 88
94. Shatzmiller, 2007
95. Shatzmiller, 1997, p. 200
96. Umri and Umri, 2008, p. 117
97. Shatzmiller, 1994, p. 352; Shatzmiller, 1997, p. 194
98. Shatzmiller, 1994, pp. 358–9
99. Shatzmiller, 1994, p. 358; Shatzmiller, 1997, p. 195
100. Shatzmiller, 1994, p. 358
101. Shatzmiller, 1994, p. 353
102. Shatzmiller, 2007, p. 112
103. Shatzmiller, 1994, p. 353
104. Shatzmiller, 2007, p. 109
105. Shatzmiller, 1994, pp. 355, 359
106. Shatzmiller, 1994, p. 363
107. Shatzmiller, 1994, p. 362
108. Umri and Umri, 2008, p. 124
109. Shatzmiller, 1994, p. 359
110. Shatzmiller, 1997, p. 196
111. Umri and Umri, 2008, pp. 118–21
112. Shatzmiller, 1997, p. 189
113. Bateman, 2023; Keddie, 2007, pp. 24–5, 29–35, 45
114. Kloss, 2023, p. 142
115. Keddie, 2007, p. 41; Kloss, 2023, p. 143
116. Kloss, 2023, pp. 149–50

117. Parker and Rathbone, 2007, p. 79
118. Shatzmiller, 1994, p. 352
119. Mernissi, 1994, p. 59
120. Spufford, 1988, p. 49; McCormick, 2001, pp. 729, 733
121. Nielson, 2012, p. 244
122. Nielson, 2012, pp. 246–7; Kloss, 2023, p. 146
123. Mernissi, 1994, p. 55
124. Mernissi, 1994, pp. 54–5
125. Nielson, 2012, pp. 248–9, 253
126. Mernissi, 1994, p. 57; El-Azhari, 2021, p. 59
127. Mernissi, 1994, p. 41
128. Nielson, 2012, pp. 248–9, 253
129. Nielson, 2012, pp. 250–4
130. Shatzmiller, 1994, p. 357; Shatzmiller, 1997, p. 192
131. Mernissi, 1994, p. 153
132. Marsot, 2007, chapter 1
133. Marsot, 2007, chapter 1
134. Marsot, 2007, chapter 1
135. Shoshan, 1981
136. Marsot, 2007, chapter 1
137. Mernissi, 1994, p. 165
138. Mernissi, 1994, p. 168
139. Mernissi, 1994, p. 169
140. Mernissi, 1994, p. 170
141. Mernissi, 1994, pp. 169–71
142. Mernissi, 1994, pp. 171–2
143. Marsot, 2007, chapter 1; Lücker and Daenschel, 2019, pp. 169–70
144. Mernissi, 1994, p. 161
145. El-Azhari, 2021, p. 205
146. Keddie, 2007, p. 26
147. Mernissi, 1994, pp. 115, 141
148. Mernissi, 1994, chapters 7–8; Lücker and Daenschel, 2019, p. 171
149. El-Azhari, 2021, p. 239
150. Mernissi, 1994, p. 149; El-Azhari, 2021, p. 241
151. Marsot, 2007, chapter 1
152. Marsot, 2007, chapter 1
153. Tauseef, 2022
154. Marsot, 2007, chapter 1, p. 28; Mernissi, 1994, p. 28
155. Tauseef, 2022
156. Mernissi, 1994, p. 91; Marsot, 2007, chapter 1; Keddie, 2007, p. 51
157. Marsot, 2007, chapter 1, p. 29
158. Keddie, 2007, p. 41
159. Mernissi, 1994, p. 89
160. Mernissi, 1994, p. 90
161. Mernissi, 1994, p. 93
162. Mernissi, 1994, p. 96
163. Keddie, 2007, pp. 45, 51–2

164. Mernissi, 1994, p. 29
165. Encyclopaedia Britannica, 2023a

CHAPTER 6: INVENTORS, WEAVERS AND SPINNERS

1. Ebrey, 2023, p. 126
2. Ebrey, 2023, p. 124
3. Glahn, 2016, p. 217; UNESCO (n.d. b); Ebrey, 2023, p. 124
4. Ebrey, 2023, p. 229; Broadberry et al., 2015, p. 372
5. The figure can be viewed at https://www.metmuseum.org/art/collection/search/42124. On horses more generally: Frankopan, 2016, p. 9; Creel, 1965, p. 658; Ebrey, 2023, pp. 74–5.
6. Frankopan, 2016, p. 9
7. Kuhn, 1984, pp. 230, 240
8. Hansen, 2011, p. 90
9. Benn, 2002, pp. 179–80
10. Benn, 2002, p. 4
11. Benn, 2002, pp. 46, 186–7
12. Morris, 2010, p. 632
13. Benn, 2002, p. 182
14. Benn, 2002, p. 183
15. Benn, 2002, pp. 184–7
16. Benn, 2002, p. 3
17. Birge, 2002, pp. 283–4
18. Birge, 2002
19. Benn, 2002, p. 36
20. Ebrey, 2023, p. 132
21. Benn, 2002, p. 36
22. Benn, 2002, p. 36; Smith, 1776
23. Benn, 2002, p. 37
24. Skaff, 2003; Hansen, 2003
25. Benn, 2002, pp. 184–7
26. Hinsch, 2021, p. 2; Benn, 2002, p. 292
27. Hinsch, 2021, p. 2
28. Hinsch, 2021, p. 4
29. Bernstein, 2009, p. 98; Ebrey, 2023, p. 146
30. Glahn, 2016, chapter 6; Benn, 2002, pp. 292–3
31. Glahn, 2016, p. 216; Deng and Zheng, 2015; Hinsch, 2021, p. 11
32. Ebrey, 2023, p. 144; Glahn, 2016, p. 235
33. Ebrey, 2023, p. 145
34. Ebrey, 2023, p. 145; Glahn, 2016, p. 233
35. Deng and Zheng, 2015; Benn, 2002, p. 293
36. Benn, 2002, p. 293; Glahn, 2016, p. 250
37. Benn, 2002, p. 293
38. Hinsch, 2021, p. 58
39. Ebrey, 2023, p. 166; Benn, 2002, p. 293; Deng and Zheng, 2015
40. Bray, 1995, p. 125
41. Glahn, 2016, p. 246

42. Bray, 1995, p. 126
43. Deng and Zheng, 2015; Benn, 2002, p. 293
44. Broadberry et al., 2015, p. 375
45. Hinsch, 2021, p. 17
46. Fan and Wu, 2023
47. Hinsch, 2021, pp. 26–7
48. Hinsch, 2021, p. 25
49. Hinsch, 2021, pp. 14, 25
50. Hinsch, 2021, p. 28
51. Birge, 2002, pp. 285–6
52. Birge, 2002, p. 227
53. Birge, 2002, p. 287
54. Birge, 2002, pp. 226, 285
55. Hansen, 1996, p. 197
56. Hansen, 1996
57. Glahn, 2016, p. 75
58. Ebrey, 2023, pp. 47–9
59. Hinsch, 2021, pp. 70–2; Ebrey, 2023, p. 170
60. Hinsch, 2021, p. 73
61. Hinsch, 2021, p. 28; Ebrey, 2002, chapter 2
62. Hinsch, 2021, p. 29
63. Ebrey, 2002, chapter 1, p. 15
64. Birge, 2002, pp. 286–7
65. Hinsch, 2021, p. 59; Birge, 2002, p. 288
66. Hinsch, 2021, pp. 58–9
67. Hinsch, 2021, p. 14
68. Hinsch, 2021, p. 19
69. Birge, 2002, p. 288
70. Birge, 2002, p. 288
71. Ebrey, 2023, p. 160
72. Encyclopaedia Britannica, 2023
73. Ebrey, 2023, p. 196
74. Birge, 2002, pp. 279–82
75. Ebrey, 2002, p. 36
76. Bawden, 2025
77. Birge, 2002, pp. 217–29
78. Birge, 2002, pp. 262–3
79. Birge, 2002, p. 264
80. Birge, 2002
81. Birge, 2002, p. 265
82. Birge, 2002, p. 268
83. Greenhalgh, 1977, p. 12
84. Greenhalgh, 1977, p. 13
85. Greenhalgh, 1977
86. Fan and Wu, 2023
87. Bray, 1995; Kuhn, 1984, p. 234
88. Bray, 1995, pp. 128–9

89. Bray, 1995
90. Brown and Satterthwaite-Phillips, 2018
91. Molony et al., 2016, p. 95
92. Elvin, 2004; Elvin, 1998, p. 6; Ebrey, 2023, p. 226

CHAPTER 7: DAIRY MAIDS, BREWERS AND SHOPKEEPERS

1. Malanima, 2009, pp. 208–11; van Zanden, 2012, p. 32
2. Headrick, 2009, p. 51
3. Ebrey, 2023, p. 144
4. Morris, 2010, p. 384
5. Marsot, 2007, chapter 1 and p. 27
6. Spufford, 1988, p. 49; McCormick, 2001, pp. 729, 733; Barker, 2023, p. 161; for a map of the primary slave trade routes, see McCormick, 2001, p. 762
7. Schiel, 2023, p. 183
8. Parker and Rathbone, 2007, p. 79; for more detail, Gordon and Hain (eds.), 2017
9. Karras, 2023, p. 219
10. McCormick, 2001, p. 776; also see Perry et al., 2021, Part II
11. McCormick, 2001, chapter 25
12. Lopez, 1964, pp. 450, 456
13. Spufford, 1988, p. 211
14. Malanima, 2009, p. 27
15. Malanima, 2009, pp. 9, 25
16. Burnard, 2022, p. 820
17. Scheidel, 2017, p. 305
18. Federico, 2001, p. 178; Bennett, 2010, pp. 12–3; Hogenboom, 2012
19. Gregory, 2023, p. 73
20. Hogenboom, 2012
21. Gregory, 2023, p. 73
22. Federico, 2001, p. 168
23. Hogenboom, 2012; Gregory, 2023, pp. 73–7
24. Gregory, 2023, p. 74
25. Scheidel, 2017, p. 311
26. Around a half of the population of England engaged in waged labour in the period 1300–1520 (Dyer, 2005, pp. 218–20); Kussmaul, 1981, p. 36
27. Scheidel, 2017, p. 305
28. Broadberry et al., 2015, p. 410
29. Scheidel, 2017, pp. 312–3
30. Schiel, 2023, p. 180
31. Slater, 2006, p. 276
32. Schiel, 2023, pp. 180–90
33. Barker, 2023
34. Schiel, 2023, p. 180
35. Karras, 2023, p. 219
36. Karras, 2023
37. McKee, 2004
38. Hagen and Hagen, 2010, pp. 40–7
39. Kussmaul, 1981

40. Voigtländer and Voth, 2013
41. Carlin, 2008
42. Kussmaul, 1981, pp. 34, 143; also see Humphries and Weisdorf, 2015, on how women gained relatively less from the post–Black Death golden age—in wage terms—compared with men
43. Kussmaul, 1981, p. 81
44. Kussmaul, 1981, pp. 82–3
45. Bennett, 1996, p. 43
46. Carlin, 2008
47. Callow, 1899
48. Bennett, 1996, p. 64
49. Bennett, 1996, pp. 66–7
50. Karras, 1996, p. 42
51. Karras, 1996, p. 14
52. Karras, 1996, pp. 6, 14
53. Karras, 1996, p. 77
54. Karras, 1996, p. 78
55. Karras, 1996, p. 81
56. Karras, 1996, pp. 79–80
57. McIntosh, 2005, p. 416
58. McIntosh, 2005, p. 410
59. Abram, 1916, p. 281
60. McIntosh, 2005, p. 417
61. McIntosh, 2005, p. 415
62. Abram, 1916, p. 278
63. Abram, 1916, p. 278
64. Kennan, 2019, pp. 64, 74
65. Kennan, 2019
66. Kennan, 2019, pp. 67, 71–2
67. Ramirez, 2022, p. 283
68. Ramirez, 2022, chapter 8
69. Mernissi, 1994, pp. 18–9
70. Mernissi, 1994, pp. 18–9
71. Lücker and Daenschel, 2019, p. 226
72. Campbell, 2005
73. Downs, 2008
74. Downs, 2008, p. 401
75. Downs, 2008
76. Lücker and Daenschel, 2019, p. 229
77. Downs, 2008
78. Zeuske, 2023
79. Lücker and Daenschel, 2019, p. 232
80. Lücker and Daenschel, 2019, p. 257
81. Zeuske, 2023, p. 384
82. The Trans-Atlantic Slave Trade Database, n.d.
83. Zeuske, 2023, p. 385
84. Romano, 2020, pp. 289–90; UNESCO, n.d. a

85. Romano, 2020, pp. 297–9, 303
86. Romano, 2020, p. 298
87. Romano, 2020, pp. 297–8
88. Romano, 2020, pp. 310–1
89. Ebrey, 2023, p. 211
90. Malanima, 2009, p. 170
91. For a detailed analysis of the economic impact, see O'Rourke and Williamson, 2002
92. Dalrymple, 2020, p. 4
93. Dalrymple, 2020, p. 8
94. Dalrymple, 2020, p. 4
95. Dalrymple, 2020, p. 4
96. Dalrymple, 2020, p. 5
97. Dalrymple, 2020, p. 3
98. Dalrymple, 2020, p. 13
99. Dalrymple, 2020, p. 14; Saberi, 2013, p. 94
100. Dalrymple, 2020, p. 14
101. Dalrymple, 2020, p. 15
102. Dalrymple, 2020, pp. 16–8
103. Hickman, 2019, p. 28
104. Hickman, 2019, p. 23
105. Hickman, 2019, pp. 17, 36
106. Hickman, 2019, pp. 17, 19, 24
107. Hickman, 2019, p. 36
108. Hickman, 2019, p. 33
109. Dalrymple, 2020, pp. 21–2
110. Dalrymple, 2020, p. 22
111. Saberi, 2013, p. 93
112. Saberi, 2013, p. 93
113. Saberi, 2013, p. 93
114. Hickman, 2019, p. 39
115. Hickman, 2019, p. 41
116. Hickman, 2019, p. 41
117. Quoted in Israel, 1989, pp. 12–3
118. Heuvel, 2007, p. 229
119. Heuvel, 2007, pp. 230–1
120. Heuvel, 2007, pp. 234–5
121. Heuvel, 2007, p. 241
122. Heuvel, 2007, pp. 225–6
123. Heuvel, 2007, pp. 136, 205
124. Heuvel, 2007, pp. 141–2
125. Heuvel, 2007, pp. 188–9, 194–5
126. Crawford and Gowing, 2000, p. 71
127. Wiesner-Hanks, 2015; Foreman-Peck, 2011
128. Kok, 2017; Keddie, 2007, pp. 39, 208
129. Keddie, 2007, pp. 35–42
130. Sommer, 2000, p. 39; De Moor and van Zanden, 2009
131. Sommer, 2000, p. 39

132. Molony et al., 2016, p. 91; Sommer, 2015, p. 10

133. Asher and Talbot, 2023, p. 157

134. For a discussion of child marriage today, see Kok (2017) and Bateman (2023). In some parts of Asia, such as in Sri Lanka and Southeast Asia, the family system was more 'women friendly' and the age of marriage was higher than in India or China.

135. De Moor and van Zanden, 2009

136. Weber, 1930

137. De Vries, 2009; for what follows, also see Bateman, 2019, chapter 2

138. De Vries, 2009

CHAPTER 8: SCIENTISTS, BANKERS AND WRITERS

1. Karras, 1996
2. Bateman, 2019, p. 25
3. Acemoglu et al., 2002
4. Hudson et al., 2020; Bryson, 2016, p. 9
5. Bryson, 2016, p. 9
6. Mokyr, 2009
7. Trinity College, n.d.
8. Mokyr, 2009
9. Rubin, 2017, pp. 13, 105–6
10. Xue and Koyama, 2018
11. Mokyr, 2017
12. Lücker and Daenschel, 2019, p. 278
13. Gregory, 2023, p. 111
14. Gregory, 2023, p. 110
15. Mokyr, 2009, p. 322
16. The Royal Society, n.d.
17. Fara, 2016
18. Lücker and Daenschel, 2019, p. 278
19. Fara, 2016
20. Jane Austen, as quoted in Irvine, 2005, p. 43
21. Stafford, 2002, p. 51
22. Nekoei and Sinn, 2021
23. Shoemaker, 1998, p. 282; Buringh and van Zanden, 2009
24. Buringh and van Zanden, 2009
25. Ferguson, 2024
26. Shoemaker, 1998, p. 285
27. Encyclopaedia Britannica, 2024c
28. Encyclopaedia Britannica, 2024c; Pink, 2006, p. 55
29. Doody, 2010, pp. 2–3
30. Encyclopaedia Britannica, 2024c
31. Irvine, 2005, pp. 12–3
32. Irvine, 2005, p. 3; Pink, 2006, p. 54
33. Irvine, 2005, p. 2
34. Irvine, 2005, p. 13
35. Irvine, 2005, p. 14
36. Encyclopaedia Britannica, 2024c; Doody, 2010, p. 25; Pink, 2006, pp. 53–5

37. Irvine, 2005, p. 15
38. Irvine, 2005, p. 15
39. Irvine, 2005, p. 15
40. Irvine, 2005, p. 15
41. Irvine, 2005, pp. 15–6
42. Irvine, 2005, p. 16
43. Irvine, 2005, p. 16
44. Shoemaker, 1998, pp. 282–95
45. Nekoei and Sinn, 2021; Sinn and Nekoei, 2021
46. Firkus, 2021, p. 6
47. Firkus, 2021, p. 6
48. Firkus, 2021, p. 9
49. Firkus, 2021, p. 13
50. Firkus, 2021, p. 11
51. Firkus, 2021, pp. 13–5
52. Firkus, 2021, pp. 15–6
53. Homestead and Hansen, 2010
54. Firkus, 2021, p. 24
55. Homestead and Hansen, 2010
56. Firkus, 2021, pp. 24–5; Encyclopaedia Britannica, 2024b
57. New York Daily Tribune, 1900
58. Homestead and Hansen, 2010
59. Firkus, 2021, pp. 25, 28
60. Firkus, 2021, p. 28
61. Molony et al., 2016, p. 78
62. Molony et al., 2016, pp. 43, 78–9
63. Molony et al., 2016, p. 104
64. Molony et al., 2016, p. 104
65. Buringh and van Zanden, 2009
66. Rostek, 2021, p. 182
67. See https://www.priscillawakefield.uk/family.html; also Rostek, 2021, p. 182
68. Rostek, 2021, p. 182
69. Rostek, 2021, p. 183. The following draws from https://www.priscillawakefield.uk.
70. Rostek, 2021, pp. 189–90
71. Quoted in Rostek, 2021, p. 192
72. Tuckniss and Mayhew, 1861, pp. xxxvi–xxxvii
73. Rostek, 2021, p. 191
74. Quoted in Rostek, 2021, p. 190
75. For this and other biographical details in the text, see Kelly, 1992
76. Kelly, 1992, p. 25
77. Kelly, 1992, p. 26
78. Wollstonecraft, 1988 [1792]
79. Wollstonecraft, 1988 [1792]
80. Kelly, 1992, p. 145
81. Kelly, 1992, pp. 145–6
82. Kelly, 1992, pp. 152–3
83. Bosker et al., 2013, p. 1424; Morris, 2010, p. 632

CHAPTER 9: FACTORY HANDS, MINERS AND MAIDS

1. Allen, 2017b, p. 107; Molony et al., 2016, p. 88, suggests an even higher percentage
2. Allen, 2017b, p. 107
3. Allen, 2009
4. Allen, 2009
5. Horrell, Humphries and Weisdorf, 2020, find evidence that it was women in particular who responded to higher wages by having fewer children, further alleviating population pressure. Also see: Foreman-Peck, 2011; De Moor and van Zanden, 2009.
6. Allen, 2017b, p. 31; Allen, 2009, pp. 39–40
7. Allen, 2009; National Trust, 2007, pp. 14–7; Ó Gráda, 2016
8. Ó Gráda, 2016, p. 231
9. Gowing, 2016; Erickson, 2008; Gowing, 2022, pp. 59–60, 88
10. Gowing, 2022, p. 82
11. Gowing, 2022, pp. 57, 85
12. Erickson, 2022
13. While women's freedom can help us explain why Britain—as a part of northwestern Europe—industrialised ahead of China, India and the Middle East (i.e. the parts of the world that had long led the world economy), it still leaves an open question: Why Britain industrialised first and not somewhere else in northwestern Europe, like the Netherlands? This has become the final frontier in regard to the question of "why Britain", making it one of the most active areas of research in economic history. I personally think that it could have been any one of the small handful of countries in the region that industrialised *first* and that a stroke of luck (on top of sharing the same main ingredients) therefore contributed to Britain coming first in the pack. Replay history and the Netherlands might have instead come first in the race, with Britain a close second. The fact that the various parts of northwestern Europe advanced economically within a few years of one another is testament to their similarities as opposed to their differences. In that sense, being able to explain why Britain—a place of little consequence in world history—managed to become the richest country in the world, with other nearby parts of Europe close behind, is of far greater significance than explaining why Britain was first and not the Netherlands.
14. Hobsbawm, 1968
15. Brown and Satterthwaite-Phillips, 2018
16. Molony et al., 2016, p. 95; Xue, 2021
17. Molony et al., 2016, p. 108
18. Raman, 2022
19. Jenkins, 1866, pp. 51, 80
20. Ó Gráda, 2016, p. 229
21. Sekers, 2013, p. 23
22. Sekers, 2013, p. 24
23. Sekers, 2013, pp. 27–8
24. National Trust, 2007
25. Sekers, 2013, p. 28
26. Sekers, 2013, p. 78
27. Sekers, 2013, pp. 24–5, 83
28. Sekers, 2013, p. 82
29. Sekers, 2013, pp. 82–4

30. Sekers, 2013, p. 82
31. Sekers, 2013, pp. 15–7
32. Sekers, 2013, fig. 8, pp. 154–6
33. National Trust, 2007, p. 13
34. National Trust, 2007, p. 19
35. Westall, 1994, "Greg's Estate"
36. National Trust, 2007, p. 19
37. National Trust, 2007, p. 20
38. Sekers, 2013, p. 156
39. Robinson, 1996, pp. 3–4
40. Robinson, 1996, p. 3
41. National Trust, 2007, p. 26
42. Sekers, 2013, p. 154
43. Sekers, 2013, p. 154
44. Robinson, 1996, p. 18
45. Robinson, 1996, p. 1
46. Sekers, 2013, p. 155; Robinson, 1996, p. 17; Westall, 1994, 'The Apprentices House'
47. Sekers, 2013, p. 155
48. Sekers, 2013, pp. 156–7
49. Sekers, 2013, pp. 158–9; National Trust, 2007, p. 25
50. Sekers, 2013, p. 160; Robinson, 1996, pp. 3, 24
51. Robinson, 1996, p. 3
52. Robinson, 1996, p. 6
53. Robinson, 1996, pp. 6–7, 16, 31
54. Robinson, 1996, pp. 9, 12, 17
55. Robinson, 1996, p. 6; National Trust, 2007, p. 25
56. National Trust, 2007, p. 27; Westall, 1994, 'Greg's Estate'
57. Robinson, 1996, pp. 14–5
58. Robinson, 1996, p. 14
59. Robinson, 1996, p. 18
60. National Trust, 2007, p. 8
61. Sekers, 2013, p. 170
62. Burnette, 2008b; also see Berg, 1993, more generally
63. Terki-Mignot, 2016; Allen, 2018; also see Horrell and Humphries, 2015, on the way in which women lost out earning-wise relative to men
64. Allen, 2009, p. 41
65. Allen, 2009, p. 41
66. Robinson, 2020 [1898]
67. Dublin, 1994, p. 89
68. Dublin, 1994, p. 78
69. Robinson, 2020 [1898], p. 5
70. Robinson, 2020 [1898], p. 12
71. Dublin, 1994, p. 89
72. Robinson, 2020 [1898], p. 39
73. Robinson, 2020 [1898], pp. 17, 31, 40
74. Robinson, 2020 [1898], p. 31

75. Robinson, 2020 [1898], p. 31
76. Robinson, 2020 [1898], p. 30
77. Robinson, 2020 [1898], p. 18
78. Dublin, 1994, p. 94; Robinson, 2020 [1898]
79. Dublin, 1994, pp. 95–6
80. Dublin, 1994, pp. 205–8
81. Rose, 1993, p. 155
82. Dublin, 1994, pp. 41–2
83. Allen, 2018; Humphries and Schneider, 2018; Muldrew, 2011
84. Dublin, 1994, p. 48 and chapter 5; Rose, 1993; Burnette, 2008a
85. Sekers, 2013, pp. 91–2, 109
86. Pargas, 2023, p. 443
87. Pargas, 2023, p. 443
88. Felder, 2020, p. 497
89. Pargas, 2023, pp. 443–4
90. Pargas, 2023, p. 446
91. Pargas, 2023, p. 446
92. Keckley, 1868, chapter 3
93. Keckley, 1868, chapter 3
94. Keckley, 1868, chapter 5
95. Molony et al., 2016, p. 148
96. Molony et al., 2016, pp. 148–9
97. Molony et al., 2016, pp. 148–50
98. Pinchbeck, 1977 [1930], p. 241
99. Molony et al., 2016, p. 148; Pinchbeck, 1977 [1930], pp. 263–4
100. Pinchbeck, 1977, p. 242
101. Pinchbeck, 1977, p. 249
102. Pinchbeck, 1977, p. 245
103. Pinchbeck, 1977, p. 247
104. Pinchbeck, 1977, pp. 250–1
105. Burnette, 2008a, p. 229
106. Hedley, 2019, pp. 9–16
107. Hedley, 2019, p. 17
108. Hedley, 2019, pp. 9–16
109. Burnette, 2008a, p. 225
110. Burnette, 2008a, p. 225
111. Mokyr, 2009, p. 321
112. Felder, 2020, p. 350
113. Burnette, 2008a, chapter 5
114. Burnette, 2008a, p. 314
115. Horrell and Humphries, 1995; Horrell and Humphries, 1997
116. Burnette, 2008a, p. 322
117. Burnette, 2008a, p. 323
118. Horrell, Humphries and Weisdorf, 2021
119. Burnette, 2008a
120. Krzanich, 2021
121. Amott and Matthaei, 1991, p. 322; Dublin, 1994, chapter 5

122. Amott and Matthaei, 1991, pp. 321–4
123. Rutterford et al., 2011
124. Rutterford et al., 2011
125. Felder, 2020, p. 475
126. Felder, 2020, p. 489
127. Wallach, 2012, p. 13
128. Wallach, 2012, p. 14
129. Wallach, 2012
130. Wallach, 2012, p. xix
131. Wallach, 2022; Felder, 2020, p. 489
132. Wallach, 2022, p. xix; Felder, 2020, p. 489
133. Elbirlik, 2021
134. Zarinebaf-Shahr, 2001

CHAPTER 10: ARMS DEALERS, PIRATES AND SEX WORKERS

1. Evans, 2020, p. 20
2. Oxley, 1996, pp. 17, 110
3. Oxley, 1996, p. 17
4. Oxley, 1996, p. 241
5. Beckett, 2013, pp. 20–1
6. Oxley, 1996, p. 17
7. Oxley, 1996, p. 20
8. Oxley, 1996, p. 20
9. Oxley, 1996, pp. 260–1
10. Oxley, 1996, p. 262
11. Oxley, 1996, pp. 119, 235, 269
12. Oxley, 1996, p. 264
13. Beckett, 2013, pp. 37–40
14. Oxley, 1996, p. 239
15. Oxley, 1996, p. 242
16. Oxley, 1996; Nicholas, 1989; Alford, 1984
17. Oxley, 1996, pp. 235–40
18. Beckett, 2013, p. 20; Oxley, 1996, p. 260
19. Dallas, 1946
20. Oxley, 1996, p. 109
21. Oxley, 1996, p. 110
22. Alford, 1984; Alford, 1986
23. Alford, 1984
24. Jacobs, 2005, p. 454
25. Jacobs, 2005, p. 454
26. Jacobs, 2005, p. 458
27. Jacobs, 2005, p. 459; Adams, 1995, pp. 23, 63
28. Mayhew and Hemyng, 1861, p. 68; on North America, see NMAI, 2009
29. Mayhew and Hemyng, 1861, p. 68
30. Kumar, 2017
31. Kumar, 2017
32. Elvin, 2004

33. Sommer, 2015
34. Harris and McKenna, 2021, p. 4
35. Harris and McKenna, 2021, p. 4
36. Harris and McKenna, 2021, p. 5
37. For this and the paragraphs that follow, Harris and McKenna, 2021
38. Harris and McKenna, 2021, p. 6
39. Harris and McKenna, 2021, p. 12
40. Harris and McKenna, 2021, p. 13
41. Harris and McKenna, 2021, p. 13
42. Dalrymple, 2020, p. xxxi
43. Dalrymple, 2020, p. xxxi
44. UK Parliament, n.d. a
45. Liddle and Joshi, 1985
46. Levine, 2003, p. 182
47. Levine, 2003, p. 180
48. Levine, 2003, pp. 180–5
49. Mayhew and Hemyng, 1861, p. 57
50. Levine, 2003, p. 179
51. Levine, 2003, p. 185
52. Levine, 2003, p. 185
53. Levine, 2003, p. 185
54. Levine, 2003, p. 195
55. Levine, 2003, p. 38
56. Levine, 2003, p. 40
57. Levine, 2003, p. 181
58. Levine, 2003, p. 181
59. Jacobs, 2005, p. 463
60. Quoted in Jacobs, 2005, p. 475
61. Levine, 2003, p. 181
62. G. T. Badsen, quoted in Ekejiuba, 1967, p. 634
63. Achebe, 2020
64. Achebe, 2020, p. 100
65. Achebe, 2020, p. 113
66. Achebe, 2020, pp. 102, 107
67. Jones, 2013, p. 182
68. Parker and Rathbone, 2007, p. 88
69. Ndzamela, 2021
70. Badawi, 2024, p. 337
71. Parker and Rathbone, 2007, p. 88
72. Parker and Rathbone, 2007, p. 82
73. Badawi, 2024, p. 337; Wheeler, 2011
74. Yemitan, 1987
75. Ekejiuba, 1967, p. 637
76. Ekejiuba, 1967, pp. 645–6
77. Ekejiuba, 1967, p. 640; Achebe, 2020, p. 111
78. Ekejiuba, 1967
79. Ndzamela, 2021

80. Abraham and Woolf, 2022, pp. 32–3
81. Ndzamela, 2021
82. Ndzamela, 2021
83. Ndzamela, 2021
84. Ndzamela, 2021
85. Ndzamela, 2021
86. Ndzamela, 2021
87. Webb, 2023
88. Cock, 1980
89. Wells, 1983a; Wells, 1983b
90. Kimble and Unterhalter, 1982; Unterhalter, 1987

CHAPTER 11: TYPISTS, TEACHERS AND ENGINEERS

1. Ortiz-Ospina, Tzvetkova and Roser, 2024
2. Goldin, 1990, p. 17
3. Glucksmann, 1990, p. 84
4. Kessler-Harris, 2003, p. 113
5. Kenez, 2017, p. 15. Note that in the Western calendar, 23 February coincides with 8 March.
6. Beevor, 2022; Beevor and Rogers, 2023
7. Kenez, 2017, p. 15
8. Kenez, 2017, p. 15
9. Kenez, 2017, p. 16; Beevor, 2022
10. Kenez, 2017, p. 15
11. Beevor, 2022
12. Kenez, 2017, p. 24
13. Kenez, 2017, p. 25
14. Kenez, 2017, p. 25; Beevor, 2022
15. Beevor and Rogers, 2023
16. Klimina, 2019, p. 116
17. Klimina, 2019, p. 116
18. Klimina, 2019, p. 116
19. Klimina, 2019, p. 117
20. Klimina, 2019, p. 117
21. Klimina, 2019, p. 121
22. Novikova and Ghodsee, 2023, p. 74
23. Klimina, 2019, pp. 121–2; Novikova and Ghodsee, 2023, p. 75
24. Kenez, 2017, p. 70; Engel, 2004, pp. xviii–xix; King, 2012
25. Goldman, 2011, pp. xvii, 286
26. King, 2012, pp. 82–3
27. Goldman, 2011, p. 1
28. Goldman, 2011, p. 11
29. Engel, 2004, p. 164
30. Novikova and Ghodsee, 2023, p. 79
31. Engel, 2004, p. 154
32. Engel, 2004, p. 163
33. Goldman, 2011, p. 5

34. Goldman, 2011, p. 19
35. Goldman, 2011, pp. 5, 8; Engel, 2004, pp. 152–3
36. Goldman, 2011, p. 23
37. Denisova, 2018, p. 152
38. Kenez, 2017, p. 94
39. Denisova, 2018, pp. 152, 155
40. Denisova, 2018, p. 154
41. Kenez, 2017, p. 114
42. Denisova, 2018, p. 153
43. Denisova, 2018, p. 150
44. Kenez, 2017, p. 100
45. Kenez, 2017, p. 96
46. Kenez, 2017, p. 95
47. Kenez, 2017, pp. 115–6
48. Kenez, 2017, p. 115
49. Engel, 2004, p. 162
50. Kenez, 2017, p. 117
51. Engel, 2004, p. xix
52. Denisova, 2018, p. 153
53. Kenez, 2017, p. 108
54. Kenez, 2017, p. 119
55. Kenez, 2017, p. 109
56. Klimina, 2019, p. 123
57. Klimina, 2019, p. 124
58. Quoted in Galbraith, 2021, p. 30
59. Crafts, 2018, p. 38
60. Galbraith, 2021, p. 32
61. Galbraith, 2021, p. 31; Goldin, 1990, p. 106
62. Bierman, 2008
63. Felder, 2020, p. 499
64. Milkman, 2016, p. 17; Desilver, 2023
65. Milkman, 2016, pp. 23–4
66. Stanley, n.d.
67. Stanley, n.d.
68. Stanley, n.d.
69. Goldin, 1990, p. 106
70. Glucksmann, 1990
71. Milkman, 2016, p. 21
72. Milkman, 2016, p. 23
73. Milkman, 2016, p. 23
74. Goldin, 1990, p. 162
75. Goldin, 1990, pp. 161–4
76. Goldin, 1990, pp. 165–6
77. Milkman, 2016, p. 25
78. Milkman, 2016, p. 25
79. Milkman, 2016, p. 27
80. Milkman, 2016, p. 33

81. Milkman, 2016, p. 32
82. US Department of Labor, 1944
83. US Department of Labor, 1944, p. 1
84. US Department of Labor, 1944, p. 2
85. Thompson et al., 2012, p. 81; Goldin, 1990, p. 153
86. Milkman, 2016, pp. 31–2; US Department of Labor, 1944, p. 8
87. Milkman, 2016, p. 34
88. Glucksmann, 1990, p. 55
89. Glucksmann, 1990, pp. 47–50
90. Blau et al., 2016, p. 80
91. Ortiz-Ospina and Roser, 2023
92. Blackburn, 1995, p. 373
93. Blackburn, 1995, p. 371
94. Blackburn, 1995, pp. 376–7
95. Cribb et al., 2014, p. 14
96. Cribb et al., 2014, p. 11
97. Felder, 2020, pp. 485, 491
98. The listing took place in the year 1987; see Felder, 2020, p. 502
99. Felder, 2020, p. 474
100. Smith, 2021, pp. 76–7
101. Felder, 2020, pp. 478–9
102. Felder, 2020, p. 479
103. Felder, 2020, pp. 489–90, 504–5
104. Blau et al., 2016, p. 117
105. Goldin, 1990; Iglikowski, 2015; Stanley, n.d.
106. Goldin, 1990, p. 17; Heckman and Killingsworth, 1986, p. 106; Blau et al., 2016, pp. 83–4
107. Thompson et al., 2012, p. 81
108. Thompson et al., 2012, p. 81
109. Goldin, 1990; Kessler-Harris, 2003
110. Blau et al., 2016, p. 84
111. Blau et al., 2016, p. 404
112. Goldin, 1990, p. 201; Phizacklea, 1982
113. Goldin, 1990, p. 27; Boustan and Collins, 2013
114. Goldin, 1990, p. 27
115. Phizacklea, 1982, p. 103
116. Goldin, 1990, p. 201
117. Felder, 2020, p. 476
118. Card, 1980, p. 218
119. UK Parliament, n.d. b
120. UK Parliament, n.d. b
121. Moss, 2015
122. Moss, 2015
123. TUC, n.d.
124. Goldin, 1990, pp. 198–201
125. Chapman, 1975, p. 40
126. Chapman, 1975, p. 44

127. Chapman, 1975, p. 44
128. Chapman, 1975, p. 43
129. Smith, 2021, p. 103
130. Castagnetti and Haines, 2023
131. Bharat, 2019, p. 27
132. United Nations, n.d.
133. Kabeer, 2004, p. 5
134. Kabeer, 2004, p. 5
135. Kabeer, 2004, p. 5
136. Wood, 1991
137. Elson and Pearson, 1981; Standing, 1989; Carswell, 2016, pp. 136–7
138. Beneria, 2007, p. 22
139. Handley, 2017
140. Ko, 1994, p. 2
141. Phillips, 2017
142. Hong Fincher, 2023, pp. 127–8
143. Hong Fincher, 2023, pp. 127–8
144. Handley, 2017
145. Handley, 2017
146. Handley, 2017
147. Handley, 2017
148. Handley, 2017
149. Handley, 2017
150. Handley, 2017
151. Hu and Khan, 1997; World Bank, 2022
152. Handley, 2017
153. Crafts, 2018, pp. 2–3, 79–85
154. Crafts, 2018, p. 91
155. Crafts, 2018, p. 108
156. Crafts, 2018, pp. 115–7, 121
157. Science Museum, 2020
158. Shetterly, n.d.
159. Felder, 2020, p. 495
160. Felder, 2020, p. 504
161. Felder, 2020, p. 486
162. Hasell, 2023
163. Goldin, 2023
164. Goldin, 2023
165. Blau et al., 2016, p. 404
166. Fukuyama, 1989

CHAPTER 12: CREATIVES, CARERS AND CLEAN-TECH INNOVATORS

1. Bogachev, 2023
2. Torkington, 2023
3. Kharas, 2023
4. World Bank, 2024, pp. xiii–xiv

5. Cited in Krugman, 2009
6. Cited in Greenspan, 2007
7. Lazarus, 2014
8. Collinson, 1987, p. 13
9. Suss et al., 2021
10. Suss et al., 2021
11. King, 2024
12. Suss et al., 2021; Cardillo et al., 2020; Arnaboldi et al., 2021
13. Lazarus, 2014; Federal Reserve, 2024
14. Federal Reserve, 2024
15. Athey and Luca, 2019
16. Scott, 2023
17. Scott, 2023
18. Scott, 2023
19. OpenAI, 2025: https://openai.com/about/
20. Kay and Jackson, 2024
21. Blackburn, 2024
22. Young et al., 2021
23. Young et al., 2021
24. Google, 2021, pp. 57–8
25. Royle, 2023; Meta, 2022
26. Apple, 2024
27. Microsoft, 2023, pp. 9, 17
28. Eurostat, 2020
29. Brixi et al., 2023
30. PwC, 2017
31. Brixi et al., 2023
32. Baral, 2024
33. Park, 2023
34. Pfizer, 2023
35. Seagen, 2022
36. Nature Biotechnology, 2023b; UK Bioindustry Association, 2023
37. Nature Biotechnology, 2023a
38. Nature Biotechnology, 2024
39. Fletcher, 2024
40. Morrow, 2024
41. Morrow, 2024
42. Morrow, 2024
43. Martin, 2024
44. UNESCO, 2022
45. Department for Culture, Media and Sport, 2023
46. Department for Culture, Media and Sport, 2023
47. Buckholtz, 2021
48. Bogachev, 2023
49. Buckholtz, 2021
50. Conteh, 2021
51. Buckholtz, 2021

52. UNESCO, 2021, p. 14
53. UNIDO, 2013
54. UNESCO, 2021, p. 17
55. Statista, 2024
56. Baer, 2023
57. UNESCO, 2022, p. 36
58. Dattani et al., 2023
59. Roser, 2024
60. Ritchie and Roser, 2024
61. International Labour Organization and World Health Organisation, 2022, p. viii
62. Skills for Care, 2023
63. Harris and Marshall, 2024
64. Harris and Marshall, 2024
65. Thomas et al., 2023, p. 12; Homer, 2022
66. Homer, 2022
67. Grimley and Horrox, 2023
68. Grimley and Horrox, 2023
69. Grimley and Horrox, 2023
70. Hoteit et al., 2024; International Labour Organization, 2016, p. 23; International Labour Organization and World Health Organisation, 2022, pp. viii, 79–80
71. International Labour Organization and World Health Organisation, 2022, p. viii
72. Quoted in Irvine et al., 2024, p. 12
73. Quoted in Irvine et al., 2024, p. 12
74. Carlin, 2024
75. Nadasen, 2015, p. 4; Blofield and Jokela, 2018
76. Nadasen, 2015, p. 1
77. Nadasen, 2015, p. 2
78. Blofield and Jokela, 2018
79. International Labour Organization—Domestic Workers Convention, 2011 (No. 189)
80. Thomas et al., 2023; International Labour Organization, 2018
81. International Labour Organization, 2018
82. International Labour Organization, 2018, p. vii
83. International Labour Organization, 2018, p. 98
84. International Labour Organization, 2018, p. 99
85. Blau et al., 2016, p. 122
86. United Nations, 2020
87. Goldin, 2023
88. International Labour Organization, 2018, p. 101; Edlund and Öun, 2023
89. International Labour Organization, 2018, p. 98
90. Regan, 2024
91. Stern and Romani, 2023
92. Stern and Romani, 2023
93. Stern and Romani, 2023
94. Stern and Romani, 2023

95. Stern and Romani, 2023
96. International Energy Agency, 2023a
97. International Energy Agency, 2023a
98. The London Sustainable Development Commission, 2018, p. 25
99. The Engineer, 2024
100. Devonshire, 2024
101. Devonshire, 2024
102. International Energy Agency, 2023b
103. World Bank, 2022; Kharas, 2023; ESPAS, 2019
104. International Labour Organization, 2016, p. 6; Halim, 2020
105. International Labour Organization, 2016; UNFPA, 2021, p. 31; CNN tracker: https://edition.cnn.com/us/abortion-access-restrictions-bans-us-dg/index.html
106. Harris, 2017

CONCLUSION

1. Wiesner-Hanks, 2019, p. 61
2. Ebrey, 2023, p. 73
3. Price, 2022, pp. 391–2
4. Spufford, 1988, pp. 49–50, 60–1; McCormick, 2001, 776; Parker and Rathbone, 2007, p. 79; Karras, 2023, p. 219
5. Saini, 2024
6. Proverbs, 31.10–25, quoted from Barber, 1995, p. 184
7. Cohen, 2016, p. 716
8. Mokyr, 2009, p. 320
9. Goldin, 1990, p. 46
10. Mercedes-Benz, 2019; Mercedes-Benz USA, 2018
11. Mercedes-Benz USA, 2018
12. Clean Energy Research Centre UBC, 2017
13. Mercedes-Benz USA, 2018
14. Mokyr, 2009, p. 320
15. Goldin, 1990, p. 44
16. Felder, 2020, pp. 495–6
17. Goldin, 1990, pp. 48–9
18. Leke, 2023
19. Barker, 2006, p. 56
20. Heuvel, 2007
21. Felder, 2020, p. 476
22. Masterson, 2024
23. Kanze et al., 2017
24. World Bank: https://data.worldbank.org/indicator/SL.EMP.SELF.FE.ZS
25. Halim, 2020
26. Muckerheide, 2023
27. Muckerheide, 2023; Halim, 2020
28. World Bank, 2024
29. Muckerheide, 2023
30. Across the world, just over a half of the working population are in waged or salaried forms of work (International Labour Organization, 2016, p. 8).

31. Burnette, 2008a; Goldman, 2011, p. 10; Molony et al., 2016, p. 148
32. Mokyr, 2009, p. 321
33. Robinson, 2020, p. 4
34. On mining, see Romano, 2020, and Mercier and Gier, 2006
35. On guilds, see Ogilvie, 2019
36. Mark, 2017
37. Brock, 1994, p. 340; https://www.historyhit.com/facts-about-agnodice-of-athens/; Kessler-Harris, 2003, p. 116
38. Goldin, 1990
39. Stanley, n.d.
40. Maxtone Graham, 2023, pp. 258–9, 265
41. Kessler-Harris, 2003, pp. 113–4
42. Kessler-Harris, 2003, p. 114
43. See the International Labour Organization's databank
44. Murray et al., 2020
45. De Moor and van Zanden, 2009
46. Kessler-Harris, 2003, p. 68
47. Blau et al., 2016, p. 117
48. European Commission, International Monetary Fund, Organisation for Economic Co-operation and Development, United Nations and World Bank, 2008, esp. p. 12
49. International Labour Organization, 2018
50. International Labour Organization, 2018
51. Humphries, 2024
52. Barrero et al., 2022
53. Blau et al., 2016
54. On this problem, see for example McCormick, 2001, pp. 741–2, and Raffield, 2019
55. Pomeroy, 1975, p. 26
56. Bharat, 2019, p. 28
57. Parker and Rathbone, 2007, p. 79
58. Schiel, 2023, p. 183
59. Zarinebaf-Shahr, 2001
60. Crawford and Gowing, 2000, p. 81
61. Earle, 1989, pp. 337, 339
62. Earle, 1989, p. 337
63. Horrell, Humphries and Weisdorf, 2021
64. Erickson, 2008
65. Erickson, 2008
66. Muncaster, 2003; Erickson, 2022, p. 43
67. Erickson, 2022
68. Nyyssölä, 2022; also Hudson et al., 2020, pp. 57–60
69. Hudson et al., 2020, p. 60
70. Nyyssölä, 2022
71. Marx, 1890 [1990 edition], volume 1, part IV, chapter 15, section 3
72. On the former, Novikova and Ghodsee, 2023, p. 72
73. Novikova and Ghodsee, 2023, p. 67

74. Calvi and Keskar, 2021
75. Adams et al., 2024
76. See Adams et al., 2024, for a discussion
77. See Chapter 10; also, Everill, 2024, p. 10
78. Brosius, 2016, p. 167
79. Barber, 1995, p. 181
80. Mieroop, 1989, p. 64
81. Romano, 2020, p. 304
82. Rose, 1993, p. 24
83. Goldman, 2011, p. 16; Ilic, 2018, p. 108
84. International Labour Organization, 2016
85. International Labour Organization, 2016, esp. pp. 23–7
86. International Labour Organization, 2016
87. World Bank, 2024, p. xiv
88. Geldard, 2024
89. Molony et al., 2016, p. 150; Kenez, 2017, p. 1

INDEX

INDEX

Credit: Courtesy of the author

Victoria Bateman has taught at the universities of Oxford and Cambridge, most recently as the director of studies in economics at Gonville & Caius College. She is a fellow of the Royal Historical Society and the Royal Society of Arts and author of *The Sex Factor* and *Naked Feminism*. She lives in Kent, UK.

RAISING READERS

Books Build Bright Futures

Thank you for reading this book and for being a reader of books in general. A
author, I am so grateful to share being part of a community of readers with
and I hope you will join me in passing our love of books on to the next genera
of readers.

Did you know that reading for enjoyment is the single biggest predictor child's future happiness and success?

More than family circumstances, parents' educational background, or inc reading impacts a child's future academic performance, emotional well-b communication skills, economic security, ambition, and happiness.

Studies show that kids reading for enjoyment in the US is in rapid decline:

- In 2012, 53% of 9-year-olds read almost every day. Just 10 years later, in 2022, the number had fallen to 39%.
- In 2012, 27% of 13-year-olds read for fun daily. By 2023, that number was just 14%.

Together, we can commit to **Raising Readers** and change this trend. How?

- Read to children in your life daily.
- Model reading as a fun activity.
- Reduce screen time.
- Start a family, school, or community book club.
- Visit bookstores and libraries regularly.
- Listen to audiobooks.
- Read the book before you see the movie.
- Encourage your child to read aloud to a pet or stuffed animal.
- Give books as gifts.
- Donate books to families and communities in need.

Books build bright futures, and **Raising Readers** is our shared responsibilit

For more information, visit **JoinRaisingReaders.com**

Sources: National Endowment for the Arts, National Assessment of Educational Progress, WorldBookDay.org, Nielsen BookData's 2023 "Understanding the Children's Book Consumer"